THE SON'S SUPREMACY

Books by Michael Whitworth

The Epic of God
The Derision of Heaven
Living & Longing for the Lord
Esau's Doom
Bethlehem Road
The Pouting Preacher
How to Lose a Kingdom in 400 Years
Splinters of the Cross
Life in the Shadow of Death

THE SON'S

SUPREMACY

A GUIDE TO HEBREWS

MICHAEL WHITWORTH

START2FINISH

ISBN 978-1-941972-12-0 (softcover)
ISBN 978-1-941972-13-7 (hardcover)
ISBN 978-1-941972-14-4 (ebook)

Library of Congress Control Number 2018911024

Published by Start2Finish
Branford, Florida 32008
start2finish.org

Printed in the United States of America

Cover Design by Dresden Design Co.

In honor of my favorite preacher

Dan Winkler

For a lifetime of exhorting us to "consider Jesus."

CONTENTS

FOREWORD

B &B. If you're engaged in a deep study of Hebrews, the nineteenth book of the New Testament, those familiar letters don't stand for "bed and breakfast." They don't represent the epistle's keyword, "better," a word repeatedly used by its unnamed author to promote the wonder of Christian living.

No, Hebrews' comforting message directs you to another B&B: the body and blood of Jesus. This uplifting epistle is self-described as a "word of exhortation" (13:22). It emphasizes one main point: if you are a Christian, then Jesus is your high priest. Right now, he's sitting next to God as a minister, seeing to your needs (8:1–2). In other words, Jesus is *at* God's side, but he is *on* your side! For that encouraging truth to be possible, two events had to occur, and both of these events give us the contextual flow of Hebrews.

First, for Jesus to serve as our high priest, he had to become and live as a man. Deity had to experience humanity in a body on earth to understand and represent humanity with deity in heaven. That's the topic of Hebrews 1–8. Jesus "was made lower than the angels" (2:9), and because of that, as "a great high priest who has passed through the heavens, ... [he can] sympathize with our weaknesses" (4:14–15). He became the "one mediator between God and men" (1 Tim 2:5) who is "able to save to the uttermost those who draw near to God through him, since he always lives to make intercession for them" (Heb 7:25).

Second, for Jesus to serve as our high priest, he had to be sacrificed for the sins of man and satisfy the wrath of God. He had to offer his own blood for humanity to appease the feelings of deity and make forgiveness possible on earth. That's the gist of Hebrews 9–13. Jesus "entered once for all into the holy places, not by means of the blood of goats and calves but by means of his own blood, thus securing an eternal redemption" and the "forgiveness of sins" (9:12, 22).

Endowed with the ability to say something of interest in an interesting way, Michael Whitworth places the finger of his readers on the pulse of the great book of Hebrews and proves why Jesus is our "hope of glory" (Col 1:27). In my years of study, Michael is one of the most gifted authors I've encountered. He combines an intelligent blend of detailed research with the charm of an engaging wit. This makes the end product of his pen understandable, enjoyable, and helpful. Such has been the case with each of his previous undertakings, and *The Son's Supremacy* does not disappoint. It will help you appreciate Jesus more deeply and strengthen the assurance you can have with our Savior sitting at the right hand of Majesty on high.

Thank you, Michael, for helping me love my Lord even more.

— Dan Winkler
Spring Hill, Tennessee

INTRODUCTION

E arly one Sunday morning, Judah made his way through Antioch's quiet streets to the cemetery on the outskirts of town. He hesitated at every junction, unsure if he was headed in the right direction. He hadn't yet memorized the route; how could he? He had never dreamed it would be necessary. This was all too new, too raw, too unexpected. As dawn's early light disrupted the darkness, Judah began questioning whether this was just a long dream, a nightmare from which he couldn't wake soon enough.

But as the graveyard came into view, the reality of it all hit home once again. Nausea washed over him. Judah could scarcely pick his way among the rocks and boulders as tears blinded his eyes. At last, he arrived at his destination—

The tomb of his only child.

His beloved son Daniel had died of a mysterious illness four months prior. A fever had taken hold of the boy at sunset; when the sun rose the following day, Judah was holding his son's lifeless body in his arms, wracked with shock and grief. He remembered the wailing of his household and neighbors. He, however, had stood there in stunned silence.

As Judah wept before his son's tomb, a voice pierced the stillness of dawn. "He would still be alive if you had not forsaken Adonai. You turned your back on the Name, and now you stand under his curse." The voice belonged to Judah's father, Azariah. *Perhaps you're right*, Judah thought to himself, though he could not yet bring himself to admit it out loud.

Three years ago, Judah and his wife, Anna, had left the traditions of their fathers and embraced faith in the Nazarene. Childhood friends had first told them of the carpenter-turned-rabbi from Galilee who had been crucified by the Romans in Jerusalem a generation prior. This same rabbi had risen from the dead and ascended into heaven—something many in Judea and Galilee had witnessed. Judah and Anna now considered themselves members of this new cult called Christians.

Membership, however, had come at a cost. First, Judah's standing in Antioch's Jewish community instantly evaporated. His business had failed, leaving them with significant debt. Members of the Christian sect had embraced them, but other lifelong friends had deserted them. Their families had shunned them. And now their son—their son was—

Their son was *dead*.

Perhaps Judah's father was right. Perhaps the Name was punishing him. Perhaps believing in the Nazarene had been a mistake. Had not Moses warned long ago of this very thing for anyone who forsook the law? For four months, a line from the Torah had been ringing in Judah's ears: "If you will not obey the voice of the LORD your God … Cursed shall be the fruit of your womb."[1]

Judah's relationship with his father had been severed once news of Judah's confession that Jesus was the Son of God had reached Azariah's ears. His father had donned sackcloth and smeared ashes into his hair and beard, acting as if Judah had died. Azariah had not spoken to his son since that day three years ago, not even when Daniel had passed. But he spoke now, and his words were laced with condemnation and bitterness in equal measure. As far as Azariah was concerned, Judah's faithlessness to the covenant had brought about the child's death.

Judah said nothing to his father. Wiping tears from his eyes, he began his trek back into the city as the sun's rays greeted the new day. Merchants, slaves, and other citizens of Antioch were starting to mill about the streets. Judah noticed none of this. One question punctuated every footstep he took towards his house. It was a question that had haunted him since his son's death. Since his business had failed. Since his friends and family had deserted him. His father's brutal allegation now made the question more poignant.

Is it worth it?

Is it worth all this to follow this crucified carpenter? Did Judah stand to inherit that much more than if he had remained loyal to the covenant?

[1] Deut 28:15, 18.

Is it worth it?

Something Judah had never been able to admit to members of his sect was that he saw little difference between being a Christian and being a Jew. Since his baptism, Judah had known little happiness and mostly heartache. He would have been better off, it seemed, had he continued in the way of Moses.

Is it worth it?

Judah spent the rest of the day sweating in a local field as a common laborer. It was exhausting, humiliating work for someone who had once had *others* working for *him*. The pay was a pittance, but it was the only employment Judah had found lately. As the sun began to set, Judah trudged home, weary as much from grief as he was from the day's grit and grime.

Assembly was that evening in the home of a neighbor, Stephen. Judah thought twice about attending. He was tired, bitter, and angry. He wasn't in a frame of mind to worship. His conversion was beginning to look like an investment gone sour. Yet something—he knew not what—prompted Judah to assemble that night with fellow members of the Way. He fumbled through the hymns; his mind wandered during prayers. When the meeting took an unexpected turn, however, his attention revived.

It wasn't every week that an out-of-town guest was present, let alone asked to speak. So Judah was intrigued when an unfamiliar face took a seat before the audience and began to teach. "Who is this man?" Judah asked the person next to him.

"Don't you recognize him?"

"No," replied Judah.

"It's Timothy, yokefellow of our brother Paul, the same who was martyred in Rome just last year."

Judah knew Timothy and Paul by reputation only. Though Paul had begun his ministry in Antioch, the apostle had long departed for Rome by the time Judah and Anna had become Christians. Judah had heard of Paul's execution, and he had also heard that Timothy had escaped from Rome soon after, but he had never met the younger man. Judah gazed upon Timothy, whom he knew to be about Judah's age yet appeared twenty years his senior. There was quiet confidence and an air of mature authority about the evangelist.

Though Judah had felt nothing while the congregation had sung and prayed, something inside his soul stirred to life as Timothy began to speak:

"Long ago, at many times and in many ways, God spoke to our fathers by the prophets, but in these last days he has spoken to us by his Son..."

>———◇———<

Like our fictional, first-century Judah of Antioch, I, too, have stood before the grave of an only son and wept. My Daniel died suddenly and unexpectedly overnight. And I won't sugarcoat it, his death made me ponder (not for the first time in my life) if following Jesus was worth it if death and grief and loss were all I had to show for it. Like Judah, I have wrestled with the questions the Accuser has always planted in the minds of the elect.

Why?

Why me?

How could God do this to me?

What did I do to deserve this?

Is it worth it?

Over the last few years, I have felt the strong current of my grief pull me away from my spiritual mooring. I have observed in my own life what it is to drift away. I know the danger of cutting ties to the Anchor of the soul. I recently remarked to a friend that most Sundays, God and I are on good terms. Occasionally on the Lord's Day, however, it seems as if God and I are two quarreling family members at a holiday get-together: we're in the same room, but we aren't speaking.

The letter to the Hebrews is unlike all the other epistles in the New Testament. Considerable mystery surrounds the book. Who is its author? Precisely to whom was it written? When was it written? None of these questions has a clear answer. In the Q&A that follows, I offer up my thoughts on Hebrews' authorship, though I have no definitive conclusions. Nor is mention of Antioch in the above story any more than conjecture. Hebrews could have easily originated in Rome, Ephesus, Alexandria, or Timbuktu.

What is more, the content of Hebrews is pockmarked with many other oddities. There are disturbing admonitions, discussion of angels, allusions to sacrificial rituals, and confusing quotations from the Old Testament with seemingly no connection to one another. Most puzzling of all is the author's fascination with the obscure Melchizedek. But Hebrews ultimately isn't about angels, sacrifices, or Melchizedek. This epistle is about one thing: the supremacy of the Son of God.

After my last book project was complete, I chose to write on Hebrews for a few reasons. First, Hebrews is unquestionably among the most majestic books of the New Testament. If one is as inexplicably drawn to complexity within majesty as I am, Hebrews might edge out Romans. Second, and with the possible exception of Revelation (though I'm not convinced Revelation is an exception in this case), there is no New Testament book more obscure or mysterious. At least with Revelation, we know who wrote it and to whom, two elements of Hebrews that remain a mystery. Yet my ultimate reason for reading, reflecting, and writing on Hebrews was an intensely personal one—

I needed to fall back in love with Jesus.

In his commentary, William Lane writes, "Hebrews is a sermon prepared in response to a crisis of faith,"[2] and is he ever right! Despite the uncertainty surrounding Hebrews' authorship, date, provenance, and destination, its audience's situation can be discerned from clues in the text.

> ›	Though there had to have been Gentiles in their midst, Hebrews' primary audience was Jewish Christians ("our fathers," 1:1).
> ›	They were second-generation Christians who had heard the gospel from others (2:3).
> ›	They were from all levels of the socioeconomic spectrum. Some were wealthy enough to be charitable (10:33–34) and hospitable (13:2), and they possessed property worth confiscation (10:34).
> ›	These Christians were at risk of falling away and losing their salvation (2:1–3; 3:12–14; 4:1, 11; 6:4–6; 10:26–31; 12:15, 25).
> ›	They had not matured in their faith as the author had hoped (5:11–6:3), though they still exhibited love and good works (6:10).
> ›	Arguably due to discouragement, some of their number were neglecting to attend the assembly of the saints (10:25).

---

[2] William L. Lane, *Hebrews* (Vancouver: Regent College, 2004), 27.

> Early on in their faith, the readers had suffered persecution but not martyrdom (10:32–34; 12:4).

Using these facts as a framework, I believe Hebrews' original audience was Christians in some locale outside of Palestine. They had initially received the gospel with gladness, and early trials had failed to rattle them. Over the years, however, the cumulative effects of temptation, trouble, and disappointment had taken their toll. Plateauing in their spiritual growth had not helped matters, nor had ostracism and boycotts from the Jewish community. There was now a predominating sentiment that these Christians would be better off if they made the "minor" adjustment of returning to Sinai and the covenant.[3] They were experiencing a crisis of faith—backtrack to Moses or double down on the Messiah? Hebrews, then, was written to urge them to maintain their faith in and confession of Jesus (3:1, 6, 4:14; 10:23).

In the aftermath of my son's death, as I began to scratch and scrape, desperate to lift myself out of grief's abyss, I realized my need to reestablish my own confidence in the Son. Burying a child was a crisis of faith I had never anticipated, so to reconnect with my soul's Anchor, I needed to hear afresh a sermon on the supremacy of Jesus. Hebrews has proven to be the cure for my affliction. The Greek word for "better" (*kreittōn*) occurs nineteen times in the New Testament, and thirteen are in Hebrews.[4] As you will discover in this book, no matter what you're going through, enduring it with Jesus makes it infinitely better, for *he* is infinitely better.

As you journey with me through this marvelous New Testament epistle, I hope you learn a great deal. I hope to illuminate certain mysterious, confusing, or ambiguous elements. I hope to excite in you a curiosity for the world of Hebrews: its author, its audience, and beyond. I hope to underscore the Old Testament's value and how it's impossible to understand the New without it. But most of all, you need to know writing this book was, as I have said, an intensely personal endeavor for me. I wrote this book for myself. I wrote this book because I needed to fall back in love with Jesus.

I invite you to behold with wonder and worship the Son's supremacy.

[3] For more on the audience of Hebrews, see Craig R. Koester, *Hebrews*, AB 36 (New York: Doubleday, 2001), 64–79.

[4] Heb 1:4; 6:9; 7:7, 19, 22; 8:6 (2x); 9:23; 10:34; 11:16, 35, 40; 12:24.

HEBREWS Q&A

In a recent interview with myself, I asked a few questions about this guide to Hebrews. I hope the answers orient you to both Hebrews and this book.

Q Who wrote Hebrews?

> **A** Wow! You don't mess around, do you? Thanks for leading off with an easy question!

Q It's my first question in every interview.

> **A** Fair enough. Well, we don't know who wrote Hebrews. As early as the third century, no one knew. Origen, a church father who died in the mid-third century, is recorded as saying, "Who wrote the epistle, in truth God knows."[1] For a long time, the author was popularly believed to be Paul,[2] yet few advocate for Pauline authorship today. Other nominees have included Apollos, Barnabas, Luke, Peter, Jude, Stephen, Silas, Epaphras, Philip, Aquila, Priscilla, Phoebe, Mary the mother of Jesus, and Clement of Rome. As you can tell, it would be easier to make a list of those who have *not* been purported to be the author. That there have been so many nominees likely means it's impossible to know for sure.

[1] Eusebius, *Church History* 6.25.14. To be fair, however, Origen said in the previous sentence, "Not without reason have the men of old time handed it [Hebrews] down as Paul's."

[2] In a New Testament manuscript dating to the early third century ($\mathfrak{P}^{46}$), Hebrews was placed after Romans. In other manuscripts, Hebrews appears after 2 Corinthians, Galatians, Ephesians, 2 Thessalonians, Titus, and elsewhere (Bruce M. Metzger, *A Textual Commentary on the Greek New Testament*, 2nd ed. [Stuttgart: German Bible Society, 1994], 591–92). For the evidence supporting Pauline authorship, see David Alan Black, "Who Wrote Hebrews? The Internal and External Evidence Reexamined," *FM* 18, no. 2 (2001): 3–26.

Q Why do so many New Testament scholars no longer consider Paul to be the author of Hebrews?

A There are several reasons. One, Paul always identified himself at the beginning of his letters and left some mark at the end to prove their authenticity (2 Thess 3:17); both are missing from Hebrews. Also, Hebrews' style[3] and vocabulary are different from Paul's (e.g., Paul uses the title "Christ Jesus" about ninety times in his thirteen letters, but it is not used once in Hebrews). The book's theology doesn't match Paul; while the apostle mentions the resurrection frequently, it occurs only once in Hebrews, and then only in passing (13:20). Moreover, the theme of Christ's high priesthood has no parallel in Paul's epistles. Yet the most convincing proof against Paul's authorship is our author's claim to have heard the gospel from others (2:3), which Paul indignantly denied (Gal 1:12).

[3] "None of Paul's other writings come close to the rhetorical finesse and stylistic polish of Hebrews. Indeed, Paul's own philosophy of preaching runs completely counter to what we encounter in Hebrews. Paul refused to rely on well-crafted rhetoric ('the loftiness of words or wisdom,' 1 Cor 2:1), insisting that the response of his audience be based on their encounter with God's power through the message; the author of Hebrews uses every rhetorical ornament in the handbooks and shows an astounding array of argumentative techniques" (David A. deSilva, *An Introduction to the New Testament: Contexts, Methods and Ministry Formation* [Downers Grove, IL: InterVarsity Press, 2004], 787).

Q If not Paul, who are some of the likely authors?

A Some have nominated Luke,[4] claiming Hebrews has a similar style to Luke and Acts; Barnabas,[5] a Levite and "son of encouragement" (Acts 4:36) who wrote a "word of encouragement" (Heb 13:22); or Apollos,[6] known for his commanding knowledge of the Old Testament and trained in Greek rhetoric in Alexandria. On the other hand, Luke was a Gentile (Col 4:10–14), and many have a hard time fathoming a Gentile as the author of Hebrews. That Barnabas was a Levite doesn't prove he *must* have written this epistle. The

[4] David L. Allen, "The Authorship of Hebrews: The Lukan Proposal," *FM* 18, no. 2 (2001): 27–40.
[5] Tertullian was possibly the first (c. 210) to ascribe authorship to Barnabas (*Modesty* 20).
[6] Apollos was first nominated by Martin Luther; while very intriguing (see Luke Timothy Johnson, *Hebrews*, NTL [Louisville: Westminster John Knox, 2006], 42–44; George H. Guthrie, "The Case for Apollos as the Author of Hebrews," *FM* 18, no. 2 [2001]: 41–56), the lack of any ancient testimony to his authorship—particularly from the church fathers of Alexandria—is critical.

author's knowledge of priestly rituals is literary, not experiential; it is based more on the Old Testament and less on personal observation.[7]

[7] For more on Hebrews' authorship, see Donald Guthrie, *New Testament Introduction*, 4th ed. (Downers Grove, IL: InterVarsity Press, 1990), 668–82; Simon J. Kistemaker, "The Authorship of Hebrews," *FM* 18, no. 2 (2001): 57–69.

Q Do you have your own theory on the authorship of Hebrews?

A There is a decent amount of evidence that Timothy is the author. I contend that Hebrews is a sermon[8] Timothy preached, one that was subsequently copied down anonymously and distributed as an epistle (the copyist's anonymity causing later confusion as to the letter's authorship). If the material is Timothy's, it would explain both its Pauline associations and the lack of Paul's vocabulary or style. Also, Timothy was raised in Greek culture yet knew the Old Testament very well (2 Tim 3:15). Finally, after the initial ending of the epistle (Heb 13:20–21), note the mention of Timothy within a second ending (13:22–25), which I take as a postscript of sorts by the person who copied down Timothy's sermon. A major problem with identifying our author as Timothy, Apollos, Barnabas, or any other is that we have no surviving documents to which we can compare Hebrews—as we can documents penned by Paul or Luke. And though I have strong opinions about Timothy's authorship, I must concede that knowing definitively who wrote Hebrews *is neither possible nor necessary*. Andrew Trotter says it best: "The church has benefited for almost two thousand years from this magisterial work without knowing with any more certainty than we do today who authored it."[9]

[8] Johnson lists four qualities indicating Hebrews originated as a sermon: (1) distinctive use of first-person plural (we/us/our), (2) author refers to speaking and hearing, not writing and reading (2:5; 5:11; 6:9; 8:1; 11:32), (3) "masterful alternation of exposition and exhortation running through the composition, a pattern that allows an orator to drive home points immediately without losing the hearers' attention," and (4) how the author introduces and develops themes, "creating a wavelike, cumulative effect" (*Hebrews*, 10).

[9] Andrew H. Trotter, Jr., *Interpreting the Epistle to the Hebrews*, GNTE 6 (Grand Rapids: Baker, 1997), 41.

Q If we don't know the author's name, do we know *anything* about him or her?

A For starters, we can rule out Priscilla, Phoebe, Mary, and any other female since the author uses a first-person masculine participle (*diēgoumenon*, "to tell") in 11:32. Second, given the prevalent use of the LXX (Septuagint) in Hebrews and several references to having received a faith handed down by eyewitnesses, the author was likely a Hellenistic Jew and second-generation Christian. The author was well educated in Greek culture, evidenced by the epistle's use of advanced rhetoric,[10] broad vocabulary (of the 1,038 distinct Greek words used in Hebrews, 169 occur nowhere else in the New Testament, and about another 100 occur only one other time), and its familiarity with the same philosophies espoused by Philo (the famed first-century Jewish philosopher in Alexandria).[11] In fact, alongside Luke, our author is considered "the most 'cultured' of the early Christian writers."[12]

[10] Andreas J. Köstenberger, L. Scott Kellum, and Charles L. Quarles, *The Cradle, the Cross, and the Crown: An Introduction to the New Testament*, 2nd ed. (Nashville: B&H Academic, 2016), 774; Harold W. Attridge, "Hebrews, Epistle to the," *ABD* 3:99.

[11] Familiarity, however, doesn't equate to agreement. Most scholars are quick to note that "the basic elements of his [i.e., the Hebrews author's] thought are far removed from the Neoplatonism and Stoicism that undergird so much of Philo" (D. A. Carson and Douglas J. Moo, *An Introduction to the New Testament*, 2nd ed. [Grand Rapids: Zondervan, 2005], 603); see also Ronald Williamson, *Philo and the Epistle to the Hebrews*, ALGHJ 4 (Leiden: Brill, 1970).

[12] Donald Guthrie, "Hebrews, Epistle to the," *ISBE* 2:664.

Q When was Hebrews written?

A Clement of Rome cited this letter in 96, making the early 90s the latest this book could have been authored. On the other hand, the congregation had been established for some time (2:3; 5:12; 10:32; 13:7), so any date circa 60–90 cannot be ruled out definitively. Fortunately, the date of authorship does not impact our interpretation of Hebrews. That said, it's difficult to believe

Hebrews was written after 70. If it were, the author surely would have mentioned the destruction of Jerusalem and the temple since it would have fit so well with his argument. However, those events and the termination of the sacrificial system seem to be future from the author's perspective (8:13; 10:1–2). Furthermore, the letter's recipients are experiencing persecution but not martyrdom (12:4), and this fits with what we know about persecution in the early church circa 60–70. "There appears to have been willingness to trade off true endurance for a compromise with their antagonistic world,"[13] and in light of this, returning to Judaism made sense for Christians in that period. Judaism was still recognized by the Empire as a permissible religion; Christianity was not.

[13] Jon C. Laansma, "Hebrews," in *Theological Interpretation of the New Testament: A Book-by-Book Survey*, ed. Kevin J. Vanhoozer (Grand Rapids: Baker Academic, 2008), 188.

Q What do we know about Hebrews' recipients or audience?

A One writer concluded that "we know less about the historical circumstances for this letter … than for almost any other New Testament book."[14] That said, most everyone agrees the epistle was written to Jewish Christians of unknown locale,[15] though the book never identifies them as such. Several sites have been proposed (e.g., Rome, Alexandria, Jerusalem, and Antioch), but none stands out. It seems the author was writing from Italy (13:24), yet his remark could just as easily refer to those living *outside* of Italy who were sending well-wishes back home. There is substantive evidence (e.g., the author's use of the LXX) that the audience was Hellenistic Jewish Christians (i.e., not from Palestine). We know the recipients had become Christians through others' influence (2:3) and had

[14] Mark Allan Powell, *Introducing the New Testament: A Historical, Literary, and Theological Survey*, 2nd ed. (Grand Rapids: Baker Academic, 2018), 449.

[15] "The simple title 'To the Hebrews' (without any authorial ascription) is first attested at the end of the second century A.D. by Pantaenus, Clement of Alexandria, and Tertullian" (Ben Witherington III, *Invitation to the New Testament: First Things* [Oxford: Oxford Univ. Press, 2013], 324).

been believers for some time (5:12). They had initially been steadfast in their faith but were now beginning to falter (10:32–36).

Q Why did you decide to write a guide to Hebrews?

A I explained that in the introduction.

Q So I should read the introduction if I haven't already?

A Yes.

Q If I don't read the introduction, what will you do to me?

A You will be mysteriously volunteered to chaperone the next youth lock-in at church.

Q Seriously?

A No. However, I strongly urge you to read the introduction.

Q Ok. What are some of the prominent themes in Hebrews?

A Three main themes come up time and again. The first is, obviously, the law of Moses; Hebrews contains fifty-six references to the law, covenant, etc. The second theme is our access to God, which is mentioned twenty-six times. Make a habit of highlighting all the times you come across the phrase "draw near." Finally, the idea of faithfulness pervades the book, appearing some fifty-four times.[16] Covenant, access, and faithfulness, then, are the three most prominent themes of Hebrews.

[16] Brett R. Scott, "Jesus' Superiority over Moses in Hebrews 3:1–6," *BSac* 155 (1998): 206.

Q Do you have any tips for reading Hebrews?

A Yes. One characteristic of this epistle is its many references— everything from direct quotations to subtle allusions—back to the Old Testament. James W. Thompson says, "the writer of Hebrews appeals to the OT more consistently than any other writer of the NT, thus becoming one of the first writers to establish the meaning of the OT for the church."[17] George Guthrie counted "roughly thirty-seven quotations, forty allusions, nineteen cases where OT material is summarized, and thirteen where an OT name or topic is referred to without reference to a specific context."[18] To appreciate each of these Old Testament references, both their original context and the way our author uses them in Hebrews, I recommend getting a copy of the *Commentary on the New Testament Use of the Old Testament*, edited by G. K. Beale and D. A. Carson, and consulting it as you read. This is an excellent resource for further study.

[17] James W. Thompson, "The Hermeneutics of the Epistle to the Hebrews," *ResQ* 38 (1996): 229.
[18] George H. Guthrie, "Hebrews," in *Commentary on the New Testament Use of the Old Testament*, eds. G. K. Beale and D. A. Carson (Grand Rapids: Baker Academic, 2007), 919.

Q What else?

A In addition to the three themes I previously mentioned, three words frequently occur in Hebrews; as you read through the epistle, I recommend highlighting their every occurrence or form. The first is "better," which is typically used to speak of the Son's supremacy. The second is "perfect," which describes Jesus, his sacrifice, and our status in him. The third is "eternal" or "forever," which characterizes not only Jesus' nature and status as our high priest but also the salvation or inheritance we have in him.

Q At times, you refer to books from the Old Testament Apocrypha. Why?

A Good question. The Holy Spirit did not inspire books like 1–2 Maccabees, Sirach, and Wisdom of Solomon, so I do not give them the same weight as I do the biblical canon. However, they are still valuable since they provide a window into the first-century Jewish world. Because many Christians are unfamiliar with these books, I refer to them only when doing so adds to the conversation.

Q Any tips for reading the New Testament epistles in general?

A Someone once said reading the epistles is like learning the answers without knowing the questions, and that's true. It's also like walking into a room where a spouse or friend is talking on the phone, and you try to discern who is on the other end and what they are discussing by listening to one side of the conversation. Plus, many Christians have been conditioned to read the epistles a few verses at a time and are thus unable to appreciate the overall message. That's why I recommend reading through the entire letter multiple times in one sitting.

Q What would be the best way to use this guide?

A I recommend a four-pass system for studying Hebrews. I'll explain. To get the most out of Hebrews 2:5–9, for example, I suggest you read (1) all of Hebrews 2, (2) 2:5–9 again, (3) that passage's section in this guide, and (4) 2:5–9 a third time. Reading the text multiple times will help cement it in your mind.

Q Similar to how rewatching a favorite movie or rereading a favorite book allows you to catch things previously missed?

A Exactly.

Q What can you tell us about how this guide came together?

A As always, I wrestled with what to include versus omit. Some scholarly debates are much ado about nothing, and sharing everything a commentator said can be more of a hindrance than a help. I wanted the reader to understand God's Word, so I tried to anticipate and answer common questions that arise from the text. Don't expect me to deal with every issue; that would exhaust us all. Besides, I don't expect you always to agree with my conclusions. I do, however, expect you to study and reflect on your own; then, and only then, should you make an informed decision. I want this guide to resemble a friendly conversation about Hebrews, albeit one-sided. Pretend you and I are sitting in a coffee shop somewhere, sipping cups of joe, and talking about Hebrews. Each chapter ends with a few Talking Points, areas of application I hope will provide practical material for lessons or sermons and spark positive discussion in a class or small-group setting. In the end, I want everyone who reads this guide to fall in love with the supreme Son and, consequently, "draw near to the throne of grace" in worship. Readers ultimately must judge for themselves whether I have succeeded.

Q Do you recommend a specific Bible translation?

> **A** No. This guide primarily uses the English Standard Version (ESV), but it always helps to read the Bible in more than one translation. I definitely recommend a good study Bible.

Q Would you like to add anything before we wrap up?

> **A** If you see an abbreviation you don't recognize, there is a list of abbreviations on page 321. All years are AD unless otherwise noted. Also, don't ignore the footnotes—at times, they are only source citations; at others, they contain elaborations, quotes that drive the point home, or a really good joke!

Q Anything else?

> **A** Did you read the introduction?

Q Yes.

> **A** Then the only other thing I would add is an encouragement to meditate on what God has to say in Hebrews. In his concluding remarks on the epistle, Ben Witherington lamented, "It is a great pity that this book has been so neglected by the church through the centuries. Perhaps in this century, this powerful sermon will finally receive the loud *amen* it deserves from its hearers."[19] I couldn't agree more. Again, I hope this study of Hebrews draws you closer to the heart of our high priest and God's supreme Son.

[19] Witherington, *Invitation*, 338.

Throughout the epistle, the term "better" is ascribed to the Lord, thus distinguishing him as better and other than mere created beings; for his sacrifice of himself, the hope that we have in him, and the promises which are ours through him are all better, not only as a matter of degree but as being of a quite different order, since he who has made these things available to us is better than all created beings.

ATHANASIUS

Chapter 1

THE LAST WORD

Joe wasn't exactly your average joe. According to many accounts, he was tall, handsome, and profoundly charismatic—everything you would want in a leader. In 1830, Joseph Smith published *The Book of Mormon*, a work purportedly translated from golden plates bearing inscriptions in an alleged ancient language Smith called "reformed Egyptian." By the time of Smith's death fourteen years later, Mormonism had nearly 25,000 followers across the world.

Among the many stories in *The Book of Mormon* is an account of how Israelites immigrated to the Americas around the time of the Babylonian Exile. The book (and Smith's subsequent writings) contains many preposterous prophecies. However, all this was secondary to Smith's primary claim: Christ had personally appeared to him and commissioned him to bring the restored gospel to the world. To this day, *The Book of Mormon* bears the audacious subtitle, "Another Testament of Jesus Christ."

Some years ago, my wife and I studied with two pairs of Mormon missionaries on separate occasions. I was impressed with their fervor and dedication to proselytizing the world. Nevertheless, I was taken aback by how adamant they were that Joseph Smith was a great prophet of God who should be heeded. They clung to this view even when I confronted them with hard evidence concerning some of Smith's most significant failed prophecies. Within Mormonism, there is a near fanatical obsession with heeding the voice of Smith, Brigham Young, and the church's other prophets and apostles.

Shake your head if you like over people's folly in buying into the erratic claims of mere mortals, but you and I do the same thing. Everyone is listening to someone. I repeat: everyone is listening to someone.

Who has your ear?

> Cable news networks like CNN, Fox News, or MSNBC and the outrage they broadcast daily into our homes?

> Social media and its "What will we be offended by today?" newsfeeds and timelines?

> Television and radio personalities like Ellen, Oprah, Dr. Phil, Dr. Oz, Glenn Beck, Sean Hannity, or Rush Limbaugh?

> Religious celebrities like Joel Osteen, Billy Graham, Rob Bell, T. D. Jakes, John Piper, Tim Keller, Francis Chan, Andy Stanley, Brian Zahnd, David Platt, or your favorite preacher?

> Pop-culture superstars like Beyoncé, Taylor Swift, Harry and Meghan, or the Kardashians?

> A favorite blogger or online personality like Matt Walsh, Ben Shapiro, or Jen Hatmaker, who writes on your pet topics (e.g., parenting, politics, religion, health) with authority and indignation?

> Family members like your mother, spouse, or older sibling?

Someone has your ear. Everyone is listening to someone, and if I spend enough time with you, I might figure out who that person is.

The opening of Hebrews is about one thing: listening to Jesus. Our author immediately begins with a call to heed the final word God has spoken to his people, one delivered via a beloved and divine Son.[1] This word isn't exactly *new*; it shares continuity with all God has spoken since creation. Still, it is an *ultimate* word.[2] All God has wished to reveal about himself (and, as it turns out, that's quite a lot) has been spoken fully and finally through Jesus.

One might think it silly to remind the church of Christ to listen to Jesus—his name is literally on the sign! Given, however, the milieu in which we find ourselves, the bride of our Lord needs to listen to her husband like never before. We need to hear what Jesus says about weakness, suffering,

---

[1] The seventy-two Greek words in 1:1–4 comprise a single sentence built around "God ... has spoken." "God has something to say to the church, and that message focuses preeminently in the person and work of the exalted Son" (George H. Guthrie, *Hebrews*, NIVAC [Grand Rapids: Zondervan, 1998], 53).

[2] "The OT is obviously the word of God, for the author appeals to it regularly. ... At the same time, the author argues consistently that God's word in the son surpasses his words of the past" (Thompson, "Hermeneutics," 232).

faithfulness, and obedience. We need to hear what Jesus says about conflict resolution, corrupting power, and becoming like little children. We need to hear what Jesus says about identifying with the meek and lowly versus high and mighty—to name a few topics. We need, Hebrews claims, to listen to Jesus. Here's why:

HEBREWS 1:1–3

The opening of Hebrews exhibits a literary artistry that can be appreciated fully only in the original language. William Barclay called it "the most stylistically impressive piece of Greek in the whole New Testament. It is a passage that any classical Greek orator would have been proud to write."[3] In his opening salvo, the author presents Hebrews' main idea: the Son's supremacy. Jesus is greater than all things, and only he reveals to us the fullness of God and enables us to enter the divine presence.

The author's reference to "the prophets" (v 1) encompasses the entire Old Testament. These men were incomplete representatives of God, who spoke to them "at many times and in many ways" through progressive revelation: riveting narratives, sacred hymns, profound proverbs, legal codes, enigmatic visions, love songs, and even a still, small voice. While we might say the prophets were God's servants, Jesus is God's Son, and though God spoke through the prophets, he never did so as fully as he has through his Son. In Jesus, all the jigsaw-puzzle-piece messages of the Hebrew Bible assemble to form a clear and complete image of the Father.

God has spoken through his Son "in these last days," which is how the Old Testament refers to the future envisioned by the prophets, the one that came to pass in the New Testament.[4] Jewish thought divided all history into two epochs, former times and end times, and the New Testament reflects this: "on [us] the end of the ages has come" (1 Cor 10:11).

After declaring that God has spoken fully and finally through Jesus, our author goes on to describe seven key elements of Jesus' person and work (vv 2–3), each of which underscores his supremacy.

---

[3] William Barclay, *The Letter to the Hebrews*, 3rd ed., NDSB (Louisville: Westminster John Knox, 2002), 13.
[4] Num 24:14; Isa 2:2; Jer 23:20; Ezek 38:16; Hos 3:5; Mic 4:1; 2 Tim 3:1; 1 Pet 1:20; 2 Pet 3:3.

Jesus as Heir. When the word "heir" comes to mind, I immediately wish upon a star and imagine what it would be like to be Jeff Bezos' heir, or Bill Gates', or Elon Musk's—really, anyone wealthy to the tune of a few billion dollars. In the New Testament, the concepts of heir and inheritance often carry this meaning. In verse 2, however, Hebrews has a different nuance in mind. To inherit (*klēronomeō*) something can mean to be granted authority to use or administer that thing (Matt 21:38; Gal 4:1)—that is, "to take possession of." A predominant way the term was used in the LXX was in reference to Israel's receiving ownership of the Promised Land (e.g., Gen 15:7; 22:17; Lev 20:24; Deut 1:39). Elsewhere in Hebrews, it says Noah inherited or took possession of righteousness by his faith (11:7), and God's people take possession of God's promises (6:12). So what is it that Jesus takes possession of by being the heir of all things?

The Old Testament speaks of God's granting authority over the earth to the first man (Gen 1:28). When Adam's dominion was lost in the fall, God granted the nations as an inheritance first to Abraham (17:5) and then to Israel's king (Ps 2:8). However, God's eternal plan was to appoint his Son as the ultimate heir of not just the nations but the entire universe, including the world to come (Heb 2:5). "Through Christ's perfect life, death, and resurrection, he earns the right to inherit the cosmos."[5] Thus Jesus has received authority from God to govern all things; he has "taken possession of" all things (Matt 11:27; 28:18).

Two verses later, we learn Jesus has inherited the name "Son" (v 4), and as fellow heirs with him, the angels minister to us (v 14). While the relationship between the Son's inheritance and our own isn't explained here, it's clear enough that the Son's inheritance has serious ramifications for our salvation.[6] For now, our author's audience is left to ponder how much better their lot will be if they remain partners with the One who will inherit, possess, and rule over all.[7] As Paul reminded the Corinthians, "Everything

---

[5] G. K. Beale and Benjamin L. Gladd, *The Story Retold: A Biblical-Theological Introduction to the New Testament* (Downers Grove, IL: IVP Academic, 2020), 369.

[6] Joshua W. Jipp, "The Son's Entrance into the Heavenly World: The Soteriological Necessity of the Scriptural Catena in Hebrews 1.5–14," *NTS* 56 (2010): 560.

[7] "Apart from Christ there is no sonship and heirship. Those therefore who desire to enjoy the privileges of the sons and heirs of God can do so only as by faith they are found *in Christ*" (Philip Edgcumbe Hughes, *A Commentary on the Epistle to the Hebrews*, NICNT [Grand Rapids: Eerdmans, 1977], 39; emphasis his).

belongs to you, and you belong to Christ, and Christ belongs to God" (1 Cor 3:22–23 NLT).

Jesus as Creator. Lest we consider Jesus to be a Johnny-come-lately, Hebrews says that he was the agent of creation. He not only was present in the beginning (John 1:1–2) but was also the force behind bringing all things into existence (John 1:3; 1 Cor 8:6; Col 1:16). Later, our author will refer to Jesus as the "builder" of the "house" (3:3). "The writer has left no room for doubt that the Son was God's agent in creating the world, at the same time equating the Son with the God of the OT."[8] This offers hope to an oppressed people looking for a supreme comforter. If Christ is the Creator of all, he can hardly be defined or subjugated by anything in his creation. Whatever power stands against us is inferior to the One who created all things and now reigns as our great high priest.

Jesus as Radiance. In the Old Testament, God's glory was synonymous with his presence.[9] As sunbeams convey the sun's power to earth, Jesus was the "radiance" of God's glory (v 3) who came to earth to show us what God is like.[10] Perhaps this was never truer than when our Lord was transfigured on the mountain, "and his clothes became radiant, intensely white, as no one on earth could bleach them" (Mark 9:3). In addition to his presence, the imagery of light and glory in Scripture often refers to God's nature.[11]

Moreover, just as there is virtually no difference between looking at a light's radiance versus the light itself, there is no difference between looking at Jesus and looking at God; "to see the Son is to view God's glory or manifest presence"[12] (see John 17:5). Consistent with his initial assertion, our author is presenting "Christ as the supreme and final revelation of the Father."[13] Not even Moses could make such a claim, for though his face shone with the glory of God as he descended Sinai, it eventually faded (2 Cor 3:13). Only Christ has retained God's glory forever.

---

[8] Calvin D. Redmond, "Jesus: God's Agent of Creation," *AUSS* 42 (2004): 297.
[9] Exod 16:7; 24:16; 33:18; Lev 9:6, 23; Num 14:10; 16:19; 20:6; Deut 5:24.
[10] Luke 9:32; John 1:14; 2:11; 1 Cor 2:8; Phil 3:21; 2 Thess 2:14.
[11] Isa 42:8; 48:11; 60:19–20; Dan 2:22; Hab 3:4; 1 Tim 6:16; Jas 1:17; 1 John 1:5.
[12] Guthrie, *Hebrews*, 48.
[13] Silva, "αὐγάζω," *NIDNTTE* 1:440–41.

Yet, while God's presence and glory in the Old Testament were often met with fear, trembling, and the subsequent command "Do not be afraid," the advent of Christ made God approachable to humanity ("fullness of God in helpless babe," as we sing). To continue the sunlight analogy, just as staring into the glory of the sun is too much for us, yet the sun's *rays* can be gazed upon safely,[14] so God's glory is too great for us, yet in Jesus we can safely behold the radiance of the Father's glory.

Jesus as Imprint. Growing up, I was often told I favored my mom, and I did. I was scrawny and lean, and I still have a few of her features (e.g., same hair color). But since college, I've morphed into a startling resemblance of my dad (which is code for "I got fat and filled out!"). With more than one person who never knew Dad, I've joked, "If you've seen me, you've seen the father."

The Greek term translated "exact imprint" (*charaktēr*) occurs only here in the New Testament. It referred to a reproduction or representation of something; in 4 Maccabees 15:4, it is used for the resemblance of children to their parents. The term is related to *charagma*, a brand for an animal (Rev 13:16; 14:9; 20:4) or a stamp used on coins and seals.[15] Just as our money bears the image of former presidents, ancient coins bore the likenesses of kings and emperors. That image on the coin was a direct imprint or image of the die or stamp used to mint the coin. Likewise, the supreme Son is the "stamp" of the Father's image.[16] Unlike myself, Jesus does not simply resemble his Father; he is *exactly like* the Father (2 Cor 4:4; Phil 2:6; Col 1:15). "Whatever God is, Christ is; the very likeness of God, the very Godhead of Godhead, the very Deity of Deity, is in Christ Jesus."[17]

Jesus as Sustainer. Atlas, a condemned Titan in Greek mythology, was believed to bear the cosmos on his shoulders. After the Olympians defeated the Titans, Zeus sentenced Atlas to uphold the universe for all time and condemned the rest of the Titans to Tartarus. Unlike Atlas, the

---

[14] Philo, *Dreams* 1.239.

[15] BDAG, s.v. "χάραγμα"; Silva, "χάραγμα," *NIDNTTE* 4:651.

[16] F. F. Bruce, *The Epistle to the Hebrews*, rev. ed., NICNT (Grand Rapids: Eerdmans, 1990), 48.

[17] C. H. Spurgeon, "Depths and Heights," in *The Metropolitan Tabernacle Pulpit Sermons* (London: Passmore, 1899), 45:389. "All the stress in this passage falls on Christ's unity with God, a traditional truth of which the readers probably needed to be reminded" (Paul Ellingworth, *The Epistle to the Hebrews*, NIGTC [Grand Rapids: Eerdmans, 1993], 100).

Son of God is not upholding the universe in the sense of bearing it on his shoulders in a static way. Instead, the verb translated "upholds" (*pherō*) can mean "to cause to follow a certain course in direction or conduct" or "to move an object to a particular point."[18] Moses complained to God concerning Israel, "I cannot carry [*pherō* LXX] all these people by myself; the burden is too heavy for me" (Num 11:14 NIV). In the context, an exasperated Moses was fed up with the Israelites' constant griping. His complaint that he could no longer carry the people meant he could not drive them toward their destination: "I can't get the job done. I can't move them to where they need to be."

Moses' example gives us a window into what our author is claiming about Christ. While it is true that, according to Paul, "all things hold together" in Christ (Col 1:17), Hebrews asserts our sovereign Lord is also driving all things (people, empires, events, trends) to their appointed end, to where his divine sovereignty has ordained them to be. What the Son has created and inherited, he now sustains.

Note also that Christ does not uphold the universe through strenuous physical effort. Instead, the Son's supremacy is demonstrated in that he does all this "by his powerful word" (NIV). Pause a moment and consider the sovereignty of a supreme Son who simply speaks and thereby sustains the universe—what theologians call the power of divine fiat.

What is true on a macro level is also true on a micro one. At this point, and not for the last time, Hebrews becomes at once profoundly theological and intensely personal. "Here the word of the Son is cosmic, but later it becomes personal, when Jesus calls people his brothers and sisters (2:11–13), speaks of obedience to God (10:5–7), and makes intercession for others (7:25; cf. 12:24). The word of Christ that bears all things also bears the listeners in their pilgrimage of faith."[19] The supreme Son is not so preoccupied with the affairs of the broader universe that he cannot empathize with our sorrows and weaknesses (4:15).

Jesus as Priest. Hebrews' most significant contribution to New Testament theology is its portrayal of Jesus as high priest. Behind this idea lies

---

[18] BDAG, s.v. "φέρω."
[19] Koester, *Hebrews*, 190.

the Old Testament concepts of the Day of Atonement (Exod 30:10; Lev 16:30) and blood covenant (Exod 24:6–8). Though he does not use the word "priest" here, our author speaks of Jesus making purification for sins before his exaltation to the Father's right hand.

It is one thing to contemplate the superlative qualities of Jesus as heir, creator, etc. Each one of these on its own ought to elicit an ineffable sense of awe. It is an altogether different thing to contemplate Jesus as priest and purifier of our sins. To get a mental image of the foulness of our sin and our need for purification, consider:

> In April 2014, the city of Flint, Michigan, switched its municipal water source to the Flint River, exposing 100,000 citizens to toxic levels of lead in the drinking water because of inadequate treatment.

> In the 1994 film *The Shawshank Redemption*, there is a repulsive scene in which inmate Andy Dufresne crawls through a half-mile of foul sewer pipes on his way to freedom.

> I had a neighbor once who installed and serviced septic tanks for a living, and he never spoke glowingly of his life's work.

> Growing up, my grandparents had an outhouse on their property. It was never pleasant to use, especially in that humid, stagnant Mississippi summer heat.

> In 1989, the tanker *Exxon Valdez* ran aground in Alaska, spilling 10.8 million gallons of crude oil into Prince William Sound. For many years, it was considered the worst oil spill in the U.S.—until 2010 when the drilling rig *Deepwater Horizon* exploded, taking eleven lives and eventually dumping over 210 million gallons of oil into the Gulf of Mexico.

> The U.S. spends an average of $38 billion annually to store its nuclear waste because no one else wants to deal with it.

Contemplate each of those facts/anecdotes and realize there is no water or sewer system, no septic tank or outhouse, no oil spill or nuclear dump that can begin to compare to or illustrate the putrid foulness that is our sin. Indeed, what has been significantly lost among some Christians is any sense of revulsion over our transgressions.

Lest we consider Jesus to be merely a more powerful cleansing agent than any that preceded him (e.g., a superior washing detergent), it must be noted that "purification" in this verse more precisely means to cleanse or purge by propitiation (see Exod 29:36; 30:10). Yes, Jesus offers a superior cleansing, but he bought it with his violent death (9:12, 14; Acts 20:28). Atonement was necessary, and the supreme Son offered it. Purification means more than being rid of putrid sin; it means we have a high priest who paid a high price for our perfection.

Jesus as King. The seventh and final element in verses 2–3 is the one to which our author has been building. After atoning for the sins of the world, Jesus was exalted to and enthroned at God's right hand.[20] This great truth has important implications. (1) Christ has "sat down," emphasizing the finality of his purification of our sins; one sits only when there remains no more work to be done (10:11–14). (2) "At the right hand" was a position of tremendous honor throughout the ancient world (e.g., 1 Kgs 2:19; Ps 45:9). Thus the Son's session (i.e., his exaltation and enthronement) means "he lives and rules with the authority and power of God himself."[21] This introduces one of Hebrews' themes: exaltation through suffering. (3) The Son is now forever exalted beyond and sovereign over his enemies. "Though men do and will continue their malice and wrath against the Lord Christ to the end of the world, as though they would crucify him afresh, yet he dies no more, being secure out of their reach."[22] Enemies of Christ's church may oppress us, but Christ—the object of Christians' worship, trust, service, and love—remains exalted and sovereign. All that we subject to—and thus secure in the possession of—the supreme Son will be shielded and kept "until that day" (2 Tim 1:12).

Of the seven elements of Jesus' character listed in verses 2–3, it is these final two that "announce the major themes of the writer's christology, i.e., sacrifice and exaltation. None of the other declarations in the opening

[20] Jesus' place at God's right hand "is one of the earliest affirmations of Christian faith" (Bruce, *Hebrews*, 49–50); e.g., Mark 12:36; 14:62; 16:19; Acts 2:33–34; 5:31; Rom 8:34; Col 3:1.

[21] William L. Lane, *Hebrews 1–8*, WBC 47A (Dallas: Word, 1991), 16. Christ shares God's "power without limitation, though always with the subordination implied in the fact that it is God who gives, and the Son who receives, this supreme status" (Ellingworth, *Hebrews*, 103).

[22] John Owen, *An Exposition of the Epistle to the Hebrews*, ed. W. H. Goold (Grand Rapids: Baker, 1980), 3:120.

paragraph will receive comparable elucidation in [Hebrews]."[23] Jesus as empathetic Priest and Jesus as exalted Son are at the heart of this epistle.

HEBREWS 1:4–14

In the remainder of Hebrews 1, our author reels off seven quotations from the Old Testament. Stringing several passages together was a standard exegetical method among first-century Jewish and Christian interpreters. This rhetorical technique was called "chain quotations" or "a string of pearls."[24] These were formed by Scriptures with conceptual links (e.g., common words, such as "Son"); the idea was to quote so much Scripture on a topic that the audience was overwhelmed and persuaded to agree. In Hebrews 1, our author's agenda is to convince his readers that Jesus is greater than the angels since his name or status, that of "Son," is superior to theirs (v 4).

But why?[25] Why was it so crucial for our author to lead off with this? Were angels objects of fascination or veneration for first-century Jewish Christians? What threat did that pose to the deity of Christ? Recall my point in the Q&A that, with the epistles, we sometimes know the answers without knowing the questions, and this is one such case. One thing is for sure: our author was not detouring on a mere for-what-it's-worth digression.[26] But neither is Hebrews solely focused on this issue; after 2:18, our author won't even mention angels again until the last two chapters, and then only in passing.

One theory is that the Hebrews audience worshiped angels, a practice to which Paul once alluded (Col 2:18).[27] However, given they were formerly Jews and thus adverse to worshiping anyone or anything but Yahweh, it

---

[23] Lane, *Hebrews 1–8*, 15.

[24] Markus Barth, "The Old Testament in Hebrews: An Essay in Biblical Hermeneutics," in *Current Issues in New Testament Interpretation: Essays in Honor of Otto A. Piper*, eds. William Klassen and Graydon F. Snyder (New York: Harper, 1962), 64; Herbert W. Bateman, IV, "Two First-Century Messianic Uses of the OT: Heb 1:5–13 and 4QFlor 1.1–19," *JETS* 38 (1995): 11–27; e.g., Acts 2:25–28, 33–36; 13:34–37; Rom 3:10–18; 9:25–29; 10:18–21; 11:8–10; 1 Pet 2:6–10.

[25] "Today's readers have little or no sense of why angels need be discussed at all, much less take the prominent place in Hebrews' argument" (Johnson, *Hebrews*, 82). See his excursus, "Why the Angels?" (*Hebrews*, 82–84).

[26] "Clearly, [the author mentions Jesus' relation to the angels] not because it might be a matter of general interest, but because the situation he is addressing demands it. The question is one of special relevance and urgency" (P. Hughes, *Commentary*, 51).

[27] T. W. Manson, "The Problem of the Epistle to the Hebrews," *BJRL* 32 (1949–50): 1–17. But nothing else of the Colossian heresy is mentioned in Hebrews (David A. deSilva, *Perseverance in Gratitude* [Grand Rapids: Eerdmans, 2000], 92, n. 20).

is highly improbable they were guilty of elevating angels to the status of deity.[28] A second theory is based on the fact that the angels had mediated the law at Sinai (Deut 33:2; Acts 7:53; Gal 3:19; Heb 2:2).[29] If the author of Hebrews could establish Jesus as greater than the angels, he could more easily present Christ as a better mediator of a better covenant (8:6; 9:15; 12:24) and worthy of greater loyalty.[30]

More likely, however, is that some first-century Jewish Christians were more comfortable ascribing to Jesus the status of an angel rather than God.[31] In other words, the issue was not the *pro*motion of angels (as in Col 2:18) but the *de*motion of Jesus. "If they would simply agree that Jesus was an angel, perhaps even the greatest of angels, but not God, they would be accepted into the synagogue and escape the awful pressure. Such a prospect was tantalizing because it did not require an outright denial of Christ, but only a different affirmation of him and his greatness as an angel."[32] After all, the Old Testament emphatically declared there was only one God (Deut 6:4) and that he did not share his glory with another (Isa 42:8). So the only other category available (as some first-century Christians thought) was that of a cosmic superhero/archangel. Moreover, the enigmatic "angel of the LORD" in the Old Testament was popularly thought by early Christians to have been the preincarnate Christ.[33] So Jesus *had* to be an angel, right? "Wrong!" says our author, and in verses 5–13, he appeals to the Old Testament for proof.

Psalm 2:7. The second psalm is about God's affirmation of the son of David who occupied the throne in Jerusalem. The wicked are portrayed as conspiring "against the LORD and against his Anointed" (Ps 2:2). Yahweh, however, mocks their foolishness and terrifies them with his fury when he declares the establishment of his anointed on the throne of Zion

---

[28] "For the Rabbis the test of the acceptability of a doctrine is its relation to belief in God. … Even in the most developed angelology the angels only serve to execute and reveal the power and deity of Yahweh" (Gerhard Kittel, "ἄγγελος," *TDNT* 1:81).

[29] Within Judaism, "Angels had taken on a very high role during the Second Temple period [c. 520 BC–AD 70], which was characterized by the absence of direct divine revelation" (Andreas J. Köstenberger, *Handbook on Hebrews through Revelation*, HNT [Grand Rapids: Baker Academic, 2020], 9).

[30] Thomas R. Schreiner, *Commentary on Hebrews*, BTCP (Nashville: Holman Reference, 2015), 60.

[31] Adolphine Bakker, "Christ an Angel? A Study of Early Christian Docetism," *ZNW* 32 (1933): 255–65.

[32] R. Kent Hughes, *Hebrews*, 2 vols., PTW (Wheaton, IL: Crossway, 1993), 1:35–36; see also Murray J. Harris, "The Translation and Significance of ὁ θεός in Hebrews 1:8–9," *TynBul* 36 (1985): 130–31.

[33] Gen 16:7–13; Exod 3:2–4; Num 22:22–35; Judg 6:11–23; 13:3–23; see "Angel of the Lord," in *A Dictionary of Early Christian Beliefs*, ed. David W. Bercot (Peabody, MA: Hendrickson, 1998), 20–21.

(vv 4–6). The psalmist depicts Yahweh saying to the Davidic king, "You are my Son; today I have begotten you"[34] (v 7).

Early Christians quickly appropriated Psalm 2 as a messianic psalm by applying it to Jesus (e.g., Acts 4:25–26; 13:33; Rev 12:5), partly because it never saw historical fulfillment in the days of Israel's monarchy. The New Testament claims that after his crucifixion, resurrection, ascension, and exaltation, the honorific title of "Son"—one Jesus had always possessed—became invested with royal meaning.[35] Only then did Jesus the Son also become Jesus the King (Acts 13:33–34; Rom 1:4). On that "day,"[36] the Father said to him, "You are my Son, today I have begotten you" (Heb 1:5), an affirmation never given to any angel.

2 Samuel 7:14. After David had established himself in his capital in Jerusalem, he desired to build the temple to honor the Lord. However, through the prophet Nathan, God informed the king that this would be a privilege reserved for David's son Solomon. Nonetheless, God made a covenant with David, swearing that Israel's throne would belong to his dynasty forever (2 Sam 7:13–14).

From this passage developed the belief of the everlasting nature of David's dynasty and God's unyielding faithfulness to Jesse's son (e.g., Pss 89:28–37; 132:11–12). "The permanence of God's covenant with David formed the basis for Israel's hope in a future king who would carry on David's line and be the inheritor of covenant promises. ... Thus, it is understandable that 2 Sam. 7 would be appropriated by later generations as a vital messianic text."[37]

Indeed, none of David's dynastic successors in Jerusalem were able to hold on to the throne forever; the promise remained unrealized. For the rest of the Old Testament, the prophets looked forward to its fulfillment:

---

[34] "I have begotten you" does not mean there was a time when the Son didn't exist. Instead, it was common in ancient Near Eastern theology for a god to call the king his son as a way of expressing "divine sponsorship, support, or assistance for the king, and by implication for his dynasty" (Joseph A. Fitzmyer, *The Dead Sea Scrolls and Christian Origins*, SDSSRL [Grand Rapids: Eerdmans, 2000], 66).

[35] "Hebrews does not know a time when Christ is not 'a son' or even when it is not appropriate to refer to him as *the* Son. It is only at God's right hand, however, that Christ is 'enthroned' as the Son and properly takes on the appointment that God has assigned him" (Kenneth Schenck, "Keeping His Appointment: Creation and Enthronement in Hebrews," *JSNT* 66 [1997]: 91; emphasis his).

[36] "This 'day' belongs, in the first place, to the event of the resurrection, but it extends also to the ascension of Christ and his glorification at the right hand of the divine majesty" (P. Hughes, *Commentary*, 55).

[37] Guthrie, "Hebrews," 928–29.

Isaiah spoke of one born of a virgin, a child who would occupy David's throne "from this time forth and forevermore" (7:14; 9:6–7); "a shoot from the stump of Jesse," a righteous branch on whom "the Spirit of the LORD shall rest" (11:1–2; see Jer 23:5; 33:15). Amos foresaw the restoration of "the booth of David" (9:11; Acts 15:16); Micah predicted the advent of a ruler of Israel from Bethlehem "whose coming forth is from of old, from ancient days" (5:2).

In the New Testament, Christ fulfilled the Davidic promise. As early as Gabriel's announcement to Mary (Luke 1:32), it was understood that Jesus would inherit David's throne. Jesus is "the root and the descendant of David" (Rev 22:16) and possesses "the key of David" (3:7). In other words, that Jesus is God's unique Son means he occupies a seat of power greater than David ever knew. He holds sway over the universe and enjoys an unrivaled position of influence with the Father. As Son and King, Jesus enjoys God's favor unlike anyone else, including the angels, and he is God's anointed Ruler, embodying the fulfillment of the Davidic promise.

Deuteronomy 32:43. Though most English translations render this verse, "Rejoice with him, O heavens; bow down to him, all gods," the LXX[38] reads, "Delight, O heavens, with him and worship him, you *sons of God*" (emphasis mine). "Sons of God" is a reference to the angels (e.g., Job 1:6, 8), while "him" refers to Yahweh. However, authors of the New Testament "often apply to Jesus texts that refer to Yahweh … since Jesus shares the same identity as Yahweh."[39]

Using this passage, Hebrews points to Jesus as God's preeminent firstborn[40] and one worthy of worship (v 6). The phrase "when he brings the firstborn into the world"[41] is a reference to Jesus' resurrection and enthronement. On that occasion, God presented the Son to the angels to be worshiped: "When the divine Son descended into the world for the

---

[38] "That our author regularly quotes the LXX is nowhere more evident than in the present quotation from Deut. 32:43, which is not found in the Hebrew Bible" (Donald A. Hagner, *Hebrews*, UBCS [Grand Rapids: Baker, 2011], 37).

[39] Schreiner, *Hebrews*, 66.

[40] The Greek *prōtotokos* can pertain to the "special status associated with a firstborn" (BDAG, s.v. "πρωτότοκος"), i.e., "priority in rank" (Lane, *Hebrews 1–8*, 26). It does not imply that Jesus was a created being but expresses his place of prominence (e.g., Ps 89:27; Rom 8:29; Col 1:15, 18; Rev 1:5).

[41] Instead of the typical Greek term for "world," *kosmos*, our author chose *oikoumenē*, which in Hebrews refers to the spiritual realm or the divine presence (e.g., 2:5).

incarnation, he was unrecognized by the angels [see Eph 3:10; 1 Pet 1:12]; but when he ascended to the right hand of the Father, he displayed his glory and received angelic homage."[42]

Psalm 104:4. The inferiority of the angels to the Son is further demonstrated in Hebrews 1:7 with a citation from Psalm 104. The statement may mean that God makes wind and fire to be his servants. It's more natural, however, to interpret this passage as claiming that God *uses* angels to *send* wind and fire at his discretion[43] (see 2 Esdras 8:21). In first-century Jewish thought, angels were closer to the presence of God than any other being. Archangels especially were believed to be in closest proximity to the throne and were known as "angels of the presence" (*Jubilees* 2.2; Luke 1:19; Rev 8:2). The Son, however, possesses an intimacy with the Father that angels never will. The angels are "hired hands," a fact our author will reiterate when he later notes that angels are mere ministers sent out to serve (v 14). Jesus is greater than the angels, however, for he is God's Son.

Psalm 45:6–7. In 1:8–9, Hebrews appeals to a psalm that might have been written to commemorate a royal wedding in Jerusalem (possibly Solomon's). In 45:6, the psalmist addresses Yahweh, but in the next verse, his attention returns to the king, God's anointed one, whom the author of Hebrews now claims is Jesus. Though this psalm was not quoted often in Jewish literature, when it was, it was always impregnated with messianic meaning.[44]

In citing Psalm 45, our author depicts Jesus as the only legitimate fulfillment of this psalm and heir of David's throne. The power (scepter) of his kingdom or throne will be in the authority (scepter) of his righteousness. The reigns of many kings have been characterized by cruelty, deceit, and selfishness; "the Son's rule, however, is dramatically different, for he rules justly and righteously."[45] In addition, this passage demonstrates that Jesus is heir to God's *eternal* throne that stands "forever and ever." Jesus is greater than the angels because God has established Jesus as king on David's throne forever to reign in unparalleled righteousness.

---

[42] Lane, *Hebrews 1–8*, 28.

[43] "Reference to the angels as 'winds' and 'flames of fire' likely evokes a connection between the angels and the Sinai theophany (Exod 3.2; 14.19; 19.9, 16–19; cf. Acts 7.30)" (Jipp, "Son's Entrance," 564).

[44] Guthrie, "Hebrews," 938.

[45] Schreiner, *Hebrews*, 72.

Psalm 102:25–27. Our author has established the Son as having an eternal existence and an eternal throne. With his sixth Old Testament quotation (vv 10–12), he uses Psalm 102 to point to the Son as integral to the consummation of all things. "Though he will be active in bringing earth and even heaven to an end, he himself will remain unchanged."[46] The constant, continuing Christ is at the heart of Hebrews' message.

The superscription of Psalm 102 identifies it as "a prayer of one afflicted, when he is faint and pours out his complaint before the LORD." The psalmist knew his days were not infinite (vv 3–11). However, he was confident of God's continued care because Yahweh is eternal, not temporal (v 12). Confidence in God's providence is rooted in his timelessness. Eventually, the psalmist found comfort that, just as all things began with God, all things will end with God (vv 25–27).

Hebrews appropriates this psalm and applies it to Christ. As with the Father, our confidence in the Son is rooted in his timelessness. "The world has no independent existence, but depends upon the power of the Son of God, who will remain when heaven and earth perish. The implication is that if faith is based on the empirical world, it is captive to the cycles of decay and death, and is therefore doomed to perish. *For faith to endure it must be placed in the Son of God, who endures.*"[47] Later in his sermon, our author will extol and elucidate the permanence of this supreme Son, who "is the same yesterday and today and forever" (13:8).

Psalm 110:1. Of all the citations from the Old Testament in the opening chapter of Hebrews, this one in verse 13 is the most foundational to the rest of the book.[48] While the psalm initially referred to a mortal king on Israel's throne in Jerusalem, the New Testament habitually applies it to Jesus, the King of kings.[49] On trial, Jesus claimed fulfillment of Psalm 110:1 for himself "when he told his judges that they would from then on see the Son of Man seated at the right hand of the Almighty [Mark 14:62; Dan 7:13]. This claim, condemned as blasphemy by the Sanhedrin,

---

[46] Ellingworth, *Hebrews*, 126.
[47] Koester, *Hebrews*, 203; emphasis mine.
[48] Ps 110 is the basis for Heb 5:6, 10; 6:20; 7:3, 11, 17, 21; 8:1; 10:12–13; 12:2. The New Testament refers to Ps 110 more than any other Old Testament text.
[49] Acts 2:34–35; 5:31; Rom 8:34; 1 Cor 15:25; Eph 1:20; Col 3:1; 1 Pet 3:22.

was held by the apostles to have been vindicated by the subsequent act of God"[50] (i.e., the resurrection).

There is a subtle reminder in verse 13 about the fate of Jesus' opponents. To become a footstool "is an image of forced submission"[51] (e.g., Josh 10:24; 1 Kgs 5:3). Jesus' enemies will be thoroughly humiliated on the final day when they are forced to worship him. Unimaginable humiliation and inescapable punishment are subjects to which our author will turn briefly at the beginning of Hebrews 2. For now, however, you and I ought to reflect on Jesus' position at God's right hand. Jesus is greater than the angels, for he will sit at God's right hand until all his enemies have been subjugated.

The angels, in contrast, are only "ministering spirits" dispatched to aid in perpetuity those set to inherit the salvation of the supreme Son (v 14). What type of help do the angels render for our benefit? Scripture teaches that, among other things, they execute God's judgment on the wicked (2 Kgs 19:35; Ps 78:49; Acts 12:23), aid in bringing the lost to a proclamation of the gospel (Acts 8:26; 10:3, 22), give strength and encouragement to the righteous (1 Kgs 19:4–8; Acts 27:23–24), offer protection to the righteous (Ps 91:11–12; Dan 6:22; Acts 12:7–11), and provide special care (as guardians?) for children (Matt 18:10). Overall, angels today do whatever God commands (Ps 103:20–21); thus, at least in theory, there is no limit to the extent and variation of their service. Indeed, "Without the spiritual assistance that God has provided through angels we could not sustain our commitment to the Son."[52]

To summarize verses 4–14, our author cites seven Old Testament passages to draw four points of contrast between Jesus and the angels:

1. His *name* is greater, for he is "Son" (v 5).
2. His *dignity* is greater, for he is to be worshiped (v 6).
3. His *nature* is greater, for he is eternal and immutable (vv 7–12).
4. His *position* is greater, for he is at God's right hand (vv 13–14).[53]

[50] Bruce, *Hebrews*, 64.

[51] DeSilva, *Perseverance*, 102, n. 38. "The [footstool] figure arose from the Oriental custom of the victor's putting his foot on the neck of the defeated enemy" (Neil R. Lightfoot, *Jesus Christ Today* [Abilene, TX: Bible Guides, 1980], 62).

[52] Lane, *Hebrews*, 37.

[53] Lane, 35

Our world is full of noise. I imagine most of us feel, at one point or another, that we are being pulled in a million and one different directions by the "voices" in our lives. At church, at school, or at work; from culture on the outside or at home on the inside—it all can be deafening.

Yet, into this cacophonous din, the Father has spoken fully and finally through the supreme Son. As Job beheld the work of God in creation, he concluded, "This is only the beginning, a mere whisper of his rule. Whatever would we do if he really raised his voice!" (Job 26:14 Msg). In Christ, God has raised his voice. The Word he speaks is both assertive and assuring. Are we listening?

As I said previously, someone has your ear. Before we continue with Hebrews, it would be appropriate to pause and ponder to whom we are listening. Is it the voice of woke outrage or cancel culture? The voice of power or identity politics? The voice of moral relativism or indiscriminate tolerance? The voice of paralyzing fear? The voice of false religion or spineless doctrine? Or is it the voice of he who created all, redeemed all, sustains all, and will conquer all? Who has your ear? "This is my beloved Son, with whom I am well pleased; listen to him" (Matt 17:5).

SUMMARY

» God's revelation in the Son shares continuity with the Old Testament, but he has spoken fully and finally through Jesus.

» As Creator and King, the Son rules with the authority of God himself.

» Jesus enjoys a position of preeminence at God's right hand.

» Because of this position, Jesus is superior to the angels and is worthy of our worship and exaltation.

TALKING POINTS

HEBREWS WILL confront us with several truths often taken for granted. First on that list may be that God has spoken. He has not left himself without witness in the world. The Lord could have left us hanging; by his eternal silence, he could have sentenced us to a cruel, lifelong, existential ignorance. Imagine how despondent it would be to live with nary a clue as to who we are, where we came from, and what our purpose is. Through both general revelation (the natural world) and special revelation (Scripture), our Creator has revealed himself and his will for us.[54] He has never spoken more fully or perfectly than through his beloved Son. As we will discover in Hebrews, God loves us enough to speak a word concerning our sin and salvation, our suffering and sanctification. Should we ever seek proof of our Father's affection for his people, we need only to revisit the first verses of Hebrews. That "God spoke" means that God loves.

>———◇———<

A FEW YEARS ago, I had breakfast with a friend, and our discussion turned to my love of the Old Testament. My friend, a deacon in the church, wondered aloud why I was so fascinated with this antiquated and irrelevant portion of Scripture. I was utterly taken aback. He summed up his sentiments with, "I'm not interested in being a good Jew." After I poured gravy in his lap and smeared butter in his hair, I reminded him that Paul declared *all* Scripture to be both inspired and profitable (2 Tim 3:16). To neglect the Old Testament is to ignore three-fourths of what God has deemed "profitable." "The manner in which the author introduces citations is significant in demonstrating how the OT now functions for the church. The citations are introduced as words of God, of Christ, or of the Holy Spirit, not of a human author. ... The words of the OT are in fact God's words to the church in the last days."[55] As Hebrews will prove, seeking to

---

[54] "The preacher confronts his ambivalent friends, troubled by the apparent silence of God in response to their desperate situation, with the indisputable fact that our God is the God who speaks. ... God is not silent, but vocal" (Lane, *Hebrews*, 29).

[55] Thompson, "Hermeneutics," 233.

understand Jesus apart from the Old Testament is to chase a shadow. Also, don't ever eat breakfast with deacons.

>———◇———<

HEBREWS NOT only affirms the importance of the Old Testament but also instructs us on how to read it. Albert Mohler notes two erroneous ways to read the Old Testament. The first is to do so "as if it is a book that does not belong to the church."[56] The Bible Jesus read does not belong exclusively to Jews. If anything, Hebrews 1:1 identifies the Old Testament saints as "our" (i.e., Christians') fathers. Nor does Hebrews leave any room for the ideas of Marcion, the ancient heretic who believed the God of the Old Testament was a different deity than the God of the New.[57] But the second erroneous way to read the Old Testament is to do so believing all of it applies to Christians today without recognizing that some things have changed with the advent of Christ. Thus Mohler calls upon us to "employ a distinctively Christological hermeneutic."[58] Earlier, he noted that Hebrews "affirms the authenticity and authority of the Old Testament. The Old Testament continues to function authoritatively for God's people. Yet at the same time, as the next verse [1:2] will show, there is something more. The Old Testament is a story in need of a conclusion—a messianic conclusion. The fathers and the prophets indeed spoke the word of God, but that word was not the final word."[59]

>———◇———<

IT'S OFTEN THE case that churches want preachers who will deliver "relevant" sermons ripe with vibrant application versus "dry" sermons stuffed

---

[56] R. Albert Mohler, Jr., *Exalting Jesus in Hebrews*, CCE (Nashville: Holman Reference, 2017), 13.

[57] "While there is a clear contrast between the old and new, there is no sense that the two phases stand in contradiction to one another. In each case it is the same God who speaks and the same message of salvation that he offers" (Harold W. Attridge, *The Epistle to the Hebrews*, Hermeneia [Philadelphia: Fortress, 1989], 38).

[58] Mohler, *Exalting Jesus*, 14. "The OT cannot be adequately comprehended apart from the crucified and exalted Christ, yet the crucified and exalted Christ cannot be adequately comprehended apart from the OT. The author interprets the OT in light of Christ because he understands Christ's crucifixion and exaltation to be God's definitive means of communication, and the OT as the shadow cast by that reality. At the same time, the author does not have unmediated access to the heavenly throne room and cannot gaze directly upon the exalted Christ. So he seeks to discern the contours of the risen Christ by examining the shadows that Christ's enthronement casts back into the Scriptures" (Koester, *Hebrews*, 198–99).

[59] Mohler, *Exalting Jesus*, 8.

with boring theology. There is much to be said for drawing attention to the "so what" of a given biblical passage. However, we shouldn't move on from Hebrews 1 without respecting the fact that our author leads off with profound theological claims concerning the Son of God. Along the way, he will draw out appropriate application for his oppressed audience. But he begins (and will continue for several chapters) with robust theological content. Later, he will shame his audience for requesting milk, not solid food (5:12–14). *The church of Christ suffers when she no longer insists that those in her pulpits deliver theologically rich sermons.* To live Scripture, we must understand it. It is impossible to grow spiritually without knowing theology. It is impossible to meet tomorrow's challenges adequately without knowing theology. It is impossible to be who God wants us to be without knowing theology. Only as we come to know God do we come to know his will for our lives (2 Pet 1:3). Sound, biblical preaching is theological preaching. The author of Hebrews believed and practiced that.

Chapter 2

THE SOUL FELT ITS WORTH

A s Timothy continued to speak, Judah stole a glance around the room at the faces in the assembly. The number of Christians in Antioch had declined of late. When Judah and his wife had joined the Way, the disciples were many. But friction with both the Jewish community and the civic leaders had taken its toll. As he noted those who were there that night, Judah thought of who was *not*.

Nicolaus, a proselyte-turned-Christian, had been among the original seven servants in Jerusalem. Many years ago, he had returned to Antioch and played a pivotal role in the church's rapid growth. More recently, however, he had been imprisoned on false charges fabricated by the local synagogue. The old man had been released after five months in chains, but only because he disavowed with strong oaths his confession of Jesus as Messiah.

Absent also was Simeon the African; he had been an influential teacher in the Antiochian assembly, one of Judah's favorites. Yet something had happened. Judah never quite understood what the fuss was about, but it seemed Simeon began to teach some things that other leaders in the assembly did not endorse. He had been a strong advocate for the circumcision of Gentiles and full participation in the festivals of the Jews. Judah, for his part, had not understood why such practices were wrong. When asked not to advance these beliefs, Simeon had forsaken the Christians with bitterness and was soon afterward seen eating with the Jews in Antioch once again.

Then there was Manaen and his family. Manaen was well connected politically and had been quite wealthy. For many years the church had met in his home. Yet, when he began to suffer financial losses, Manaen and his household had turned their backs on the church and returned to the synagogue. The Christians were forced to find a new meeting place, this time in the home of Stephen, Judah's neighbor. It seemed to Judah that Manaen's return to Judaism had been a smart move; his business had quickly recovered, and his losses reversed soon after.

The attrition of former Christians in Antioch had been steady and demoralizing. Each departure had a different story but ultimately circled back to one reason: it had become too challenging to maintain allegiance to the Nazarene. Judah wondered how soon it would be before he joined them.

It isn't worth it anymore.

He struggled to provide for his household. He struggled with the rift between himself and those friends who had remained loyal to Moses and the covenant. He struggled with being shunned by his father.

It isn't worth it anymore.

Judah remembered the miracles he had witnessed years ago; they had been one of the reasons he and his wife had converted. He had been particularly impressed with eyewitness accounts of the dead being raised, and one story stood out: that of a woman named Dorcas in Joppa. A man called Cephas, one of the Twelve, had brought her back to life—a miracle!

Where were such wonders when I needed them? Judah thought resentfully. Four months ago, when the fever had struck his son at dusk, Judah had prayed fervently for healing. He did not consider his petition audacious; healing from disease was common among the Christians at Antioch. So Judah was confused when no one appeared to heal his son, nor was his prayer answered by the Most High.

When it was clear his son was dead, Judah had stood in stunned silence. Something in his mind prevented him from accepting the permanency of it all. No one had come forward to heal his son, true. But this was undoubtedly because resurrection from the dead was a more powerful witness to Messiah's message than recovery from disease. Now that his son was dead, someone would surely step forth to raise him in the name of Jesus Christ of Nazareth that all might glorify the Most High.

It never happened.

Perhaps God intends to raise my son once he is already in the tomb just as he raised his own Son, Judah had thought. Thus, most every morning for four months, he would make his way to the tombs outside the city, daring to believe he would find his beloved Daniel perched on a boulder, waiting for him with outstretched arms and an enthusiastic shriek of "Abba!"

Yet every morning, Judah was crushed to discover God still silent and death still a tyrant.

It isn't worth it anymore.

As Timothy proclaimed in his homily the eternal rule of God's supreme Son, Judah wrestled with the dissonance of it all. *Jesus? King? What proof is there?* His recent experiences argued otherwise, and he knew for a fact he wasn't the only Christian in Antioch who felt this way. The days of signs and wonders seemed too long ago; all the church had known of late was darkness and doubt.

He had confided in no one, but Judah was seriously considering withdrawal from the Christians. He would make no flashy exit; he wasn't one to be a fly in the ointment. No, he would slip away quietly. Judah had told his plan to nary a soul. That's why he was startled to find Timothy looking intently at him: "We must pay much closer attention to what we have heard, lest we drift away..."

>———◇———<

As mentioned previously, Judah is entirely fictional. While Nicolaus, Simeon, and Manaen were real Christians associated with Antioch in the book of Acts, their "rest of the story" is a product of my imagination.

What *is* real—too familiar, even—is the cognitive dissonance so often felt due to the "yes, but not yet" nature of Christianity. Lofty thoughts concerning the supreme Son of God can excite the mind and quicken the heart. However, when we, like Peter (Matt 14:30), take our eyes off Christ to behold the storm surrounding us, Jesus, Heir of all; Jesus, Creator of all; Jesus, Sustainer of all; Jesus, King of all, fades until he seems as much a fabrication as our Judah of Antioch.

In Hebrews 2, our author begins to merge two themes introduced in the first chapter: Jesus' position as Son over the angels and Jesus' ministry as our high priest. Turning again to the Psalms, he extols both Jesus' sovereignty and his submissiveness. It is through our Lord's subjugation and suffering, our author says, that Jesus became supreme. His supremacy is not for accomplishing a selfish agenda but for the emancipation of and intercession for the children of God, whom he has chosen to call "brothers." Before he can proceed to these magnificent truths, however, our author must raise a word of warning.

HEBREWS 2:1–4

Throughout this sermon, there are several "warning passages" in which the author temporarily steps aside from his theological discussion to admonish his audience. The opening four verses of Hebrews 2 comprise the first such interlude (see 3:7–4:13; 5:11–6:8; 10:26–31; 12:25–29).[1] But this is not to say the theological and practical in Hebrews are disconnected. For example, if Jesus enjoys a superior name and position to the angels, the message he speaks is also superior to theirs.

Thus we should "pay much closer attention to" that message (v 1). The verb translated "pay attention" (*prosechō*) is used on several occasions in the New Testament when people heeded the Word of God upon its presentation (e.g., Acts 8:6; 16:14; 1 Tim 4:13; 2 Pet 1:19). It is in the present tense here, meaning this heeding is to be a continuous action. There is never a time when we can afford *not* to pay attention to what God has to say through his Son. While our author doesn't say specifically what is amiss in his audience, "it is clear they are in danger of moving from a spiritual vantage point where the gospel is the focus."[2]

Along with *prosechō*, which was used in Greek literature to describe bringing a ship to port,[3] "drift" (*pararreō*) also carried a nautical connotation. The idea was that of a boat "in peril of being carried downstream past a fixed landing place and so failing to gain its security."[4] As we will discover later, the alternative to drifting is to secure ourselves to the anchor of the soul (6:19).

The "message declared by angels" (v 2) refers to the law given at Sinai. As already mentioned, it was commonly accepted in Jewish tradition that

---

[1] For an excellent overview of how Hebrews' warning passages have been interpreted by recent scholars, see Robert A. Peterson, "Apostasy in the Hebrews Warning Passages," *Presb* 34 (2008): 27–44.

[2] Guthrie, *Hebrews*, 84.

[3] Herodotus, *Histories* 9.99; Euripides, *Orestes* 362.

[4] Bruce, *Hebrews*, 66; e.g., Herodotus, *Histories* 2.150.

the covenant had been delivered or mediated by angels. If that "message" proved reliable, the gospel is even more so.[5] Since Jesus is superior to the angels, rejecting his gospel carries a surer penalty than rejecting the message borne by these divine servants.[6] Note the use of "transgression" and "disobedience" (v 2), both of which "involve a deliberate rejection of the divine will."[7] What begins as drifting away eventually becomes decided antagonism against the Son's gospel of grace. Considering some of the punishments for disobedience that were meted out in the Old Testament (you can brush up on the covenant curses in Lev 26 or Deut 28), the punishment for such under the New Testament is too terrible to contemplate.

This brings us to "neglect" (*ameleō*) in verse 3. This neglect isn't an innocuous, absent-minded forgetfulness to do something but "a gradual, unthinking movement away from the faith."[8] To be guilty of neglect, one does not have to actively rebel against or despise Jesus' saving gospel; it just means we treat it as inconsequential.[9] In one of Jesus' parables, *ameleō* is applied to those who didn't take seriously an invitation to a lavish wedding feast (Matt 22:5), and though different terms are used, the theme of heedlessness continues in other parables related to Judgment Day (Matt 24:37–39; 25:1–12). That's why Maclaren draws particular attention to this specific word: "not *reject*; not *fight against*, simply 'neglect.'"[10] Spurgeon warns us not to downplay the severity of the term: "Neglect is as ruinous as distinct and open opposition."[11]

Suppose we neglect this unparalleled deliverance offered by a holy God through the suffering of his supreme Son. In that case, we will not "escape" (*ekpheugō*), a term often used in the context of retribution awaiting

---

[5] In 2:2–3, our author makes an *a fortiori* argument, meaning it moves from the lesser to the greater (e.g., "If this lesser thing is true, how much more is this greater thing true?"). He will use such an argument several more times (8:6; 9:13–14; 10:28–29; 12:9, 25).

[6] Our author does not mean that rejecting the gospel will incur a stiffer penalty for even the wilderness generation was lost eternally. Instead, "the judgment of those faithless to the Son is even more *certain* than the absolutely certain judgment of those disobedient under the OT revelation" (Gareth Lee Cockerill, *The Epistle to the Hebrews*, NICNT [Grand Rapids: Eerdmans, 2012], 121; emphasis his).

[7] Lane, *Hebrews 1–8*, 38. "If there is any distinction between [these terms], it is not that of deliberate and unintentional sins, but that of sins of commission and sins of omission" (Attridge, *Hebrews*, 65).

[8] Koester, *Hebrews*, 206.

[9] Cockerill, *Hebrews*, 120.

[10] Alexander Maclaren, *Expositions of Holy Scripture* (Grand Rapids: Baker, 1984), 29:212; emphasis his.

[11] C. H. Spurgeon, "An Earnest Warning against Unbelief," in *The Metropolitan Tabernacle Pulpit Sermons* (London: Passmore, 1910), 56:477.

those outside of Christ on the final day (Matt 23:33; Luke 21:36; Rom 2:3; 1 Thess 5:3). As assured as our salvation is in Christ, so is the destruction awaiting those who neglect the gospel. Our author will return to this theme later in his homily (10:28–29; 12:25).

The three-fold admonition to pay attention to, not drift from, and not neglect the gospel is based on the superiority of both the Son and the gospel itself. The gospel of the Son is superior to the "gospel" of Sinai for three reasons explained in verses 3–4. It is superior because of (1) the One who declared it—not the prophets, nor the angels, but the supreme Son now at God's right hand. If we reject Jesus as Savior and Lord, we will not escape him as Judge and King.

The gospel is also superior because (2) it was passed on to us by those who heard the teachings of Jesus for themselves. Mohler reminds us, "We do not believe myths and legends about Jesus. The message of the gospel has come down to us from the credible eyewitness testimony of the apostles."[12]

Finally, the gospel is superior by virtue of (3) its confirmation by signs, wonders, miracles, and gifts from God. There is historical importance in the phrase "signs and wonders" (v 4), for they were the means by which God delivered Israel out of Egypt (Deut 4:34; 6:22; Ps 135:9; Jer 32:20–21). In the New Testament, these same "signs and wonders" were divine affirmation of the ministries of Jesus and the apostles (Acts 2:22; 14:3; Rom 15:19; 2 Cor 12:12). "Thus 'signs and wonders' affirmed not only the validity of God's word in the Son but the continuity of this word with his Sinai revelation and with the gospel preached throughout the world."[13]

>———◇———<

There is a pronounced tension in these verses that must be addressed. It is unsettling, after exalting the Son's majesty, to hear our author "bully" his readers into obedience by invoking the covenant and consequences of Sinai and by threatening that, if they fall away, their punishment will be more certain than their ancestors'. Such a tactic is no doubt at odds with the love and grace of a merciful God who stands at the center of Christianity. Right?

---

[12] Mohler, *Exalting Jesus*, 27.
[13] Cockerill, *Hebrews*, 122.

This is precisely the moment when I must acknowledge an important truth: if I don't fear God, I don't know him very well. To the argument that we should not "scare people into heaven," our author would surely shake his head. He understood Jesus' message to be a matter of life and death, and as is the case with any good teacher, he was concerned with his audience's knowledge of the truth and their reaction to it.

Guthrie aids our understanding of this first "warning pause" by summarizing the author's three points in 2:1–4. His outline helps us appreciate how a better covenant necessitates stern warnings. First, "the author calls his audience to personal commitment and responsibility."[14] As will be discussed later, our author is not undermining eternal security—just the opposite! He is calling them to evaluate their confession of, connection with, and commitment to the Son of God; their eternal destiny depends on their maintaining all three. If our author did not love his audience, or if their dedication were not bound up with their worship and honor of the supreme Son, he would not have bothered to exhort them.

Second, "the preacher motivates his listeners through threat of punishment."[15] Granted, John says, "perfect love casts out fear" (1 John 4:18). However, those to whom our author spoke were not yet mature in their faith (5:11–6:3). To say it is *never* appropriate to "scare people into heaven" is to call into question the motivational methods of none less than the Holy Spirit. Can such a motivational tactic be employed abusively? Of course. But so can any of the things God utilizes to move us to faithfulness. Few of the devil's devices are original to him as much as they are a dark and twisted manipulation of the strategies of the Spirit of Light. And what kind of love is it to know people are headed for destruction yet refuse to warn them?

Third, though the threat of punishment is a negative, the gospel itself is positive.[16] That gospel is the word God has spoken in and through Jesus, his supreme Son. It is a great salvation. Thus, to keep from drifting, we must be diligent to "pay much closer attention to," "consider," or look "to Jesus" (2:1; 3:1; 12:2).

[14] Guthrie, *Hebrews*, 88.
[15] Guthrie, 88.
[16] Guthrie, 89.

HEBREWS 2:5–9

It may seem as if Hebrews now returns to the theme of chapter 1—the exalted nature of the Son.[17] But it would be a mistake to consider 2:1–4 to be an excursus having little in common with verses 5–9. Just as verses 1–4 were connected to Hebrews 1 (the Son's supremacy demands we "pay much closer attention"), they are also the perfect preface to what follows. Our author is about to expound on how Christ has made our salvation "great," a topic that will dominate the remainder of Hebrews.

What else sets Christ apart from the angels? Though the idea is never fleshed out fully, the Old Testament hints that angels once governed the world. In the Song of Moses, the LXX reads, "When the Most High distributed nations as he scattered the descendants of Adam, he set up boundaries for the nations according to the number of the angels of God" (Deut 32:8; see also Dan 10:13, 20; Rom 8:38).

However, a new sheriff is in town (Eph 1:20–23; 1 Pet 3:22). Unlike the present world, "the world to come" was entrusted to Christ upon his enthronement. Elsewhere in Hebrews, this coming world is described as our "homeland" (11:14), a coming city in a better, heavenly country (11:16; 13:14), "the heavenly Jerusalem" (12:22), and "a kingdom that cannot be shaken" (12:28). In one sense, this coming world exists now—our author will say we "*have* come" or entered into this new world (12:22; emphasis mine) and will speak of this new kingdom in present-tense language (12:28). At the same time, though, the coming world "is not yet present in its fulness; its consummation awaits the time when Christ will appear to bring his people into the final blessings of the salvation which he has procured for them"[18] (9:28).

To prove the Son's supremacy in the world to come, our author appeals to Psalm 8,[19] which focuses on the honored place human beings possess as the crown jewel of God's creation. As David—perhaps lying in a field with his father's sheep—gazed up at the moon and stars (Ps 8:3), he wondered

---

[17] The phrase "of which we are speaking" (v 5) "underscores the continuity in thought between 1:5–14 and the resumption of the exposition at this point" (Lane, *Hebrews 1–8*, 45).

[18] Bruce, *Hebrews*, 71–72.

[19] "It has been testified somewhere" (v 5) doesn't mean the speaker is ignorant of the statement's origin. Instead, by omitting the name of the author, Hebrews stresses the divine origin of Scripture. Philo used a similar phrase for rhetorical effect (e.g., *Drunkenness* 61; *Unchangeable* 74).

how a marvelous Creator could give any regard to something as insignificant as mankind. Despite that, he affirmed that humanity had been crowned "with glory and honor" and granted "dominion" over all the earth (vv 5–6). Whether standing at a viewpoint on the rim of the Grand Canyon, before an alpine lake in the shadow of the Matterhorn, or in the sandy surf of the Pacific Ocean—it's difficult to believe that the massive expanse of the natural world doesn't dwarf us in God's eyes. Yet that's precisely what Psalm 8 claims.

Lingering in the background of this psalm is God's command to Adam and Eve to fill the earth, subdue it, and reign over it (Gen 1:28). "Human beings were destined to rule the entire world for God. Everything was supposed to be under the rule and dominion of human beings, but sin intervened to frustrate this rule. … The glory designed for human beings has not become a reality in human history. Instead, human history is littered with the wreckage of destruction and death—a world gone mad."[20] Maclaren puts it this way: "If that psalm be God's thought of man, the plan that He hangs up for us His workmen to build by, what a wretched thing my copy of it has turned out to be!"[21] Hebrews, however, seizes upon this psalm to argue "that the divine commission of Adam as king over God's creation ultimately has been fulfilled in Christ, the eschatological last Adam."[22] Jesus succeeded where man has failed miserably, thus demonstrating his supremacy.

No sooner is the final phrase of Psalm 8:6 out of our author's mouth than he realizes it requires explanation. "Are all things really under the feet of the Son of Man?" his audience might have asked, perhaps incredulously. "Yes," says our author. All things means *all* things; "he left nothing outside his control" (Heb 2:8). On the one hand, the ink is scarcely dry on 1:13, where it is implied that Jesus' *complete* sovereignty remains a *future* reality ("until…"). On the other hand, the first half of verse 8 seems to indicate the Son's sovereignty is a *present* reality. Factor in the human experience, which indubitably demonstrates all things are *not* in *total* subjection to Christ, and it's easy to question, "Jesus? King? What proof is there?"

---

[20] Schreiner, *Hebrews*, 89.
[21] Maclaren, *Expositions*, 29:214–15.
[22] Guthrie, "Hebrews," 946.

This is not a modern conundrum, as Hebrews proves. In another book also dating to the late first century, the author of 2 Esdras marveled at creation as David did. At the same time, he wondered aloud why God, if he created the world for his people, allowed their enemies to succeed.

> All this I have spoken before you, O Lord, because you have said that it was for us that you created this world. As for the other nations that have descended from Adam, you have said that they are nothing, and that they are like spittle, and you have compared their abundance to a drop from a bucket. And now, O Lord, these nations, which are reputed to be as nothing, domineer over us and devour us. But we your people, whom you have called your firstborn, only begotten, zealous for you, and most dear, have been given into their hands. If the world has indeed been created for us, why do we not possess our world as an inheritance? How long will this be so?
>
> 2 ESDRAS 6:55–59 NRSV

Indeed, how long, O Lord?

This is one of many moments when Hebrews becomes both profoundly theological and intensely personal. Like the anonymous author of 2 Esdras, we can't help but wonder from time to time, as we endure suffering, whether Jesus truly reigns over all things with sweeping sovereignty, particularly given the circumstances of his people. Many of us were taught to sing as children, "He's got the whole world in his hands." But where is the evidence? You and I have been there.

› In the ICU, we have wondered whether Jesus is greater than sickness or cancer.

› As markets crashed, jobs were lost, or mortgages went unpaid, we have wondered whether Jesus is greater than turmoil.

› Beset by seemingly unquenchable desires, we have wondered whether Jesus is greater than temptation.

› Hearing of another mass shooting, we have wondered whether Jesus is greater than hatred.

› Watching two planes fly into the World Trade Center, we have wondered whether Jesus is greater than terror.

› At the grave of a loved one, we have wondered whether Jesus is greater than death.

These Hebrew Christians lived all of this (albeit on a more severe scale) as they faced scorn and derision from their neighbors and mounting persecution from civil authorities. Surely they, like us, looked to the heavens at times and asked, "Just how important are we to You, anyway?"

In these and all other painful moments, Hebrews assures us Jesus is Lord of all, "but that the full subjugation of all things lies in the future."[23] Our author acknowledges the cognitive dissonance. While it's easy to read on without noticing, he has included a little word in his statement—one bursting with anticipation and possibilities—that deserves reflection. The entire section hinges on the word "yet" (*oupō*, v 8), meaning the quoted psalm is a prophecy slated for future fulfillment, "a legal decree, the realization of which is yet deferred."[24] We have already been told that Jesus is the heir of all things (1:2). That promise is now reiterated in that all things will yet be subjected to him. The Son's supremacy is a *fait accompli*; it is one of many Christian truths that fall into the "yes, but not yet" category.

We may not see everything presently in subjection to the Son, but we *do* see Jesus himself. Instead of obsessing over our lousy lot in the land of "yes, but not yet," we ought to focus intently on the person of Jesus—a strategy our author will commend to us time and again.[25] In our despondency, we ought to focus particularly on Jesus being "crowned with glory and honor." What we failed to achieve (Gen 1:28), Jesus has accomplished (1 Cor 15:27; Eph 1:22), "and with this the possibility of man's fulfilling God's ultimate intention is made possible. Christ's glorification is our foothold in glory."[26]

While all we have known on earth is a status "lower than the angels," our Lord was at this stage only "for a little while"—a phrase given an

---

[23] Guthrie, "Hebrews," 947.

[24] Lane, *Hebrews 1–8*, 48.

[25] "When the author says we 'see' Jesus, he anticipates exhortations to 'consider' him later in the book (3:1; 12:1–2). These exhortations focus both on Jesus' earthly obedience to the Father and his subsequent exaltation. To 'see Jesus,' therefore, does not mean a physical perception, but rather a spiritual perception, recognizing both the witness of his earthly endurance and his present exalted position" (Guthrie, *Hebrews*, 99).

[26] R. Hughes, *Hebrews*, 1:59.

emphatic position in the Greek text. From when he quoted Psalm 8:6a in verse 7 to when he repeats it in verse 9, our author has altered the location of "for a little while," moving it from the middle of the phrase (v 7) to the beginning (v 9).[27] He thereby draws attention to the fact that, although Jesus was subjected to living in the world of "yes, but not yet," it was only "for a little while." We, too, can take comfort in the fact that life here is not forever but "for a little while." In Christ, every ill effect of the fall is temporary. We may not see Jesus "crowned with glory and honor" with our eyes of flesh, but we can see such with the eyes of faith. Focus on Jesus; focus on the glory and honor in which he is now enthroned.

Focus also on *how* he achieved his status as the supreme Son: "because of the suffering of death, so that by the grace of God he might taste death for everyone" (v 9). This is a startling claim. The only way humanity can reclaim the place of prominence first bestowed upon us is to identify with the suffering and death of Jesus. Only in Christ—in being crucified and buried with him—do we realize our "glorious destiny designed by God."[28] The path to Jesus' exaltation was Jesus' humiliation (12:2; Phil 2:6–11), which our author describes as tasting death.

When I think of "taste," I associate it with lightly sampling something (e.g., "I just want a taste"). If you peruse an English dictionary, this nuance is confirmed with definitions such as "sample or test" and "eat or drink a small portion of." If, however, we infer from our author's words that Jesus had only a tiny sample of death (as some, including Chrysostom and Luther, concluded), we are dreadfully mistaken.[29] Jesus did not "sample" death in part but experienced it fully in all its helplessness and horror. The "taste" metaphor is predicated on the idea of drinking the cup of suffering. Just as Socrates was executed by forcibly drinking hemlock poison, God in the Old Testament often swore to make the nations (including Israel and Judah) drink the cup of his poisonous wrath on account of their sins (e.g., Isa 51:17; Jer 25:15; Lam 4:21).

---

[27] Without the advantage of bold, italics, or underline, Greek authors designated significant words/phrases by placing them at the beginning or end of a clause or sentence.

[28] Lane, *Hebrews 1–8*, 49.

[29] The verb "taste" (*geuomai*) appears in the LXX in the sense of tasting food (1 Sam 14:24; Job 34:3), yet it also means to experience something (Ps 34:8)—a distinction reflected in English as well—and this is the sense in which Jesus used it (Matt 16:28; John 8:52). It is also the sense it carries here in Hebrews.

In his comments on Obadiah 16, another passage where this idea is present, Paul Raabe explains:

> The image of drinking the cup points to the full amount of divine wrath that the recipients experience. They do not receive just a little bit of punishment; they receive it to the full extent. Almost every text emphasizes this point. The recipients drain the cup filled with Yahweh's wrath down to the dregs and become drunk. Ezekiel 23 pictures the cup as deep and wide, so huge and containing so much that others laugh at it. ... When Yahweh's wrath comes, it is irresistible and unstoppable.[30]

At the cross, Jesus drank the cup of his Father's wrath "for everyone" (Heb 2:9). Though he had asked that the cup pass from him, he resigned himself to the will of his Father (Matt 20:22; Mark 14:36; John 18:11).

All this—the Son's humiliation and our subsequent restoration to our primeval glory over creation—was "by the grace of God." The Son's suffering was not due to any anger the Father harbored against the Son; it was due to his affection for us that he freely decreed his perfect Son would suffer for us. Perhaps our author emphasizes God's grace lest we conclude that Jesus' death was due to the impotence of God. Never in time or space was God's sovereignty or the Son's supremacy considered more dubious than when Christ was hung on a tree as an enemy of the Empire and buried in a borrowed tomb like a pitiful indigent. The cross, however, "which appeared to be the extinction of all his power, was nonetheless the sovereign expression of his power" (John 10:18).[31]

HEBREWS 2:10–13

With Jesus' humanity and suffering in focus, our author now asserts that Christ is greater than the angels because of his solidarity with God's people. This solidarity has two extraordinary results. First, as Jesus' brothers and sisters (vv 11–13), we have been emancipated from death's tyranny

---

[30] Paul R. Raabe, *Obadiah*, AB 24D (New York: Doubleday, 1996), 238.
[31] P. Hughes, *Commentary*, 87.

(vv 14–15). Second, Jesus has been perfected by this camaraderie, qualifying him to be our high priest (vv 16–18). Before we explore these two facts, though, there is much in verse 10 that merits extensive reflection.

God as Creator. Our author depicts God as the one "for whom and by whom all things exist" (v 10; see Rom 11:36; 1 Cor 8:6). God is not only the Creator of the universe but also the Author of its unfolding drama. Though Adam and Eve plunged the planet into chaos when tempted by the devil, the Origin and End of all things could not bear the thought of forsaking his creation and letting it waste away to nothing from the effects of the fall. No, our Creator devised a scheme for the redemption of the crown of his creation (Eph 1:3–12), a design planned and promised "before the ages began" (Titus 1:2), a blueprint drawn up before it was made necessary by the sin of our first parents.

God's Goal in Redemption. This blueprint's goal was to bring "many sons to glory," to restore to humanity what was lost in the fall. "Crowned with glory and honor," and with everything in subjection to them, Adam and Eve squandered it away through their sin. Thanks be to God that our Creator desired to restore to us the glory and honor of sonship, and he did so through Christ. There is more to the biblical idea of "glory" than receiving honor or praise; as mentioned previously, "glory" is also synonymous with the divine presence. "Those who entered into glory entered the sphere where God's presence was manifest."[32] Thus God planned to bring many sons into his presence. This constitutes the first mention of one of the grandest themes in Hebrews: access to God or the act of drawing near (4:16; 7:25; 10:1, 22; 11:6).

Jesus as Founder. Hebrews has a rich reservoir of titles for Jesus, including "founder" (*archēgos*). Translations render this word widely: "source" (HCSB), "author" (NASU), "pioneer" (NIV), and "captain" (NKJV). Its underlying definition is "he who is the first, who stands at the head of, who leads." In its thirty-five occurrences in the LXX, its range of meaning includes "head," "leader," "prince," "supervisor," "confidant," "family representative," or even "physician."[33] All four occurrences of *archēgos* in the New

---

[32] Koester, *Hebrews*, 228.
[33] Paul-Gerd Müller, "ἀρχηγός," *EDNT* 1:163.

Testament (Acts 3:15; 5:31; Heb 2:10; 12:2) refer to Christ and always in the context of his death and resurrection. Given how widely *archēgos* is translated, and that it has to do with Jesus, we should dig deeper.

Somewhat controversially, Lane argues the translation "champion" is consistent with Greek culture and the literary context of verse 10 and verses 14–15. He then invokes the "divine hero" concept in ancient literature—one who descends from heaven to help the people of earth (e.g., Hercules): "Locked in mortal combat with the one who held the power of death, he [Jesus] overthrew him in order to release all those who had been enslaved by this evil tyrant."[34] So if by *archēgos* Hebrews means "champion," it's comparable to someone today referring to Jesus as our Superman.[35]

Against Lane, Cockerill concedes that the Greek term *could* mean "champion" if it occurred in verses 14–15 but not in verse 10. The bigger issue, he claims, is that "champion" is inconsistent with the Jewish background of Hebrews.[36] Instead, Cockerill argues for the translation "pioneer": Jesus leads his people to "their divinely appointed glory."[37] "Pioneer" seems to be a better fit when we consider how *archēgos* is used in both the LXX and the immediate context of Hebrews 2:10.

The problem is that when I think of "pioneer," I think of travelers along the Oregon Trail and whether I want to ford the river or caulk and float. I doubt this is what our author intends. So while my head is drawn to "pioneer," my heart is drawn to "champion." I will concede that "champion" isn't as consistent with the term's use in the Old Testament. On the other hand, there is something to the argument that *archēgos* invokes the Old Testament's divine warrior motif (e.g., Exod 15:3; Josh 5:13–15; Isa 42:13; 49:24–26).[38]

Our culture is littered with larger-than-life champions, the real (Davy Crockett, Chuck Norris) and the imagined (Paul Bunyan, Jack Bauer). Add to these the adventures of Superman, Batman, Spiderman, Ironman,

---

[34] Lane, *Hebrews 1–8*, 57. He adds that this depiction of Jesus [in Hebrews] "was calculated to recall one of the more famous labors of Hercules, his wrestling with Death, 'the dark-robed lord of the dead'" (*Hebrews 1–8*, 57; citing Euripides, *Alcestis* 843–44).

[35] Guthrie, *Hebrews*, 108.

[36] Cockerill, *Hebrews*, 137–38, n. 60.

[37] Cockerill, 138–39.

[38] See "Divine Warrior" in *Dictionary of Biblical Imagery*, eds. Leland Ryken, James C. Wilhoit, and Tremper Longman III (Downers Grove, IL: InterVarsity Press, 2000), 210–13.

Aquaman, Thor, Hawkeye, Hulk, Wolverine, Flash, Green Lantern, and countless others—seriously, how many movies can Marvel and DC make? That our culture has so many champions betrays the fact that we still crave a Superhero to end all superheroes, and I'd contend Christ is the hero we seek. He is the one who can restore our status lost in the fall; he is the one who conquered the grave, crushed the serpent's head, and delivered us from the dark domain (Col 1:13).

Perhaps "champion" versus "pioneer" is a distinction without a difference. If you haven't caught on already, no single English word can capture all the nuances, Greek or Jewish, of *archēgos*. While I'm tempted to coin a new term ("championeer"?), I don't think it's necessary. When I was a kid, America's pioneers *were* my superheroes, specifically Crockett (at least the Fess Parker iteration). Perhaps "champion" and "pioneer" are two sides of the same coin. Think of the images elicited by both terms:

> - Blazing a trail into the great unknown
> - Going where no man has gone before
> - Leading others to a better land across the river and beyond the mountains
> - Neutralizing threats with cunning
> - Vanquishing enemies with superhuman strength
> - Killing a bear when he was only three

Ok, so maybe that last one doesn't apply to Jesus, but you get the idea. More to our author's point in the context, Jesus is the champion who pioneers the way to our destiny, the way into the immediate and intimate presence of God. Most significantly, Christ has become our champion by becoming a pioneer through death back into life.

Christ's Consecration. The scheme of redemption was accomplished via our Lord's suffering. As our champion-pioneer, Christ was made perfect through suffering to fulfill God's plan. So acutely aware are we of Jesus' divine nature that it seems borderline blasphemous to suggest that Jesus needed to be made perfect. How was he ever *im*perfect?

The idea of "perfection" in Greek is that of completeness, wholeness, or maturity. In religious contexts, we often think of the moral aspect of "perfect" (i.e., the absence of moral or ethical failure). However, "perfect"—in the New Testament broadly and in Hebrews specifically—carries both a telic and a cultic quality.[39] It is the cultic quality that our author has in mind in verse 10. The verb employed here (*teleioō*) was used in the LXX to refer to priests' consecration for the priesthood.[40]

Likewise, Jesus was consecrated for his ministry through his suffering; Christ's passion qualified his priesthood. "In no place is it suggested that Christ was high priest eternally, or that he became high priest during his earthly life, before or independently of his death."[41] To become our savior par excellence, Jesus had to endure pain. Later, our author will explain how Jesus' suffering allows him to identify with our weaknesses and deal gently with us (4:15; 5:2); here, he argues that the suffering of the supreme Son gives him solidarity with the frail children of God (2:11).

Entirely Appropriate. Go back to the beginning of verse 10 and read our author's words carefully: "it was fitting." So critical was this idea to our author's point that, for emphasis, he placed it first in the sentence. Our Creator—the one we failed in the fall—considered it "entirely appropriate" (CSB) to make our Savior suffer. Say these words slowly to yourself: *the Father found it entirely appropriate to make his Son suffer for us.* Put another way, Jesus' suffering was neither a frivolous choice nor a logical obligation forced upon God; it was "an appropriate expression of the divine character."[42]

Some first-century readers of Hebrews would have likely recoiled at the notion that making his divine Son suffer was something God considered "fitting." Attridge calls our author's use of this term "a rather bold move, since in Greek and Greco-Jewish theology it would not have been thought 'proper' to associate God with the world of suffering."[43] If God is indeed sovereign over all, they would have reasoned, "such eminence in

---

[39] "Telic" has to do with completeness; "cultic" refers to a system of religion. Ellingworth provides a helpful chart of the uses of *teleioō* ("to make perfect") in Hebrews. He believes all three nuances of "perfect"—ethical, telic, and cultic—are in view when the verb is used in v 10. "By undergoing death, God accomplished his purpose whereby the Son would become a high priest, able to cleanse God's people from their sins, thus enabling them to approach God in true worship" (*Hebrews*, 162).

[40] Exod 29:9, 29, 33, 35; Lev 4:5; 8:33; 16:32; Num 3:3; see Silva, "τέλος," *NIDNTTE* 4:477.

[41] Ellingworth, *Hebrews*, 186.

[42] Cockerill, *Hebrews*, 137.

[43] Attridge, *Hebrews*, 82.

being should remove God far from the realm of suffering."[44] Paul acknowledged this obstacle: "We preach Christ crucified: a stumbling block to Jews and foolishness to Gentiles" (1 Cor 1:23 NIV). Yet this plan of God was entirely consistent with his person and purpose. How so?

First, the cross was fitting because God is *love*, and love is not selfish. It seeks the good of others and "never fails" (1 Cor 13:5, 8). God's love hung his Son on the cursed tree. Second, the cross was fitting because God is *faithful*. This is perhaps why, after saying, "it was fitting," our author refers to God in creation language. As our Creator, he is responsible for us, even in our selfish rebellion, and thus made provision for us to be reconciled to him. God's faithfulness hung his Son on the cursed tree.

Finally, the cross was fitting because God is *glorious*. The ultimate reason God does anything is to bring himself the glory and exaltation due him. Centuries ago, Athanasius asked, "Since, then, human beings had become so irrational and demonic deceit was thus overshadowing every place and hiding the knowledge of the true God, what was God to do? … Or what profit would there be to the maker God, or what glory for him, if human beings, brought into being by him, did not revere him but reckoned others to be their makers? For God would be found creating them for others and not for himself."[45] Because of his love, God could not bear to see his creation ruined. Yet, to a greater degree, his glory was also at stake. God's love and God's glory are not polar but two sides of the same coin. Maclaren declares that what some may consider "Almighty selfishness … is really the expression of Almighty love."[46] Whatever God does for his glory is also for our good (Rom 8:28). Maclaren then adds, "The purpose of God that all creation should redound to His honour, and be 'for Him,' reaches its end through the suffering of Jesus Christ, and in Him, and in His death God is glorified."[47] God's glory hung his Son on the cursed tree.

One subtle strand running through this magnificent tapestry is arresting to consider. One of Hebrews' presuppositions is the fact that God—the

[44] Johnson, *Hebrews*, 95.
[45] Athanasius, *Incarnation* 13.
[46] Maclaren, *Expositions*, 29:237.
[47] Maclaren, 29:237; emphasis his.

same God mighty enough to create all things by simply speaking them into existence; the same God who used elementary grammar, not elbow grease, to fashion cosmos, canyons, and creatures—is a God who could not by his power or word alone effect the restoration of our squandered status. At least not in a way and to a degree consistent with his person and purpose. No, to draw us near and lead us to glory, God knew the suffering and sacrifice of a supreme Son was necessary, one who would first unite with us in life and death that we might be reunited with God in the Son's resurrection and exaltation.

His creative agency is not the highest exhibition of His power. Creation is effected by a word. The bare utterance of the divine will was all that was needed to make the heavens and the earth. ... But the bare utterance of will is not enough here. If men are to be brought to glory, they cannot be brought by the mere desire of God to bring them, or by the mere utterance of His will that they should be brought. This work needs a process, needs that something should be done. This work needs the humiliation, the suffering, the death, resurrection, ascension, and session at the right hand of God, of the Captain of our salvation and the Prince of our life. ... *Omnipotence has made the world, the Cross has redeemed it.*[48]

Jesus' Solidarity. Lest we falsely conclude that Jesus was never on board with this scheme but rendered his obedience in a belligerent or begrudging manner, our author moves a step further in affirming Jesus' willful incarnation. Jesus, he who sanctifies us, has the same source as we do, and thus is proud to call us his "brothers" (v 11). "In the great mind of God," Spurgeon once said, "it is not Christ alone, and his people alone, but Christ and his Church who are regarded as 'all of one.' They are fitted, constituted, designed for each other; they are the complement of each other."[49]

It is one thing for God to be so committed to our redemption and restoration that he would ordain his supreme Son to experience the cross' immense agony and humiliation. It is an altogether different matter for Christ to desire such complete concord with his brothers that he would

---

[48] Maclaren, 29:237–38; emphasis mine.
[49] C. H. Spurgeon, "All of One," in *The Metropolitan Tabernacle Pulpit Sermons* (London: Passmore, 1895), 41:290.

consent to this. Both the Father and the Son desired "to create a family that is so unified and so deeply interwoven and empathetic"[50] that there is nothing we feel that Father and Son cannot. That's why God considered Jesus' death "fitting." Our author will revisit this point beginning in 4:15. Here, though, he cinches his claim about Jesus' solidarity by quoting in verse 12 a line from Psalm 22.

This psalm is famous for its messianic tone. For the first twenty-one verses, David complains of God's distance and silence amid the king's distress (vv 1–2), yet his faith in Yahweh's deliverance is sustained by memory of God's past faithfulness to David's ancestors (vv 3–5). The wording of verse 21 is ambiguous as to whether David has been delivered already (past tense) or is confident of deliverance (future tense); either way, the first word of thanksgiving comes in verse 22. David's use of "your name" is an allusion to God's power to save; the king promises that, among God's people, he will praise God's name for God's deliverance.[51]

There is little doubt that the New Testament writers considered Psalm 22 to be a prophecy concerning Jesus.[52] By citing a single line from the psalm, our author invokes its entirety. In his suffering and death, Jesus willingly chose to identify with humanity and their distress and sorrow. For the sake of sinners, the Son agreed volitionally to be forsaken by the Father. But he endured this humiliation in complete confidence that he, like David, would be delivered and vindicated by the Father, and he did so to bring praise to God's name.

Our author focuses on two phrases from Psalm 22:22. Jesus praises God's greatness and power (1) "to my brothers" and (2) "in the midst of the congregation." Jesus and the people of God have the same source; he is thus proud to be numbered among us while retaining preeminence as the firstborn (Heb 1:6). The divine rescue mission was carried out by Christ, motivated not just by his love for the Father and desire to honor him but also by his love for his lost brothers.

---

[50] John Piper, "Our Captain Made Perfect Through Sufferings," *Desiring God*, 2 June 1995, http://www.desiringgod.org/messages/our-captain-made-perfect-through-sufferings.

[51] Guthrie, "Hebrews," 948.

[52] For example, compare Ps 22:1 with Matt 27:46, Ps 22:7–8 with Matt 27:39–44, Ps 22:14–15 with John 19:31–36, and Ps 22:18 with John 19:23–24 and Matt 27:35.

After echoing Psalm 22, our author cites a passage from Isaiah 8. The connection between the two Scriptures is rather subtle. Isaiah speaks of God "hiding his face from the house of Jacob" (8:17), yet the prophet maintains his hope in God. In Psalm 22:24, David affirms that God "has not hidden his face from" his suffering servant. These passages speak of God's people as "brothers" of the Messiah (Ps 22) and his "children" (Isa 8). Both speak of the Messiah as living among his people; both refer to the Son's suffering and his trust in God during his suffering. "Consequently, they [Ps 22 and Isa 8] are appropriate for the author's purposes, especially when understood against a fertile backdrop of early Christian messianic interpretation."[53]

In Hebrews' second quotation from Isaiah, the prophet identifies himself with the faithful in Israel, saying they together will be a sign to others in Israel, an example of trusting God in troubled times (8:18). Both Jesus' suffering and his example of faithfulness amid that suffering help him identify with our humanity. Our author's point is that Jesus has a connection with us, not only because we have the same Father, but also because he knows what it's like to be faithful in trying times.

The broader context of Isaiah 8:17–18 contains two exemplary messianic prophecies. The first is 7:14 (the prophecy of Jesus' virgin birth), and the second is 9:6—"For to us a child is born, to us a son is given; and the government shall be upon his shoulder, and his name shall be called Wonderful Counselor, Mighty God, Everlasting Father, Prince of Peace." In another statement alluding to the coming Christ, Isaiah speaks of a "stone of offense" and "rock of stumbling" (8:14; see also Rom 9:33; 1 Pet 2:6, 8). In addition, and as Isaiah did in 8:18, Jesus referred routinely to those whom God had "given" him (e.g., John 6:37–39; 10:29; 17:2–9).

Therefore, the Hebrews author had good reason to see Jesus standing in the background of Isaiah 8. As in Psalm 22, Isaiah affirmed both his trust in the Father and his fraternity with the faithful children of God. These twin themes undergird much of Hebrews' message. Despite suffering the effects of weakness, temptation, and mistreatment, Jesus entrusted himself entirely to God (1 Pet 2:23). As great as Jesus' commitment was to identify fully with life "down here," even greater was his commitment

---

[53] Guthrie, *Hebrews*, 110.

to have faith in the One "up there." Jesus is an older brother worth emulating on account of his love for and faithfulness to us, as well as his love for and faithfulness to the Father.

HEBREWS 2:14–18

Since the fall, those of us who are made of "flesh and blood" (v 14) have been slaves to the tyranny of death and the devil. The Creator warned our first parents of the consequences of violating the one prohibition he gave them (Gen 2:17). Through their disobedience in Eden, sin and death entered the world and spread as an international contagion to infect and subjugate "all men" (Rom 5:12)—"Death as death is no part of the divine order."[54]

To err is human, so they say. But to die is also human. Everyone dies, even those who eat right, exercise, and avoid high fructose corn syrup and Yellow #5! Everyone has an appointment with death that cannot be postponed forever (Heb 9:27). Death is a part of life. "Death prevents human beings from obtaining the rule over the world promised in Psalm 8. Human beings can hardly serve as God's vice-regents over the world if they die under Satan's domain."[55]

Thus, to share solidarity with us, Jesus became mortal flesh and blood. This solidarity or fraternity with us is why Jesus came to live. Yet it's also why he came to *die*.[56] Let me express that again so that you'll pause and ponder these words. The purpose of Jesus' birth, the purpose of his life, the purpose of the incarnation was to die. Only through the death of the supreme Son of God was death's tyranny terminated and the devil destroyed (2 Tim 1:10; 1 John 3:8).

Many of you reading these words know good and well "the basic plot" (to quote George Costanza) of our faith. From the earliest days of our childhoods, we were told the story of Jesus. We sang "Jesus Loves Me." Red and yellow, black and white—we were taught that Jesus died for, rose for, and loves all the little children of the world. With the aid of

---

[54] Brooke Foss Westcott, *The Epistle to the Hebrews* (Grand Rapids: Eerdmans, 1967), 53.

[55] Schreiner, *Hebrews*, 104.

[56] "Jesus' death was the logical consequence of his determination to identify himself so completely with his brothers and sisters that there would be no aspect of human experience which he did not share" (Lane, *Hebrews 1–8*, 61).

flannel-board Jesus, we learned about the gospel—the powerful miracles of Christ, the parables of Christ, and the passion of Christ. So as adults, it is often difficult to appreciate just how precious this good news is. Consider these words by F. F. Bruce; I hope the thought helps you, as it did me, stand in awe (perhaps for the first time in a long while) of the message spoken fully and finally by God through his Son.

> It calls for an exceptional effort of mind on our part to appreciate how paradoxical was the attitude of those early Christians to the death of Christ. If ever death had appeared to be triumphant, it was when Jesus of Nazareth, disowned by the leaders of his nation, abandoned by his disciples, executed by the might of imperial Rome, breathed his last on the cross. Why, some had actually recognized in his cry of pain and desolation the complaint that even God had forsaken him. His faithful followers had confidently expected him to be the destined liberator of Israel; but he had died—not, like Judas of Galilee or Judas Maccabaeus, in the forefront of the struggle against the Gentile oppressors of Israel, but in evident weakness and disgrace—and their hopes died with him. If ever a cause was lost, it was his; if ever the powers of evil were victorious, it was then. And yet—within a generation his followers were exultingly proclaiming the crucified Jesus to be the conqueror of death and asserting, like our author here, that by dying he had reduced the erstwhile lord of death to impotence. The keys of death and Hades were henceforth held firmly in Jesus' powerful hand, for he, in the language of his own parable, had invaded the strong man's fortress, disarmed him, bound him fast, and robbed him of his spoil (Luke 11:21f.). This is the unanimous witness of the New Testament writers; this was the assurance which nerved martyrs to face death boldly in his name. This sudden change from disillusionment to triumph can only be explained by the account which the apostles gave—that their Master rose from the dead and imparted to them the power of his risen life.[57]

He who hung accursed on the tree, the perfect and faithful Son forsaken by his Father; he who had died a pauper and been placed in another's tomb—this same Jesus mopped the floor with death and the devil. At

---

[57] Bruce, *Hebrews*, 85.

dawn on the third day, the Father kept his oath that the Son's body would not see decay (Acts 2:31). "Death could not keep its prey!"

As a preacher's kid, I admit I've been jaded at times when it came to Scripture, the gospel, and our faith. The proverb has proven true: "Familiarity breeds contempt." But whenever I find myself face to face with the Son's supremacy over the grave, I lose it. I do. I can be sitting in a public place (e.g., coffee shop), casually reading my Bible or a commentary, and nothing is wrong. However, I start crying if I stumble upon a quote such as the one above or biblical passages such as Hebrews 2:14–15. I have to choke back the tears and clear my throat (because it's weird for a grown man to weep in public for no apparent reason). Only in Christ is death subjugated forever; only in Christ can we grieve with hope; only in Christ can we punch our ticket to the marriage supper of the Lamb before the Lion of Judah treads the winepress of his Father's fury. *If the thought of an empty tomb doesn't excite you, you've never wept beside a grave.*

Yet there is a nuance to the verb "destroy" in verse 14 that must be acknowledged. The verb *katargeō* doesn't exactly mean "destroy," as in "annihilate" or "exterminate," which is the way we use "destroy" in English. This is the Greek term's only occurrence in Hebrews, but Paul often used it to indicate rendering something powerless or ineffective (e.g., Rom 3:3, 31; Gal 3:17). Elsewhere, the apostle spoke of how the Lord Jesus Christ "abolished" (*katargeō*) death (2 Tim 1:10) and would "bring to nothing" (*katargeō*) the lawless one at the Second Coming (2 Thess 2:8). Hebrews has already explained that Jesus is now enthroned at God's right hand, though he still awaits the occasion of seeing all his enemies placed under his feet (1:13; see also 10:12–13), and, as Paul reminds us, "the last enemy to be destroyed [*katargeō*] is death" (1 Cor 15:26).

So has Christ "destroyed" (as we commonly use the word) death and the devil? As is true for many of the New Testament's claims, "Yes, but not yet." Our author's precise affirmation is valid: Jesus has rendered the devil "powerless" or "ineffective." "Though the devil still lives, and constantly attempts our ruin, yet all his power to hurt us is destroyed or restrained."[58]

[58] John Calvin, *Commentaries on the Epistle to the Hebrews*, trans. John Owen (Grand Rapids: Eerdmans, 1949), 72.

"At present," however, "we do not yet see everything in subjection to" Christ (v 8). Though we know the end of the story, we await its consummation. It is a daunting task to live this life "in between"—between promise and fulfillment, between faith and sight, between Good Friday and Easter Sunday.

However difficult this life "in between" can be, we can live it liberated from the fear of death our forefathers once knew. On the one hand, yes, death itself has yet to be annihilated once and for all. Our *fear* of death is another story. There is no reason for us to be enslaved to this fear; no longer can the devil bully us mercilessly with death's inevitability. There is life beyond the grave—life in the immediate presence of God. This is partly what is in view when we consider how Jesus restores humanity to its place of prominence, "crowned with glory and honor."

The despair with which death has blanketed the human race is evident in both Scripture and ancient literature. Solomon lamented, "Anyone who is among the living has hope—even a live dog is better off than a dead lion!" (Eccl 9:4 NIV). In one of the tragedies penned by the Greek playwright Euripides, the main character asks Phrygian, "You are a slave, Phrygian, and death will release from slavery. Why be afraid of death?" Phrygian replies, "Because, my lord, even a slave feels good to see the sunlight."[59] Arguably the best expression of death's inevitability comes from the Stoic philosopher Epictetus: "Where can I go to escape death? Show me the country, show me the people to whom I may go, upon whom death does not come; show me a magic charm against it. If I have none, what do you wish me to do? I cannot avoid death."[60]

We all have been oppressed at some point by our fear of death. The audience of Hebrews certainly felt that oppression; though our author will later say they had "not yet resisted to the point of" death (12:4), the operative word there was "yet." Martyrdom would come soon enough. Christians, however, have a champion-pioneer who has liberated them from the fear of death.

>———◇———<

[59] Euripides, *Orestes* 1522.
[60] Epictetus, *Discourses* 1.27.9–10.

There are two words in verse 14 that left me scratching my head because they made little sense. The part about Jesus destroying death and the devil, I understand. More than that, I rejoice in it! For all those who have spent time in the shadow of death, nothing will bring us to our knees in worship more swiftly than the thought of Jesus rising as a victor over the dark domain. When you are forced to put a loved one six feet into the earth, you long for the day when Christ our champion crushes the serpent's head for good.

It's my association of Christ with champion or superhero that leaves me scratching my head over those two words in verse 14—"through death." It was through death that Jesus destroyed death and the devil, our author claims, as well as through death that he delivered us from our fear of death. It seems paradoxical at best and asinine at worst to suggest that *death* was the means of defeating death. If Hebrews had said Jesus defeated death by *life*, I could understand that. Yet that's not our author's claim.[61] I think there are three ways to understand how Jesus defeated death through death, and they are not mutually exclusive.

First, his death was the only one that was not a result of the fall. As the perfect, voluntary sacrifice of atonement, Jesus broke Satan's power over his brothers, whom he now leads to glory. In Christ, we lay claim to his victory—we join the winning team—and inherit the advantage Jesus gained over the devil.

Second, "through death" may be parallel to "through suffering" (v 10). "Jesus does not conquer death by avoiding it or commanding its disappearance, but by *experiencing* it in the manner of other human beings."[62] In both Jesus' suffering and his death, the devil hurled every assault, every temptation, every arrow at our Lord to persuade him to abandon the Father and frustrate God's eternal purposes. But Christ defeated death and the devil by absorbing the sting fully, yet faithfully.

Third, Jesus defeated death through death by rising back to life and ascending to the Father. "Unlike others, Jesus did not encounter death as a slave, but as an assailant; he intruded into death's domain in order to

---

[61] Those who draw parallels here between Greek heroes (e.g., Hercules) and Jesus miss the point. Christ "conquers through death itself, though his victory was validated by his subsequent resurrection/exaltation" (Cockerill, *Hebrews*, 148; see also Attridge, *Hebrews*, 79–82).

[62] Johnson, *Hebrews*, 100; emphasis his.

overcome it. By dying and being raised, Jesus showed that death's power is not absolute, but is subject to the power of God."[63] Think of death as a dark cave that all are eventually forced to enter, engulfed in what seems to be eternal blackness. Death intimidates us with both its finality and the uncertainty of what lies beyond. Jesus, however, has blazed a trail to the other side as a champion-pioneer, proving the cave is not a cave at all but a tunnel, a path to the world to come.

This metaphor, for all its inadequacies, is perhaps our author's point. For an audience harassed by neighbors and civic leaders, and with the threat of death ever before them, this vision of their ultimate destiny—vindication, victory, and eternal glory—is compelling. Our destiny is found only in Christ, in identifying with his life, his sufferings, and his death. Just as he defeated the devil *through* death, Jesus offers us deliverance not *from* death but *through* death (i.e., by leading us through the cave and out the other side into the glorious presence of the Father). Suffering and death are nothing to fear if they bequeath to us the destiny appointed to us by our Creator in the beginning.

What does the Son's supremacy mean for us? Why should we "pay much closer attention" to the Son's gospel (2:1)? Why should we care that this message was declared "first by the Lord" (v 3) and not by angels (v 2)? Why does it matter that Jesus "for a little while was made lower than the angels" (v 9)? What is it about Christ's salvation that makes it so great?

The Son's supremacy is seen in that Christ has chosen to identify with God's people (i.e., "the offspring of Abraham"[64]) versus the angels (who never die and thus have no fear of death). Most translations of verse 16 say that Jesus "helps" the offspring of Abraham, though a better rendering would be, "It is not of angels that he *takes hold*, but he *takes hold* of the offspring of Abraham" (v 16; emphasis mine). The verb *epilambanomai* can mean "to be concerned about," yet its more natural meaning is "to grasp" or "to take hold of"[65] (e.g., 8:9). I prefer the translation "take hold" or "grasp"

[63] Koester, *Hebrews*, 239–40.
[64] This phrase refers to the spiritual, not physical, descendants of Abraham (Gal 3:7).
[65] BDAG, s.v. "ἐπιλαμβάνομαι."

because the idea is more immediate and intimate than "help." Our Savior does not aid from afar but personally extends his pierced hands to lift us from the mess that is our circumstances. The verb is in the present tense, meaning the grasp Jesus has on Abraham's offspring is ongoing.

Maclaren points out that *epilambanomai* is used in the story of Peter's attempting to walk on water. Beginning to sink, he cried out to Jesus for deliverance, and the Lord "immediately reached out his hand and took hold [*epilambanomai*] of him" (Matt 14:31). The word's sense of "rescue" is apparent here: "Here we are all, the whole race of us, exposed to the pelting of the pitiless storm, and ready to sink beneath the waters, and Jesus Christ stretches forth His strong, gentle hand and lays hold of our tremulous and feeble fingers, and keeps us up above the surges which else would overwhelm us."[66]

This grasp in which Jesus holds us is made possible by his incarnation, in becoming "like his brothers." God knew humanity would not be aided much by a superhero unacquainted with the ordinary, a divine champion who had never been brought low. Having overcome death and the devil through his faith and obedience to the Father, the supreme Son takes hold of us as he ascends and assumes his destiny. And Jesus didn't merely become like us but like us "in every respect" (v 17), a phrase stressed in the Greek text. There is not a single facet of the human experience that Jesus did not face. Emotions, temptations, weaknesses, disappointments—the supreme Son condescended to endure them all. He was not selective of those aspects of humanity to which he would subject himself.

The lengths to which Jesus went to identify with us were necessary if he was to qualify as our high priest,[67] and a merciful and faithful one at that. Only through total solidarity could the supreme Son understand our plight. "The Son could not have represented men before God, offering, as their high priest, the sacrifice of himself on their behalf and in their place, had he not first become their fellow man. Representation requires identification."[68]

---

[66] Maclaren, *Expositions*, 29:253.

[67] Verse 17 is the first of ten times that "high priest" is applied to Jesus in Hebrews. "The development of the argument in Hebrews ... suggests that υἱός ['Son'] was a name already known and recognized by the first readers of Hebrews, while ἀρχιερεύς ['high priest'] was a new title for which they had to be prepared" (Ellingworth, *Hebrews*, 185).

[68] P. Hughes, *Commentary*, 120.

Jesus' incarnation was also necessary to atone for our sins. The exact term is "make propitiation" (*hilaskomai*). This verb doesn't have a sole English equivalent. God's wrath over sin is real, making us enemies of God (Rom 1:18; 5:10). Jesus, however, satisfied this wrath with his death. In one sense, then, *hilaskomai* can mean "peace offering." And lest we think reconciliation was Jesus' idea alone, remember that redemption is found in "Christ Jesus, whom *God* put forward as a propitiation by his blood, to be received by faith. This was to show God's righteousness, because in his divine forbearance he had passed over former sins" (Rom 3:24–25; emphasis mine). In the Son's life and death, the Father was appeasing his own wrath over sin and reconciling us to himself (2 Cor 5:19).[69]

With the final verse of the chapter, our author clarifies the application of all that has preceded. To Christians drowning in their doubts and fears, he radios the comforting message: "The supreme Son—heir and King of all—knows exactly how you feel. Every bitter moment of the human experience was laid upon him. He walked this road; he endured this pain; he drank this cup. The siren call of selfishness wasn't muted until his faith and obedience to the Father were complete. Even now, from his Father's right hand, your brother offers you his grasp that will bear you through to the destiny appointed to you since before the foundation of the world—a crown of glory and honor!"

SUMMARY

» The punishment for rejecting Jesus and his gospel is more certain than the punishment for rejecting the law of Moses.

» In his suffering and death, Jesus reclaimed our glory and honor that was ours before we lost it in the fall.

» Jesus' suffering made him "one of us" and qualified him to be high priest.

» In his death, Jesus destroyed death and the devil and began to reverse the consequences of sin.

[69] God "is both the provider and the recipient of the reconciliation" (Silva, "ἱλάσκομαι," *NIDNTTE* 2:538).

TALKING POINTS

IN AN EFFORT to defend the doctrine of "once saved, always saved," some contend that the warning passages of Hebrews were written, not out of any legitimate concern that the readers could fall away from their salvation, but merely to offer an encouraging word not to do so. These passages were preventative, they argue, not prescriptive. However, it will become increasingly clear that "our author was afraid that his readers, succumbing to more or less subtle pressures, might become liable to those sanctions [mentioned in Heb 2]—if not by an overt renunciation of the gospel, then possibly by detaching themselves increasingly from its public profession until it ceased to have any influence upon their lives."[70] Some in the church have gone so far in the *opposite* direction of "once saved, always saved" that they have come to deny a person can be sure of salvation at all. This, too, is unbiblical; our author will soon urge confidence in our confession and salvation (3:6, 14). The incorrect response to false doctrine is to take up the polar position by default; the correct response is to think biblically about the issue. God wants us to be confident in drawing near to him (as Hebrews will go on to advocate). But this does not make losing our salvation an impossibility, and it is irresponsible to suggest so. Guthrie, a Southern Baptist professor, warns that "those of us who have preached 'once-saved, always-saved' to the neglect of teachings on accountability have done a disservice to the body of Christ and her members, offering an unbalanced view of a right relationship to God. We must never maximize the grace of God to the neglect of the holiness of God and God's desire for the holiness of his people."[71]

>———◇———<

DO NOT RUSH through Hebrews 2 without reflecting on what it means to drift away from Jesus and his gospel. Most Christians lose their salvation, not in a single moment of major moral failure, but as part of a "slow fade." C. S. Lewis asked rhetorically, "If you examined a hundred people who had lost their faith in Christianity, I wonder how many of them would turn out

[70] Bruce, *Hebrews*, 68.
[71] Guthrie, *Hebrews*, 87.

to have been reasoned out of it by honest argument? Do not most people simply drift away?"[72] The drift is almost imperceptible; we never realize it's happening (due to neglect) until it's too late. That's why our author calls us to "pay much closer attention." The Christian life requires active vigilance (Matt 25:1–13; 26:41). Reflecting on this, Maclaren mentioned three "currents" that can cause us to drift away from Christ: (1) *The passage of time.* The longer we live, the more difficult it is to remain vigilant and faithful (e.g., Eccl 12:1–13). (2) *One's knowledge of the truth.* There's a reason for the proverb, "Familiarity breeds contempt." Being well-versed in the faith does not mean one will be well-versed in faithfulness. (3) *The daily stressors of life.* If it didn't take tragedy or disaster to make the little boy Alexander want to move to Australia, then it won't take the same to lead us astray. As they fall to earth, snowflakes are itty-bitty and impotent; in accumulation, however, an avalanche can be a destructive force.[73]

><———◇———<

WHAT DOES it mean in real terms to "pay much closer attention" to the message God has spoken through the supreme Son? Regular and diligent study of the Word should be first on the list. Later in Hebrews, our author will talk about how the Word pares us down, splits us open, and exposes the holes in our holiness (4:12). Add to that the need to reflect on what we read and study. It isn't enough to read what God has said; we must savor and enjoy it like a delicious meal. There is a reason the Lord calls us to meditate on his Word "day and night" (Josh 1:8; Ps 1:2). As Maclaren puts it, "If we had more honest occupation of thought with, and more quiet feeding like a ruminant animal upon, the truths of the gospel, we might bid defiance to all the currents to sweep us away."[74] Another strategy is to be constant in prayer. Prayer has a way of connecting us to what God is doing in the world and in our lives, prompting us to live in faith and confidence versus fear or presumption. Only after we have committed ourselves to regular study and reflection of Scripture, as well as faithful prayer, are we equipped to examine

---

[72] C. S. Lewis, *Mere Christianity* (New York: HarperCollins, 2001), 141.

[73] Maclaren, *Expositions*, 29:206–7.

[74] Maclaren, 29:210.

ourselves (2 Cor 13:5). Is the Spirit bearing his fruit in our hearts (Gal 5:22–23)? Are the Christian virtues being added to our lives (2 Pet 1:5–8)? Is sin promptly confessed and repented of (1 John 1:6–10)? Is our faith in God and love for others growing more and more (2 Thess 1:3)?

><>—<

THE COMMANDS to pay attention, don't drift, and don't neglect become joys, not chores, when placed in perspective. The author of Hebrews isn't calling us to pay attention to what is a bane or a bore but a blessing! "It's not as if he is saying, Don't neglect your arthritis. Or: Don't neglect your dandelions. Or: Don't neglect your spinach. He is saying don't neglect your *salvation*. Your *great* salvation. So it's as if he said, Don't neglect your steak dinners. Don't neglect your cancer-healing therapy. Don't neglect your sunrises and sunsets. And don't neglect your Butterfinger Blizzards or your new baby's smile, or your Rocky Mountains, or your Boundary Waters' breezes under the full night sky, or your safe warm bed. It's *like* that."[75] Indeed, it helps to think of not neglecting our salvation as one obsessing over a passion or hobby. I don't find it a chore to "pay much closer attention" to college or pro football; as soon as the Super Bowl ends, I'm eager for the start of Training Camp. I don't find it a chore to "pay much closer attention" to landscape photography; researching new locations to shoot is an itch I can never scratch to my satisfaction. The more we reflect on what makes our salvation "great," the less of a chore the Christian life becomes; the more fertilized and cultivated our hearts become for the Spirit's fruit.

><>—<

THE SIGNS AND wonders performed by Christ and the apostles confirmed their message. But, and as Paul had predicted (1 Cor 13:8), those miracles did not last. When our author mentioned these signs (2:4), it likely sparked a question in the minds of some: "Where are those miracles now?" If those signs were evidence of God's power to deliver his people, why were his people presently suffering verbal and physical harassment?

[75] John Piper, "Spoken, Confirmed, Witnessed: a Great Salvation," *Desiring God*, 5 May 1996, http://www.desiringgod.org/messages/spoken-confirmed-witnessed-a-great-salvation; emphasis his.

Why did God not act to deliver once again? Our fictional Judah couldn't have been the only first-century Christian to be discouraged when, after believing partly because of miracles, he saw none wrought in his own life. Hebrews will argue that the proper response to suffering is enduring faith, not an expectation of miraculous deliverance (10:35–39). This is because, along with the rest of the Spirit's fruit, *enduring faith in a Christian's heart is superior proof of Christianity's authenticity versus any miracle.* Though God wrought many miracles in Israel, only to see the Israelites become unfaithful, the suffering of countless Christian martyrs has seen the borders of the kingdom expand. Perhaps in our suffering, we should not demand that God do something until we've resolved what *we* will do.

THE QUESTION "What is man, that you are mindful of him?" rings as a shrill echo within the moral madness of our present culture. On the one hand, we argue whether the unwanted unborn can be legally murdered; on the other, we argue whose lives matter more: black or blue? Yet Scripture presents all humanity as the crown of God's creation, and Hebrews 2 is ripe with evidence. Such a reminder was desperately needed by saints who must have felt "like an unwanted speck among the millions of the Roman Empire. But that is an illusion. The reality is, ... as God's children they are objects of astounding attention."[76] For example, nowhere are the angels called Jesus' brothers. It is not the angels who are led to glory via the Son's suffering; it is not the angels to whom Jesus offers personal help. Perhaps the two greatest arguments for our worth are the twin scenes at the heart of Hebrews: Christ on the cross and Christ on the throne. In the former, we see our worth in God's eyes in that he sacrificed the supreme Son to restore our primeval destiny; in the latter, we see actualized what was promised to us in the beginning—dignity and dominion.[77]

---

[76] R. Hughes, *Hebrews*, 1:59–60.
[77] Maclaren, *Expositions*, 29:228.

PHILO ONCE wrote, "Nothing is so calculated to enslave the mind as a fear of death, arising from an excessive desire of living."[78] Our emotional attachment to the material realm feeds our fear of death like sugar fuels a toddler. People may *say* they don't fear death, but how they *live* reveals the truth. Our fear of death is a subtle thing; rarely do we feel it acutely. Instead, it is chronic, "and therefore more fundamentally shapes human choices."[79] Consider that we fear death because (1) the guilty conscience is terrified of meeting God in judgment,[80] (2) we associate it with pain (physical and emotional), and (3) what lies beyond it is unknown to the human experience (i.e., we "know" what lies beyond by faith, not sight). In light of our fear, we chase riches, success, or pleasure and think some concoction of the three will either delay death indefinitely or dull our senses to the anxiety and pain associated with it.[81] We seek ways to build a selfish legacy beyond our lifetime, or we engage in self-sabotage under the banner of *carpe diem* hopelessness. Jesus frees us from the tyranny of our fear by (1) purging the conscience clean (9:14), (2) teaching us how to live for more than ourselves, (3) revealing the redemptive purpose of pain: perfection and glorification, and (4) reminding us that joy awaits us on the other side of death if we are faithful. In light of Philo's comment, we realize we must learn to cherish "the reproach of Christ" and reject the "treasures of Egypt" (11:26) if we want to feel the grave's death-grip on us loosen.

---

[78] Philo, *Good Person* 22.

[79] Johnson, *Hebrews*, 101.

[80] David G. Peterson, *Hebrews*, TNTC 15 (Downers Grove, IL: IVP Academic, 2020), 96.

[81] In Western Christianity especially, "we have become committed to relieving the pain behind our problems rather than using our pain to wrestle more passionately with the character and purposes of God" (Guthrie, *Hebrews*, 104).

Chapter 3

REST OR WRATH?

T imothy's mention of death and its destructive power caused Judah's mind to wander back to the tomb of his son. Nothing had been the same since Daniel's death. Everything now seemed harder—too hard, in fact. Judah's confession of Jesus as the Messiah had triggered family shunning and social ostracism, as it would for nearly any Jew. Though this was painful, Judah had taken it in stride. He had expected it. He had even accepted the failure of his business with grim resignation; the same had been happening to other members of the Way in Antioch.

But his son's death had been the back-breaking straw. Adhering to the covenant of his fathers now seemed a safer course. What had he gained by betraying his family and turning his back on Moses to embrace the Nazarene? Christs, after all, were a denarius a dozen farther south in Judea and Galilee. *I'm a fool*, Judah thought, *for casting my lot with this one. Doing so has cost me my family, my friends, my future—and now my child. Everything I had with Moses, I've lost with this Messiah.*

Even as he thought these words, Judah questioned whether he believed them. He had been second-guessing so much of late that he felt confident of very little at present. External pressures and internal pain had reduced his boldness and resilience to rubble. While blessing and confidence had once inhabited his heart, bitterness and callousness now poisoned it.

Judah was exhausted—physically, emotionally, spiritually. He was exhausted by the uncertainty, exhausted by the grief, exhausted by the numb indifference his pain had produced in his heart in such a short amount of time. Judah's mind refocused on the homily as he heard Timothy say, "Consider Jesus…"

>———◇———<

It would be difficult to overstate the veneration first-century Jews held for Moses. He was "the liberator and lawgiver of Israel, the most important person in the OT. While Abraham may be regarded as the founder of Israel's faith, Moses is the founder of Israel's religion."[1] The Old Testament tells us that Moses spoke to God face to face (Num 12:8) and saw the glory of Yahweh, which set his face aglow for a time (Exod 34:29–30, 35). Moses was deeply respected by his enemies (11:4). After his death, it was said that Israel never again saw a prophet of his caliber (Deut 34:10–12).

By the first century, Moses was even approaching a quasi-divine status in the minds of at least some Jews. Sirach claims God "made him equal in glory to the holy ones [i.e., angels]" (45:2), and Philo referred to him as "the god and king" of Israel.[2] Even the earliest Christians held Moses in high regard, as seen in Peter's and Stephen's sermons (Acts 3:22; 7:20–44). "To the Jews, it would have been impossible to conceive that anyone ever stood closer to God than Moses did, and yet that is precisely what the writer of the Hebrews sets out to prove."[3]

Hebrews will help us discover that the covenant of Jesus has superseded the covenant of Moses and that, although access to God was limited through Moses, we are now invited to "draw near" to God with boldness through Jesus (4:16). Despite all the uncertainty and suffering confronting his readers, our author assures them that they are indeed a part of God's family if they maintain their confession, conviction, and confidence in Christ.

HEBREWS 3:1–6

This section builds on the previous one (2:10–18); Jesus, as our high priest, can help us because he shared in the human experience. Therefore, just as he descended in the incarnation and sanctified us (2:11, 17), we now can rise to "share in a heavenly calling" (3:1). The word translated as the verb "share" (*metochos*) is actually a noun that can refer to a companion (1:9) or business partner (Luke 5:7). As many sons being led to glory, Christians

[1] James K. Hoffmeier, "Moses," *ISBE* 3:415.
[2] Philo, *Moses* 1.158; *Dreams* 2.189; see also Exod 7:1. "The rabbinic tradition provides ample evidence for the belief that Moses was held in higher esteem than the angels" (Scott, "Jesus' Superiority," 203, n. 17).
[3] Barclay, *Hebrews*, 35.

are partners in a joint endeavor: "a heavenly calling." With these words, our author wants his readers "to see themselves 'at home' with God and one another and in no need of the home, honor, hope, and security they left behind when they converted to membership in this group."[4] Since we enjoy this privileged position of belonging or "at-homeness" because of Jesus, we should consider him.[5]

Our author identifies Jesus as "the apostle and high priest of our confession." These two titles are used nowhere else in the New Testament in reference to our Lord, but that does not mean the ideas are foreign to New Testament theology. That Jesus is our apostle and high priest is among the most fundamental claims of the Christian faith. The twin terms mark Jesus "as being both God's representative among human beings and their representative in the presence of God,"[6] and this confession thus forms the foundation of the church.

In this passage, "apostle" does not carry its technical New Testament meaning (i.e., one of the Twelve) but is a general designation of "one who is sent" or a messenger "with extraordinary status"[7] (e.g., Moses, Exod 3:10 LXX). In the Gospels, primarily John's, Jesus describes himself as sent by the Father (4:34; 5:23–24, 6:29).[8] But Jesus wasn't just any messenger; he was a plenipotentiary, "an ambassador with full powers."[9] Bearing in himself the full and final word spoken by God, Jesus proved his faithfulness to the Father by accomplishing the mission assigned to him (17:4).

Christ is also a high priest who faithfully intercedes for his people at God's right hand. In the Old Testament, Moses performed both roles: He was an apostle assigned a mission by God, and he was a faithful priest and intercessor to God on behalf of the people.[10] "Moses was a priest especially favored by God, because he alone was called into the divine presence, where he spoke to God 'face to face.' This tradition of Moses' intimate

---

[4] DeSilva, *Perseverance*, 133.

[5] "The urgent invitation for the [author]'s hearers to give Jesus their full attention in v. 1 sets the direction for the rest of this sermon" (Cockerill, *Hebrews*, 157).

[6] Bruce, *Hebrews*, 91.

[7] BDAG, s.v. "ἀπόστολος."

[8] See James Swetnam, "ὁ ἀπόστολος in Hebrews 3,1," *Bib* 89 (2008): 252–62.

[9] Scott, "Jesus' Superiority," 205.

[10] Exod 17:10–12; 24:4–8; 32:11–14, 31–32; Num 14:13–19; Ps 99:6; Jer 15:1.

encounter with God underwent further development in Hellenized Jewish circles and among the rabbis. In these various traditions Moses becomes the intermediary par excellence between God and humanity, the sort of claim made for Jesus in Hebrews."[11] Since the central section of Hebrews unpacks the high priesthood of Christ, I will not explore that theme here. Note our author's subtle point, however: compared to Moses, Jesus is a superior priest who provides superior intercession in every way.

The reference to Moses as "faithful in all God's house" (vv 2, 5) comes from Numbers 12, where Miriam and Aaron challenged Moses' leadership of Israel. In the verbal dressing-down God delivered to Moses' upstart siblings, he identified Moses as his chosen leader and reminded them that he spoke to Moses plainly and directly versus in obscure visions and confusing dreams (12:6–8). This meant Moses was an honorable and faithful steward over the household of God (Exod 14:31; Num 11:11; Deut 3:24; Josh 1:2).

The word translated "servant" (Heb 3:5) is not the typical Greek *doulos* but *therapōn*, occurring only here in the New Testament. It carries a more specific meaning than "servant" or "slave"; it referred to "one who renders *devoted* service"[12] and was used of Moses three times in the LXX (Exod 4:10; 14:31; Num 12:7). While *doulos* had a pejorative connotation of forced servitude,[13] *therapōn* "speaks of service that is of a nobler and freer character."[14] "Further in the background may lie the distinction between a steward, set over a household, and a servant, who is merely a member of the household."[15]

As much honor as Moses deserves as a faithful steward, however, Jesus deserves greater honor because "the builder of a house has more honor than the house itself" (v 3). In other words, the Creator is always greater than his creation. Whenever we behold an architectural marvel, we applaud the architect. Even when we praise the building itself, "the

---

[11] Attridge, *Hebrews*, 105. "If the servant's (Moses') prayers offered on behalf of the people were answered, 'how much more' will the prayers of the Son offered for believers be answered. The closeness of the Son to the Father is passed on to those who believe, so that they receive greater access to God than Moses experienced" (Scott, "Jesus' Superiority," 210).

[12] BDAG, s.v. "θεράπων"; emphasis mine.

[13] Attridge, *Hebrews*, 111, n. 82.

[14] Scott, "Jesus' Superiority," 209, n. 54.

[15] Ellingworth, *Hebrews*, 207.

designer is praised by implication."[16] Seen from a different perspective, and as the text makes clear, Moses was faithful *in* God's house (v 5), but Jesus is *over* God's house (v 6).

Moses was a faithful steward particularly in that "he looked forward to when God would speak a better and final word through his Son"[17] (v 5). Without explicitly referencing them, our author surely has in mind the lawgiver's words to Israel: "The LORD your God will raise up for you a prophet like me from among you, from your fellow Israelites. You must listen to him" (Deut 18:15 NIV). A few verses later, the Lord foretold through Moses, "I will raise up for them a prophet like you from among their fellow Israelites, and I will put my words in his mouth. He will tell them everything I command him. I myself will call to account anyone who does not listen to my words that the prophet speaks in my name" (vv 18–19 NIV).

The final verses of the Pentateuch acknowledge that no such prophet had yet arisen after Moses (Deut 34:10–12), which foreshadowed the day when One greater than any servant or prophet would appear. We might say Moses was "a shadow of the good things to come" (Heb 10:1). Hebrews is showing Moses the honor he deserves while also noting that Moses pointed forward to the advent of One greater than he (Luke 24:27; John 5:46). Note that our author has deftly managed to exalt Jesus here without denigrating Moses. He could have thrown Moses under the bus by calling attention to his *un*faithfulness (e.g., Num 20:12), but he does not. "There is no need to belittle Moses, for the greater Moses is, the more the Son's superiority will be magnified."[18]

As were the angels (1:7, 14), Moses was a faithful *servant*, but Christ is a faithful *Son*. "Servants have an obligation to faithfulness, but sons have a special, vested interest in and authority over the house"[19] (e.g., John 8:35). And while Moses was a faithful intercessor, Jesus is a faithful and great high priest who creates for us an intimacy with God that Moses

---

[16] Johnson, *Hebrews*, 109.

[17] Schreiner, *Hebrews*, 118. "This would be an encouragement to those first-century Jewish believers to remain faithful to Christ, even in the midst of the tough trials they were experiencing. Instead of going back to Moses, they should *imitate* Moses and be faithful in their calling" (Warren W. Wiersbe, *The Bible Exposition Commentary* [Wheaton, IL: Victor, 1989], 2:286; emphasis his).

[18] Cockerill, *Hebrews*, 168.

[19] Guthrie, *Hebrews*, 128.

never could. Likewise, just as Israel was the household of God in the old economy, the church comprises God's household in the new—a common claim by the apostle Paul.[20] On the other hand, Hebrews says individual Christians remain a part of God's family only as long as they "hold fast" or maintain their confidence and boasting (vv 6, 14). What does this mean?

"Confidence" (*parrēsia*, see also 4:16; 10:19) was used by Josephus and Philo[21] of the boldness one should have before God. In its everyday use, it referred to freedom of speech that results from self-assurance.[22] Within the context of Hebrews, "confidence" and "confession" (4:14; 10:23) are somewhat interchangeable. Therefore, our author may be saying, "Hold fast to the boldness that enables you to speak freely about the object of your faith and hope." As we will see throughout this epistle, it was not a foregone conclusion that the audience of Hebrews would persevere to the end; they had to keep a tight grip on their confession.[23]

The word translated "boasting" (*kauchēma*) has more to do with what we are boasting about than the act of boasting itself.[24] It relates to the subject, not the attitude (Prov 17:6; Rom 4:2). In what do Christians boast? Hope! More specifically, hope that God will do what he has promised: crown us with glory and honor (Heb 2:5–10), purify us from sin through our high priest (6:19; 10:19–23), and beckon us to approach his throne of grace (4:16; 7:19). Hope, however, by its very definition is an as-yet-unrealized reality, a "not yet" (11:1). Thus readers of Hebrews are urged to be faithful, as were Jesus and Moses, looking forward to what is to come.

Our author was speaking to an assembly of saints facing discouragement and pressure from various directions. The temptation was real to return to Moses and the law in order to find relief from their heartache. True relief, however, could be found only in holding onto Jesus. "At one time the 'holy brethren' openly made a confession of faith in Jesus [v 1]. Such confession must be continued if they are to continue to be counted as

---

[20] 1 Cor 3:16; 6:19; 2 Cor 6:16; Gal 6:10; Eph 2:19, 21; 1 Tim 3:15; see also 1 Pet 2:5; 4:17.

[21] Josephus, *Antiquities* 2.52; 5.38; Philo, *Heir* 5–7.

[22] Both Ellingworth (*Hebrews*, 211–12) and Koester (*Hebrews*, 247–48) have excellent discussions of the nuances of this term.

[23] Note that the clause "we are his house, if indeed…" (v 6) is conditional.

[24] Ellingworth, *Hebrews*, 212; "that which constitutes a source of pride" (BDAG, s.v. "καύχημα").

members of God's house."[25] Indeed, to forsake Jesus was to forsake Moses because the servant pointed to the Son. What greater way to illustrate this call to confidence in the face of difficulty than to evoke a tried-and-true anecdote about the audience's ancient, apostatized ancestors?

HEBREWS 3:7–11

If a picture is worth a thousand words, then an apropos verbal illustration or anecdote must be worth at least five hundred. As a speaker and writer, I appreciate the knack narrative often has for smuggling truth in through the back door of our hearts and into our minds before we know what hit us. A good sermon will often begin with an illustration and a good chapter with a story. Why tell an audience something when you can "show" them, albeit verbally?

Having issued a call to hold fast in confidence, our author addresses a significant threat to one's ability to "hold fast" (v 6): a hard heart. Since Jesus is greater than Moses, we cannot afford to reject Jesus' word as Israel did Moses' (2:2–3). By appealing to the example of Israel in the wilderness,[26] our author wants his audience to realize that steadfastness is not dependent on God's goodness (his grace to Israel in the desert was great) but on our faith and obedience. In other words, God's grace is constant; our faithfulness is the variable.

To emphasize this, our author quoted Psalm 95. That Hebrews attributes the psalm to the Spirit is a fact not to be ignored. First, by appealing to the words of the Spirit, our author is laying claim to a greater authority than his own. If his audience rejects his words, it is the Spirit of God they are rejecting. Second, the present tense—"as the Holy Spirit *says*" (v 7; emphasis mine)—highlights the urgent relevancy of the matter. That the Spirit speaks today, not just a long time ago, means we should listen

---

[25] Gareth L. Reese, *Hebrews* (Moberly, MO: Scripture Exposition Books, 2008), 43.

[26] By invoking the wilderness generation, our author was using an established rhetorical tool of his day. "Examples from historical precedents were especially valued by orators in deliberative situations, in which the goal was to convince the hearers that a certain course of action would entail certain consequences. ... How could one convince people concerning events yet to happen? The 'quickest method of securing assent' was to point the audience to historical parallels, for which the consequences are now a matter of record" (deSilva, *Perseverance*, 141).

carefully to what has been said.[27] Our author will soon speak of how God's word is living and breathing (4:12).

Psalm 95 begins with a call to praise the Lord with a "joyful noise" (v 1) and songs (v 2) for what he has done for his people, particularly as Creator of the universe (vv 4–6), sovereign King above all things (v 3), and Shepherd of his flock (v 7). In verse 8, David admonishes his listeners not to harden themselves against such a benevolent God and King, as their ancestors did in the wilderness at Meribah and Massah.

The background of Psalm 95 is Israel's departure from Egypt. Following the Ten Plagues and the Red Sea crossing, Israel bitterly complained about a lack of water in the desert, alleging they had been liberated from slavery only to be brought out into the desert to die (Exod 17:3). Yahweh provided Israel with water by telling Moses to strike the rock. Though they had just been miraculously delivered from Pharaoh's hand, Israel did not have faith to believe God would provide for them in the wilderness. Theirs was a "fair-weather, herd-instinct faith—good until the first trial, when it dissolved in unbelief."[28]

Also in David's mind was Israel's rebellion due to the spies' report at Kadesh (Num 13–14). Though Joshua and Caleb espoused faith that Israel could conquer Canaan by the power of God, the other ten spies said, "No way!" The people rebelled, triggering the Lord's wrath arguably like never before. "Not a single person of those who saw my Glory, saw the miracle signs I did in Egypt and the wilderness, and who have tested me over and over and over again, turning a deaf ear to me—not one of them will set eyes on the land I so solemnly promised to their ancestors. No one who has treated me with such repeated contempt will see it" (Num 14:22–23 Msg). Over time, the wilderness generation in general (and Israel's faithlessness at Kadesh specifically) became the go-to illustration among biblical authors for disobedience and rebellion (e.g., Neh 9:15–17; Ps 106:24–26; 1 Cor 10:1–12).

---

[27] "'Today,' when David wrote this Psalm [95:7], was a reference to his own generation. But, when the writer of Hebrews applies this Psalm to his readers, 'Today' means now, right at the present. The very time when the command is heard by the readers is the time it is to be obeyed. God's voice must not be neglected or ignored, or put off till tomorrow. Immediate action is imperative" (Reese, *Hebrews*, 44). "God never says to anyone, Hearken to my voice and obey my precepts tomorrow. His command is, Do it now; at the very moment that you hear his voice and know his will" (Robert Milligan, *The Epistle to the Hebrews* [Nashville: Gospel Advocate, 1981], 145).

[28] R. Hughes, *Hebrews*, 1:100.

According to David, then, to harden one's heart against the Lord is to question his goodness and faithfulness after he has so clearly acted in the past to deliver (e.g., "my works," Ps 95:9). A mindset of "What have you done for me lately?" leads only to stubborn rebellion, which in turn leads to being turned away from entering God's rest because we have tested his and provoked his wrath. Note the inclusion of "always" in Hebrews 3:10, indicating "that Israel's wandering from the Lord was not temporary or occasional but was the constant refrain of their lives"[29] (see Num 14:22). Time and again, they treated Yahweh like an enemy instead of a savior. Since God knew that this was Israel's way, he swore in his wrath, "They shall not enter my rest"[30] (Num 14:30; Deut 2:14). An entire generation dropped as corpses in the desert because they did not trust and obey.[31]

Our author was deliberate in using the wilderness generation, and more specifically Psalm 95, to illustrate his point. This psalm was read at the beginning of synagogue services on the Sabbath,[32] meaning the Hebrews audience would have been familiar with it. Understandably, a Sabbath call to worship would conclude with a call to soften one's heart to the voice of God and hear his word while one had the opportunity.[33]

HEBREWS 3:12–19

Desiring that none in his audience follow their wilderness ancestors, our author warns them to "take care" (literally "look" or "watch out") that their[34] hearts not become "evil" and "unbelieving" (v 12). As Attridge notes, a literal translation would be "a wicked heart of faithlessness."[35] When our

---

[29] Schreiner, *Hebrews*, 123.

[30] The Greek text of Heb 3:11 is an incomplete conditional statement, "if they should enter into my rest." "This idiom suggests the need for an impossible conclusion to be supplied, such as 'I would not be God', to reinforce the seriousness of the proposition" (Peterson, *Hebrews*, 113).

[31] Jewish rabbis deduced from Ps 95:11 and Num 14:35 that the wilderness generation would have no part in the world to come (*Sanhedrin* 110b).

[32] Lane, *Hebrews 1–8*, 85; Marvin E. Tate, *Psalms 51–100*, WBC 20 (Dallas: Word, 1990), 499.

[33] Guthrie, "Hebrews," 953.

[34] "Every single person should take the admonition seriously, for he directs it to 'any of you.' No member of the church is exempted from the warning" (Schreiner, *Hebrews*, 126).

[35] Attridge, *Hebrews*, 116, n. 42. "Unbelief springs from the heart but becomes real in the concrete act of refusal to trust God (3:18). *[Our author] envisions no faith that does not lead to obedience, nor does he conceive of any obedience that does not stem from faith*" (Cockerill, *Hebrews*, 183; emphasis mine).

hearts refuse to trust God and obey him, they become a Petri dish for the most vicious heart diseases of the spiritual sort.

This sort of heart will make us "fall away from the living God." For the original audience, falling away from Christ to return to Judaism was worse than Israel's rejecting God and mentally turning back to Egypt (Num 14:3–4; Acts 7:39). "It would not be a mere return to a position previously occupied, but a gesture of outright apostasy, a complete break with God."[36] Put another way, the falling away our author has in mind here is an active rebellion. "Falling away," according to Bruce, "is a more positive activity than the English words themselves might suggest; it denotes rebellion against him [i.e., God]. When the Israelites at Kadesh-barnea repudiated Moses and Aaron's leadership, they revolted in effect against God, who had appointed these two men to be their leaders. And for Christians to repudiate the apostle and high priest of their confession, similarly appointed by God, would be if possible an even more outrageous revolt against the living God."[37]

This raises another important point. More significant than the action (falling away) is *from whom* we fall away—"the living God" (v 12). This language, when coupled with so severe a warning, seems to have been God's way of reminding his people that their rebellion wasn't against a lifeless code of conduct; it wasn't just non-compliance with policies and procedures. To turn away from the living God is to forsake a relationship, to break a heart—as Attridge puts it, "['living God'] gives expression to the vital reality that is the object of faith."[38]

In the context of Hebrews, I'm convinced "living God" refers particularly to Jesus. Our author has already appropriated Old Testament passages concerning God and applied them to the Son. It is the Son from whom these Hebrew Christians were tempted to fall away. Ever closer draws the Day when the Son will humiliate and destroy any who reject him (1:13; 6:4–8; 10:13; 12:25–29), meaning the consequences of apostasy for Christians will make the fate of the wilderness generation look like a short run

---

[36] Bruce, *Hebrews*, 100.

[37] Bruce, 100.

[38] Attridge, *Hebrews*, 117; e.g., Num 14:21, 28; Josh 3:10; 1 Sam 17:26; 2 Kgs 19:4, 16; Jer 10:10.

of bad luck. It "is not a dead idol, but a living, eternal, all-powerful being" whom the Hebrews audience is about to abandon.[39] Indeed, "Falling away from the true and living God is an unmitigated disaster."[40]

The way to avoid cultivating such a heart is to "exhort one another every day" (v 13). Our author takes the word "today" in Psalm 95 literally—tomorrow isn't guaranteed. "The fact that the 'today' of the psalm is also the 'today' of the church gives a special urgency to the church's response."[41] The word translated "exhort" (*parakaleō*) is used widely throughout the New Testament, often with the meaning to "urge strongly" or to "make a strong request"[42] (e.g., 2 Cor 10:1; 1 Thess 5:11). Given the verb's tense (present continuous) and meaning, the kind of exhortation our author has in mind is mutual, ongoing, and passionate. "Believers should gather together, as the author says later (10:25), to strengthen and encourage one another. They should be reminded of the goodness of God and the dangers of unrepentant sin. *Occasional encouragement does not suffice.*"[43]

Suppose this encouragement is not mutually extended daily to members of the Christian community. In that case, they will become dangerously susceptible to a heart hardened by "the deceitfulness of sin."[44] Sin isn't just a lie, and Satan isn't simply a liar. A lie is something factually inaccurate. On the other hand, deceit is a lie packaged with just enough truth that it becomes believable. A lie is when your kids tell you a bird flew into the house through an open window, knocked over the expensive vase, and then flew out; a lie is telling the preacher you loved his sermon though it was clear to everyone you were sleeping through most of it! Deceit, however, is plausible, believable, even attractive. A lie makes you think, "I wasn't born yesterday. I can see right through this." Deceit is something you swallow hook, line, and sinker.

[39] Reese, *Hebrews*, 48.

[40] Schreiner, *Hebrews*, 127.

[41] James W. Thompson, *Hebrews*, PCNT (Grand Rapids: Baker Academic, 2008), 93.

[42] BDAG, s.v. "παρακαλέω."

[43] Schreiner, *Hebrews*, 127; emphasis mine.

[44] "It seems likely, in this context, that the arguments presented to the minds of the Christians why it would be wise to abandon Christianity and go back to Judaism, are what are called 'the deceitfulness of sin.' The deceit is so plausible, the mind becomes insensitive to the heinous nature of the act (i.e., that by such an act you are falling away from the living God)" (Reese, *Hebrews*, 49).

If sin comes to us as sin, we are swift to hate it, and strong to repel it, by the grace of God. When we are walking with God, we only need to know that an action is forbidden, and straightway we avoid it; we shun the evil thing when it is plainly evil. But sin puts on another dress, and comes to us speaking a language which is not its own; and so, even those who would avoid sin as sin, may, by degrees, be tempted to evil, and deluded into wrong.[45]

That's how sin works. Satan doesn't lie to us outright as much as he attempts to deceive (Rom 7:11). He is too crafty; he wraps his lie in just enough truth that we believe it. The prince of this world is very, very good at this. Sin deceives by telling us:

> "It's not that bad."
> "It's just this once."
> "No one is being hurt."
> "You can quit whenever you want."
> "I can reconcile my rebellion with God later."

Even though:

> Sin is always worse than imagined.
> Seldom is a sin committed "just this once."
> Someone is always hurt, even if it's only you.
> Sin enslaves; you can never quit whenever you want.
> Your rebellion separates you from God's grace.

Paul warned the Corinthians, "I am afraid that as the serpent deceived Eve by his cunning, your thoughts will be led astray from a sincere and pure devotion to Christ" (2 Cor 11:3). I don't know about you, but I've fallen for some of these deceitful lies far too many times. I've seen sin's deceit harden the nerve center of my spiritual self until my entire being nearly became sclerotic. As the witness of Scripture bears out in stories and stipulations, the human heart can become so hardened that it loses its ability to believe the word of God, even when spoken for our good.

---

[45] C. H. Spurgeon, "The Deceitfulness of Sin," in *The Metropolitan Tabernacle Pulpit Sermons* (London: Passmore, 1890), 36:97–98.

In Hebrews 3:1, our author had referred to his audience as those "who share in a heavenly calling," and he uses the same word (*metochos*) in verse 14. Unlike in verse 1, however, our author now places a condition on sharing in Christ: "if indeed we hold our original confidence firm to the end." We consider something that is "firm" to be valid or guaranteed.[46] The blessings we enjoy by sharing in Christ[47] are dependent on our daily submission to Christ.

The word our author uses for "confidence" in verse 14 (*hypostasis*) isn't the same as that used in verse 6. Instead of connoting boldness as before, the term our author chooses here refers to "the essential or basic structure/nature of an entity."[48] At times, it referred to a title deed—tangible proof of an intangible reality; it's the same word used in 11:1 ("assurance") and 1:3 ("nature"). *Hypostasis* can also describe the resolve of a soldier or martyr; it "does not indicate the act of endurance or resistance but the determination that produces such endurance."[49] Our author uses it here to say that we will share in Christ "if we continue to consider our initial resolve or the beginning of this new reality to be guaranteed or legitimate until the end."

>———◇———<

After repeating Psalm 95:7–8, our author shifts his focus back to the wilderness generation. Asking himself a series of rhetorical questions in 3:16–18 (each taken from Ps 95), and drawing a conclusion in verse 19, he reveals four aspects of Israel's desert apostasy.

Israel was guilty of *rebellion* (v 16). As we previously noted, what we might consider a passive withdrawal from God (i.e., "fall away") is really active and open rebellion against him. When our author says those who rebelled were "all those who left Egypt led by Moses," he is reminding us that the very ones who rejected God had been the beneficiaries of his deliverance and witnesses to his mighty acts. Israel had no excuse. More inexcusable is Christians' hard-hearted rebellion against the same Lord

---

[46] Koester, *Hebrews*, 260–61.

[47] Enrique Nardoni, "Partakers in Christ (Hebrews 3.14)," *NTS* 37 (1991): 456–72.

[48] BDAG, s.v. "ὑπόστασις."

[49] Attridge, *Hebrews*, 118; e.g., Polybius, *Histories* 6.55.2. Attridge adds, "This pregnant expression serves as a paraphrase for faith. As the whole of Hebrews will indicate, faith puts the Christian in touch with what is ultimately true and real. Being in touch with that reality enables the life of fidelity to God that Christ exemplified and made possible" (*Hebrews*, 119).

who, by his violent death, redeemed us and atoned for us that he might bring us to God. Though he may be criticizing ancient Israel, our author intends for us to sober up and heed the Spirit's warning.[50]

Israel was guilty of *sin* (v 17). Israel refused to obey God's command to enter Canaan because they feared death if they did so. But "the consequences were disastrous. ... they experienced death because they didn't do what he mandated."[51] For forty years—a startling duration when the trip should have taken a mere few months—the Israelites did little more than provoke ("put ... to the test," v 9) the Lord. Punishment was often dispensed for Israel's sin, but the most severe was that meted out at Kadesh: all those over twenty years of age would die before entering the Promised Land (Num 14:28–32). Well did Paul write, "For the wages of sin is death" (Rom 6:23).

In verse 17, Hebrews does not use *sōma*, the typical Greek word for "body," but *kōlon*, meaning "corpse." More specially, it referred to "dead bodies that were left unburied (1 Sam 17:46; Lev 26:30), which connoted an accursed death. ... This was deemed suitable for apostates (Isa 66:24). People went to great lengths to ensure that the righteous were properly buried (Tob[it] 1:16–19). In the Greco-Roman world, many believed that those whose bodies remained unburied would find no rest after death."[52]

Israel was guilty of *disobedience* (v 18). By this, our author is not referring to a solitary violation of some arcane command of the covenant, but to a habitual and wholesale rejection of God's calls to faith and obedience (Exod 17:2–3; Num 11:1; 12:1; 14:1, 22). "The author, as will be evident throughout the letter and especially in chapter 11, believes faith and obedience are inseparable."[53] To an entire generation of Israel who refused to obey, God swore they would never enter "his rest"—a phrase that refers to Canaan but also to much more than that, as we will soon see.

[50] P. Hughes, *Commentary*, 153–54. "Who was it that God was angry with? It wasn't a different people, Gentiles, pagans, people outside the family God had chosen and called out of Egypt, a different people who weren't descended from Abraham, Isaac and Jacob. No: it was his own people, who had gone against his word, who heard what he said and did the opposite. Again, the writer is insisting: this warning isn't for the person standing next to you. It's for you. Yes, you" (N. T. Wright, *Hebrews for Everyone*, NTE [Louisville: Westminster John Knox, 2004], 33).

[51] Schreiner, *Hebrews*, 130.

[52] Koester, *Hebrews*, 261–62; see Gen 40:19; Deut 28:26; 1 Kgs 14:11; 21:24; 2 Kgs 9:10, 34–35; Jer 7:33; Homer, *Iliad* 23.70–71; Virgil, *Aeneid* 6.316–83).

[53] Schreiner, *Hebrews*, 131.

Israel was guilty of *unbelief* (v 19). Though the author has not said as much, Hebrews' original audience would have known why Moses himself did not enter God's rest—it was because of the lawgiver's own rebellion, sin, and disobedience (Num 20:12). Or, as our author says here, Israel (along with Moses) failed to reach God's rest "because of unbelief." The term "unbelief" (*apistia*) literally means "lack of faith" and refers to "rejection of the veracity of God's promises and the reality of his power."[54] In a sense, "unbelief" encompasses rebellion, sin, and disobedience—Westcott referred to disobedience as "unbelief [that has] passed into action."[55]

Westcott is right. Think about the last time you were tempted to rebel against, sin against, or disobey the word of God. You resisted that temptation based on how much trust you had in God, specifically trust or faith that God would keep his promises. I've noticed such in my young children. If I tell them to do or not do something (and they are already aware of the consequences of disobedience), their obedience usually depends on their level of confidence in what I said.

"Does he really intend to spank us if we disobey? Maybe not."

"Will he really bring home a treat if I clean my room? Maybe not."

"Was he serious when he told me that the stove was hot and that I'd burn myself if I touched it? Maybe not."

Doubt in God's word is the root of rebellion, sin, and disobedience. All are due to unbelief that God will do what he has promised. Consider again the deceitful things Satan whispers in our ear:

> ›　"It's not that bad"—but God said it is.
> ›　"It's just this once"—but God said not to do it at all.
> ›　"No one is being hurt"—but disobedience breaks God's heart.
> ›　"You can quit whenever you want"—but this is not the way to use the freedom God gave you!
> ›　"God still loves you and will forgive you"—but is this any way to treat the One who has adored you since the foundation of the world?

[54] Cockerill, *Hebrews*, 194.
[55] Westcott, *Hebrews*, 87.

Rebellion against God is a repudiation of his promises. Like the wilderness generation, the Hebrews audience found themselves in that space between promise and fulfillment, redemption and rest, Egypt and Canaan. To a group of Christians tempted to turn their back on Christ and return to Moses—in the same way their ancestors longed for a return to Egypt—our author gave the exhortation to hold fast their confession and confidence. Abandoning Jesus would exhibit faithlessness in God's promise. To be guilty of unbelief is to forfeit access to God's rest and experience the same fate—death—as Moses and the wilderness generation. Such is a terrible thing to miss out on because Jesus, as our champion-pioneer, has secured for us a rest with God that far exceeds any real estate in Palestine.

HEBREWS 4:1–10

At the beginning of this sermon, our author stressed the connection between his audience and Old Testament Israel (1:1); as the New Testament church, we share continuity with the saints of old, and the same offer to enter God's rest that was extended to the wilderness generation is also proffered to us.

> In Hebrews 3 we see how entering into 'rest' in the Old Testament pointed to the people of Israel entering the land of promise. That land of promise was more than just a piece of territory. The land was indicative of God's promise to Abraham and signified God's plan to restore creation after the fall corrupted it. Thus, entering the promised land meant more than just entering a piece of real estate. It meant enjoying and entering God's plan of salvation and inhabiting the very place where God set his dwelling.[56]

Like the wilderness generation, we may fall short[57] of reaching the promised land if we continue in unbelief. The promise or offer of God's rest is not held out indefinitely ("while the promise ... still stands," v 1). This is why our author says fear is justified in this case. He is not referring

---

[56] Mohler, *Exalting Jesus*, 55–56.

[57] The verb translated "failed" (*hystereō*) can mean to "stop half way, stop short" (Ellingworth, *Hebrews*, 240). The idea in this context is that Christians can journey a long way in their spiritual walk yet still fall short of the goal if they give in to rebellion and unbelief.

to an anxious or paralyzing phobia but a healthy fear—reverence and awe rooted in the holiness and majesty of God. "The fear commanded here is a stimulus to action, like the fear that motivates mountain climbers to ensure all their equipment is working properly, provoking readers to enter God's rest and stimulating them to believe and obey."[58]

The failure of the wilderness generation was not the fault of the message they heard; "they heard good news just as you have," our author says in effect. They failed to enter God's rest because they did not respond to the message with faith (v 2). "Hearing a message of good news does not guarantee that what has been promised will be received. Only faith as confident expectation for the future can secure the promised reality"[59] (Rom 10:16–17; Gal 3:2, 5). Whatever flaws one might perceive in Christianity are never intrinsic—there is nothing faulty about the Son or what he has accomplished on our behalf. No, the problem is always user error. We must respond to Christ with faith, "and if that faith is a genuine faith, it will be a persistent faith."[60]

Again, our author's words were profoundly practical for his audience. They had had a solid start to their Christian lives before pressure from the world around them planted the deceit in their minds that their faith was foolish, that no promise remained for them. Our author assures them God's rest is very real, though it remains a future reality. Meanwhile, they should not despair in the present but rather respond to the promise with faith, something far greater than private obedience or mental consent to a set of beliefs. Genuine, biblical faith prompts the believer to be sensitive to God's word (v 7) and obedient to it (3:18); such faith persistently identifies with the great crowd of witnesses[61] (11:2–12:1), as well as with the present community of faith (the church). Only by this genuine, biblical faith can we enter the rest of God.

What exactly is that rest? In the Old Testament, "rest" referred to the land sworn to the patriarchs and given to Israel (Deut 12:9; 1 Kgs 8:56); of

---

[58] Schreiner, *Hebrews*, 134.

[59] Lane, *Hebrews 1–8*, 98. He adds, "Already in its first occurrence in Hebrews πίστις, 'faith,' is clearly confident expectation for the future (cf. 6:12; 10:38–39; 11:1). It is a quality of response that appropriates the divine promise and recognizes the reliability of God" (*Hebrews 1–8*, 98).

[60] Bruce, *Hebrews*, 106.

[61] Cockerill, *Hebrews*, 204.

course, our author does not intend for God's "rest" in Hebrews to refer to Canaan in a literal sense (v 8).[62] We get better clues to what "rest" means here by noting that the term in the Old Testament also referred to the resting place of the ark of the covenant. Once Israel had been granted reprieve from her enemies in the land, Solomon was allowed to build the temple, including the inner sanctuary, which served as a resting place for the ark (Ps 132:8, 13–14). Likewise, entering God's rest in Hebrews is to follow Jesus, our forerunner behind the curtain, into the presence of God (6:19–20).

> [Hebrews] uses two types of imagery to describe the place where God's people enter his presence. When he is urging them to persevere until final entrance at the return of Christ, he uses Promised Land language to describe that reality—"rest" (4:1–11); "homeland" (11:13–16); and "City" (11:9–10; 12:22). When he encourages them to draw near in the present so that they can receive grace for perseverance, he speaks of the Most Holy Place that has been opened for the people of God through Christ's high priesthood (4:14–10:25).[63]

Broadly, we may say entering God's rest is entering into the new covenant inaugurated by Jesus and maintaining our confession of such. More specifically in our present passage, entering God's rest means participating in or enjoying the type of rest God has experienced since the final day of creation (vv 3–4; Gen 2:2).[64] The reason the wilderness generation did not enter God's "rest" was not that his rest was *unavailable*, or not "open for business"—it had been open since the beginning! The reason they did not reach it was *unbelief*. "The repetition [Heb 4:5] of the warning words of Ps. 95:11b after the Genesis quotation emphasizes the identification of the one rest with the other: God's rest has remained open to his people since the work of creation was finished, but it will be forfeited by disobedience."[65]

---

[62] The Old Testament considers the promise of rest in Canaan to be fulfilled (Josh 21:44; 22:4; 23:1).

[63] Cockerill, *Hebrews*, 197. One thing to which God's "rest" does *not* refer is any sort of end-times, pre-millennial kingdom on earth. This view, posed by Walter Kaiser and advocated by John MacArthur (among others), places "rest" in the physical world and thus in contradiction to the orientation of our author. See deSilva's deconstruction of this view (*Perseverance*, 157–62).

[64] "When God spoke in Genesis 2:2 about resting from all his works in creation, it was a sign of his gracious intention for humanity" (Peterson, *Hebrews*, 126).

[65] Bruce, *Hebrews*, 107.

David's reference to "today" in Psalm 95 and our author's reminder here are evidence that God's rest remained open both in David's day and in our author's day (i.e., the first century). It remains available now and for as long as our Lord delays his return. This is also evidence that God's rest in Hebrews 4 cannot be Canaan. From David's perspective, Israel had yet to enter God's rest when Psalm 95 was penned, though they had occupied Canaan for four hundred years when David wrote those words! Our author argues that if Joshua had delivered Israel to God's true or final rest, then David would not have indicated that entrance into God's rest remained open. Instead, entering God's rest means entering into the immediate presence of his eternal repose.

There we[66] will cease from our work as God did from his.[67] No more striving, no more frustration, no more weariness. All the things that drain us physically, emotionally, and spiritually will be no more (Rev 14:13; 21:4). Even in this life, we cannot escape dangers, toils, and snares, but in Christ, we can begin to experience the rest of God in part while the full experience awaits us in the world to come. To a persecuted church, this is indeed good news. "It won't be like this forever," our author effectively says.

> The Canaan rest for Israel is a picture of the spiritual rest we find in Christ when we surrender to Him. When we come to Christ by faith, we find *salvation* rest (Matt. 11:28). When we yield and learn of Him and obey Him by faith, we enjoy *submission* rest (Matt. 11:29–30). The first is "peace with God" (Rom. 5:1); the second is the "peace of God" (Phil. 4:6–8). It is by believing that we enter into rest (Heb. 4:3); it is by obeying God by faith and surrendering to His will that the rest enters into us.[68]

Another aspect to God's rest is buried within our author's use of "Sabbath rest" in verse 9. The Sabbath was more than a day of rest for the Jews; it was one of praise and celebration—one of worship (2 Maccabees 8:27).

---

[66] It's possible that the "whoever" of 4:10 refers to Christ (Nicholas J. Moore, "Jesus as 'The One who Entered his Rest': The Christological Reading of Hebrews 4.10," *JSNT* 36 [2014]: 383–400).

[67] How can we say God is at rest (a claim made in Hebrews) when God still speaks and works in the world (also a claim made in Hebrews)? Even Jesus said that the Father is working (John 5:17). God's being at rest means he is not at work any longer in the same way he was during the six days of creation. He works in the world via providence, but this "work" is of a very different sort.

[68] Wiersbe, *Bible Exposition*, 2:289; emphasis his.

Psalm 92, which is filled with praise and thanksgiving, is identified in its superscription as a psalm for the Sabbath. Likewise, "Sabbath rest" here points to that day in eternity when God's people will both rest from their labor and congregate around the throne in celebration and worship (12:22–24). "Sabbath rest" anticipates "the festival of the priestly people of God in the heavenly sanctuary, celebrating in the presence of God the eternal Sabbath with unceasing praise and adoration."[69] Though that Sabbath rest remains a future reality in terms of its fullness, the people of God experience a foretaste when the earthly church assembles to worship.[70]

To summarize, God's "rest" in Hebrews 4 refers generally to the new covenant and the spiritual promised land Christians long for "across Jordan"; specifically, it points to the immediate presence of God. But it also refers to the eschatological celebration around God's throne, of which the worship assembly of the church on earth is a foretaste.

Yes, God's rest awaits us on the other side of Jordan. It is not the physical land of Canaan; it is a land fairer than day that we see by faith from afar. Though it is a full reality only in the hereafter, God's rest offers us safety and security here and now. "Though Satan should buffet and trials should come," we hold fast our confidence and our hope of eternal rest with God. Those who share in Christ will come to sing the song of Moses and the Lamb (Rev 15:3–4) "and dwell with Jesus evermore."

But if we, as did Old Testament Israel, test God's patience and presume upon his goodness, we are like a ship ignoring a safe, sure harbor in a stormy sea.[71] At some point—we know not when—"today" will pass, and "tomorrow" will prove too late (2 Cor 6:2).

HEBREWS 4:11–13

Our author concludes this section concerning Moses and the wilderness generation by calling upon his audience to strive to enter the rest of God. That he has a mutual striving in mind (i.e., "We're all in this together") is

---

[69] Lane, *Hebrews 1–8*, 102.

[70] See Randall C. Gleason, "The Old Testament Background of Rest in Hebrews 3:7–4:11," *BSac* 157 (2000): 281–303.

[71] R. Hughes, *Hebrews*, 1:107.

evident by his stated goal: that no one in the congregation should succumb to the same disobedience as the wilderness generation (v 11). In other contexts, the Greek *spoudazō*, translated here as "strive," could mean "hurry" (e.g., 2 Tim 4:9, 21; Titus 3:12) but more broadly meant "be eager" or "take pains."[72]

The wilderness generation was destroyed because they did not heed God's voice; Hebrews warns that God's word today is no less potent than it was then. Lest anyone think themselves capable of slipping into God's rest undetected, we are reminded that all façades are torn down by the sword that is the word of God (v 12). Note five paramount truths about this "word"[73] from this passage.

The word is "living and active." That is, "it possesses the power to effect its own utterance."[74] Inherent within God's every word is what is known as the power of divine fiat. God merely speaks, and what he decrees or commands happens (Ps 107:20; Isa 55:11). Hebrews has already said that all things are driven to their appointed end by his spoken, powerful word (1:3), and it will go on to say that God spoke the universe into existence (11:3). Because of the vigorous potency of his word, we can be sure that what God promises will come to pass.

The word is "sharper than any two-edged sword." Paul, too, refers to the word of God as a sword (Eph 6:17). Polybius described the sword carried by a Roman soldier as "excellent for thrusting, and both of its edges cut effectually."[75] That the word is likened to a two-edged sword might be an allusion to its twin capabilities, "that while God's word is a word of promise to those who would enter God's rest, it is also a discerning word of judgment"[76] (John 6:63; 12:48). More important, however, is the sharpness the word is said to possess.

---

[72] BDAG, s.v. "σπουδάζω."

[73] Among patristic (e.g., Athanasius, Chrysostom) and medieval commentators, it was common to equate the "word" of God with Christ, but this explanation has mostly fallen out of favor, and I understand why. It doesn't fit, either in this immediate passage or in Hebrews as a whole. Jesus is said to wield a sword (Rev 1:16; 2:12; 19:15), but he is never said to *be* a sword. A better understanding, given the context, is that our author is referring to the word of God generally (anything he has uttered), to the biblical canon particularly, and to the "voice" of Ps 95 specifically.

[74] Lane, *Hebrews 1–8*, 103.

[75] Polybius, *Histories* 6.23.6–7.

[76] Guthrie, *Hebrews*, 156.

In first grade, I joined the Boy Scouts of America as a Tiger Cub Scout. I soon underwent the ultimate initiation into scouting: the trafficking of that very addictive drug, Boy Scout popcorn. I didn't sell much that first year, but it was just enough to win for myself the one thing I coveted most—a pocketknife. I remember receiving that prized knife at an awards ceremony in my elementary school cafeteria. My dad gave me the strict warning, "Be careful, or it will cut you!" I opened it up as we left the cafeteria, and before we had gotten to the car, I had already sliced my finger open.

Like my first pocketknife, the word of God can slice us open before we know it. "The Word of God is so sharp a thing, so full of cutting power, that you may be bleeding under its wounds before you have seriously suspected the possibility of such a thing. You cannot come near the gospel without its having a measure of influence over you."[77]

The word pierces "to the division of soul and of spirit, of joints and of marrow." Any time someone attempts to draw a sharp distinction between the soul and spirit of man, especially based on this passage, they are missing the point.[78] Our author is engaging in a bit of hyperbole since "strictly speaking there is no one point at which joints and marrow may be separated."[79] If there *is* any real distinction between the soul and spirit of a person, they are but two sides of the same coin—distinct but inseparable (and I doubt it's within us to understand the distinction). This is our author's point: the word of God is so sharp that it "can penetrate precisely to those places where human knowledge cannot—what human can accurately distinguish between soul and spirit?"[80] However, what is indistinguishable to us lies exposed to God, for nothing is hidden from his sight! In the only psalm attributed to Moses, the lawgiver confessed, "You spread out our sins before you—our secret sins—and you see them all" (Ps 90:8 NLT), and Proverbs claims, "The eyes of the LORD are in

[77] C. H. Spurgeon, "The Word a Sword," in *The Metropolitan Tabernacle Pulpit Sermons* (London: Passmore, 1888), 34:115–16.

[78] "It is not apparent elsewhere from the OT or the NT that clear distinctions should be erected between the soul and spirit. In some popular and devotional literature, this verse is used to justify distinguishing between the soul and the spirit, and sometimes a whole spirituality springs up that separates the spirit, the soul, and the body. These tripartite understandings of human beings are speculative, testifying to the creativity of their authors more than they reflect the teaching of the NT" (Schreiner, *Hebrews*, 147).

[79] L&N, s.v. "μυελός."

[80] Johnson, *Hebrews*, 134.

every place, keeping watch on the evil and the good" (15:3; see Job 26:6; 28:24; Ps 33:13).

The word discerns "the thoughts and intentions of the heart." The word translated "discerning" (*kritikos*) derives from *krinō*, meaning "to judge legal cases."[81] Not only can God's word see everything in our heart with 20/20 vision—distinguishing what humans cannot—but it also criticizes or judges what it finds.[82] Both "piercing" and "discerning" infer the idea "of an extreme power of penetration. ... The discrimination of the heart's thoughts and intentions entails a sifting process that exhibits the penetrative and unmasking potency of the word."[83]

It is an abiding truth that the Bible knows us better than we know ourselves. One thing that happens to all of us is that we become experts at self-deception and self-manipulation. We can talk ourselves into or out of almost anything. Avoiding the gym. Ordering dessert. Remaining in a toxic relationship. Retaining a destructive habit. Making an ill-advised purchase. We get good at lying to ourselves—and the Bible calls us on it. "The heart is deceitful above all things," the prophet Jeremiah lamented, "and desperately sick; who can understand it?" (17:9). On the other hand, "Scripture untangles the human heart and unearths sin like no other book can. No other book can discern the thoughts and intentions of our hearts. Only God's Word can do that."[84]

The word judges thoroughly and righteously. We cannot escape the judgment of God (v 13; 1 Cor 4:5). The audience of Hebrews was tempted to turn their backs on Christ in favor of a return to Judaism or any other option that left them less at odds with their neighbors and the local authorities. Yet it was not the judgment of their peers that should have concerned them as much as their ultimate appointment before the judgment seat of God[85] (9:27). More specifically, our Lord said that it will be his word that judges us all on the final day (John 12:48).

---

[81] L&N, s.v. "κριτικός."

[82] Luke 16:15; Acts 1:24; 15:8; Rom 8:27; 1 Cor 4:5; 1 Thess 2:4.

[83] Lane, *Hebrews 1–8*, 103.

[84] Mohler, *Exalting Jesus*, 61.

[85] Hagner wonders "whether the readers contemplated some form of compromise that was meant to veil what was actually apostasy" (*Hebrews*, 74).

Before the Judge of all the earth, everyone stands "naked and exposed." The latter term, *trachēlizō*, literally meant "to seize the throat." It could refer to how a priest bent back an animal to slit its throat for sacrifice,[86] to a wrestling move (e.g., a chokehold) that rendered an opponent helpless,[87] or to "how a man being led to execution had a knife placed beneath his chin so that he could not bow his head in shame away from the gaze of the people."[88] All three word pictures are apt relative to our status before the judgment throne of God.

> › Our necks are laid bare before him because we—not an innocent animal—deserve to be executed for our sins.
> › We have been rendered helpless before the greatness and power of a superior, and we have no means of escape.
> › We stand in shame before the One who has every right to take our lives as punishment for our lawlessness.

"The language here forces us to imagine ourselves naked, held helpless, exposed, in God's grip, close to his omniscient eyes, and so we must give account. He cannot be fooled. Duplicity and hypocrisy will not work. Happily, this means he will miss no good thing. But to the sinning, self-righteous heart, apart from the grace of God, this brings nothing but unmitigated terror."[89] If such isn't clear already, our author's words are intended to unsettle his audience, to imagine themselves vulnerable—utterly defenseless—before the Lord.

>———◇——<

This section began by exalting the supreme Son as a perfect model of faith and obedience (3:1–6). Our author implores his readers to emulate Jesus' faith and obedience that they may be numbered with Moses among all the faithful servants in the household of God. Once upon a time, Israel's wilderness generation encountered "today"—they were confronted with

---

[86] Theophrastus, *Characters* 27.6.
[87] Philo, *Dreams* 2.134; *Rewards* 29; Plutarch, *Antony* 33.
[88] R. Hughes, *Hebrews*, 1:123; see Philo, *Cherubim* 78.
[89] R. Hughes, *Hebrews*, 1:124.

the word of God and forced to choose whether that word would prove to be one of promise or punishment for them. Through their rebellion and unbelief, they chose punishment. "It is now your turn," our author says, "to embrace the word as a word of promise and enter into God's promised rest." You and I choose promise over punishment, rest over wrath, by living out 4:2—by responding to the good news with faith. This guarantees that the word of God will bring us untold benefits.

If we follow in the path of our wilderness ancestors, we can expect the word of God to search us and sift us as wheat, leaving us stripped bare before the fearful throne of judgment. Worse, the promise of punishment will come to pass because that living, active word does not return empty to the One who speaks. Rebel in our unbelief and we will join those in Revelation who begged to buried by the mountains: "Fall on us and hide us from the face of him who is seated on the throne, and from the wrath of the Lamb, for the great day of their wrath has come, and who can stand?" (6:16–17).

When we consider our many sins, wrath—not rest—seems sure. Who can stand before the throne? Our author immediately offers a word of comfort and hope to our hearts that stand eager to condemn us.

SUMMARY

» As God's faithful Son, Jesus is superior to Moses, who served as God's faithful steward.

» We need daily mutual encouragement in order to resist sin and remain faithful.

» Rebellion against God is a repudiation of his promises.

» Jesus secures a better "rest" for us than Moses or Joshua did for Israel.

» We will fail to reach that "rest" if we are faithless like wilderness Israel.

» Without Jesus, standing before God's judgment throne is terrifying.

TALKING POINTS

IF ONE WERE forced to reduce Hebrews to a single short command, it would have to be "consider Jesus" (3:1). The verb doesn't simply mean to look at something but to fixate the attention and contemplate.[90] Hebrews beckons us to consider carefully the supreme Son and to keep doing so, for there are infinite riches thereby to be discovered. Realize that this call to consider is given to Christians, not unbelievers. Even one as spiritually mature as Paul still yearned to "know [Christ] and the power of his resurrection" (Phil 3:10). But what does "consider" mean in practical terms? (1) We consider Jesus *by learning more about him*. Commune with the Lord in the Gospels. Study his person and work. Particularly in Hebrews, Christians are urged to consider Jesus' restoration of our squandered destiny, his example of faithful obedience in suffering, and the priestly ministry he discharges on our behalf. (2) We consider Jesus *through prayer and obedience*.[91] Paul wanted to know Christ, not simply know *about* Christ. Jesus is our brother and partner in this venture, so communication is important, as is constant evaluation of our submission to his lordship. From this is formed the faithful endurance we need to withstand sin's deceitfulness.

>———◇———<

JESUS' BROTHER once admonished his fellow Christians, "How do you know what your life will be like tomorrow? Your life is like the morning fog—it's here a little while, then it's gone" (Jas 4:14 NLT). There are many references in this section of Hebrews to "today." Whether in Psalm 95 or Hebrews 3–4, "today" is the time when God's people hear his voice speak. We might say the "today" of this passage is perpetual, but it is certainly not infinite (3:13). We presently live in an age of salvation, grace, and patience (2 Pet 3:9), but the day approaches when that age will end without a tomorrow. Whether it be the certainty of death or the imminence of our Lord's return, "today"

---

[90] "There must be no languid look, as between half-opened eyelids, as men look upon some object in which they have little interest, but there must be the sharpened gaze of interested expectancy, believing that in Him on whom we look there lie yet undiscovered depths, and yet undreamed-of powers, which may be communicated to us" (Maclaren, *Expositions*, 29:259).

[91] Guthrie, *Hebrews*, 144.

is all we have been promised. There came a day when God closed the door on the wilderness generation and banned them eternally from his presence; it wasn't the sword of the Canaanites that kept them out of Canaan as much as the sword of the Lord (Num 14:44–45). Likewise, there comes a day when an unfaithful Christian reaches a point where return is impossible (Heb 6:4–6; 12:16–17). Thus "now is the day of salvation" (2 Cor 6:2).

>———◇———<

MINISTERS CAN be among those most negligent of the Word of God. Nearly every minister I've known who lost his ministry to burnout or scandal at some point stopped studying the Word for his personal benefit and cracked it open only to prepare for lessons (and sometimes not even then!). Any Christian, including ministers, can become like faithless Israel. It is thus imperative that we be diligent in heeding God's voice "today." How? (1) We must commit ourselves to regular Bible study, the sole purpose of which is personal edification (not lesson preparation). "The antidote to unbelief, indecision, and disobedience is exposure to the trenchant judgment of God's living word" (4:12–13),[92] and we must subject ourselves to that trenchant judgment long before we even think of subjecting any in our audience to it. (2) We must lead the way in confessing personal sin to one another and offering mutual encouragement (Jas 5:16) in an urgent manner. When did you last listen to biblical teaching and seek earnestly to apply it to yourself rather than someone else in the audience? When did you last repent? When did you last read the Word and tremble with fear or weep in godly sorrow? (3) We must at all times guard our heart (Prov 4:23) and examine it to see what is lacking in our obedience (2 Cor 13:5). As we resist Satan's schemes, his deceit only grows more devious and more difficult to resist. Above all, we must guard against a calloused heart, one that "no longer hears the admonition of God. Such a heart steels itself against the stabs of conscience that bring one back to God."[93]

>———◇———<

---

[92] Lane, *Hebrews*, 71. "Instead of allowing sin to make them resistant to the word of God, the listeners are to allow the word of God to make them resistant to sin" (Koester, *Hebrews*, 259).

[93] Schreiner, *Hebrews*, 127.

GOD'S OATH that Israel's wilderness generation would not enter Canaan is a key theme in this section, and that he swore such an oath in his wrath is deeply unsettling. Reese reminds us, "God is not passive when He sees sin; … [instead,] He springs into energetic action to see that the sin is properly recompensed."[94] On the other hand, it is cause for great confidence and jubilant celebration that God has also sworn another oath to us and has done so in his compassion rather than his rage. Later in Hebrews, our author will speak of how God's trustworthiness enables us to endure as heirs of the promises: "The certainty of the divine oath, here established, also undergirds the adequacy of God's provision for entrance into his blessing (6:13–20). His oath (Ps 110:4) has made Christ the absolute 'Guarantor' of salvation for those who faithfully persevere (7:20–22). The God who pronounces unremitting judgment on the faithless promises unfailing grace to the faithful."[95]

><——◇——<

WE LIVE IN A remarkable age. Instead of waiting until the morning newspaper delivery or the evening newscast, breaking news and headlines are always just a tap away via the web. But for all the advantages of living in the information age, our culture is awful at making judgments. When an alleged crime is committed, our culture immediately choses sides and adjudicates the case in the court of public opinion. Very often, we get it wrong. I hear the phrase "wrong side of history" thrown around; the inference is that if you do not side with the majority opinion today, you'll be "cancelled" tomorrow. In the starkest contrast, Hebrews draws our attention away from the court of public opinion and toward the court of the Judge of all the earth.[96] It is God who scrutinizes us perfectly; it is God to whom we will ultimately answer. The judgment of this world is as fickle and faulty as it is fleeting. We'd do well to spend less time worried about being on the wrong side of history versus the wrong side of *His story*.

[94] Reese, *Hebrews*, 47.

[95] Cockerill, *Hebrews*, 193.

[96] "By subjecting the faithful to physical abuse, prison, destitution, and death, the unbelieving world seeks to degrade them … yet Hebrews denies that the world has the right to pass judgment" (Koester, *Hebrews*, 519–20).

Chapter 4

NOBODY KNOWS

A ll his life, Judah had been familiar with the wilderness generation, those Israelites who, en route to the Promised Land, had died in the desert due to disobedience. Yes, they had suffered. Yes, they had succumbed to the Angel of Death. They had brought their fate upon themselves. It was the adults who had died, not the children. The children had been spared.

Judah's son had not.

Those called Christians in Antioch were a supportive lot. The despair of being disowned by family upon their defection from Judaism had been mitigated in part by the new friendships Judah and Anna made. Their fellow Christians called each other "brother" and "sister" as if a new family had been forged from the splintered remains of former ones. When Daniel died, their new family had done their best to sympathize with the devastated parents.

But they have no idea what this feels like, Judah often thought to himself. He knew their care and concern were sincere, just not helpful. All the care and concern in the world couldn't bring his son back. It couldn't remove the sting or soften the blow. Judah's frustration had been nursed into bitterness, and bitterness into emotional and spiritual isolation. He felt increasingly detached from other members of the Way. Whereas they all had formerly commiserated in their shared trouble, Judah now felt like the sole outcast living in self-imposed exile. *Even lepers have their own communities,* Judah had thought. *Yet these people have no idea how I feel—no idea how much this hurts.*

I wish someone could understand...

This was the thought running through Judah's mind as he heard Timothy say, "We do not have a high priest who is unable to sympathize..."

———◇———

The concepts of priests and the priesthood are foreign to many Protestant traditions. The entirety of the Old Testament Israelite cult[1] that stands in Hebrews' background has received scant attention from twentieth-century Protestant commentators on Hebrews; for such, we have had to rely primarily on Catholic scholarship.[2]

In his excellent book on the biblical priesthood, Andrew Malone expresses this unfamiliarity: "All the formative decades of my own life were spent in churches with a congregationalist structure, mostly Baptist. A 'priest' was some guy from another denomination who dressed up and led his church in liturgy (and often using a book other than the Bible). Natural suspicion of anything different suggested that here was someone leading a crowd who did not quite worship God in the 'right' way."[3]

Malone is right. For many of us, priests and priesthood are foreign concepts to our religious experience and ones most often greeted with suspicion if not disdain. This makes the world of Hebrews more confusing since "we cannot without considerable elaboration begin to think of Christ as our 'representative' before God: we have *no* modern analogy to this concept of his priesthood."[4] That doesn't mean we haven't tried, however. Piper explains:

> If you try to skip the Old Testament and interpret Jesus within your own context first without the Biblical-historical context and categories, you may make him a coach or a therapist or a good example or a guru or a mentor or a hero or a trailblazer. And there may be some truth in each of these. But they will not be as true and deep and authoritative and helpful as the categories that the Bible itself uses. … God planned centuries of history with Israel, recorded in the Old Testament, so that we would have a context for understanding this category. That means he thinks it is really important. We would impoverish ourselves and swerve from the

---

[1] Most people associate "cult" with a small group of people with strange or sinister practices. Yet the word's *primary* meaning in the dictionary is neutral, indicating a system of religion. This definition is how the term is used in biblical studies, especially in literature on the book of Hebrews.

[2] William G. Johnsson, "The Cultus of Hebrews in Twentieth-Century Scholarship," *ExpTim* 89 (1978): 104.

[3] Andrew S. Malone, *God's Mediators: A Biblical Theology of Priesthood*, NSBT 43 (Downers Grove, IL: InterVarsity Press, 2017), 1.

[4] Johnsson, "Cultus of Hebrews," 107; emphasis his.

truth if we said, "Well, that's too old-fashioned and irrelevant for today. Nobody knows what a high priest is; so let's just translate Jesus into one of our familiar categories, say, defense attorney." Instead what we need to do before we jump to contemporary analogies is to go back to God's context, God's history and God's book, and learn some deep and wonderful things that we might otherwise miss.[5]

Because the priesthood of the supreme Son is Hebrews' greatest contribution to New Testament theology,[6] and because drawing near and having access to God are so fundamental to Hebrews' message, it is worth exploring the function of this Old Testament office to appreciate how Jesus fills this role for God's people today. A priest "is the person through whom and through whose ministry people draw near to God."[7] The entire concept of "priesthood springs out of the deepest need of the human soul."[8] While we need access to God when we are in the depths of sorrow or discouragement, our high priest is most necessary when it comes to forgiveness. "Men are sinful … and without some kind of mediation they cannot draw near to God at all."[9]

I suggest pausing to read that last line again. The previous section of Hebrews ended with a fearful reminder of God's omnipotence and omniscience (4:12–13). It is one thing to think about that future day when we will stand before a holy, all-knowing King to give an account of our deeds. It is infinitely more terrifying to realize we presently have no access to God in this life—none at all—outside the supreme Son. The faithful advocacy of our merciful high priest mitigates any fear we have as we stand before the excoriating judgment seat of God. Only in Christ do we not stand condemned (Rom 8:1).

---

   [5] John Piper, "Draw Near to the Throne of Grace with Confidence," *Desiring God*, 15 September 1996, http://www.desiringgod.org/messages/draw-near-to-the-throne-of-grace-with-confidence.

   [6] "The significance of Christ's priesthood is the essence of the Epistle's argument. On the priesthood and its adequacy depend, in the author's mind, the whole question of whether a man can really gain access to God. The priesthood of Christ, and His sacrificial death that went with it, opened heaven (cf. 10:19ff.). For the author, therefore, the nature of the priesthood defined the nature of the religion" (Lightfoot, *Jesus Christ Today*, 100).

   [7] James Denney, "Priest in NT," in *A Dictionary of the Bible*, ed. James Hastings (New York: Scribner's, 1911–12), 4:98.

   [8] William G. Moorehead, "Priesthood," in *International Standard Bible Encyclopaedia*, ed. James Orr (Grand Rapids: Eerdmans, 1939), 4:2445.

   [9] Denney, "Priest in NT," 4:98.

HEBREWS 4:14–16

As an avid landscape photographer, I've done my fair share of hiking. In September 2018, I scored a permit to photograph an area on the Utah-Arizona line known simply as the Wave. Reaching the Wave isn't easy. There is no marked trail, and rangers are diligent in knocking over cairns. The route is a couple of miles long over nondescript slickrock and sand. It is usually hot, and the threat of dehydration is real. People have died out there. The Bureau of Land Management provides each hiker with a brochure featuring some general directions and pictures of landmarks to note in order to stay on track. Before I left the parking lot, however, I had studied a "bird's eye view" of the route, compliments of Google Earth, and that's what helped the most.

Hebrews 4:14–16 constitute a critical moment in the flow of Hebrews. It is a rare opportunity to pause, come up for air, and be reminded of the big picture afforded by a "bird's eye view." Guthrie calls these verses "a crystallization of Hebrews' main message, a snapshot of the sermon."[10] On the one hand, they are a fitting summary to 3:1–4:13; on the other, they reintroduce the theme of Jesus' high priesthood.

For the past few years, I've conducted grief seminars across the country. If there is one thing I've learned, it's that a person experiences the grief process for more than just death. We grieve divorce, job loss, and any number of other tragedies and setbacks in life. If the Hebrews audience was anything, it was a community in crisis. Though bloodless (12:4), their persecution had cost them something (10:32–34). It's likely, then, that they were experiencing many of the emotions associated with grief: anger, bargaining, and depression. Most of all, they felt unsettled and uncertain, and to counteract this, our author implored them to "hold fast [their] confession" (v 14). *Our ability to hold fast and endure faithfully depends upon the priestly work of "Jesus, the Son of God."*

Unlike Moses and Aaron, who were only servants, Jesus was "declared to be the Son of God in power according to the Spirit of holiness by his resurrection from the dead" (Rom 1:4). Following his resurrection, this supreme Son ascended to the Father's right hand (i.e., "passed through the heavens,"

---

[10] Guthrie, *Hebrews*, 173.

v 14; see also Eph 4:10). He went to the heavenly Most Holy Place (Heb 6:19–20; 8:1–2; 9:24) to assume his role of high priest. The themes of divine sonship and kingship would have harmonized well in the minds of our author's audience; the king of Israel (as well as almost every other sovereign in antiquity) was often thought of as God's son. But they would *not* have expected God's Son (i.e., the King) to be a high priest also, for the two offices were never united in one person in Israel, and when such was attempted, it proved disastrous (e.g., 1 Sam 13:8–14; 2 Chr 26:16–21).

Hebrews has already referred to Jesus as *archiereus* or "high priest" (2:17; 3:1); in 4:14, and for the only time, he is called our "great high priest" (*archiereus megas*). In the LXX, Israel's high priest was often called the *hiereus megas* ("great priest," e.g., Lev 21:10; Num 35:25, 28; Zech 6:11), so to say Jesus is our "great high priest" is redundant, no different than saying "great, great priest" or "high, high priest."[11] Such a redundancy, though, is an emphatic way of elevating Jesus far above the high priests from Aaron's line and signifies his belonging to a wholly different order than Aaron.

Also unlike Aaron's descendants, our great high priest can completely "sympathize with our weaknesses" (v 15). This was a startling claim compared to the Greek philosophies of the first century. Stoics considered one of God's primary attributes to be apathy, a lack of feeling; Epicureans believed God was detached from the world.[12] Our Lord, however, is neither apathetic nor detached. "Sympathize" is a translation of the Greek *sympatheō* and carries the idea of "to suffer with." Jesus suffered and was tempted as a human being (2:18); having walked much more than a mile in our shoes (Isa 53:4), our high priest feels the same emotions we feel when we hurt physically, emotionally, and spiritually. "Christ's earthly life gives him inner understanding of human experience, and thus makes him ready and able to give active help."[13] Colloquially, Jesus is both *sym*pathetic and *em*pathetic.[14] He knows just how we feel.

---

[11] Cockerill, *Hebrews*, 223.

[12] R. Hughes, *Hebrews*, 1:129–30.

[13] Ellingworth, *Hebrews*, 268.

[14] Though the English "sympathize" has been watered down, the Greek *sympatheō* "suggests a stronger 'common feeling' among those who are suffering. At the very least, the term as used by Hebrews should not bear the slight air of condescension carried by the English 'sympathize,' for it is precisely this composition's point that Christ entered fully into the human experience of suffering" (Johnson, *Hebrews*, 140–41).

In my grief seminars, I emphasize why a person shouldn't compare losses. I particularly take issue with the phrase "I know just how you feel." I've buried a father and a son, but when offering comfort to a person who has lost one or the other (or both), I never claim, "I know just how you feel." No two people grieve the same way. Though you and I may have both lost a father, our relationships with our dads were different. Moreover, our emotional makeups are different. I may know *some* of what you feel, but I don't know *all* of it. I sometimes will say, "I don't know exactly how you feel, but I know enough to know this is terrible."

The Son of God, however, knows exactly how we feel. Our author's contention that Jesus was tempted "in every respect ... yet without sin" (v 15) means he felt every human weakness and sinful compulsion and was subjected to every one of Satan's schemes[15] (see Matt 4:1–11; Luke 4:1–13)—arguably to a degree greater than anything we will face. In response to the ridiculous objection that Jesus, since he never sinned, could never have been tempted as we are, C. S. Lewis wrote in *Mere Christianity*:

> A silly idea is current that good people do not know what temptation means. This is an obvious lie. Only those who try to resist temptation know how strong it is. ... A man who gives in to temptation after five minutes simply does not know what it would have been like an hour later. That is why bad people, in one sense, know very little about badness. They have lived a sheltered life by always giving in. ... Christ, because He was the only man who never yielded to temptation, is also the only man who knows to the full what temptation means—the only complete realist.[16]

That Jesus was without sin[17] means he can plead our case to the Father uninhibited. But it also means he felt all the emotions so often triggered by dangers, toils, and snares. Like us, he experienced uncertainty, anger, and even the crippling loneliness from being abandoned by God. We do not feel an emotion our Lord has not also felt. "When he represents us before

---

[15] Given the context of Hebrews, our author likely has in mind the audience's temptation to abandon God under the strain of severe suffering (Guthrie, *Hebrews*, 179).

[16] Lewis, *Mere Christianity*, 142.

[17] Luke 23:41; John 7:18; 8:46; 14:30; 2 Cor 5:21; 1 Pet 1:19; 2:22; 3:18; 1 John 3:5, 7.

the father, he isn't looking down on us from a great height and being patronizing about those poor creatures down there who can't really do much for themselves. He can truly sympathize. He has been here. He knows exactly what it's like."[18] In other words, he knows just how we feel.

We must not falsely assume that Jesus' ascension and enthronement signaled the end of his humanity; quite the contrary! Among the New Testament's most understated claims is that "Jesus remains fully and gloriously human, and that it is as a human being that he rules the world"[19] (Acts 1:11; Phil 3:21; 1 Tim 2:5). The same man who was born in Bethlehem, traveled homeless through Galilee, wept at loved ones' tombs, and was crucified unjustly outside Jerusalem is the one interceding for us as our high priest in the heavenly places. He knows just how we feel.

Nor should we assume Jesus' empathy elicits, at best, a passive "Bless your heart" or, at worst, an eye roll. Citing several passages from Jewish literature, Lane notes that there is a nuance to *sympatheō* that "extends beyond the sharing of feelings (i.e., compassion). It always includes the element of active help [see 10:34; 4 Maccabees 5:25; 13:23]. ... In this context, the stress falls on the capacity of the exalted high priest to help those who are helpless."[20] Jesus acts to help us because he knows just how we feel.

Jesus' high priesthood makes possible two things: holding fast our confession (v 14) and drawing near to God's throne (v 16). "The former speaks to our need for stability in the world, the latter to our need for access to resources beyond this world in order to gain that stability."[21] Rather than holding fast and drawing near, the Hebrew Christians were turning loose and shrinking back; opposition from neighbors and government officials was leading them to renounce their confession and distance themselves from Jesus, the Son of God, and thus from God himself.

How much better it would be to hold fast and draw near in confidence. We can do so because of our Lord's solidarity with humanity. To borrow a famous line from Joan Osborne, "What if God was one of us?" Hebrews declares that Jesus, the Son of God, is just that. As our high

---

[18] Wright, *Hebrews*, 44.
[19] Wright, 44.
[20] Lane, *Hebrews 1–8*, 114.
[21] Guthrie, *Hebrews*, 179.

priest, he "is able to help those who are being tempted" (2:18) since he became "like his brothers in every respect" (2:17). Jesus knows just how we feel because he's been where we are.

Proximity of experience affects the level of emotion we feel. If war, famine, plague, or natural disaster strike on the other side of the world, it might elicit a "That's too bad" and nothing more. As 9/11 demonstrated, however, we feel a stronger, greater pain when it happens in the United States. If a tornado hits Kansas and you live in Maine, your sympathy may not be strong. But what if Kansas were your home and where family still lived, the names of the devastated communities representing people you knew and loved? Your hurt would be great because you would have a personal connection to a place you know well and to people among whom you once lived. You've been there.

If you are told that someone has just been diagnosed with aggressive cancer for the third time, it might not elicit as much grief if you've never lost someone to that terrible malady. If you have, however, your heart sinks. If you've watched cancer devastate the body of someone you love, the emotions of grief return like a torrent. If you've held someone's hand through chemo treatments and hospice care, the pain is palpable. You've been there. I hurt, of course, when I hear people's stories of losing a spouse. Yet the pain reaches a far deeper level if they have buried a child or parent, especially if the latter was "well before their time." I hurt because I've been there.

Since Jesus is one of us—because of the shared feelings of suffering we have with Christ—we can "draw near"[22] to God's throne "with confidence" to receive mercy, grace, and help when we need it most (v 16). Our solidarity with the Son lends us unprecedented and unfettered access to God himself. We have through the Messiah what we never had through Moses: indiscriminate, immediate intimacy with the Father.

There is much to say about the amazing privilege of drawing near to God, but our author's second use of the Greek word *parrēsia* ("confidence," v 16; 3:6) is especially noteworthy. "The English language has not

---

[22] This verb is in the present tense, "indicating that drawing near to God constitutes an ongoing aspect of the Christian's relationship with God: 'let us constantly approach'" (Guthrie, *Hebrews*, 176).

one word to render the various shades of meaning covered by [this Greek noun]."[23] In the Gospel of John, it refers to an outspokenness or plainness of speech (7:13; 10:24; 11:14; 16:25), "a use of speech that conceals nothing and passes over nothing."[24] As mentioned in the last chapter, the word essentially means "to say everything." Embedded in *parrēsia* are two separate nuances: "the free right to approach God, given in the sacrifice of Christ, which is the essence of the Christian faith, and the open confession of this faith, which is an unshakable hope. These two sides are an inseparable unity. In the situation in which the Christians live they need it as a gift and a task."[25] In short, bold speech before the Lord mandates bold speech before the world.

Such confidence or boldness seems impossible before God's throne, particularly since we all stand naked and exposed before that throne (v 13). Throughout Psalms, God's throne is synonymous with justice and righteousness (9:4, 7; 45:6; 89:14; 97:2), and in ancient literature the throne of the gods represented power, authority, and condemnation. The ark of the covenant typified Yahweh's throne (2 Sam 6:2; 2 Kgs 19:15; Pss 80:1; 99:1), and it was inaccessible except to the high priest and only one day each year. Yet, because Christ has torn the veil in two and sprinkled his blood above the new mercy seat in heaven on our behalf, we are beckoned to intrude boldly into the divine presence. Jesus' high priestly ministry has transformed a throne of wrath into a throne of grace; "righteous judgment has been replaced with radical mercy."[26]

Whatever our struggle, Jesus' high priesthood enables us to speak freely at the throne[27] (John 14:13; 15:7; 16:24). Because he was and is a man, the Son is able to communicate to the Father the fullness of our pain. Thus God is the only one fully prepared to deal with our emotions. Though our petitions will not always be answered precisely as we wish,

---

[23] W. C. van Unnik, "The Christian's Freedom of Speech in the New Testament," *BJRL* 44 (1961–62): 469. He expresses his preference for translating *parrēsia* as "freedom of speech" ("Christian's Freedom," 469).

[24] BDAG, s.v. "παρρησία." The word is derived from *pas* ("every") and *hrēsis* ("word") (Silva, "παρρησία," *NIDNTTE* 3:657).

[25] van Unnik, "Christian's Freedom," 485.

[26] Mohler, *Exalting Jesus*, 68.

[27] "This isn't arrogance. Indeed, if we understand who Jesus is, what he's done and what he's still doing on our behalf, the real arrogance would be to refuse to accept his offer of standing before the father on our behalf, to imagine that we had to bypass him and try to do it all ourselves" (Wright, *Hebrews*, 45).

ours is the assurance that mercy and grace are always available upon request. A supreme Son and sympathetic Priest who qualifies us to draw near to get the help we need when we need it—that is a significant reason for confidence and hope!

HEBREWS 5:1–4

As I stated at the beginning of this chapter, priests and priesthood are foreign concepts to many of us. This section is a terrific description of the form and function of Israel's priesthood. In the Old Testament, the high priest was a mediator between the people and God (v 1), made offerings for sin (vv 1, 3), was chosen from among men by God (vv 1, 4), and was, like his constituency, profoundly human (vv 2–3).

The priest was a *mediator*. Though the word is not used in this passage (see 8:6; 9:15; 12:24), this is what is meant when our author says the priest acted "on behalf of men in relation to God" (v 1). It means the priest was a mediator, or bridge builder. This is the aspect of the priesthood that Protestants struggle most to comprehend, so accustomed are we to the priesthood of all believers (1 Pet 2:5–9) and Jesus' now being the only mediator between man and God (1 Tim 2:5). Yet this has not always been so. Before Christ, there was no direct access to God available to his people; "the very existence of a priesthood and a system of sacrifices gave evidence that man is estranged from God."[28] On the other hand, divine access here and now is among the greatest privileges of Christianity.

Outside of religion, mediators aren't often known as such. Instead, we will say we have an "in" or "I got a guy," someone who can "hook us up" or get us to "the inside." Mediators give us *access*; they connect us to those who can take care of our situation. Mediators give us *advantage*; we benefit by proxy from their harmonious relationships with those who can help. Mediators give us *answers*; our case is addressed and resolved, hopefully in our favor. Access, advantage, answers—this is what a priest provided Israel, and it's what Jesus provides us.

---

[28] Wiersbe, *Bible Exposition*, 2:291.

The priest was a *human* mediator. The priest excelled as a mediator because he, too, was "beset[29] with weakness" (v 2; Isa 53:6) and offered sacrifices for both his sins and those of the people (v 3). That is, he had solidarity with them (see "from among men," v 1; "from among the people," Exod 28:1). Like the people, the priest sinned; like the people, the priest died. Thus the priest was able to "deal gently" with them (v 2). He was one of them.

The word translated "deal gently" (*metriopatheō*) occurs only here in the New Testament. It had to do with exercising moderation, "the golden mean between indifference and mawkish sentimentality."[30] E. K. Simpson acknowledges that it almost can't be translated—that rendering it as "to treat considerably" ("deal gently" ESV, "have compassion" NKJV) "is an inadequate rendering, yet we can devise no better."[31] Bruce added that the term

> indicates more particularly forbearance and magnanimity on the part of people who are subject to great provocation and who could, if they wished, give way to unmoderated anger and meet the provocation with the utmost severity. A high priest could not make fitting expiation for sins which filled him, at that very time, with feelings of indignation and exasperation against those who were guilty of them. Aaron is credited with exemplary forbearance in face of the repeated provocation and envy of those on whose behalf he served as high priest—although in this respect, as in most others, he falls behind his brother Moses.[32]

The mention of Aaron and Moses at the end of Bruce's statement hints that *metriopatheō* is better illustrated than defined—pictures, a thousand words, and all that. So back to the Old Testament we go.

Upon the return of the spies in Numbers 14, the conduct of Moses and Aaron was exemplary. While the nation ungratefully "grumbled against" them (14:2), the two responded by falling "on their faces before all the

---

[29] The word translated "beset" (*perikeimai*) can mean "to be surrounded by" (12:1) or "to wear something" (Herodotus, *Histories* 1.171.4; Josephus, *Life* 334; 4 Maccabees 12:2), as well as "to be burdened" (Mark 9:42; Acts 28:20). Thus our author speaks of the high priest as being surrounded, burdened, or clothed by "all the weaknesses and infirmities common to our fallen nature" (Milligan, *Hebrews*, 187).

[30] E. K. Simpson, "The Vocabulary of the Epistle to the Hebrews," *EvQ* 18 (1946): 37.

[31] Simpson, 37.

[32] Bruce, *Hebrews*, 120.

assembly" (v 5), and Moses interceded on their behalf (vv 13–19). To be sure, there were times when both Aaron and Moses lost their cool or caved to the people's demands (e.g., Exod 32:19, 24). Yet, in Numbers 14 and similar passages, both demonstrated remarkable restraint and moderation. These two brothers had every right to throw the nation under the chariot but chose not to since they recognized the people's human frailty.

This is what Hebrews has in mind when it uses *metriopatheō*. "As high priest [Jesus] is concerned with men, but His concern for them never drives Him to the point of irritation or annoyance with them. He is always gentle and patient and ready to bear with them in their mistakes."[33] In contrast to a high priest who can only "deal gently," however, ours does far more. The verbs *metriopatheō* (v 2) and *sympatheō* (4:15) aren't exactly synonymous;[34] recall that the latter possesses the nuance of "active help," while *metriopatheō* does not. With a nail-scarred hand, our priest in his empathy offers personal aid to Father Abraham's many children (2:16).

The priest was an *appointed* human mediator. No one was allowed by the law to claim the priesthood for himself; such an office was filled by divine—not human—appointment. The Old Testament explicitly bears out that Aaron and his descendants held the high priesthood by God's election.[35] "No one chooses to be the high priest. It isn't a democratic office in which one puts forward his name, nor is it an elected office in which people choose the high priest. The high priest is called and chosen by God."[36]

Such had not been the case in Judaism of late, however. In 174 BC, the Greek overlord of Palestine, Antiochus IV, deposed Onias III from the priesthood and installed first Jason, then Menelaus—neither of whom was a Levite—as his puppet priests. The Hasmoneans gained the priesthood by decree of Antiochus' son, Alexander Balas, in 152 BC, and they continued to hold it by another decree of the Jews beginning in 140 BC. With the end of the Hasmoneans, high priests were appointed by Herod the Great (37–4 BC), Archelaus (4 BC–AD 6), Roman governors (6–41), and the Herodian

[33] Lightfoot, *Jesus Christ Today*, 106.
[34] Attridge, *Hebrews*, 143–44.
[35] Exod 28:1; Num 16:5; 17:5; 20:23–29; 25:10–13; Ps 105:26.
[36] Schreiner, *Hebrews*, 160.

line (41–66).[37] According to Josephus, the last high priest before Jerusalem's destruction, Phanas, was elected by the people.[38] In stark contrast, and as our author will soon underscore, Jesus, the Son of God, holds his office of high priest by a divine appointment that shall never be rescinded.

The priest was an appointed human mediator *for sin.* Foremost in our author's mind is the sin offering made by the high priest on the Day of Atonement. While our author will later draw several distinctions between Aaron's practice and Christ's, he wants us here to realize that the high priest in the Old Testament could offer atonement for the sins of the people only *after* he had made such a sacrifice for himself and his family[39] (Lev 16:6, 11)—and that sacrifice was limited in its duration.

A subtle though important nuance exists in both the Old Testament and the New concerning what sins were forgiven. Both the law and our author are referring to sins committed out of ignorance and weakness (v 2), not those done intentionally. "It was for just this type of person—the person who, because of human moral weakness, has unintentionally wandered off the path of right living—that God designed the old covenant sin offerings. The defiant sinner, however, blasphemes God and thus finds no such provision."[40]

HEBREWS 5:5–10

All of Hebrews to this point has been an exposition of sorts of Psalm 2:7 (see Heb 1:5; 5:5). Likewise, our author's quotation of Psalm 110:4 in 5:6 signals a new emphasis[41] that will continue through the rest of Hebrews. Put another way, verses 5–6 link the two halves or themes of Hebrews: the sonship of Christ and the priesthood of Christ.

---

[37] Bruce, *Hebrews*, 122, n. 19.

[38] Josephus, *Antiquities* 20.227.

[39] The high priest's "technical or Levitical purity was jealously guarded, and his life had to be as morally blameless as unflagging discipline could make it—nevertheless he remained a fallible mortal, and no orthodox son of the Old Covenant would ever have regarded him in any other light" (R. A. Stewart, "The Sinless High-Priest," *NTS* 14 [1967]: 126).

[40] Guthrie, *Hebrews*, 188.

[41] Our author has already quoted v 1 of Ps 110 (Heb 1:13) and used it as it commonly was in early Christianity. His *application* of this psalm, however, is unique. "No other Christian writer of this period drew attention to Ps 110:4, but in Hebrews there are more references to Ps 110:4 than to any other biblical text" (Lane, *Hebrews 1–8*, 118).

In his Pentecost sermon, Peter pointed out that David's claim in Psalm 16:10, "You [God] will not … let your holy one see corruption," had never been fulfilled by David since David was still dead (Acts 2:29). Hebrews makes a similar argument here. Psalm 110 cannot refer to Israel's past kings since they were all unqualified for the priesthood—none was descended from Aaron. On the other hand, by linking Psalm 2:7 with 110:4, our author claims that the Father has appointed his Son (unlike past kings) as King and Priest over his people.

What qualifies Jesus to be our high priest? (1) *He was appointed to it* (vv 5–6). Just as Aaron and his sons did not exalt themselves but were appointed by God, so Jesus did not exalt himself (John 8:50, 54; Phil 2:6–8)—though he could have. As Lane put it, "He does not cling to the privileged status that his unique sonship implies but receives it from the Father only after he has suffered the humiliation of death on the cross (cf. 12:2)."[42]

What else qualifies Jesus to be our high priest? (2) *He knows what it is to suffer as only humans suffer* (vv 7–8). The phrase "loud cries and tears" (v 7) is meant to express "the intensity of his grief."[43] In this, he experienced the deepest depths of the human experience. Rather than exalt himself, Jesus subjected himself to suffering, and it was in his suffering that the identities of sonship and priesthood merged. It's unclear whether our author means to take us back specifically to the scene in Gethsemane. None of the Gospels explicitly say Jesus wept in the garden, and the phrase "in the days of his flesh" might refer to his entire life as opposed to his final hours. Jesus struggled for a long time with his appointed suffering, begging his Father for another way (John 12:27). This was even the point of contention behind the last two temptations of Satan in the desert. One was for Jesus to skydive off the temple's highest point, and when the Father inevitably dispatched angels to preserve him lest he stub a toe or twist an ankle, onlookers would eagerly acclaim him to be the Son of God (Matt 4:5–6). The other temptation offered Jesus authority over all the earth (one of the objectives of the incarnation); all Jesus had to do was worship Satan, to take a shortcut (Matt 4:8–9). He could gain what he came for without the pain of the cross.

---

[42] Lane, *Hebrews 1–8*, 121.
[43] Calvin, *Hebrews*, 121.

So there's a sense in which all of Jesus' life is in view here. Yet it is also true that everything our author evokes in verse 7 was exhibited in Gethsemane (Matt 26:38; Mark 14:33–34; Luke 22:44). That none of the evangelists depicts Jesus weeping in the garden doesn't mean it didn't happen. In grief and agony, the Son petitioned the Father not to make him drink the cup of his Father's poisonous fury, the cup of suffering (Mark 14:36; John 18:11). Jesus petitioned the only One "able to save him from death, and he was heard" (v 7).

But how? How was Jesus' subsequent crucifixion an affirmative answer to his petition for deliverance? If anything, it seems heaven's door was slammed in the Son's face (Matt 27:46). Is that what it means to be "heard" by the Father? One answer to this perplexing inquiry is that Jesus' desire to be reverent and obedient (John 17:4) was greater than his wish to be rescued from the cross' agony and the humiliation of bearing the world's sins. Put another way, Hebrews considers the prayer "Let this cup pass" to have been ignored, while the subsequent "Your will be done" was heard and answered; the second request set aside the first.

An alternative is to consider our Lord's resurrection and subsequent exaltation to be the Father's affirmative answer to Jesus' request, to recognize that Jesus was not delivered *from* suffering but *through* suffering. He was not rescued *from* death but *out of* death.[44] This is what Peter had in mind at Pentecost when he spoke of God's releasing Christ from the pain of death because of his ancient promise not to allow his "Holy One [to] see corruption" (Acts 2:24, 27). "Jesus did not pray in order to be saved from dying; he prayed in order to be saved out of death through the resurrection."[45]

This interpretation makes even more sense when we remember that "salvation" within Hebrews means more than eternal life or deliverance from a bad situation; salvation is uninterrupted fellowship with the Father in his glory and rest by virtue of unwavering obedience, even obedience in the face of the most horrific death imaginable (Phil 2:8). Only in this way, obedience in suffering, could Jesus obtain his appointment as our high

---

[44] The preposition *ek* in v 7 more often means "out of," while the preposition *apo* means "from." When the Greek New Testament speaks of "saving from" (e.g., Matt 1:21; Acts 2:40; Rom 5:9), it uses *apo*. But since *ek* is used here in v 7, it's better to say Jesus was saved "out of" (*ek*), not "from," death.

[45] Mohler, *Exalting Jesus*, 75.

priest. For us, this means that when we suffer as Jesus did—even though we may pray for deliverance and not receive it—we can be confident that God has something grander in mind: the restoration of our glory and honor in his eternal rest.[46]

That said, I believe there is a third way of interpreting the confusion surrounding verse 7, the question of how Jesus was "heard" though he was not saved "from death." Jesus' ultimate prayer in the garden was not for the cup to pass, nor was it passive resignation to the Father's will, but a request that he be qualified for priesthood for our sake. Knowing the Father had the ability "to save him from death," and in spite of his exalted status as the supreme Son, our high priest nonetheless asked to suffer in order to be "made perfect." Jesus' ultimate request in Gethsemane was that his death qualify him for a permanent priesthood so he could always live to make intercession for us (7:24–25). You and I—selfish squanderers of our primeval status—were the subject of his selfless, sacrificial prayer. "And he was heard because of his reverence."[47]

This brings us to Jesus' final qualification for priesthood: (3) *He learned obedience in his suffering.* It is arresting to read that Jesus is supposed to have *learned* something. How can this be if God is perfectly omniscient? The verb *manthanō* can carry the simple meaning of gaining "knowledge or skill by instruction" (1 Cor 14:31; 1 Tim 2:11). But it can also refer to coming "to a realization, with implication of taking place less through instruction than through experience or practice."[48] In other words, it refers to learning through experience, not explicit instruction (Phil 4:11; 1 Tim 5:4; Titus 3:14). Herodotus put *manthanō* in the mouth of Croesus, who (foolishly, as it turns out) had urged the Persian king Cyrus to attack the Massageteans (a tactic that led to Cyrus' death). "Disaster has been my teacher," Croesus said afterward.[49]

---

[46] "The fact that the cup was not removed qualifies him all the more to sympathize with his people; when they are faced with the mystery and trial of unanswered prayer they know that their high priest was tested in the same way and did not seek a way of escape by supernatural means of a kind that they do not have at their disposal. At no point can the objection be voiced that because he was the Son of God it was different, or easier, for him" (Bruce, *Hebrews*, 130).

[47] For a more detailed breakdown of 5:7, see Neil R. Lightfoot, "The Saving of the Savior: Hebrews 5:7ff.," *ResQ* 16 (1973): 166–73.

[48] BDAG, s.v. "μανθάνω."

[49] Herodotus, *Histories* 1.207.1.

Hebrews claims that in the incarnation God experienced something heretofore foreign to him. Never in the eternal history of the Most High was it necessary to obey anyone for any reason. The very notion of God's obedience is diametrically opposed to his utter sovereignty. Sovereigns do not obey. Sovereigns do not submit. Sovereigns do not kneel. In the Son's suffering, however, a part of the triune God did just that. He tasted "every consequence of obedience"[50]—or, as Maclaren put it, "He felt the reluctance of the flesh to enter upon the path of suffering, the perfectly natural human shrinking from all that lay before Him. But that shrinking never made His purpose falter, nor made Him lose His son-like dependence upon the Father's will and submission to the Father's will."[51]

Plus, "The Son's obedience revealed a dependence on God's power and assurance of his promises that was the antithesis of the wilderness generation's faithless disobedience (3:18; 4:11)."[52] Christ learned obedience both to qualify as our high priest and to model for us as our champion-pioneer how to hold fast our confession when obedience carries a high cost in the physical realm. Instead of unbelief, Jesus exhibited faith in his Father's word and thus did not fall victim to disobedience, sin, and rebellion. Our Lord understood that there is something far worse than physical death: broken fellowship with the Father due to our disobedience. The atonement his suffering secured for us makes possible the indwelling of God's Spirit, who empowers us to endure obediently in the worst of circumstances. In modeling obedience for us, Jesus "learned obedience" that he might know precisely what to request on our behalf at the throne of grace that dispenses timely help.

Our author claims that Jesus "offered" his prayers to the Father as a part of his suffering. The word translated "offered" in verse 7 (*prospherō*) commonly referred to offering sacrifices (e.g., Matt 5:23; Mark 1:44; Acts 7:42). Just as Israel's high priest offered gifts and sacrifices, our high priest offered prayers along "with loud cries and tears." These prayers, accompanied with groaning and weeping, epitomized the Son's utter dependence

---

[50] James Burton Coffman, *Commentary on Hebrews* (Austin: Firm Foundation, 1971), 110.
[51] Maclaren, *Expositions*, 29:347.
[52] Cockerill, *Hebrews*, 248.

on and obedience to his Father, dependence and obedience that climaxed at Golgotha. The order of Aaron offered to God gifts and sacrifices; Christ, in the order of Melchizedek, offered to God nothing less than himself and did so in every sense.

The implication for our author's audience is clear. With his call to hold fast, Jesus is not asking of his people anything he has not undergone.[53] He knows what it means to be obedient to the Father to the point of death. Sonship and suffering are not mutually exclusive—a thought to which our author will give full attention later in his sermon (12:5–11). When we find ourselves beset on every side by trials, temptations, and turmoil, we can be confident that Jesus intercedes for us, saying, "I know just how they feel." Jesus' obedience in suffering qualifies him for his priesthood.

Put another way, by learning obedience through suffering, Jesus was "made perfect" (2:10).[54] As with his obedience, this does not mean he was previously *im*perfect (i.e., flawed); remember that "perfect" in Hebrews means more than being without moral blemish. If you remember from our discussion of Christ's consecration in 2:10, *teleioō* ("made perfect") in the LXX refers to consecration of Levitical priests. That Jesus was "made perfect" means he was consecrated or qualified for his ministry as our high priest.

In sum, what qualifies Jesus to be our high priest? It was his (1) divine appointment, (2) human suffering, and (3) perfect obedience.

Obedience to the Father's will amid suffering made Jesus "the source[55] of eternal salvation to all who obey him" (v 9; Rom 5:19). Note, first, that this salvation is *eternal*. It is without end. It stretches infinitely into the future. Once realized, it can never be stripped from us. But second, this eternal salvation is available to all who *obey* him. Our author has already spoken of how the authority of the Son's kingdom is one of righteousness

---

[53] "The listeners had previously received the message of salvation (2:3–4), but this message was called into question because of the ongoing experience of friction with the wider society (10:32–34; 13:13) and internal malaise (5:11; 6:12; 10:25). Here the author reminds listeners that the source of salvation is the Christ who suffered. Suffering does not negate salvation, but is the way that God brings about salvation" (Koester, *Hebrews*, 299).

[54] Jesus' "perfection was an abstraction until he obeyed God in the concrete realities and travails of everyday human experience" (Schreiner, *Hebrews*, 165).

[55] "His role as 'source' (*aitios*) of eternal salvation is parallel to his role as 'pioneer' (*archēgos*, 2:10; 12:2) and 'forerunner' (*prodromos*, 6:20)" (Thompson, *Hebrews*, 117).

or obedience (1:8–9; Ps 45:6–7). For all of Hebrews' confusion or mystery, it's clear on one thing: "there is no salvation apart from obedience."[56]

The subject of obedience is where our author now turns, though not before he arouses curiosity in his readers by mentioning the most mysterious Melchizedek (v 10). This priest of old holds the key to understanding how Jesus is the "source" of our salvation, but that will be delayed for another chapter or so. Our author must first address his readers' arrested development.

It is in this pivotal section of Hebrews that our stories and Jesus' merge. When we suffer, our pain can be exaggerated by the thought that we suffer alone, that no one knows how we feel. Empathy is often in short supply. Not so with Jesus, our author insists.[57] The individual agonies of the human experience are an opportunity to share in Jesus' identity as a suffering, obedient Son.

Our fictional Judah almost allowed his heartache to isolate him from Jesus' people, and I nearly did the same. What prevented me from snipping the final thread of connection was the realization that we are never more like Jesus than when we continue to trust and obey though the heavens fall. Even in his honest-to-God divine abandonment on the cross—most evocatively expressed in the cry *Eli, Eli, lema sabachthani?*—Jesus rejected the temptation to call ten thousand angels or curse God and die.

So committed was he to become qualified to be the priest we need—
So committed was he to understand the depths of our pain—
So committed was he to know the trouble we've seen—
He endured.

---

[56] Schreiner, *Hebrews*, 166. "There is something appropriate in the fact that the salvation which was procured by the obedience of the Redeemer should be made available to the obedience of the redeemed" (Bruce, *Hebrews*, 133).

[57] "As Christians we look not in the sky to a possible God for comfort, but in history to the suffering servant. God is not distant, aloof, or insensitive to our suffering" (Kevin DeYoung, "Divine Impassibility and the Passion of Christ in the Book of Hebrews," *WTJ* 68 [2006]: 50).

SUMMARY

» Jesus' ascension to heaven was necessary to serve as our high priest.

» Because he is fully human, Jesus always knows exactly how we feel.

» Jesus' priesthood makes God's throne a place of grace, not judgment.

» Jesus' appointment, suffering, and obedience qualified him to be our heavenly advocate.

TALKING POINTS

ONE OF MY college Bible teachers once deadpanned that there is God the Father and God the Son, and the Holy Spirit is like the family uncle no one wants to talk about. I feel the same way when it comes to certain events of the gospel. Christ's crucifixion and resurrection have enjoyed lots of attention in church history, while the ascension has often seemed an afterthought. When did you last read a Christian bestseller on the ascension? Or sing a hymn on the subject? Or hear a sermon? In contrast, Hebrews considers Christ's passage through the heavens to be critical to maintaining our confession (4:14). And why? Because the Son's return to the heavenly throne room was the fulfillment of his Father's oath in Psalm 110:1, 4—the promise of glorification as supreme Son and permanent Priest. His crucifixion and resurrection alone were not enough; "the present sequence suggests that the exaltation is the basis for the saving significance of Jesus' death."[58] Only an ascended, exalted Jesus can atone for sins, draw us near to God, offer timely help, deliver us from death, and lead us to glory. Only an ascended, exalted Jesus "is fit for our worship and attention and … can help us persevere in the Christian life."[59] Let's give more attention to Jesus' ascension and exaltation!

>———◇———<

ONLY AN ASCENDED, exalted Lord can take the crippling vulnerability of 4:13—"all are naked and exposed to the eyes of him to whom we must give account"—and transform it into grace to help "when we need it most" (v 16 NLT). As Maclaren put it, "We see a divine omniscience shining upon us through the merits of the great High Priest, full of light and hope, and because all things are naked and open to the eyes of Him who is our High Priest; therefore the right grace will be most surely given to me to help me in time of need."[60] Yes, we receive help from the Lord at just the right time and not a moment sooner. "It will not come as quickly as impatience might

---

[58] Thompson, *Hebrews*, 71.
[59] Guthrie, *Hebrews*, 65.
[60] Maclaren, *Expositions*, 29:341.

think it ought, it will not come so soon as to prevent an agony of prayer, it will not come in time enough for our impatience, for murmuring, for presumptuous desires; but it will come in time to do all that is needed."[61] As Hebrews will continue to demonstrate, the supreme Son and perfect Priest makes all the difference.

>———◇———<

BY VIRTUE OF our ascended, exalted Lord, we are beckoned to enter into the divine presence "with confidence" (4:16). What does this confidence look like? I'm not entirely sure; I'm still figuring it out. It's something less than saying to God, "I'm gonna tell you what to do, and you're gonna do it." Yet it's something more than timidly pleading like Oliver Twist, "Please, sir, more." I know that our level of confidence rises the more we understand the advantages of Jesus' high priestly ministry. For example, (1) contemplating our *pardon* will increase our confidence. If we are in Christ, the favor that the Father extends to the Son is also extended to those whom the Son calls brothers. Our confidence grows knowing God delights in (versus despises) us. (2) Considering our *proximity* to the throne will increase our confidence. "We are not shouting across a great gulf. We are not trying to catch the attention of someone who has little or no concern for us."[62] Our confidence grows knowing we are heard. (3) God's *promise-keeping* will increase our confidence. Like the boy who cried wolf, a faithless god would inspire no confidence whatsoever. On the other hand, God has never broken his word or proven faithless (6:17–18). Our confidence grows knowing the Lord is reliable and trustworthy. (4) Our *persistence* will increase our confidence. With every visit to the throne, we discover more of God's goodness. The distant "man upstairs" becomes a compassionate Father. Not every prayer is answered as we like, but time spent in his presence changes us. Our confidence grows as we learn to see prayer and worship as opportunities to deepen the relationship versus only make requests. Thank God for the boldness we can have before him through Jesus Christ!

---

[61] Maclaren, 29:341.
[62] Wright, *Hebrews*, 45.

Chapter 5

ARRESTED DEVELOPMENT

Obedience. The word rang sharply in Judah's mind, and he knew why. Over the last four months, Judah had often thought of ancient Job. The patriarch had suffered enormous calamity—much worse than Judah had, if he were honest with himself. Through it all, Job had maintained his integrity. However, there was one line from Job's story that had always unsettled Judah: "I will argue my ways to his face."[1]

He had never felt confident enough to approach the Most High with his grief, let alone to argue his case. No, Judah had grown accustomed to being bitter and dwelling in his darkness, lamenting how terrible was his fate. Judah's self-pitying mantra, *No one knows how I feel*, had become an excuse to drift away from Jesus and his people in Antioch. Yet the real reason for his being adrift was this: Judah was regressing spiritually.

He thought back to that day's labor. He had spent most of the afternoon clearing a field that had stopped yielding for his master. Where there had once been robust plants, only thorns and briers remained. He realized the field was a metaphor for his life of late. *I was like a fertile field when I joined the Way*, he thought. At some point, however—perhaps before his son's death, but he wasn't sure—Judah had stopped growing.

His growth had been strangled by *sadness*. He had sought comfort for his heartache in some wrong places.

His growth had been strangled by *selfishness*. His focus had been on little more than himself: his grief, his pain, his miserable circumstances, and the formidable challenges that lay ahead of him.

His growth had been strangled by *sin*. His temper had become short, and he often cursed in anger—and that was just for starters.

---

[1] Job 13:15.

Judah knew he had not been obedient. He closed his eyes as immense guilt again rippled through him. He shuddered despite the warm night air, and a knot formed in his stomach as he recalled his many covenant violations since he had become accountable. Converting to the Way had given him a brief reprieve from his demons, but they had returned. They always did.

His ancestors had been led out of Egypt on the night when Pharaoh's son had been struck down because the king had defied God. Judah wondered, not for the first time, *Was my son taken from me because of my own disobedience?* As Timothy cited verse after verse from the psalter, Judah thought of a particular line he had read years ago: "When you discipline us for our sins, you consume like a moth what is precious to us. Each of us is but a breath."[2]

>———◇———<

I get the oddest junk mail. AARP registration information (though I'm nowhere near retirement). Offers for auto loans (both of my cars are paid off, and I'm in no rush to assume another monthly payment). Coupons and discounts for oil changes, pizza, and timeshares. I even receive the occasional magazine to which I've never subscribed. The oddest of all, however, is sales information about hearing aids. Solidly in my mid-thirties, I assure you I do not suffer from hearing loss—though I admit to some "selective hearing" when my wife needs me for a honey-do!

While hearing loss is a mark of growing older, dullness of hearing is a mark of spiritual immaturity. Our author has arrived at the main point of his sermon: the high priesthood of Jesus Christ. Some in his audience should have already known about the wondrous implications of Jesus' intercession. Instead, they had become lazy and dull of hearing, and were scarcely able to discern black from white in a world of gray.

Fundamentals and first principles are essential, mind you, but they're not the final destination. Our author is about to issue one of the harshest warnings in all of Hebrews. Failure to make it past the ABCs of all things Jesus will leave us spiritually anemic and in imminent danger of falling

---

[2] Ps 39:11 NLT.

away from the faith. Perhaps irreparably. If our spiritual development is arrested, we share the destiny of a fruitless field: "worthless and about to be cursed, and at the end will be burned" (6:8 CSB).

HEBREWS 5:11–14

These verses launch another of our author's strategic pauses.[3] Mention of the mysterious Melchizedek in verse 10 means he wants to explore further the issue of Jesus' high priesthood, and he will do so beginning in 6:20. Our author is frustrated, however, knowing that some listeners won't be able to handle it. We should not be surprised by this pause. He has already chided and urged his audience:

- › "pay much closer attention" (2:1)
- › "consider Jesus" (3:1)
- › "do not harden your hearts" (3:8)
- › "take care" (3:12)
- › "let us fear" (4:1)
- › "strive to enter that rest" (4:11)
- › "hold fast our confession" (4:14).

Nowhere else in Hebrews do we come closer to perceiving what was amiss with the original recipients. "Heb. 5.11–14 is the only place in Hebrews where the author uses the second person plural indicative form to accuse them directly. In other places, he warns of a possibly shameful future (e.g., 3.12: 'watch out, lest you may have an evil and unbelieving heart …') but in Heb. 5.11–14 he directly accuses them of past failure."[4]

There is an emphasis in verse 11 that is obscured by most English translations. As awkward as it is, a literal translation of the Greek would be "much to us the word and difficult to explain," with the emphasis placed on "word."[5] This emphatic "word" is the doctrine of Jesus' high priesthood.

---

[3] Guzmán and Martin argue persuasively that while 5:11–14 is a digression for our author, 6:1–20 is not (Ron Guzmán and Michael W. Martin, "Is Hebrews 5:11–6:20 Really a Digression?" *NovT* 57 [2015]: 295–310).

[4] Peter S. Perry, "Making Fear Personal: Hebrews 5.11–6.12 and the Argument from Shame," *JSNT* 32 (2009): 104.

[5] Cockerill, *Hebrews*, 254.

Our author wants to tell his audience something substantial and essential about Jesus.

That "word" was "hard to explain" not because the subject is intrinsically dense or complex (or that our author could not explain it adequately) but because the audience was "dull of hearing." The word translated "dull" (*nōthros*) refers to a lazy or sluggish person,[6] such as an out-of-shape athlete, and that is its meaning later in 6:12. But in 5:11, it refers to the readers' "inattention to the public proclamation of biblical teachings."[7] We might say that "dull of hearing" refers to someone spiritually ignorant, and willfully so,[8] because of a lack of desire to learn more. Perry goes so far as to argue that (*nōthros*) in 5:11 and 6:12 means "unambitious," and more specifically "slow to recognize and act on advantages."[9] In apathy, the Hebrew Christians had been slow to take advantage of the spiritual blessings found in Christ and closed their ears to God's voice, leading to an erosion of the community's faith and hope.[10]

We know what it means to be dull of hearing. We listen—but do we *really* listen—when

> ›   the flight attendant describes safety procedures?
> ›   music plays over the speakers in an elevator?
> ›   the teacher gives instructions for homework or a test?
> ›   the pharmaceutical commercial lists the drug's many side effects?
> ›   announcements are made at the end of worship?
> ›   someone drones on and on about a subject you find boring?
> ›   your spouse asks you to do something he or she considers important, but you don't?

That's what it's like to be dull of hearing.

[6] BDAG, s.v. "νωθρός"; e.g., Sirach 4:29; Polybius, *Histories* 31.23.11. The term serves as bookends for 5:11–6:12, suggesting everything in between ought to be read through the lens of spiritual sluggishness.

[7] Guthrie, *Hebrews*, 202.

[8] "Their problem was an *acquired* condition characterized by an inability to listen to spiritual truth. They were not naturally 'slow,' they were not intellectually deficient, but they had become spiritually lazy" (R. Hughes, *Hebrews*, 1:146; emphasis his).

[9] Perry, "Making Fear Personal," 109. Later, he notes that *parrēsia* ("boldness") stands opposite of *nōthros* in Hebrews ("Making Fear Personal," 110).

[10] Lane, *Hebrews 1–8*, 136.

"By this time," our author says, his audience should have been teachers (v 12), but they had allowed sin and discouragement to rob them of their hunger for further study. God's desire for his people is for us to learn the truth so intimately that we can teach it to others—that's precisely what the Thessalonians had done (1 Thess 1:8). The Hebrews audience, however, wasn't there yet, and it was their fault.

Worse than stagnation, they had begun to regress in their understanding ("you need someone to teach you again"). Imagine how humiliating it would be for a football team, once considered a favorite to win the Super Bowl, to perform so poorly that the head coach made them relearn the fundamentals of blocking and tackling. When our author mentions "basic principles," he employs a phrase used by other Greek authors to refer to the alphabet.[11] The Hebrews audience needed to relearn their spiritual ABCs (e.g., "the ABC of God's oracles" NEB), some of which our author will rattle off in 6:1–2. To further emphasize their need for remedial training, our author chastised, "You need milk, not solid food" (v 12), which is among the harshest criticisms in the New Testament. But sometimes a strong rebuke is necessary to awaken us from spiritual lethargy. "The writer's grotesque images are meant to shock and to motivate some of his hearers to pull out their thumbs and say, 'I'm no baby.'"[12]

This won't come as a shock to anyone, but I've never breastfed a child, nor have I ever been too motivated to learn more about the subject. However, a child's necessary and inevitable transition from milk to solid food intrigued me when I came to this passage. What does medical science have to say? As luck would have it, a lifelong friend works in women's health and was willing to give me a crash course. (If I get any of these facts wrong, it's because I was dull of hearing!)

A mother's milk offers a child initial immunity that is necessary for healthy growth. Breast milk contains an incredible and complex combination of vitamins and enzymes. The problem is that this immunity lasts only for a child's first few months and then declines gradually. In

---

[11] BDAG, s.v. "στοιχεῖον"; LSJ, s.v. "στοιχεῖον"; Philo, *Prelim. Studies* 149–50. "The phrase in Greek may be translated woodenly as 'the basic principles of the beginning of the words of God'" (Guthrie, *Hebrews*, 202).

[12] R. Hughes, *Hebrews*, 1:149.

particular, iron levels in breast milk start to decline at around six months, making it even more necessary to introduce solid food to children around this point. Solid food encourages independence, motor skills, and recognition of colors and shapes. Solid food helps to teach simple actions such as chewing and aids in developing teeth and the gastrointestinal system. To deny solid food to a child would constitute an appalling, even abusive, act of negligence. Without solid food, a child's weight would plateau, he or she would become too dependent, development would be stunted, and malnutrition would wreak havoc.

My son, Daniel, was born two and a half weeks early and was underweight. Constant feedings were necessary to help him grow. Each night, bottles had to be washed and sanitized, and going places was a chore in that we had to make sure enough formula and bottles were in tow to meet his needs. Milk was important, but it was also a pain in some ways. How much better it was when he was able to eat solid food! Certain daily chores disappeared, and life became more manageable.

My point is that it is healthy and natural (not to mention crucial) for a child to transition from milk to solid food. Yet, while we feel a sense of urgency as we anticipate a child making this transition (and would be deeply disturbed if it never happened), the same sense of urgency is often lacking when it comes to a Christian making an identical transition spiritually. "Why is it, in the twenty-first century as in the first, that so many Christians are not only eager to stay with a diet of milk, but actually get cross at the suggestion that they should be eating something more substantial?" N. T. Wright wonders.[13] Churches more or less leave responsibility for growth to the individual Christian, and seldom is there great alarm when someone fails to make the jump to solid food. However,

> › Is worship attendance dwindling? Call a special meeting.
> › Is the church under budget? Call a special meeting.
> › Is an influential member upset? Call a special meeting.

On the other hand,

---

[13] Wright, *Hebrews*, 52.

> › Are Jack and Jill members in "good standing" but also chronic malcontents and continually griping? Silence.
> › Has Jane been a Christian for forty years but never attempted to evangelize? Crickets.
> › Is John an elder in the church but maintains an infamous, volatile temper? We'll get back to you.

Such people are children and "unskilled in the word of righteousness" (v 13), a phrase that refers to the ability to discern the right course of action. More specifically, and given the context of Hebrews, "word of righteousness" refers to Jesus' high priesthood and its practical implications for Christians (i.e., perseverance in the life of faithfulness).[14] "The 'milk' of the Word refers to what Jesus Christ did on earth," Wiersbe says, "His birth, life, teaching, death, burial, and resurrection. The 'meat' of the Word refers to what Jesus Christ is now doing in heaven. We begin the Christian life on the basis of His finished work on earth. We grow in the Christian life on the basis of His unfinished work in heaven."[15]

Having not yet proven themselves capable of digesting the "meat" of Jesus' high priesthood, the audience of Hebrews was stuck in arrested development. While milk was acceptable for Peter's audience (1 Pet 2:2), it's because they were new Christians. The Hebrews author expected more from his readers because they should have been more mature at this stage. The ability to digest solid food was evidence of spiritual discernment (i.e., the ability to "distinguish good from evil"), and such would be sorely needed for what lay ahead. Compared to an adult, a baby has no discernment:

> › Babies will put anything in their mouths without discrimination. They cannot chew, so they swallow immediately. Immature believers will listen to any voice or message. They can't identify whether it is consistent with the Word of God, so they believe or digest almost anything without a second thought.
> › Babies cannot eat meat; they cannot discern what is food, what is gristle, and what is bone. Immature believers cannot handle

---

[14] Cockerill, *Hebrews*, 258–59.
[15] Wiersbe, *Bible Exposition*, 2:295.

spiritual meat; they cannot discern what is true, what is false, and what is deceitful; what is white, what is black, and what is gray.

› Babies cannot resist or repel threats because they cannot discern a proper course of action in those situations. There's a reason we use the phrase "like taking candy from a baby." Immature believers cannot resist temptation or patiently endure hardship because they cannot discern the path before them.

Perhaps all the reasons Hebrews was written narrow here into one: a lack of discernment that was bearing within the hearts of the audience the rotten fruit of insecurity, guilt, unbelief, disobedience, spiritual abandonment, and more. They had become spiritually malnourished to the alarming extent that their moral integrity was presently in jeopardy.

Like us, the Hebrews audience needed discernment if they were to grow. It requires discernment to look at the fallen world around us and the difficult circumstances of life yet to believe we, as esteemed children of God, were destined for something far greater—honor, glory, and rest. It requires discernment to suffer from the cruel tyranny of death and the devil yet to believe every enemy will be made a footstool for our King. It requires discernment to believe that despite the immense guilt hammering our consciences day after day, there is now no condemnation for those in Christ Jesus. It requires discernment to believe that when there is no more hope in our lives, we have a priest who even now intercedes for us at the Father's right hand. It requires discernment to believe that what we think is meant to punish us is instead intended to train us. It requires discernment to walk by faith, not by sight.

HEBREWS 6:1–3

Several years ago, my wife and I built a house. If you've never done so, the entire process is an "experience" unlike any other. A lot is involved: selecting a site, a builder, and a floor plan; signing the contract; preparing and pouring the foundation; rain delays; erecting the walls and roof; adding the exterior; more rain delays; finishing out the interior; mortgage company dragging its feet; finalizing an amount and date for closing; mortgage company losing your paperwork; finalizing a different amount and date for closing; mortgage company asking for paperwork you've sent three times already. ...

You get the idea.

One of the highlights of this "experience" was watching the foundation being laid. Maybe it's the "big boy, big toys" thing, but I loved watching one cement truck after another pour the foundation and the workers set it. As thrilling as it was to watch the foundation be poured, I wouldn't have been the least bit happy if that's where things had stopped. Foundations are great; foundations are important. But you don't stop building with the foundation. You move forward.

The Hebrews audience was being called to leave behind the spiritual milk they desired "and go on to maturity." The word translated "maturity" (*teleiotēs*) is similar to the one translated "make perfect" (*teleioō*) throughout Hebrews. Recall from our discussion of 2:10 that "perfection" has a moral ("sinless"), cultic ("consecrated"), and telic ("whole") nuance. It is the telic meaning—bringing something to its intended goal—that our author has in mind here. Holding fast our confession and entering into God's rest require that we "go on to maturity" versus stopping with the foundation.

What does our author have in mind specifically when he speaks of "the basic principles of the oracles of God" (5:12) and "the elementary doctrine of Christ" (6:1)?[16] With no intention of being exhaustive, he suggests:

Repentance from dead works. In the first-century document *Didache* 5.1, the "way of death" is described as "murders, adulteries, lusts, fornications, thefts, idolatries, magic arts, sorceries, robberies, false testimonies, hypocrisy, duplicity, deceit, arrogance, malice, stubbornness, greed, foul speech, jealousy, audacity, pride, boastfulness." Paul warned the Romans that "the end of those things is death" (6:21).

Thus the New Testament's earliest cry was one of repentance (Mark 1:4, 15; Acts 2:38; 20:21). Repentance "is the first step on the road which

---

[16] The Greek phrase *tēs archēs tou Xristou logon* literally means "the word of the beginning of Christ" or "the beginning word of Christ." "What is being left behind is not 'the word of Christ' as such, but the 'word' of Christian initiation" (Ellingworth, *Hebrews*, 311).

leads the sinner back home to the Father. It is the moment when he 'comes to himself' (Lk. 15:17), and in doing so turns away from the course he has pursued to this point."[17] Our author considers turning from sinful acts to be an elementary practice of the Christian faith; later he will explain that it is from these same dead works that the conscience must be cleansed (9:14).

Faith toward God. "If repentance means turning away *from* dead works, faith means turning *to* the living God."[18] The importance of faith has already been stressed with the illustration of the wilderness generation; we will later learn that it is impossible to please the Lord without faith (11:6). The fact that faith is essential and elementary does not make it unimportant; our author will soon dedicate an entire chapter of this epistle to the topic. Faith is the foundation of the Christian experience; what good is a foundation, though, if nothing is ever built upon it?

Instruction about washings. It's not certain that our author refers to baptism here, especially since the noun he uses is plural.[19] But since no other "washing" is a part of "the elementary doctrine of Christ," it's safe to assume he has baptism in mind. It seems some in our author's audience were spending too much time on the topic of baptism long after theirs had taken place and to the neglect of greater truths.

Laying on of hands. In the New Testament, the laying on of hands had three purposes: (1) There was a non-miraculous form that represented ordination or the bequeathing of authority to another (Acts 6:6; 1 Tim 4:14; 5:22). (2) A miraculous laying on of hands saw the Holy Spirit's gift passed from an apostle to another Christian after baptism (Acts 8:17–18; 19:6; 2 Tim 1:6). (3) Laying on of hands was also done to heal the infirmed (Acts 9:17–18; 28:8). Since the phrase in 6:2 is connected to Christian baptism, it's assumed Hebrews is referring to laying on of hands to impart the postbaptismal miraculous gift of the Spirit.

---

[17] P. Hughes, *Commentary*, 197.

[18] Koester, *Hebrews*, 305; emphasis his.

[19] The Greek *baptismos* occurs only three other times in the New Testament, referring to ceremonial Jewish washing (9:10; Mark 7:4) and Christian baptism (Col 2:12). Hebrews may use the plural because "a single person could conceivably have undergone, in sequence, a proselyte baptism, circumcision, John's baptism, and baptism into the Jesus movement. An instruction concerning baptisms, therefore, could well involve the distinctions between other washings and baptism into Christ" (Johnson, *Hebrews*, 159).

Resurrection of the dead. "Dead" is plural, and thus our author has in mind the raising of all the dead, not just Christ. The final resurrection, denied by both the Sadducees (Matt 22:23) and Greek philosophers (Acts 17:31–32), is another elementary teaching of Christianity (Mark 12:18–27).

Eternal punishment. Implicitly connected with the resurrection of the dead is the doctrine of the final judgment, the time when the deeds of all will be adjudicated by the supreme Son (Matt 25:31–46; Acts 17:31; Rom 2:6–10). When Hebrews uses "eternal" here, it's to remind us that such judgment will be final with no second chances.[20]

Our author wanted to move beyond these elementary principles[21] and lead his audience into the majesty that is the doctrine of the high priesthood of Jesus Christ, and he affirms that they will do so "if God permits" (v 3). The phrase may be nothing more than "a pious cliché"[22]—writers of the day often used it this way.[23] Given, however, that the Spirit inspired these words, they indicate a sincere submission to the will of God. In other words, our author affirms here that only by God's help (John 15:5) will his audience move beyond their foundation, away from the danger of apostasy, and into the grand cathedral of the doctrine of the Son's perfect and permanent priesthood. While spiritual maturity requires our cooperation, growth must always be attributed to God (1 Cor 3:6; Heb 13:20–21).

I want to stress a few points here. First, moving beyond these "elementary" doctrines in no way belittles their importance; it only means they are presupposed. When a child moves "beyond" the ABCs, it doesn't mean the alphabet itself is now inconsequential. It's just that a foundation either exists or it doesn't.[24] Our author laments the need to lay "again a foundation" (v 2) because he's frustrated by the redundancy.

---

[20] Schreiner, *Hebrews*, 177.

[21] "It is striking that the six items mentioned all find parallels within Judaism. This may suggest that the readers were attempting somehow to remain within Judaism by emphasizing items held in common between Judaism and Christianity. They may have been trying to survive with a minimal Christianity in order to avoid alienating their Jewish friends or relatives" (Hagner, *Hebrews*, 87).

[22] P. Hughes, *Commentary*, 206.

[23] Josephus, *Antiquities* 20.267; Plato, *Alcibiades* 1.135d.

[24] P. Hughes, *Commentary*, 196.

More significantly, and peeking ahead in Hebrews, our author doesn't want to leave these ideas behind per se as much as connect them in his readers' minds to their source. You must understand this: *our author wants us to see how these Christian principles are rooted in Christ.*[25] Before I unpack that idea, let me explain why it's so important.

If we aren't careful, we can fixate too much on a good thing at the expense of seeing what lies behind, beneath, or beyond it. Consider baptism as an example. If we fixate too much on this act, there is a tendency to take what is a glorious union of the believer to Christ and reduce it to a ritual of initiation—akin to confusing a wedding with pledging a fraternity or sorority. Fixating on the act and *our* role in it dims our view of what *God* is doing through it. When baptism is seen merely as a way to join a group versus the way to identify with the Son of God, the result will be a Christian stuck in arrested development.

The audience of Hebrews had forgotten that Jesus had everything to do with every teaching and principle and word they had heard and learned since their first day of faith. In their rush to return to Moses, or at least to make their connection to the Messiah appear ambiguous or ambivalent, these Christians were eroding the foundation beneath their feet. To use a different building metaphor, what they thought was a minor cosmetic facelift to the interior was, in reality, the removal of all the support beams and bearing walls. Their spiritual house would soon collapse.

Some of them surely wondered, "What does Jesus have to do with repentance?" "Everything!" our author booms. What does Jesus have to do with your faith? Your baptism? The Spirit indwelling you? Your resurrection and judgment? Everything! Jesus is the one who turned you around from death to life. Jesus is the one who gave you faith and a reason to hope. Jesus washed your conscience clean and gave you a helper in the Holy Spirit. Jesus is the one who will return to raise you back to life. And when you stand in judgment, he will plead your case as only a perfect Priest and supreme Son can.

---

[25] "Each of the six articles [in vv 1–2] is related to the high priestly christology developed in the subsequent chapters, which makes explicit the christological structure of the foundation. ... Accordingly, in 6:1–2 the writer is not asking the community to discard one aspect of Christian instruction for another but to build upon the solid foundation already laid for them" (Lane, *Hebrews 1–8*, 140).

As for elementary teachings, "Use these things as a launch point into the deeper things of Christ," Hebrews says to us. Don't focus on them solely for their own sake. Focus on them only as they beckon you deeper into the doctrine of Jesus Christ, the Son of God, your faithful and merciful high priest.

HEBREWS 6:4–8

This is Hebrews' most troubling passage. Barclay calls it "one of the most terrible passages in Scripture."[26] In early Christianity, misunderstanding of this passage led some to delay their baptism until their deathbed, believing any sin after baptism triggered irrevocable damnation—a sort of theological Monopoly Chance card: "Go to hell, go directly to hell. Do not pass Go, do not collect $200."

I agree with Bruce when he claims the warning of this passage "has been both unduly minimized and unduly exaggerated,"[27] though such extremes are difficult to avoid. On the one hand, there is an absolutist tone to our author's words ("it is impossible") that leaves no room for equivocation. "The term clearly means that something cannot happen."[28] Plus, I reject the suggestion that our author's warning is an improbable hypothetical.[29]

On the other hand, the passage's claim seems to contradict one of the most fundamental tenets of Christianity: that God can forgive any sin if we repent and turn to Christ. These words naturally inspire fear in readers' hearts; who among us has not sinned since we first became Christians? If we fall away, is there indeed no hope of restoration? To fully understand what our author is saying with these somber words, let's break the passage down by answering three questions.

---

[26] Barclay, *Hebrews*, 66.

[27] Bruce, *Hebrews*, 147.

[28] Guthrie, *Hebrews*, 218.

[29] Of "have fallen away" (v 6), Wuest wrote, "The participle is a conditional participle here presenting a hypothetical case, a straw man" (Kenneth S. Wuest, "Hebrews Six in the Greek New Testament," *BSac* 119 [1962]: 52). However, "The danger of apostasy, it must be emphasized, is real, not imaginary; otherwise this epistle with its high-sounding admonitions must be dismissed as trifling, worthless, and ridiculous. Certainly, in our author's judgment, the situation is one of extreme gravity" (P. Hughes, *Commentary*, 206).

1. Of whom is he speaking? Some contend that he is thinking of non-Christians[30] or, more precisely, those who are *almost* Christians.[31] But his reference to a foundation of "the elementary doctrine of Christ" in verse 1, plus his descriptions in verses 4–5, make it clear he has true Christians in mind. For example,

> - "enlightened" means having come to a knowledge of God's truth concerning his Son (10:32; 2 Cor 4:6; Eph 1:18).
> - "tasted the heavenly gift" means experiencing all the spiritual blessings God offers us in Christ (Eph 1:3).
> - "shared in the Holy Spirit" means possessing his indwelling, which is a mark of being a Christian (Acts 2:38; Rom 8:9, 11; Gal 4:6).
> - "tasted[32] the goodness of the word of God" means experiencing the benefits of God's Word (Pss 34:8; 119:103).
> - "powers of the age to come" reminds us the gospel was confirmed by "signs and wonders" (2:4; 1 Cor 2:1–5; Gal 3:1–5).

Attridge calls these descriptions "broadly evocative of the conversion experience,"[33] and even Charles Spurgeon, a Calvinist, acknowledged that "a child, reading this passage, would say, that *the persons intended by it must be Christians.* If the Holy Spirit intended to describe Christians, I do not see that he could have used more explicit terms than there are here. How can a man be said to be enlightened, and to taste of the heavenly gift, and to be made partaker of the Holy Ghost, without being a child of God?"[34] Our author has genuine Christians in mind.

---

[30] This is the Calvinist view: "The persons here intended are not *true and sincere believers,* in the strict and proper sense of that name. ... There is in their full and large description no mention of faith, or believing" (Owen, *Hebrews,* 5:84; emphasis his).

[31] For a defense of this view, see Wayne Grudem, "Perseverance of the Saints: A Case Study from the Warning Passages in Hebrews," in *Still Sovereign: Contemporary Perspectives on Election, Foreknowledge, and Grace,* eds. Thomas R. Schreiner and Bruce A. Ware (Grand Rapids: Baker, 2000), 133–82. David L. Allen gives an excellent rebuttal (*Hebrews,* NAC 35 [Nashville: B&H, 2010], 350–54).

[32] As with tasting the heavenly gift, our author does not mean "taste" as in a small sampling but total experience or participation (see 2:9).

[33] Attridge, *Hebrews,* 170.

[34] C. H. Spurgeon, "Final Perseverance," in *The New Park Street Pulpit Sermons* (London: Passmore, 1856), 2:170; emphasis his.

2. What does our author mean by "fallen away"? The verb used (*parapiptō*) refers to failing to "follow through on a commitment."[35] While this is the verb's only occurrence in the New Testament, it is used in Ezekiel to refer to faithlessness to the law of Moses (14:13; 15:8; 18:24; 20:27 LXX).

By "fallen away," then, we are not talking about well-intentioned doctrinal error or sins such as a momentary lapse in moral judgment (Gal 6:1), the kind that make us almost immediately say, "I've made a huge mistake." That the people under consideration have been "enlightened" (v 4) precludes ignorance, doctrinal or otherwise, from being in view here (see 1 Tim 1:13). And our author's prior mention of drifting, neglect, and sluggishness (2:1, 3; 5:11) seems to indicate that, while such behavior can *lead* to falling away, it's not the same. His readers may be sluggish, but our author considers them better than apostates (6:9; 13:19).

No, our author has in mind a willful repudiation of the gospel: its principles, its teachings, and its Lord. He is referring to an evil, unbelieving, calloused heart that has turned away from God. In the original context, he may have been directly pointing to those who had publicly denied the Lord for personal advantage (Mark 8:38).

3. Is there indeed no chance of restoration once a person falls away? Our author says it is impossible "to restore them again to repentance." It's often alleged that, by "impossible," our author means "difficult," but this is unfounded. Whenever Hebrews uses "impossible" (*adynatos*), our author has in mind a zero percent chance of an event occurring (6:18; 10:4; 11:6). It ain't gonna happen. "Impossible" is at the beginning of the sentence in verse 4, meaning our author wants to emphasize it. But what does he mean by "impossible" in this particular context?

In biblical interpretation, it is critical never to make the exception the rule. That is, it's unwise to hang a doctrine or interpretation on the single nail of one verse and ignore or exclude all other relevant passages. If we are to say that should a child of God sin, then they can't be restored at all, what are we to do with the example of David's restoration? Or Peter's? What of

---

[35] BDAG, s.v. "παραπίπτω." "Hebrews has in mind here a fundamental and conscious rejection of the Church" (*EDNT*, s.v. "παραπίπτω").

God's claim that "he will abundantly pardon" (Isa 55:7)? That he who turns from sin and obeys "shall surely live; he shall not die" (Ezek 18:21)?

How do we reconcile these verses?

Answering this challenging question requires us to look ahead in Hebrews to the book's claim: that the Son of God, as our high priest, has offered perfect atonement for our sins once and for all. No other atonement is needed. None other is effective. So, when Christians renounce Jesus, they forfeit their only means of forgiveness. That renunciation is a grave one "since they are crucifying once again the Son of God to their own harm and holding him up to contempt" (v 6).

Note that at the end of verse 6, our author switches to the present tense ("they are crucifying") as if it is a condition of this impossibility.[36] *As long as* a person scorns the supreme Son, there remains no means of repentance, restoration, or access to God, for, according to Hebrews, the Son is the final word spoken by the Father. Restoration is impossible for the continuing apostate since Christ is our only avenue of atonement, our only road to repentance and redemption.[37] Restoration is impossible *if it doesn't go through Jesus.*

The impossibility of restoration spoken of here isn't due to a psychological "mind block" in which people can't bring themselves to repent (though this can certainly happen, as both Scripture and common experience can attest). No, our author is speaking of a theological impossibility. There is no other way to draw near to God but through the Son (John 14:6). To renounce the Son, therefore, makes eternal salvation quite impossible (Acts 4:12).[38]

Turning away from Christ means more than passively dismissing him. "Apostasy concedes that Jesus should have been crucified, that the penalty was warranted."[39] An apostate doesn't cause the supreme Son physical pain, for Jesus is now enthroned above the world. He is both sovereign over, and out of the reach of, any who might do him harm. Yet apostates, by their rebellion, unite with that first-century mob who cried, "Crucify him!"

---

[36] J. Keith Elliott, "Is Post-Baptismal Sin Forgivable?" *BT* 28 (1977): 330–32.

[37] "This does not mean that the efficacy of his sacrifice reaches only into the past and not into the future, but that once Christ and his sacrifice have been rejected, there is nowhere else to turn" (Ellingworth, *Hebrews*, 323).

[38] Having renounced the Lord, can an apostate be restored if he returns to faith in and obedience to Christ? Yes, for Peter did so (Mark 14:66–72; John 21:15–19).

[39] Schreiner, *Hebrews*, 189.

By their faithlessness, apostates also incite others to scorn our Lord. Koester reminds us of the "public character" of falling away. Just as the grotesque and public shame of crucifixion was designed to deter others from crime, so also the repudiation or "crucifixion" of a person's relationship with Christ can deter others from faith and move them to show contempt for the Christ whom we have rejected.[40] The act of faithlessness is made even more emphatic by our author when he reminds us that it is not simply "Jesus" or "Christ" or "our Lord" that we crucify afresh, but none less than the supreme "Son of God."

>——◇——<

In many of his parables, Jesus presented dual examples for his audience to consider: a faithful versus prodigal son, a wise versus foolish builder, prepared versus unprepared virgins, and a grateful versus ungrateful debtor. One particular parable tells of servants reaping a field yielding both worthless weeds and valuable wheat. "Should we pull the weeds now?" the servants ask their master. "Not yet," he says. "Wait until the harvest; then we will separate what is valuable from what is worthless" (Matt 13:28–30). In another parable, Christ presented four types of soil as representative of four types of people and their receptivity to the good news (Matt 13:1–9, 18–23).

To understand Hebrews 6:7–8, it would also help to recall the Song of the Vineyard in Isaiah 5. More than seven centuries before Hebrews was written, the prophet poetically depicted Israel as a vineyard prized and loved by its owner. It was blessed with every agricultural extravagance imaginable. Stones were cleared, a watchtower and wine vat were installed, and vines were planted that would win first prize at the county fair. The landowner waited expectantly for the field to yield superior grapes but instead received "worthless grapes" (Isa 5:2 csb).

In that tradition, our author paints a verbal picture of two fields for his audience to envision. The first absorbs rainfall and does with it what was intended: it produces a healthy crop. Such a "field," our author says, will enjoy God's blessing. The second field also has had its fill of rain but gives

---

[40] Koester, *Hebrews*, 322–23.

the appearance of being perpetually dry—a field full of nothing but thorns and thistles that will soon be deemed worthless. This is the kind of field, our author says, that makes a farmer want to cuss it out, then soak it in diesel, set it aflame, and watch with pyromaniacal wrath as that Godforsaken patch of dirt (literally, in this case!) scorches away to nothing.

By "near to being cursed," our author does not mean that a curse *might* happen, but that it is *soon* to happen ("about to be cursed" CSB). He will use the word translated "near" (*engys*) later in 8:13 to describe an inevitable event.[41] Likewise, the word rendered "worthless" (*adokimos*) is used elsewhere in the New Testament of those who will be judged and condemned by God on the final day (Rom 1:28; 1 Cor 9:27; 2 Cor 13:5–7; 2 Tim 3:8; Titus 1:16.). Fire in Hebrews is also representative of the final judgment (10:27; 12:29). While a farmer might burn a field to clear or restore it (i.e., to start over), God's fire in 6:8 is punitive, not restorative. The destiny of an unfruitful field or unfruitful Christian is fiery judgment and eternal punishment under God's curse.

Recognize that in this illustration, both fields receive ample rain from above. Their yield (or lack thereof) is not a result of different amounts of precipitation (blessings). No one field has an inequitable advantage over another. Neither the seed's quality nor the farmer's skill is in focus, only the quality of the harvest. God's blessings fall on all of us—perhaps to varying degrees, but how we have been blessed relative to another "field" is not the point. The point is what kind of "harvest" the Lord will gather from us.

Let's not forget that the truth revealed by the agricultural illustration of verses 7–8 is essential to the argument of verses 4–6 (note "for" in v 7). Isaiah's Song of the Vineyard went on to identify Israel as God's vineyard (Isa 5:7), which had been given every blessing or advantage—"Can you think of anything I could have done to my vineyard that I didn't do?" (5:4 Msg). When the "field" proved worthless, the landowner destroyed it and denied it every blessing, including rain (5:5–6). In Hebrews, the worthless field represents a person who obeys the gospel and is added to the church—thus sharing in all the blessings God rains down on his people—only to lead a life at odds with his confession of the supreme Son. In doing

---

[41] Herbert Preisker, "ἐγγύς," *TDNT* 2:331; e.g., Homer, *Iliad* 22.453.

so, such a one holds the Son in open contempt. Upon such a one, our author says, God's blessing will be replaced with God's curse; judgment will be pronounced, and the fiery wrath of the Holy One will descend.

HEBREWS 6:9–12

Right when it seems our author is content to rake his audience over the coals, he stops short and sounds a note of hope. As previously suggested, his words are those of prevention, not prescription. His audience had not *yet* fallen away due to sluggishness or immaturity, though they were at risk of doing so. This "not yet" status gave our author hope for "better things." He echoes the same confidence expressed by Paul to various churches, including the most problematic ones (2 Cor 7:4; Gal 5:1, 7–10). Like Paul (Phil 1:6), our author was convinced God's work in his audience would one day be completed. Why was our author so "sure of better things"?

First, he was confident because "God is not unjust" (v 10). The Lord is neither forgetful nor neglectful; he remembers (Gen 8:1; Exod 2:24; Ps 25:7). Our Father always does what is good and right (Gen 18:25; Rom 3:5); we can count on him to act always for our good and his glory (Rom 8:28). Given their trials and Christ's intercession, our author knew the Father understood his listeners' present weaknesses (Ps 103:14; Matt 12:19–20). God takes all things into account. He would not excuse or overlook their immaturity, but neither would he overlook their good deeds.

Second, he was confident because his audience loved to glorify God's Name (v 10). Their good deeds were rendered not in a futile attempt to win God's favor under challenging circumstances but to bring him honor (Matt 5:16).[42] "The author was persuaded that men who would show such kindness to Christ's followers were not the sort who would lift Him up to public contempt."[43] Although we disparage good intentions by saying they pave the path to hell, they nonetheless count for something. Our

---

[42] "Deeds of kindness done to the people of God are reckoned by God as done to himself, and will surely receive their reward from him" (Bruce, *Hebrews*, 151).

[43] Lightfoot, *Jesus Christ Today*, 128.

weaknesses are never irredeemable if, with a pure heart, we yearn to magnify God to the ends of the earth.

In their desire to show honor and love for the Name, these saints were looking for opportunities to serve one another (Matt 25:40). It's easy to imagine that, given the oppression they were enduring, such opportunities were abundant.[44] Our author will later specify some of these good deeds (10:32–34). I'll admit that the church today has its fair share of problems (and more than a few of our own doing), though I have seen it proven time and again that we know how to care for our own. The church of Christ never shines brighter than when we "bear one another's burdens, and so fulfill the law of Christ" (Gal 6:2).

Third, our author was confident because the same eagerness to serve, if applied to holding firm their confession and hope, would see them safely to the "end" (v 11). Just as their works proved their love, our author wants them to "show" their faith and hope by their earnestness, which is the remedy for spiritual sluggishness (5:11). I know Christians, and you do also, whose servant-hearts appear otherworldly. They constantly seem to be thinking of others and how to help them. They prepare food for the needy. They hold the hands of the lonely. In their spare time, they seek even more opportunities to serve. Yet veterans of the spiritual disciplines will tell you there is a dark side to this, as Satan sows vice among even the greatest of virtues.[45] In seeking to serve many, we, like Martha, can neglect ourselves and our own pursuit of God—the "one thing [that] is necessary" (Luke 10:42).

Our author's earnest desire[46] (v 11) was that his audience "not grow weary of doing good" (Gal 6:9), but that they take the same enthusiasm for glorifying the Name with good deeds and invest it also in "the full assurance of hope"—hope that although things aren't OK now, they will be someday because the tomb is empty. Hope that even in these present

---

[44] "This implies that their coming to the assistance of their brethren is evidence of their willingness to identify themselves with the stigma attaching to the name of Jesus, and thus of the genuineness of their love for him" (P. Hughes, *Commentary*, 226).

[45] "Wonderful as works of benevolence assuredly are, pure benevolence, however lavish, is no substitute for faithful adherence to the word and doctrine of Christ" (Coffman, *Hebrews*, 129).

[46] The verb "desire" (*epithumeō*) referred to a strong desire (e.g., Matt 13:17; Luke 15:16; 22:15; Rev 9:6), and even lust in sexual contexts (Matt 5:28; Gal 5:17).

circumstances, tough as they may be, we will get through them because we have a faithful and merciful high priest interceding on our behalf. Hope that he who began a good work in us "will bring it to completion at the day of Jesus Christ" (Phil 1:6). Hope that our champion-pioneer will see us through to our destiny.

———◇———

Why must Christians not remain in a state of arrested development? Why must we move beyond the foundation toward maturity, toward our destiny? Because the only alternative to moving forward is falling away, the consequences of which are too terrible to contemplate. Because if we yield a worthless versus useful harvest, there is "a fearful expectation of judgment" (10:27). Because the overcast skies of spiritual sluggishness will cloud out our hope and plunge us into despair's abyss.

How do we invest in such hope? How do we move from wishful thinking to "full assurance" (v 11)—a "state of complete certainty"[47]—that God will do all he has said? By rejecting sluggishness and immaturity in favor of focusing on the truth that all those who have hoped in God's promises have never been disappointed (v 12).

SUMMARY

» God expects Christians to grow in their knowledge of spiritual things.

» Spiritual maturity improves a Christian's discernment and endurance.

» If a person rejects Jesus, there is no other means of access to God.

» Those who reject Jesus will suffer God's terrifying judgment.

[47] BDAG, s.v. "πληροφορία."

TALKING POINTS

AT ITS CORE, the gospel is a simple message. Most people can grasp that they are great sinners and Jesus is a great Savior. Though the gospel itself is simple, however, no one should remain in willful ignorance of Christianity's more profound truths. Over a century ago, one homiletician lamented, "It is pitiful and painful to reflect upon the prevalence of spiritual obtuseness in our own age. How many Christians are perfectly content and self-satisfied having only the barest rudiments of Scripture truth! Some even pride themselves in holding 'the truth,' as though they had grasped and mastered all truth; and in their firm adherence to 'the simple gospel,' as though there were no profundities and sublimities in the gospel of Jesus Christ."[48] It is the personal responsibility of all Christians to push themselves deeper into the Word of God and seek to understand it. Some have excused their biblical ignorance by claiming "the secret things belong to the LORD" (Deut 29:29), but such an appeal is a gross abuse of that verse. It is shameful to blame God for our ignorance when it is clearly his desire that we grow in our knowledge of his Word. Indeed, if Hebrews 5:11–14 teaches anything, it's "that our ignorance of God's Word is a moral problem, not an intellectual one."[49] Refusing to deepen our knowledge of God's truths may reflect less what God has withheld from us (knowledge) and more what *we* are withholding from God (faithfulness).

>———◇———<

AS WE PUSH ourselves deeper into understanding God's Word, our ability to discern good and evil, truth and falsehood is sharpened. "A good illustration is the way bank tellers learn to distinguish real money from counterfeit. They learn what authentic bills feel like by repetitive handling. There is no need to learn what counterfeit bills look and feel like. The tellers become so familiar with authentic bills that when they touch a counterfeit, they can

[48] W. Jones, "Hebrews," in *The Pulpit Commentary*, eds. H. D. M. Spence and Joseph S. Exell (Grand Rapids: Eerdmans, 1950), 21:148.

[49] Mohler, *Exalting Jesus*, 79.

easily tell the difference."[50] There is black and white in this world, but there is also a lot of gray—recall our discussion in 3:12–19 about sin's deceitfulness. There is not a "Thus saith the Lord" for every issue; the "red letters" in our Bibles don't explicitly speak to every possible scenario. Sometimes I wish God would send me an email or text to communicate his specific will in my particular circumstances, but it doesn't work that way. The more we grow in the Word, however, the more oriented we become to God's truth versus Satan's deceit. That orientation is critical for sustaining hope and enduring faithfully to the end. To return to the wilderness generation, faithless Israel had no discernment; they could not appreciate that God does not command where his grace will not provide. Knowing the Word will sustain our hope during seasons of turmoil; because we know from Scripture how God was present with his people in tough times, we can greet the future with certain hope he is with us today. Knowing the Word will help us recognize darkness when it is shrouded in light; because we know Scripture, we can be wise in perplexing times (Ps 119:97–104). Indeed, a deeper understanding of God's Word trains our powers of discernment.

>———◇———<

AS INCUMBENT as it is that a Christian actively endeavor to grow and remain faithful, we must never for a moment believe that such happens by our own power. Maturity and endurance are always products of God's work in our lives. Our author acknowledges such with the words "let us … go on to maturity" (6:1), which in Greek can be interpreted as passive; Hebrews desires for its readers "that they allow themselves to be moved by the power of God through a proper appropriation of Christ's high-priestly ministry."[51] Two verses later, our author uses the words "if God permits" (6:3). In his closing benediction, he will pray "[May God] equip you with everything good that you may do his will, working in us that which is pleasing in his sight" (13:21). From beginning to end, a Christian's growth and endurance are God's work. This has three important implications. (1)

[50] Cynthia Dianne Guy, *Journey to a Better Place: A Women's Guided Study of Hebrews* (Nashville: Gospel Advocate, 2017), 50–51.

[51] Cockerill, *Hebrews*, 262.

Since it's God's work, growth and endurance are developed over a lifetime. Spiritual maturity cannot be microwaved. We must be *patient*. (2) Since it's God's work, our faithfulness is not a trophy of our spiritual superiority, but an endorsement of the grace and mercy of God. We must not be *proud*. (3) Since it's God's work, he expects the results to be something grand. We cannot settle for what we might think is "good enough" but rather strive to achieve God's grandest intentions for our lives. We must be *productive*.

><———◇———<

MY DAD SPENT most of his childhood summers visiting his grandparents in rural East Texas. He'd often tell the story of how, at the beginning of summer, the bottoms of his feet were soft and tender, and walking barefoot on those hot Texas roads was painful. By the end of the summer, however, he'd developed callouses on the bottoms of his feet so that he no longer felt the searing-hot pavement. If we aren't careful, the same thing can happen to our hearts. Sin hardens the heart until it is no longer sensitive to spiritual pain (1 Tim 4:2). We can reach a point where we have repented and regressed over and over and over until the whole thing seems silly to us. We lose our ability to turn from sin. It's still possible for us to be restored if we were to turn to Jesus, but we never do so. The gospel no longer moves us. As Lightfoot puts it, we become "void of conscience" and lose our "repenting-apparatus."[52] If we never want to be in danger of this, we must remain sensitive to the Word and dependent on Christ's help. We must consider repentance as an opportunity to learn to hate our sin as much as God does. On the other hand, the longer we indulge our temptations—the more we walk on searing-hot pavement—the sooner the callouses form, and we perhaps pass a point of no return.

[52] Lightfoot, *Jesus Christ Today*, 126.

Chapter 6

SOLEMNLY SWEAR

Promises. That word, the latest one Timothy had spoken, always left Judah feeling anxious and unsettled.

What good are promises if they're always broken? he thought to himself.

Judah instantly felt engulfed in a maelstrom of bitter memories. In his youth, he had been betrothed to a young girl in Antioch's Jewish community, one who was very beautiful and came from a respected family. Many a time, Judah had thanked the Most High for this blessing. A few months before the wedding, however, while adding adjacent living quarters to his father's house for his bride-to-be, there had been a falling-out with his future father-in-law, and the wedding was called off, the relationship severed. Judah was crushed. He had been promised a wife.

What good are promises if they're always broken?

His mind drifted to thoughts of Israel's beloved patriarch and Judah's arch-ancestor. "The promises of Abraham, the promises of Abraham." The refrain rang in Judah's head. The synagogue elders of Judah's youth would often beat their chests and laud the promises of Abraham. Just the same, Judah had often been skeptical. Father Abraham had been promised a special son yet waited twenty-five years to see that child born into the world. Abraham had been promised divine protection but seemed to suffer threats from every side. He had been promised a certain land the Lord would show him, except he died owning no real estate save the family cemetery.

What good are promises if they're always broken?

Four years ago, Judah had found himself embroiled in a property dispute with another landowner in the synagogue. The case was brought before the leaders, and Judah's rival had sworn by heaven and the temple that he had never moved the boundary stone. Such a strong oath had been rather intimidating to Judah, and he backed down from his claim. The elders ruled in his rival's favor. Two weeks later, however, witnesses came forth proving the other landowner had sworn falsely, and a minor scandal ensued.

What good are promises if they're always broken?

Judah had confessed his doubts to no one, but the promises the Most High made to Father Abraham and Israel had always seemed a bit untrustworthy. The land had been promised and given, only then to be taken away. For five hundred years, God's people had been dispersed throughout the world instead of living in sovereign territory. The Torah taught explicitly that sacrifices brought about forgiveness of sins, yet Judah had heard from his fellow Christians that only Jesus could forgive sins.

What good are promises if they're always broken?

If he were honest with himself, Judah had broken more than a few promises of his own. Since he didn't trust himself, he eventually found it difficult to trust others, including the Most High. In his heart, Judah knew this had loosed him from his spiritual mooring. With nothing to stand on and nothing to anchor him, he tended to drift in whatever direction the wind and current dictated. Broken promises had cost him a bit of his faith—

And more than a little of his hope.

Judah realized his eyes had been locked on the ground for quite a while, and as he raised them back to the evangelist, Timothy said, "We have this as a sure and steadfast anchor of the soul, a hope…"

>———◇———<

Do you remember the first time you were disappointed? For me, it was Christmas 1994. That year, I desperately wanted a Super Nintendo and asked Santa for one. The reason I yearned for a Super Nintendo was that all of my friends had Super Nintendos.

I, on the other hand, had only a regular Nintendo.

Christmas morning dawned crisp and clear at our home in north Alabama. I made sure to wake up extra early to get some quality gaming in before having to hit pause and go to church. Christmas fell on Sunday that year, something my nine-year-old self considered to be cruel and unusual punishment.

So at an earlier-than-usual hour, I sprang out of bed and scurried down the hallway, through the kitchen, and into the den where stood our Christmas tree. With giddy anticipation, I was greeted by a treasure trove of gifts straight from Santa's workshop—

None of which was a Super Nintendo.

Think about the word *disappointed*. It means you appointed (or decided) something would be, but it never "becomes." My girls use the word when they don't get their way: "I'm so disappointed." It's usually said after I've told them that they can't go to the park that day, that they've watched too much television for now, or that no, they can't have cheesecake for supper. In response to their pouting, I usually mutter under my breath, "If that ends up being your greatest disappointment in life, you'll be just fine."

If only…

Our childhood disappointments eventually give way to grown-up ones. We are disappointed when our love is rejected, when a medical test comes back positive, or when a promotion goes to someone else. We are most disappointed when promises are broken. Disappointment comes from unmet expectations. We appointed something to be, but it never "becomes."

Into that gap—the chasm between reality and expectation—each of us places something. Some people place fear there. Others place doubt, anger, or rebellion. Christians, however, are called to respond to disappointment with faith and hope, especially when we are disappointed with God.

Our author is speaking to a group of distraught, disappointed Christians. Some had seen their businesses fail or their property seized. Many had experienced family expulsion or social ostracism because of their confession that Jesus is the Son of God. Nearly all had entertained the notion at some point, and to whatever degree, that their adverse circumstances were the result of God's disappointment with *them*!

They were struggling, yes. Still, our author assures them he is confident of "better things" (6:9), that the spiritual lethargy overwhelming them can give way to an earnest imitation of their spiritual heroes. The funny thing about God's promises in the Old Testament is that they often seem broken into pieces. Can one really say God kept his promise of land to Abraham when the patriarch lived and died without owning a single divot of sod save the field he bought to bury his dead? Can one really say David's throne endured forever when, at the time of our author, no king had occupied that throne for over six centuries? What of the glory and honor promised to us in the beginning? What of God's promised rest? God appointed something to be, but it never "became."

What good are promises if they're always broken?

In what follows—obscured somewhat by a lot of talk about oaths and anchors, patriarchs and priests, sanctuaries and sacrifices—our author stresses a few critical facts: (1) God does not break his promises. Ever. It's impossible. He'll even swear by himself to prove it. (2) Just when you think God is breaking his promise, you discover he's been at work for a long time to fulfill it. Be patient. (3) God gives us what we need, not necessarily what we want. This always works to our benefit, which means (4) God always over-delivers. He fulfills his promises beyond our wildest expectations. Always has. Just ask Abraham.

HEBREWS 6:13–20

At the end of the previous section, readers were encouraged to continue in their patient faith until they inherited the promises (v 12). Our author has already given his audience an example *not* to follow: the wilderness generation. For a positive role model, he now sets before them the father of Israel.

Abraham's story is integral to the narrative of Scripture. The patriarchal promises in Genesis lay at the heart of the Old Testament, to say nothing of the New. For good reason, many biblical writers used Abraham as a paradigm of faith, as did non-inspired authors of Jewish literature.[1] Thus the patriarch's story would have resonated deeply with the original audience. They were struggling, as Abraham had at times, to hold tightly to God's promises, especially when it looked like God was not coming through for them. Was their faith in the God of their fathers misplaced?

Moreover, the story our author alluded to, the sacrifice of Isaac (v 14; Gen 22:1–18), was an occasion when Abraham had to have felt like God

[1] Rom 4:1–22; Gal 3:6–29; Jas 2:21–23; Sirach 44:19–21; 1 Maccabees 2:52.

was sending mixed signals. Isaac was the fulfillment of God's promise, so why must Abraham sacrifice his son? What kind of God gives so graciously, only to rip his gift away? Perhaps the audience of Hebrews felt like "the circumstances and sufferings of life suggest that God's promises are a charade, that they are disconnected from reality."[2] What assurance did they have, then, that God's oath concerning his Son (5:6, 10) was trustworthy?

In ancient times, similar to our "signing on the dotted line," swearing an oath was done to support a statement's veracity or assure a promise's fulfillment. The law allowed for oaths to be sworn in God's name (Deut 6:13; 10:20), and lying under oath was thus verboten (Exod 20:7; Lev 19:12; Zech 5:3–4). When we swear an oath in court, we do so with the phrase "so help me God." Outside of court, some will explicitly "swear to God." Others might swear on the Bible or "on my mother's grave." All these oaths are an appeal to something or someone greater than ourselves. These oaths are also a wish that something catastrophic should happen to the thing or person we swore upon (as well as to us) if we do not tell the truth. Surely swearing by something as significant as God's name would preclude lying.

Not even God is above swearing by his own name. Notice that after Abraham had proven his willingness to sacrifice Isaac, God answered, "By myself I have sworn, declares the LORD" (Gen 22:16). God's sworn oath is key to Hebrews:

> › He swore the wilderness generation would not enter his rest (3:11).
> › He swore his Anointed would be a priest forever in the order of Melchizedek (5:6, 10; Ps 110:4).
> › He swore he would keep his promise to Abraham (6:13–14).

Our author notes that God "had no one greater by whom to swear" (v 13) when he made an oath to Abraham. Seeing as how God is as great as it gets, unparalleled and unsurpassed, the buck stops with him. When God swears, he swears by himself.

The burning question now becomes why God needed to swear an oath at all. If God can't lie (v 18; Titus 1:2) or deal unfaithfully, why an oath?

---

[2] Schreiner, *Hebrews*, 200.

It was not because his integrity was suspect but because of the frailty and skepticism of human beings. People are prone to lie; again, that's why we swear by something greater than ourselves to convince another we are truthful. By swearing an oath via himself—"I swear to Me"—God was acknowledging our suspicion when it comes to promises.[3]

Another reason God swore an oath is along these same lines. Like today, it was not uncommon in ancient times to reserve the right to change a promise (e.g., a will) made to one's heir(s).[4] The Lord, however, has done more than make a promise to his heirs. He has sealed that promise with an oath. He will not go back on his word.

Twice in Genesis, God swore an oath and went the extra mile to assure his covenant partner that he, the Lord, was trustworthy. After the flood, God swore to Noah never to destroy the world with another flood, and he sealed the oath by hanging a bow in the sky (9:8–17). In Noah's day, people would swear an oath by holding a warrior's bow pointed toward themselves as if an imaginary arrow were drawn and aimed at their head. They would then swear the oath. The implication was that if they did not keep their word, they called upon themselves the curse of death. In Genesis 15:7–21, God did something similar for Abraham. Walking between the halved carcasses of animals was a standard method in the patriarch's time of swearing oaths and sealing covenants. The implication was that if either party did not keep their word, they called upon themselves the curse of death.[5]

When it came to his promise concerning the high priesthood of his supreme Son, God went the extra mile, as he did in Genesis, to assure his faithfulness. "His *oath*, though unnecessary, is the double assurance that he cannot lie. Truth has sworn by itself that its truth shall truly be fulfilled. There is no more possibility of God's promises failing us than of God falling out of Heaven! His Word is eternally sealed with the double surety of promise and oath."[6] As he did with Noah and Abraham, he swears to us,

---

[3] "God does not need the oath, but humans do, especially in the face of circumstances that present evidence contrary to the promise" (Johnson, *Hebrews*, 170).

[4] S. R. Llewelyn, *New Documents Illustrating Early Christianity* (New South Wales: Ancient History Documentary Research Centre, Macquarie Univ., 1992), 6:41–47.

[5] Michael Whitworth, *The Epic of God: A Guide to Genesis*, rev. ed. (Bowie, TX: Start2Finish, 2014), 67, 116–17.

[6] R. Hughes, *Hebrews*, 1:177; emphasis his.

"May I die if I don't keep my promise." God can't die, of course, but neither can he break his promise, and that's precisely the point.

Because the patriarch believed God and patiently waited, he "obtained the promise" (v 15)—unlike faithless Israel in the wilderness. Likewise, our author wants his audience to wait with patience to obtain their promise. The word translated "patiently waited" (*makrothumeō*) could refer to persevering through trial without complaint (1 Cor 13:4; 1 Thess 5:14), as well as anticipating the fulfillment of a promise (Jas 5:7–8). Both ideas are in view in this passage: Christians should follow Abraham's example by persevering through the trials of life without complaint as we anticipate God's assured fulfillment of his promises.

In the meantime, we "hold fast to the hope set before us" (v 18). It is a terrible feeling when we realize we got our hopes up for nothing; someone gave us their word, only to prove untrustworthy.[7] Those who hope in the Lord, however, will never be disappointed in the end. Hope in the Lord's promises isn't a fool's errand. Because of his nature, God must honor his word, for "God is not man, that he should lie, or a son of man, that he should change his mind. Has he said, and will he not do it? Or has he spoken, and will he not fulfill it?" (Num 23:19).

The immutability of God's person and purpose—that he won't lie and won't change his mind—is the hope and refuge of every Christian. In ancient times, people often sought refuge or sanctuary in the temples of their gods;[8] in Israel, refuge was sought at the altar or in the cities of refuge among the Levites.[9] According to Hebrews, the Christian's refuge is in "two unchangeable things" (v 18) about which God cannot lie or be unfaithful. What are those two unchangeable things? God's promise and God's oath. "God cannot lie when he makes a promise, and he cannot lie when he makes an oath" (v 18 NCV).

What is this promise of which our author has been speaking? It's that Jesus Christ, the supreme Son of God, is our high priest (vv 19–20; 8:1). This

---

[7] The low point of Jeremiah's lament over Jerusalem's destruction is this: "My strength is gone, and I have no hope in the LORD" (Lam 3:18 NCV).

[8] Herodotus, *Histories* 2.113; 5.46; Tacitus, *Annals* 3.60.

[9] Num 35:25–28; Deut 4:42; 1 Kgs 1:50; 2:28. The Greek word for "refuge" in Heb 6:18 (*katapheugō*) is the same as that used in the LXX for the cities of refuge.

is God's pledge, and he has sworn to it. Our author will unpack this idea in Hebrews 7, though not before his call for us to seek refuge in this promise—refuge beyond the curtain, in the Most Holy Place, upon the horns of the altar where Jesus has performed the high priestly service of atoning for our sins. On earth, we may be foreigners and transients (11:9, 13), but we have a home, a place of refuge and security, beyond the curtain in the immediate presence of the Father[10]—and that will never change.

The final two verses of Hebrews 6 can be confusing since our author mixes metaphors with wild abandon. We are first asked to focus on the nautical imagery of an anchor. The scene then shifts immediately to that of the tabernacle and the curtain that separated the Holy Place from the Most Holy Place. Add to that a third metaphor of a journey with a forerunner or advance scout, and it's easy for our heads to spin! So let's take these metaphors one at a time.

No matter what storms come upon us in life, our author assures us we have a "sure and steadfast anchor of the soul" (v 19), something that secures us from drifting towards destruction. Though this is the only time "anchor" is used metaphorically in the New Testament, such usage was common in Greek literature.[11] A metaphorical anchor was something that gave safety or steadfastness in life—what we might call endurance or "staying power." The anchor symbol has been found inscribed numerous times in the Roman catacombs by early Christians dating to the second century. "Its appearance on epitaphs verifies that the dead were interred 'in the sure and certain hope of the Resurrection.'"[12]

Late in the first century, Epictetus, a Stoic philosopher, said, "We ought neither to fasten our ship to one small anchor, nor our life to a single hope."[13] Our author would disagree. The Christian's sole anchor—our sole hope—is not established upon or invested in a thing but in a *he* (1 Tim 1:1). Within the raging storm of cognitive dissonance inherent in the life of faith—the tension between promise and fulfillment, between

[10] Koester, *Hebrews*, 328. "The characterization ... provides a sharp image of readers who are *not* sure of their place in the world and are in need of what is stable and secure" (Johnson, *Hebrews*, 171–72; emphasis his).

[11] Virgil, *Aeneid* 6.3–5; Plato, *Laws* 12.961c; Euripides, *Helen* 277.

[12] Charles A. Kennedy, "Early Christians and the Anchor," *BA* 38 (1975): 115–24.

[13] Epictetus, *Fragment* 89.

homeless refugees of earth and glorified children of God[14]—our anchor is Christ's presence behind the curtain, interceding for us at his Father's right hand. In other words, "His continual priestly prayer for us is the medium for our survival."[15]

However, there are two significant differences between a literal anchor and the anchor available to Christians. First, a physical anchor is cast downward beyond the "curtain" of the depths of the sea, whereas ours is cast upward beyond the "curtain" of the heights of heaven. Second, while a ship's anchor by nature does not move and prevents what is connected to it from moving (as in "drift away," 2:1), our anchor in Christ beckons us forward to the realization of our destiny, forward into the divine presence.

Turning to the tabernacle, our author says our hope enters "behind the curtain" into the Most Holy Place. He will use various forms of the verb "enter" (*erchomai*) repeatedly in his sermon to refer to Christ's entering the Father's presence (vv 19–20; 9:12, 24–25; 10:5), our approaching God in praise and prayer (4:16; 7:25; 10:1, 22; 11:6), and our arrival in the heavenly city (12:22). Negatively, our author used this verb throughout Hebrews 3–4 when he spoke of being denied access or entrance into God's rest. Thus the tabernacle curtain (separating the Holy Place from the Most Holy Place) is a symbol of "that which encloses the presence of God."[16] It separates the physical realm from the spiritual, the material from the transcendent.

Behind that curtain and into that transcendent, unshakeable realm, Jesus has gone as a "forerunner on our behalf" (v 20). The word translated "forerunner" (*prodromos*) literally means, as we might expect, "one who runs ahead." It occurs only here in the New Testament, but in classical Greek, it referred to advance military scouts or heralds who announced a party's arrival.[17] This is not the first time in the epistle that Christ has been spoken

---

[14] DeSilva, *Perseverance*, 251.

[15] R. Hughes, *Hebrews*, 1:179. "The aptness of the figure of an anchor appears in the fact that an anchor is not doing any good at all as long as it is visible. It is only when it disappears in the deep beneath that it stabilizes and protects the ship; how beautiful the imagery of Christ's also being out of sight from Christians, having disappeared into the unseen world, but who is nevertheless connected with Christians by the strong and effective cable of his love, just as the anchor, though unseen, is connected to the ship by a mighty chain" (Coffman, *Hebrews*, 134).

[16] Attridge, *Hebrews*, 185.

[17] Herodotus, *Histories* 1.60; 4.121–22; 7.203; 9.14; Polybius, *Histories* 12.20.7.

of with this type of language (e.g., "founder," 2:10; "apostle," 3:1; "source," 5:9). As our forerunner, Jesus' presence behind this foreboding curtain is the assurance that we will join him in the inner sanctuary where God is (10:19, 22).[18] Those *in* Christ will be *with* Christ (John 14:1–4).

Jesus provides us with better access to God, access that neither Moses nor his law could ever offer. This is where our hope, our confidence, our assurance rests as Christians. As surely as God cannot lie, as surely as Jesus is now behind the curtain at God's right hand, so will we inherit every one of God's promises.

HEBREWS 7:1–10

A few years ago, I took my wife on a special trip to the islands for our tenth wedding anniversary. On that excursion, I went snorkeling for the first time. It was a fantastic adventure to swim through coral reefs and among the most exotic fish and marine life I'd ever seen. It was also a little intimidating. I've always been a good swimmer and never afraid of water, but being under the surface for such long periods was unnerving. More than once, I had to come up to breathe and get my bearings. The payoff, however, was more than worth a little unease.

Beginning with Hebrews 7, we are entering the most difficult chapters of this epistle. There is much in these chapters that is both fascinating and intimidating, the Melchizedek discussion arguably being the greatest in both categories. It will help as we move forward to "come up for a breath of fresh air" from time to time. Keep in mind that though these chapters talk about Melchizedek, the tabernacle, the old covenant, the heavenly sanctuary, and blood sacrifices, they're just decoration for the main exhibit. Don't get so bogged down in the details that you lose sight of our author's main point: we have a faithful and merciful—a promised, permanent, and perfect—high priest (8:1).

The payoff for your patience will be more than worth it.

>———◇———<

---

[18] Lane, *Hebrews 1–8*, 154.

Having first mentioned the mysterious Melchizedek in Hebrews 5 and naming him again at the close of Hebrews 6, our author finally gets around to elaborating on what he means that Jesus is an eternal high priest in the order of Melchizedek. Hebrews 5:1–10 had to do with Jesus' qualifications for the priesthood, and that conversation is resumed in Hebrews 7. Barclay captures well the importance of this section: "This priesthood after the order of Melchizedek is the most characteristic thought of Hebrews. Behind it lie ways of thinking and of arguing and of using Scripture which are quite strange to us and which we must try to understand."[19] To get on the same page as our first-century audience, let's go back to the beginning—or close to it.

In Genesis 14, Abraham learned Sodom had been sacked, and his nephew Lot had been hauled off as a POW. The patriarch saddled up a posse and led the successful liberation of the captives. Upon Abraham's return, Melchizedek, king of Salem (i.e., Jerusalem, Ps 76:2), came out to greet and bless him. In response, the patriarch honored Melchizedek by giving him a tenth of the spoil he had captured in his rescue mission.

Our author wants us to be impressed with the significance of Melchizedek's name and title. His name, a combination of the Hebrew *melek* and *sedeq* ("king" and "righteousness," respectively), is not the only factor that should remind us of Jesus. Melchizedek was also the king of Salem, a name that means "peace." "These concepts of righteousness and peace are appropriate for one who prefigures the Messiah, who would make righteousness and peace possible for the people of God."[20]

Though Melchizedek is an enigmatic figure in the Old Testament, our author did not need to jog his readers' collective memory as to the king's identity. The Dead Sea Scrolls discovery revealed that Melchizedek had become the object of significant fascination and speculation within Judaism by the first century. One scroll (c. early first century) depicts Melchizedek as an angel and central player of the end times (11QMelchizedek 2.6, 13). In the pseudepigraphal *2 Enoch* (also c. first century), the child Melchizedek is rescued from Noah's flood and transported by the archangel Michael to Paradise, where he serves as a priest forever (*2 Enoch* 71–72). Other

---

[19] Barclay, *Hebrews*, 75.
[20] Guthrie, *Hebrews*, 253.

documents from this period identify Melchizedek as the archangel Michael and claim he is "the highest archangel in charge of the heavenly priesthood."[21] Readers of Hebrews would have been familiar, to varying degrees, with the speculation concerning Melchizedek, just as most any American has heard tall tales about Davy Crockett, Clark Kent, or Chuck Norris.[22]

However, just as abruptly as Melchizedek appears on the pages of Scripture, he disappears, never to be mentioned again in Genesis. "He crosses the sky like a meteor, nobody knowing where he comes from or where he is going to."[23] His sudden appearance/disappearance is what our author is alluding to when he says of Melchizedek, "He is without father or mother or genealogy, having neither beginning of days nor end of life, but resembling the Son of God he continues a priest forever" (v 3). This doesn't mean Melchizedek was a mythical character[24] or a divine figure versus a flesh-and-blood person, though this has been hotly debated through the centuries.[25]

No, our author uses an argument from silence to present Melchizedek as a priest of a different sort, of an order unlike Levi's. If no mention is made of his parents in Scripture,[26] the logical conclusion is that Melchizedek held his office by virtue of something other than his birth and lineage—and he did! His priesthood was by virtue of God's call, as is Jesus' (5:5–6). In contrast, priests of Levi had to authenticate their right to serve by presenting evidence of their lineage (Num 3:10; Ezra 2:61–63). For our author, this divergence established Melchizedek's priesthood as greater than the priests descended from Levi.

---

[21] D. C. Allison, Jr., "Melchizedek," *DLNT* 730.

[22] "While the author is not directly dependent on the secondary literature on Melchizedek, he is probably responding to conversations that were taking place in the first century AD" (Thompson, *Hebrews*, 146). For more on Melchizedek in first-century Jewish thought, see the excursus in Attridge, *Hebrews*, 192–95.

[23] M. Delcor, "Melchizedek from Genesis to the Qumran Texts and the Epistle to the Hebrews," *JSJ* 2 (1971): 115.

[24] "It is very likely that the verse [v 3] has to be interpreted as: he did have a genealogy, though not the required one. … Obviously, Melchizedek did have parents. But he did not have the right of kingship or priesthood on account of his descent" (M. J. Paul, "The Order of Melchizedek (Ps 110:4 and Heb 7:3)," *WTJ* 49 [1987]: 205, 207). "While our author was probably inspired to engage in his treatment of Melchizedek by contemporary speculation on the shadowy figure of the ancient priest, his own handling of the topic is tantalizingly restrained. Ultimately he is concerned not so much with Melchizedek as with Christ, and what he says of the former is influenced heavily by what he firmly believes of the latter" (Attridge, *Hebrews*, 187).

[25] Bruce, *Hebrews*, 159–60, n. 20.

[26] Melchizedek's story is not introduced by a genealogy, as are other major characters' accounts in Genesis.

Indeed, in verses 4–10, Melchizedek's superiority to both Abraham and Levi is emphasized. "See how great this man was," our author invites (v 4). He considers Melchizedek great for at least three reasons. First, Melchizedek blessed Abraham, the great patriarch "who had the promises." Abraham was important, no argument—he was a "prince of God" (Gen 23:6) and called "my friend" by God (Isa 41:8; 2 Chr 20:7; Jas 2:23). Yet Melchizedek was greater since the superior always blesses the inferior (v 7).[27] This alone was a startling claim, for Abraham was held in the deepest reverence by the Jews. On the other hand, Melchizedek was "of such importance that he could bless Abraham, even when Abraham appears to be the most blessed human being on the planet."[28]

Second, the Israelites gave their tithes to "mortal men," priests destined for the grave. "But Abraham paid tithes to a priest who, the Scripture says, 'lives'" (v 8 Msg). What we need, our author argues, is a living priesthood, and "Melchizedek points to Jesus Christ as the resurrected one. Do the readers want to attach themselves to priests who die or to a great high priest who has conquered death and lives forever?"[29]

Finally, the Israelites paid tithes to the Levitical priesthood as a form of honor (Num 18:21–24, 28; Neh 10:38–39), and it could be said that Levi indirectly paid tithes to Melchizedek for the same reason (vv 9–10). If so, the order of Levi must be inferior to the order of Melchizedek.[30]

>———◇———<

What does Hebrews mean when it says Christ is a high priest after the order of Melchizedek? Before I list three answers to that question, it might help us for a moment to invert the statement and see *Melchizedek* as a high priest after the order of Jesus Christ, the Son of God. "The direction of thought is important: the Son of God is not like Melchizedek; rather,

---

[27] Our author's logic initially seems suspect; there are plenty of examples in Scripture of an inferior blessing a superior (e.g., Deut 8:10; 2 Sam 14:22; 1 Kgs 8:66). In Genesis, however, a superior almost always blesses an inferior (i.e., fathers blessing their sons).

[28] Mohler, *Exalting Jesus*, 103.

[29] Schreiner, *Hebrews*, 213.

[30] One might ask, "If Levi honored Melchizedek through Abraham, couldn't the same be said for Christ, since he also descended from Abraham?" No, because as our Lord made clear, "Before Abraham was, I am" (John 8:58). Jesus is the eternal Son of God, without beginning or end.

Melchizedek is like the Son of God, who is the principal reality."[31] As far as we know, our author was the first Christian writer to elucidate Psalm 110:4 as prophesying the high priesthood of Christ, especially in light of that priesthood's connection to Melchizedek. His choice of words (Christ "after the order of Melchizedek") likely reflects the fact that our author was trying to explain to his audience an unknown concept (the priesthood of Christ) using an understood one (the priesthood of Melchizedek). However, two thousand years removed from the world of Hebrews, we are more familiar with Jesus than with Melchizedek, so it might help us to think of Melchizedek as a priest after the order of Christ.

But back to our question: how is Christ a high priest of the order of Melchizedek? First, Christ is like Melchizedek *in terms of order and rank*. Melchizedek is the first priest mentioned in Scripture; his priestly order was superior to Levi's because it came first chronologically.[32] Melchizedek's priesthood was also first in rank. He was both priest and king. In contrast, no monarch of Israel ever held both offices. Even more, Melchizedek was a king of righteousness and peace.[33] So Christ, following Melchizedek as Psalm 110 claims, tops Levi in both order and rank.

Second, Christ is a high priest like Melchizedek in that *he does not have a priestly lineage*. He holds his office by God's appointment, not by genealogy. If translated literally, verse 3 reads, "fatherless, motherless, genealogy-less." This phrase in Greek was a bit of a slur in the first century, at least when it referred to a mortal; otherwise, it implied divine status.[34] Of course, Jesus of Nazareth had a father, a mother, and a genealogy (Matt 1:1–16; Luke 3:23–38; Rom 1:3), though it has already been established in Hebrews that the supreme Son of God preexisted all things and will outlast all things (1:2, 10–12). His earthly lineage has no bearing on his heavenly priesthood.

Third, Christ is a high priest like Melchizedek because *he is eternal*. Priests of the order of Levi were mortal. When Aaron died, the garments

---

[31] Koester, *Hebrews*, 343.

[32] Both Philo (*Alleg. Interp.* 3.79) and Josephus (*Wars* 6.438) claimed Melchizedek was an archetype for all priests since he came first.

[33] "Clearly, Melchizedek as a priest-king of righteousness and peace typifies the qualities that are characteristic of Messiah's kingdom" (Lightfoot, *Jesus Christ Today*, 138; Ps 72:7; Isa 9:6–7; Jer 23:5; John 14:27; Rom 5:1; 2 Cor 5:21; Eph 2:14–17).

[34] Koester, *Hebrews*, 342, 348.

of his office were passed to Eleazar (Num 20:22–29). Aaron's *priesthood* was perpetual, but the *priests* were not; neither Aaron nor his descendants served forever. That makes our author's phrase "having neither beginning of days nor end of life" (v 3) particularly striking. In Greek literature, this phrase implied divine status,[35] and in ancient Judeo-Christian literature, it unequivocally referred to God.[36]

This begs the question: did our author imply that Melchizedek of Genesis was a divine being (rather than human)? Again, no. Our author is making an argument from the silence of Scripture; Melchizedek was a shadow of the Son of God[37] ("resembling," v 3). Intriguingly, our author does not regard Melchizedek as a rival to Christ as he did Moses, Aaron, and the angels. If Melchizedek were indeed more than human, one would think Hebrews would downplay him in contrast to Christ. As it is, "Hebrews extols Melchizedek, not for his own sake, but to convey the greatness of the Son of God, whom he prefigures."[38]

HEBREWS 7:11–19

Moving forward, it will help to bear in mind that our author is thinking of two spheres of reality (earth versus heaven, mortal versus immortal), not just two places on a timeline (old versus new).[39] Having established Melchizedek's—and Christ's—superiority to Abraham (who held the promises) and Levi (who held the priesthood), Hebrews now argues that the law is also inferior and that Jesus inaugurates a better covenant, one granting perfection.

Remember that "perfection" in Hebrews carries not only a moral nuance ("without flaw") but also a telic one ("arriving at a desired end/

[35] Jerome H. Neyrey, "'Without Beginning of Days or End of Life' (Hebrews 7:3): Topos for a True Deity," *CBQ* 53 (1991): 439–55.

[36] Richard Bauckham, "The Divinity of Jesus Christ in the Epistle to the Hebrews," in *The Epistle to the Hebrews and Christian Theology*, eds. Richard Bauckham et al. (Grand Rapids: Eerdmans, 2009), 30–32.

[37] "The exalted Christ is like a person who stands before the sun and casts a shadow upon earth. Those who look at the shadow can discern in it the contours of the one who made it. Similarly, Hebrews considers Melchizedek to be an earthly shadow that the risen Christ casts back on the page of OT Scripture, and the author will speak about Melchizedek in order to bear witness to the Son of God whom he represents (7:3)" (Koester, *Hebrews*, 346).

[38] Koester, 350.

[39] James W. Thompson, "The Conceptual Background and Purpose of the Midrash in Hebrews VII," *NovT* 19 (1977): 217, n. 26.

reaching a goal"). In verse 11, this perfection or desired end is "the establishment of right relationship with God through the cleansing of the conscience and the consummation of this relationship in everlasting glory, rest, and celebration in God's heavenly city."[40] If the law and the Levitical priesthood had been able to make us perfect in that sense, another covenant/priesthood would have been unnecessary.

Later, we learn the law was inadequate—weak and useless, our author claims—and was thus "set aside" in favor of a new covenant (vv 18–19), one that gives us hope of perfection and offers unfettered access to God. The term translated "set aside" (*athetēsis*) referred to legal annulments and debt cancellations.[41] It is a more forceful word than that used in verse 12, which is "change" (*metatithēmi*). The law was annulled because it was useless to accomplish God's purpose for his people—not because God is weak or makes mistakes, but because he never intended it to be more than a shadow of a grander reality. The reality is not at odds with the shadow; it is the shadow's perfection or fulfillment.[42]

By extension, if the law was inadequate or imperfect, so was Aaron's priestly order (v 11), for the two were inextricably intertwined. A change in the law necessitated a change in the priesthood. The inverse is also true, our author says. If there is a change in the priesthood, as Psalm 110:4 implied would happen, the law must also change (v 12). If God appointed a priest that was not from Levi (vv 13–14)—which the law prohibited—it means he must have annulled the entire old covenant, our author reasons.[43] And as it was with the old, so it is with the new: in the order of Melchizedek, covenant and priesthood are still inextricably intertwined. Far from being useless, however, this new covenant is perfect in that it brings to fulfillment God's purposes for his people: cleansing, access, glory, and rest.

The Hebrews audience can't be blamed for asking, "How can God set aside the old covenant in favor of a new one and expect us to believe it will

[40] Koester, *Hebrews*, 353.

[41] BDAG, s.v. "ἀθέτησις"; Silva, "ἀθετέω," *NIDNTTE* 1:160; e.g., Gal 2:21; 3:15; 2 Maccabees 14:28.

[42] Moisés Silva, "Perfection and Eschatology in Hebrews," *WTJ* 39 (1976): 68.

[43] "The appointment as high priest of the exalted Christ is not merely an incident which concerns an individual: it entails the setting up of a whole new order; as chaps. 8–9 will express it, a new covenant, with consequences for all believers" (Ellingworth, *Hebrews*, 378).

hold? How do we know this new covenant (and, by extension, Jesus' priesthood) is permanent? Wasn't Aaron's priesthood to be permanent?"[44] When our author invokes Psalm 110:4 in verse 21, he expounds on two words, "forever" and "sworn." He argues that a change in the priesthood is apparent because our high priest descended from Judah, not Levi (vv 13–14). This means Jesus' priesthood is by God's appointment, and this provides our author an opportunity to discuss another aspect of Jesus' priesthood: its permanence.

Jesus "has become a priest … by the power of an indestructible life" (v 16). What *appeared* to be true of Melchizedek in Genesis is *actually* true of Christ. He has "neither beginning of days or end of life, but … continues [as] a priest forever" (v 3). The grave prevented any priest of Aaron (or Melchizedek, for that matter) from serving in perpetuity, yet Jesus has conquered the grave (vv 23–24). Subsequently, "where there is a priest forever there is obviously no necessity for a law regarding priestly succession, for the very idea of succession is ruled out in the case of him whose priesthood is forever."[45] Christ's eternality, or permanence, makes the old covenant unnecessary.

I want to call attention to three words our author employs in verses 14–16 to stress Jesus' permanence. His choice of *anatellō* ("descended," v 14) is odd given its meaning "to rise/spring up." When Paul speaks of Jesus as being "descended" from David (Rom 1:3), he uses the more common verb *ginomai*. Moreover, *anatellō* was never used in classical Greek or the LXX in reference to one's genealogical descent. It *does* make an appearance in the LXX in messianic passages (e.g., Num 24:17; Jer 23:5; Mal 4:2). "Even when referring to Christ's human ancestry [Hebrews] must distinguish him from those whose priesthood was dependent on their genealogy. They may have descended from a particular tribe, but he, even in his incarnation, 'arose.' He receives no authority from his ancestry."[46] Most New Testament uses of *anatellō* refer to sunrise, and Mark 16:2 is especially tantalizing: "Very early on the first day of the week, when the sun had risen [*anatellō*], they went

---

[44] Exod 40:15; Num 18:19; 25:13; 1 Maccabees 2:54; Josephus, *Antiquities* 2.216.

[45] P. Hughes, *Commentary*, 264.

[46] Cockerill, *Hebrews*, 320; see also Schreiner, *Hebrews*, 219–20.

to the tomb." Sunrise on Easter morning found our high priest had risen to die no more.

Jesus' resurrection qualified his priesthood, a fact that "becomes even more evident when another priest *arises* in the likeness of Melchizedek" (v 15; emphasis mine). The verb *anistēmi* ("arises") here is the book of Acts' favorite way of referring to Jesus' resurrection (e.g., Acts 2:24; 3:26; 17:31). Granted, in verse 15 and elsewhere (e.g., Acts 7:18), it means "to come/appear to carry out a function or role,"[47] but the dual meaning can't be coincidental. Jesus rose from the dead to assume his role as high priest.

Our author's third word for Jesus' permanence is *akatalytos* ("indestructible," v 16). The term occurs nowhere else in the New Testament. Jesus' life was not destroyed by his crucifixion—far from it. Instead, the resurrection, ascension, and exaltation of the supreme Son of God demonstrated and declared his indestructibility. In turn, Jesus' indestructibility means his priesthood is superior in rank to Aaron, for it belongs to a different realm (heaven, not earth; immortal, not mortal).[48]

In verses 18–19, our author brings his point to a climax. He uses a stock Greek construction, the combination *men ... de*, which is translated "on the one hand, ... but on the other hand." When Greek writers used such a phrase, their emphasis was always on the *de* or "the other hand."[49] The law was set aside because it was weak and useless; it could not accomplish God's purpose: perfection for his people. The law could not give hope; the law could not cleanse; the law could not draw us near to God in confidence and boldness.[50] What God has replaced it with—the permanent priesthood of the supreme Son ("but on the other hand")—has achieved what God purposed all along. "It is in this great truth—the fact that Jesus Christ is the High Priest of Christians—that the treasures of forgiveness, access to God, strength, consolation, and care are to be found."[51] This is the "better hope" of which our author speaks. How we draw closer to God will

[47] BDAG, s.v. "ἀνίστημι."

[48] Lane, *Hebrews 1–8*, 184. "It must be emphasized that this 'indestructible life' is not a description of but the basis and cause of his all-effective priesthood" (Cockerill, *Hebrews*, 323).

[49] Lane, *Hebrews 1–8*, 185.

[50] Schreiner, *Hebrews*, 226.

[51] David J. MacLeod, "Christ, the Believer's High Priest: An Exposition of Hebrews 7:26–28," *BSac* 162 (2005): 331–32.

be explained later (10:19–22), but the fact that we now have access to God in Christ makes his new covenant greater than the old.[52]

HEBREWS 7:20–28

Recall our question from a few paragraphs ago: "How do we know this new covenant and new priesthood are permanent?" The permanence or eternal nature of Jesus' priesthood is supported by (1) his indestructibility and (2) the Father's oath. Granted, God had made a covenant with Israel (the law) and Aaron (the priesthood). However, just as it was popularly understood that the maker of a will had the right to change it later as long as he was alive, our author assumes that "the living God" has the prerogative to change his covenant with his people.[53]

Yet the new covenant, which establishes Jesus' priesthood, is backed by an oath from none other than God himself (v 21). Our author makes a big deal about this.[54] The Levitical priests were not installed via an oath, only a command (Exod 29:35). Here, though, "the divine oath verifies the absolute reliability of the priesthood of Christ, upon which the hopes of the Christian community are anchored (6:18–20)."[55] Unlike with the perpetuity of Aaron's priestly order, God will not change his mind on this. Recall our author's words in 6:17: God swears an oath when he wants to assure us that he will not change his mind. "If you are looking for an oath as a sign of certitude," our author says, "Jesus has it, and they don't!"[56]

Therefore, "this makes Jesus the guarantor of a better covenant"[57] (v 22). A guarantor (*engyos*) provided surety that a promise would be kept or

---

[52] Bruce, *Hebrews*, 169–70.

[53] Koester, *Hebrews*, 361. He later quotes one of the Oxyrhynchus Papyri (#492.9): "So long as I live I am to have power … to make any further provisions or new dispositions I choose and to abrogate this will, and any such provisions shall be valid" (*Hebrews*, 373).

[54] "He uses the double negative, 'not without an oath,' to affirm the reality of this oath in the most emphatic way. … The word order and economy of style evident in these verses allows the emphasis to fall on the phrases 'not without an oath' (v. 20a); 'without an oath' (v. 20b); and 'with an oath' (v. 21a). The magnitude of the Son's having been made priest by the divine oath breaks all bounds" (Cockerill, *Hebrews*, 328–29).

[55] Lane, *Hebrews 1–8*, 187.

[56] Johnson, *Hebrews*, 191.

[57] This is the first occurrence of "covenant" (*diathēkē*) in Hebrews, and it will become a key term in 8:1–10:18, occurring fourteen times.

an agreement honored;[58] the term carries the same idea as "anchor" in 6:19. Unlike a mediator (*mesitēs*, see 8:6; 9:15; 12:24), a guarantor had a heavier responsibility since he staked "his person and his life on his word"[59] (e.g., Gen 43:1–14). Sirach's words are especially helpful here: "A good person will be surety [*engyos*] for his neighbor, but the one who has lost all sense of shame will fail him. Do not forget the kindness of your guarantor [*engyos*], for he has given his life for you" (29:14–15 NRSV). Ironically, Proverbs warns of the risk of providing surety for another (17:18; 22:26; see also Sirach 29:19). Yet Jesus has done precisely that—he "guarantees God's fidelity and faithfulness."[60]

It's then that we come to the majestic "so what" of this entire chapter. Jesus' priesthood is superior to Aaron's, but not because his is new and the other is old. As I mentioned before, Jesus isn't better because of his placement on the historical timeline. Jesus is supreme because of the realm he occupies.[61] In verses 23–24, our author once again uses the Greek construction *men ... de* ("on the one hand, ... but on the other hand"), though it is left untranslated in most English versions. The construction places in sharp contrast the fact that the Levitical priesthood was limited by the priests' own mortality (v 23). Not only does the book of Numbers record Aaron's death (20:22–29), but it also presupposes that the death of the high priest would be a frequent event (35:25, 28, 32). Jesus, on the other hand,[62] defeated death through death (Heb 2:14) and thus "holds his priesthood *permanently*, because he *continues* forever" (7:24; emphasis mine).

"Permanently" (*aparabatos*) occurs only here in the New Testament and has as its root the verb *parabainō*, meaning "to go beyond or transgress." The prefix "a-" in Greek turns something into a negative (e.g., an "a-theist" is someone who negates or denies God); thus, *a-parabatos* meant something that could *not* be transgressed, passed over, superseded, etc. A legal decree that was *aparabatos* was absolute. In Jesus' case, his priesthood

[58] Plutarch, *Alcibiades* 5.2–3; Xenophon, *Taxes* 4.20.

[59] Lane, *Hebrews 1–8*, 188.

[60] Schreiner, *Hebrews*, 230.

[61] "The levitical priesthood belongs to the sphere of death; because of the exaltation, Christ now is in the sphere of life" (Thompson, "Conceptual Background," 216).

[62] "Like Israel's priests, Jesus did die, yet death did not terminate his priesthood, but rather inaugurated it" (Koester, *Hebrews*, 371).

is *aparabatos*, meaning it "will not be replaced. It is not relative but absolute in character."[63] It cannot be superseded; it cannot be defeated; it cannot be undone. Ellingworth goes so far as to suggest a link with 12:27—Christ's priesthood "cannot be shaken."[64]

The verb translated "continues" (*menō*) occurs throughout the LXX in reference to God[65] (e.g., Pss 9:8; 102:12; Dan 6:26), particularly his perpetual presence as the "living God." Without beginning or end, the Father simply *is*. He remains or continues, as does the Son (1:11–12; 13:8). The Jews anticipated that their Messiah would remain forever (John 12:34), and Jesus does. He is the living Son of the living God.

It is precisely because Jesus "continues" (v 24) in his permanent priesthood that "he is able to save to the uttermost those who draw near to God through him" (v 25). The word translated "uttermost" (*pantelēs*) means "completely" or "totally" but also "forever" or "for all time."[66] The salvation available only through Jesus is total and forever. This is the emphasis of the verse. There is no limit to the *degree* or *duration* of the salvation offered to us by our faithful and merciful high priest.

God's sworn oath backs this great truth. As certain as he kept his oath to Abraham and David (Gen 22:16–17; Ps 89:35–36), as certain as he kept his oath to leave a generation of Israelites to rot in the wilderness for their rebellion (Ps 95:11), as certain as he kept his oath to deliver Israel from Assyria (Isa 14:24–25), as certain as he kept his oath to exile his people to Babylon (Jer 22:5), as certain as he kept his oath to humiliate the enemies of his people (Jer 49:13; 51:14), as certain as he will one day fulfill every one of his mysteries and purposes (Rev 10:6–7), as certain as he will one day fulfill his promise to see every knee bow and tongue confess (Isa 45:23)—that is the certainty we have that our high priest continues forever and will save us to the uttermost.

Do not move beyond verse 25 without appreciating its final clause. Jesus is "able to save to the uttermost" *only* because "he always lives to

---

[63] Johnson, *Hebrews*, 193. In similar usage, Plutarch held "the course of the sun to be fixed and unchangeable [*aparabatos*]" (*Obsolescence of Oracles* 3).

[64] Paul Ellingworth, "The Unshakable Priesthood: Hebrews 7.24," *JSNT* 23 (1985): 125–26.

[65] Friedrich Hauck, "μένω," *TDNT* 4:574–75.

[66] BDAG, s.v. "παντελής."

make intercession for them." Our salvation is due not just to Jesus' sacrifice at the cross or to his resurrection but to Jesus' crucifixion, resurrection, *and* ongoing intercession on our behalf at the Father's right hand. Our salvation is dependent on the permanency of Jesus' priesthood. "Who is to condemn? Christ Jesus is the one who died—more than that, who was raised—who is at the right hand of God, who indeed is interceding for us" (Rom 8:34).

In Jewish literature, the verb rendered "to make intercession" (*entynchanō*) often meant "to pray" when directed to God.[67] Have you ever considered the fact that Jesus "prays" for us? Even now, Jesus is praying to his Father on our behalf, and he will continue to do so into the ages. The Scottish preacher Robert Murray McCheyne once said, "If I could hear Christ praying for me in the next room, I would not fear a million of enemies. Yet the distance makes no difference; He is praying for me."[68] For the distraught Christian, the prayerful intercession of Christ means everything since "his advocacy is the safeguard of his church."[69]

As a final note, there is no limit to the degree or duration of Jesus' salvation, but there is a limit to its *demographic*. It extends only to "those who draw near to God through him." Jesus' atonement was for the whole world (1 John 2:2), but the efficacy of that atonement is accessible only to those who approach the Father (John 14:6) *and continue to request it*. Piper notes that "draw near" is a present continuous action versus a single past action. The passage "is not saying: God is able to save those forever who once drew near to him, but who go on drawing near to him. If we do not go on drawing near to God we have no warrant for thinking that we are being saved by the Lord Jesus."[70] To his audience, the Hebrews author was adamant: "If you turn your back on Jesus and return to Moses, you forfeit the advocacy and intercession Jesus provides as your high priest. Do not turn your back on your superior high priest!"

---

[67] Wisdom of Solomon 8:21; 16:28; BDAG, s.v. "ἐντυγχάνω."

[68] Robert Murray McCheyne and Andrew A. Bonar, *Memoir and Remains of the Rev. Robert Murray McCheyne* (Edinburgh: Oliphant, 1894), 158.

[69] Simpson, "Vocabulary," 187.

[70] John Piper, "Jesus: From Melchizedek to Eternal Savior," *Desiring God*, 1 December 1996, http://www.desiringgod.org/messages/jesus-from-melchizedek-to-eternal-savior.

In the chapter's final verses, our author merges the themes of intercession and perfection as a means of transitioning to the theme of Christ's
self-sacrifice in 8:1–10:18. Piling synonyms atop one another, he says Jesus
was "holy, innocent, unstained, separated from sinners, and exalted above
the heavens" (v 26). These first three terms, which could be translated as
"covenant keeping, without evil, without blemish,"[71] describe Jesus' relationship with God, others, and himself, respectively.[72] There isn't much
nuance between these terms, but in the LXX, the word translated "holy"
(*hosios*) "describes those whose relationship to God and to others reflects
fidelity to the covenant."[73] "Innocent" (*akakos*) connotes pure motives or a
lack of guile, and "unstained" (*amiantos*) refers to purity or "freedom from
blemish and spot."[74] Despite his total immersion into the human experience, these terms testify to the sinlessness of our high priest.

The last two phrases allude to Jesus' present status. Christ is "separated
from sinners" in that he no longer lives among sinful men by virtue of his
ascension and exaltation "above the heavens" to God's right hand.[75] Jesus'
permanence means his people have no reason to fear that he might one
day have to relinquish his priesthood to an inferior successor. There is no
chance that Jesus can lose his priesthood in the future by sinning. He will
never be disqualified from his office. However, though Jesus' place at God's
right hand has removed him from earth in a physical sense, there is no re-
moteness between him and his brethren; Christ remains spiritually present
and personally involved with us and our struggles.[76]

Note again the author's use of the phrase "it was indeed fitting" (v 26).
He previously used this phrase to describe God's decision to perfect the
Son through suffering in order to lead us to glory (2:10). But it is here
that we learn *why* the Son had to be perfected: it was so that, in our weakness, we might have access to a high priest who is supremely qualified in
all things. God considered it fitting to lead us to glory. He also found it

---

[71] Cockerill, *Hebrews*, 338.

[72] MacLeod, "Christ," 335–37.

[73] Lane, *Hebrews 1–8*, 191; e.g., Pss 12:1; 18:25; 32:6; 79:2; 132:9, 16; 149:1.

[74] MacLeod, "Christ," 337.

[75] Lane, *Hebrews 1–8*, 192.

[76] Lane, 193.

fitting to give us someone who can help us along the way, a high priest from whom "the faithful can expect sympathetic, effective, and assured intercession."[77]

What our author has said implicitly in verse 26, he makes explicit in verse 27. Jesus is superior to the Levitical priests in a spiritual and moral sense because, unlike them, he does not need to atone for his own sins before atoning for those of his people (5:3; Lev 16:6). Nor does he need to offer sacrifices *daily*. The Son's intercession continues forever, but his propitiation was "once for all."[78]

Imagine you were tried and justly convicted for a capital crime. After some time on death row, your execution is imminent. But as the eleventh hour nears, your case is taken up and advocated by someone who knows the governor personally. Given a choice, would you rather this advocate, your last hope, be someone who had experienced a falling-out with the governor years prior, someone against whom the governor bore a long-standing, completely justified grudge? Or would you prefer an advocate with a harmonious relationship with the state's chief executive? What about the governor's beloved, perfectly obedient, one-of-a-kind son? In Jesus, we have such an advocate. Because Christ did not need to atone for his own sins before atoning for ours, he was able upon his ascension to slide seamlessly into the role of eternal and favored intercessor.

Recall that at the end of verses 1–10, we asked, "What does it mean that Christ is a priest of the order of Melchizedek?" It means he is (1) a priest who is first in order or rank, (2) a priest by God's appointment, not by lineage, and (3) a priest who serves forever without end. Similarly, the chapter's final verse provides an excellent summation of all our author has said concerning Jesus' priesthood. It is:

> › **Promised.** The law made Aaron a priest; Christ has been appointed such by God's sworn oath.
> › **Permanent.** Aaron was a mortal, lowly man; Christ is the indestructible, supreme Son who serves forever.

---

[77] Attridge, *Hebrews*, 212.

[78] This is the common translation of the adverb *ephapax* (9:12; 10:10; Rom 6:10), which means "taking place once and to the exclusion of any further occurrence" (BDAG, s.v. "ἐφάπαξ").

> › **Perfect.** Aaron was weak and sinful; Christ "has been made per-
> fect forever" (v 28), making his priesthood first in rank.

To a large extent, these three themes of Jesus' priesthood apply to all
Hebrews has to say on the subject. In 5:1–10 and 6:13–20, our author
demonstrated how Christ was appointed by God's oath or *promise* versus
"from among men" by the law. Much of chapter 7 has been spent exploring
how Christ is like Melchizedek: as a priest without beginning or end, he
holds his office *permanently*. In what follows, our author will further expound upon the *perfection* of Christ versus the weakness of Aaron and his
sons (9:1–10:18). For now, however, it is abundantly clear that "alongside
this heavenly advocate, Melchizedek has no place."[79]

SUMMARY

» God has sworn an oath that Jesus is our high priest forever, and God is
trustworthy. His faithfulness provides refuge for his people.

» Jesus is a priest like Melchizedek in terms of order (first), rank (king-
priest), lineage (none), and duration (forever).

» A new priesthood required a new covenant. This new covenant accomplished what the old covenant never could.

» The permanence of Jesus' priesthood means we are saved to the uttermost—completely and forever.

---

[79] Lane, *Hebrews 1–8*, 190.

TALKING POINTS

HEBREWS DEPICTS Christians as having "fled for refuge" (6:18) to Christ and his church. "The author wants them to consider themselves coming to the church not as shoppers trying out a new philosophy, but as refugees, fleeing from the certified catastrophe of eschatological judgment."[80] If nothing in the soul responds to the thought of Jesus as our anchor; if nothing within us wells up in excitement at the notion of God's unyielding fidelity to his oath, then it can be reasonably asked: Are we aware of the swift and frightful fury headed our way? We hold fast to something only when we realize that utter destruction awaits those who lose their grip. That is why God in his mercy erodes our foundations in life—money, status, family, intellect, talent, experience, power, politics—until we recognize them as sinking sand and are forced to flee for refuge. On the other hand, "If we cleave to Jesus Christ we have anchored ourselves in the fastnesses of the divine nature. We have struck the roots of our hopes deep into the very being of God; and all that is majestic, all that is omnipotent, all that is tender, all that is immutable in Him goes to confirm to my poor heart the astounding expectation that whatsoever Christ is I shall become, and that wheresoever Christ is there will also His servant be. Oh! how this rock-foundation on which we may build makes all the other foundations upon which men rest their ruinable hopes seem wretched and transitory."[81]

>————◇————<

FAR DEADLIER than any biological contagion known to us, hopelessness has become an international pandemic. The playwright Jean Kerr wrote, "Hope is the feeling you have that the feeling you have isn't permanent."[82] When Hebrews speaks of hope, does it have in mind the sort of wishful, fleeting thinking reflected in Kerr's line? Hardly. Christian hope is not subjective but objective; it isn't grounded in ourselves (e.g., our attitude) but in the atonement and advocacy of Jesus. This is the "hope set before us" (6:18) as a

---

[80] DeSilva, *Perseverance*, 252.

[81] Maclaren, *Expositions*, 29:399–400.

[82] Jean Kerr, *Finishing Touches*, act III.

gift from the Spirit (Rom 15:13). Not wanting us to be plagued by hopelessness, Jesus has acted and is acting to give us hope. He has acted—sin is the source of all suffering in the world, and he has dealt with sin decisively. He is acting—whatever threatens to rob us of hope is brought to the Father's attention by his faithful advocacy. In return, the Lord wants us to trust that he is both sovereign and immutable—in control and unchanging. We grow hopeless when we believe ourselves ill-suited for what lies ahead, but Christ our atonement and Christ our advocate is sufficient provision for the unknown. For now, it is only our hope that has pierced the veil between heaven and earth, entering behind the curtain into God's immediate presence.[83] But that unseen realm is more real than the world we see around us presently. Thus the Christian's hope is not wishful thinking but confident assurance anchored deep in Him who remains and continues sure and steadfast.

>———◇———<

IT CAN BE confusing to consider, on the one hand, that God cannot lie (6:18) and, on the other hand, that he nullified his covenant with Israel and Aaron in favor of a new and better covenant. Are God's integrity and the notion of a new covenant mutually exclusive? Not at all. The covenant of Moses was conditional on Israel's faithfulness; legally, God was not bound to uphold his part of the covenant if Israel rebelled against him (and Hebrews has demonstrated that they did). In contrast, two factors make God's promise concerning Jesus' priesthood unimpeachable. (1) God has sworn that Jesus will be our high priest forever, though he never swore such an oath to Aaron (7:20–21). Before you object that this is a technicality (as in a child saying, "Well, I promised, but I didn't pinky-promise!"), consider that (2) Jesus' priesthood under the new covenant isn't conditional. Our faithlessness does not remove Jesus from office; it only restricts us from laying claim to the benefits of his office. Put another way, this new covenant or contract with God—one "brokered" (mediated) through Jesus—is as safe a bet as can be imagined. None less than the supreme Son himself is the Father's guarantee that he will not violate his oath (7:22). If we ignore the world's call to

[83] DeSilva, *Perseverance*, 252.

abdicate our confession and instead maintain our allegiance to Jesus, God will surely reward us far beyond our wildest imaginations.

>———◇———<

IN ONE SENSE, our salvation was secured by Christ's death on the cross. In another sense, his death had no efficacy to save were it not for the resurrection. But we must add to that the reality that it is now his present intercession that continues to secure our salvation (7:25). No singular action on Christ's part effected our salvation as much as a combination of his death, resurrection, and ascension. Our victory over sin is a product of Jesus' present intercession on our behalf. On the night before his death, Jesus told Peter, "Satan has asked to sift you like wheat. But I have prayed for you that your faith may not fail" (Luke 22:31–32 csb). "If it be asked what form his heavenly intercession takes, what better answer can be given than that he still does for his people at the right hand of God what he did for Peter on earth?"[84] We can also consider our spiritual growth to be a result of Jesus' intercession. Though the phrase is not present in the chapter, John 17 is often known as the "High Priestly Prayer." In it, Jesus prayed for his followers, that God would keep them in his name (v 11), that he would protect them from Satan (v 15), that he would sanctify them with the Word (v 17), and that they would be united (vv 11, 21). There is no reason to believe that our Lord does not make the same requests now while ministering on our behalf at God's right hand.

>———◇———<

THOUGH THE high priesthood of Jesus may seem at first glance to be a deep concept with no practical application, it actually serves to meet our most basic needs. In his famous multi-volume exposition of Hebrews, John Owen noted eight of those needs that are reflected in Hebrews. (1) *Atonement:* We need a high priest who can pay the price for our sins (2:17). (2) *Purification:* We need a high priest who can cleanse our consciences (9:14). (3) *Acceptance:* We need a high priest who can make us acceptable to the

[84] Bruce, *Hebrews*, 174.

Father (10:19). (4) *Administration:* We need a high priest who can administer the spiritual blessings that provision our faith, worship, and obedience (13:15, 21). (5) *Assistance:* We need a high priest who can help when we are in need (2:17–18; 4:15–16). (6) *Protection:* We need a high priest who can protect us from spiritual threats (7:25). (7) *Answer:* We need a high priest who can answer our call for help (2:18). (8) *Final Salvation:* We need a high priest who can shepherd us until death and into eternal life (13:20–21).[85]

>———◇———<

STUDYING AND reflecting on Christ's priesthood has the potential to do extraordinary things for your faith. It has mine. Specifically, my focus on Christ's priesthood these past few years has affected my prayers, peace, and persistence. (1) *My prayer life has grown stronger.* For as long as I can remember, private prayer was difficult for me because I felt so inadequate. What right did I have to approach the Most High with my petitions? In Christ, I discovered I have *every* right—not due to anything I have done, but because the favor the Father shows his Son is extended to me by proxy. Contemplating the fervency of Jesus' prayers has given mine a boost of confidence. (2) *My inner peace has grown stronger.* Jesus' advocacy (7:25; 1 John 2:1) is the means of my salvation. Whatever guilt I feel for past sins is unnecessary if I have repented. The Son has convinced the Father to forgive *and* forget those sins. Instead of falling into the abyss of shame, I move forward from my sin in gratitude that Jesus continues to plead my case. (3) *My persistence in faith has grown stronger.* According to 2:18, Jesus, as high priest, gives me strength when I am tempted. In 4:16, this strength is described as timely help. Given the context of Hebrews, "One aspect of Christ's intercessory ministry is prayer for believers struggling with ... the temptation to deny the faith under persecution."[86] Later, our author will speak of how Jesus disregarded the cross' shame in favor of the joy that was before him (12:2). As I reflect on the faithful, obedient determination Jesus had to do the work appointed to him by the Father, I am encouraged to be faithful in my own life. Our Lord is the ultimate inspiration for faithful living.

[85] Owen, *Hebrews*, 5:548; see also MacLeod, "Christ," 334.
[86] Guthrie, *Hebrews*, 268.

Chapter 7

IT IS FINISHED

Throughout his youth, Judah had often accompanied his father to Jerusalem for the three annual feasts. One year, they made the journey south for the Feast of Booths a week early to be there for the observance of Yom Kippur (the Day of Atonement). He remembered watching with rapt attention as the high priest, dressed in special clothes reserved for only that day, faced west and placed his hands on the head of a bull, then a goat, and offered three prayers. The first was for the sins of the high priest and his family: "O Lord, I have committed iniquity, transgressed, and sinned before you, I and my house. O Lord, forgive the iniquities, transgressions, and sins, which I have done by committing iniquity, transgression, and sin before you, I and my house. As it is written in the Torah of Moses, your servant, 'For on this day shall atonement be made for you to clean you. From all of your sins shall you be clean before the Lord.'" The crowd responded, "Blessed is the name of the glory of his kingdom forever and ever."

The second prayer was for the sins of the high priest, his family, and the entire priesthood. Following the second prayer, the crowd again responded, "Blessed is the name of the glory of his kingdom forever and ever." Before the final prayer, the high priest placed both hands upon the scapegoat and confessed all Israel's sins. After the third prayer, the crowd fell prostrate on the ground and said, "Blessed be the name of the glory of his kingdom forever and ever."[1] It was then that the high priest made his annual journey beyond the sacred curtain to perform the ceremony of atonement in the Most Holy Place.

As a child, Judah had been in awe of the annual ritual and the priests' solemnity as they went about their work. As an adult, however, he couldn't

[1] *Yoma* 3.8; 4.2; 6.2.

help but be struck by the futility of it all. Instead of making him feel as if his sins were forgiven, Yom Kippur had always unnerved Judah with the oppressive realization of just how sinful he was. Every year, he resolved to live more in line with the Torah's teachings; each Yom Kippur marked another year of failure. One of the things he had loved about membership in this new sect called Christians was the absence of a yearly reminder of his own futility and failure. Other than that, he had never quite understood the difference between this new covenant and that of his fathers.

Judah noticed Timothy's voice growing in earnest: "…the covenant he mediates is better, since it is enacted on better promises."

>———◇———<

We have come to the heart of Hebrews, but it is undoubtedly the most foreign to a twenty-first-century Western mindset. In this section, our author explores several specifics of the old covenant, demonstrating in every instance how the new covenant of the supreme Son is better. As your guide through Hebrews, I'll do my best to keep you from getting bogged down or having your eyes glaze over. I've done enough hiking in unfamiliar country to appreciate the help landmarks or reference points can provide. To keep us from getting lost in this exotic jungle, note the seven ways our author will say the new covenant is better than the old:

1. It is based on better *promises* (sins forgiven *and* forgotten versus merely forgiven).
2. It effects a better *purity* (of the conscience versus only the flesh).
3. It offers a better *inheritance* (eternal versus temporal).
4. Christ enters into a better *sanctuary* (heaven versus earth).
5. Christ offers a better *sacrifice* (his blood versus an animal's).
6. Christ's sacrifice is a better *atonement* (once for all time versus for a day or a year).
7. We face a better *fate* when he returns (salvation versus judgment).

Everything our author says in this section ultimately comes back to his understanding of Jeremiah 31, which spoke of a new and better covenant six hundred years before the Word became flesh. It will help to keep that in mind.

That said, I want to urge you to take your time with this chapter. This is not a section of Hebrews one should rush through. As a prodigious fan of our national parks, I rank the Grand Canyon among my favorite places in the world. Of the over six million annual visitors, very few ever venture below the rim to get a close-up view of all the Grand Canyon has to offer. Instead, most make the hour-long drive from the interstate to the prominent overlooks at the South Rim and then leave.

Don't do that with this part of Hebrews. Take a walk down into this "canyon." Notice the intricate detail and rich color on display. Find a place in the shade to pause and ponder what you discover, a place to reflect and rejoice. Wrestle with it, then worship. Along the way, you'll notice that our author's discussion seems to circle back to a few essential themes: purification of the conscience, the certainty of our redemption, and the unprecedented access we now have to God through Christ. Our author is intentionally repetitive with these themes; he has to be, given this complex material overflowing with such eternal truths. Maybe the repetition is God's way of urging us to seize these better promises and hold fast our confession.

HEBREWS 8:1–7

Jesus is our high priest, and much of Hebrews 1–7 has been employed to establish that fact (8:1). In the previous chapter, our author focused on Jesus' superior priesthood; specifically, he connected the themes of priesthood and *sonship* in 7:28. In 8:1–2, he links the themes of priesthood and *session*[2] (i.e., Christ's exaltation and enthronement). He speaks to Jesus' superior ministry in a superior sanctuary (8:1–5) before transitioning to the superior covenant (8:6–10:18).

Jesus' priestly ministry is superior because he is seated at God's right hand in the heavenly sanctuary. Christ is an *enthroned* priest, our author

[2] Lane, *Hebrews 1–8*, 205.

says. "Not only did the high priest of Israel never sit down in the tabernacle, but he never sat down *on a throne*."[3] Yet Zechariah had foreseen one who "will build the LORD's temple; he will bear royal splendor and will sit on his throne and rule. There will be a priest on his throne, and there will be peaceful counsel between the two of them" (Zech 6:13 csb).

Hebrews also considers Jesus' session as a place of work. Christ is an *engaged* priest, our author says, "a minister in the holy places" (v 2). The word translated "minister" (*leitourgos*) was derived from a verb (*leitourgeō*) that means "to perform a public service" (e.g., Rom 13:6), particularly religious service of some kind and usually at one's personal expense[4] (e.g., Rom 15:16). At this moment, Jesus is engaged in work on behalf of his people. "While Christ's atoning work is finished, his advocating work is not. This mediatory work is the primary occupation of Christ in heaven."[5] I believe this is what our author is referring to when he mentions that every high priest needs something to offer (v 3; 5:1). In other words, if Jesus is our high priest, he has to be doing more than sitting around and marking time until the Second Coming. A priest offers something, and though the nature of Jesus' offering isn't explored until 9:14, our author would have us pause and ponder how wonderful it is that we have so great a high priest working even now on our behalf.

That Jesus serves in the heavenly versus the earthly sanctuary is also proof of his superiority. Talk of a heavenly tabernacle may be confusing to us today—where else would Jesus be ministering but in heaven? However, some in our author's time believed certain things on earth were only material copies, or shadows, of spiritual realities. They thought that an earthly thing had a spiritual counterpart (a philosophy originating with Plato). This idea is certainly reflected in the Jewish literature of the time. Guthrie draws attention to sources from the first century, including texts from the Dead Sea Scrolls, that spoke of a new Jerusalem and a new temple in the spiritual realm. Similarly, Paul referred to "the Jerusalem above" (Gal 4:26). John saw the holy city descend (Rev 21:1–22:5), though note that

---

[3] Wiersbe, *Bible Exposition*, 2:304; emphasis his.
[4] BDAG, s.v. "λειτουργέω"; Silva, "λειτουργέω," *NIDNTTE* 3:104–7; Johnson, *Hebrews*, 198.
[5] Mohler, *Exalting Jesus*, 120.

John says, "I saw no temple in the city, for the Lord God Almighty and the Lamb are its temple" (21:22 NLT).[6]

That there is no temple in the heavenly city makes sense. Recall that the tabernacle (and later the temple) represented God's presence among Israel (Exod 25:8; 1 Kgs 6:13). Correspondingly, our high priest ministers and intercedes on our behalf in the Father's presence (9:24), but because Jesus is in the *immediate* presence of God—in reality, not in a representative or shadowy way—his priestly work is inherently superior.[7] By "true tent" (v 2), our author does not mean the earthly one was false (as it would have been if it were pagan or illegitimate). At the same time, however, by calling the heavenly sanctuary "true," he nonetheless identifies the earthly tent as inferior (2 Cor 5:1). Since he is an eternal priest ministering in heaven, Jesus' ministry will not end, as will that of an earthly priest, for his is performed in a transcendent, unshaken realm versus a transient, volatile one (12:27–28).

That last point is underscored by the fact that the Levitical priesthood, the tabernacle, and the sacrificial system were an earthly "copy and shadow" (a phrase Lane renders as "a shadowy suggestion"[8]) of what is in heaven. The word translated "copy" (*hypodeigma*) can refer to a sketch or outline. We're familiar with two-dimensional blueprints used by builders or three-dimensional models of proposed complexes such as airports, hospitals, or universities. Such a blueprint or model is essential, but it's not the same as the real thing. In fact, a sketch or model scarcely compares to the real thing when you think about it.

God showed Moses a "sketch" of the tabernacle on Sinai (v 5; Exod 25:9, 40), and this was the blueprint used for its construction. Yet the earthly tabernacle was an incomplete model, a "shadow" (*skia*) of the heavenly tabernacle—clear enough to point to it but faint enough not to be mistaken for it. Though he was referring to feasts, kosher laws, and Sabbath observances, Paul's words to the Colossians are relevant here: "These are a shadow of the things to come, but the substance belongs to Christ" (2:17).

---

[6] George H. Guthrie, "Hebrews," in *Zondervan Illustrated Bible Backgrounds Commentary: Hebrews to Revelation*, ed. Clinton E. Arnold (Grand Rapids: Zondervan, 2002), 4:48.

[7] "The logic is impeccable. If what defines a sanctuary is the presence of God, where God essentially and eternally exists must be the real 'holy place.' All of the subsequent argument flows from this simple imaginative premise" (Johnson, *Hebrews*, 198).

[8] Lane, *Hebrews 1–8*, 206. "Copy" and "shadow" in v 5 are synonymous (Ellingworth, *Hebrews*, 406).

The idea of earthly copies and shadows was common in the philosophies of Plato and Philo. In the former's parable of the cave, the famed Athenian philosopher described people seeing shadows on a cave wall and mistaking those shadows for reality. Our author may be borrowing this idea in a general sense, but this is where the similarities end between Plato and Hebrews.[9] For our author, the concept of earthly versus heavenly sanctuaries is not a philosophical exercise or metaphysical puzzle. It is an expression of what our high priest is accomplishing on our behalf even now. Our author isn't being philosophical but rather theological and practical. His audience was flirting with a return to what was superficial and transient; he wanted them to remain tethered to their anchor, to what is as true as it is spiritual, as real as it is supernatural, and as permanent as it is profound.[10]

"This is what we have," our author essentially says. "A superior priest (Jesus), seated in a superior position (the right hand), ministering in a superior place (the heavenly sanctuary)." Such is proof that our priest mediates a superior covenant based on superior promises (the dual use of "better" in v 6 is emphatic). With this, our author turns his attention to delineating the new covenant's superiority and detailing what comprises those superior promises.

HEBREWS 8:8–13

This is not the only place the New Testament speaks of a new covenant. However, the theme is nowhere else as fully developed as it is in Hebrews. So far, we have seen our author use Psalm 95 extensively throughout chapters 3–4, Psalm 110 throughout chapters 5–7, and Genesis 14:17–20 in chapter 7. Now, in what is the most extended Old Testament quotation in the New Testament, our author uses Jeremiah 31:31–34[11] as

---

[9] Williamson, *Philo*, 557.

[10] "There is indeed some affinity with Platonic idealism here, but it is our author's language, and not his essential thought, that exhibits such affinity. For him, the relation between the two sanctuaries is basically a temporal one" (Bruce, *Hebrews*, 184; see also Attridge, *Hebrews*, 222–24; Cockerill, *Hebrews*, 428–29).

[11] "This is the only OT passage which explicitly refers to a new covenant" (Ellingworth, *Hebrews*, 414). In contrast, first-century Judaism was convinced God's covenant with Moses was everlasting (Sirach 17:12; 2 Esdras 9:36–37; Philo, *Moses* 2.14–15).

a springboard of sorts for his comments in 9:1–10:18. This passage is a reminder that God always intended to introduce a new and better covenant than the one instituted at Sinai—Jeremiah's "the days are coming" had been realized with the advent of the Son ("in these last days," 1:2). Though this new covenant carries several promises, the ultimate one is this: "I will remember their sins no more" (8:12). This promise will dominate our author's attention through 10:18.

There is a discrepancy in how the beginning of verse 8 should be rendered. Almost every translation renders the Greek as if God found fault with "them" (i.e., "the people" NIV), and this is why he gave notice of a new covenant. Contextually, however, it makes more sense to take our author's words beginning in verse 7 as, "If that first covenant had been faultless, there would have been no occasion for a second; for he finds fault (with that first covenant) when he says to them. ..."[12]

That said, the difference between "it" (covenant) and "them" (people) may not be of any significance. God found fault with the old covenant, but not because there was something wrong with it intrinsically (Rom 7:12–13). The problem was the people. Their hearts were not wholly able to love God, and their subsequent sins made the old covenant ineffective. It provided no mechanism or process to atone entirely for the people's sins so that their sins might be forgiven and forgotten. The law was incapable of restoring to us our primeval destiny (Rom 3:20). "What was needed was a new nature, a heart liberated from its bondage to sin, a heart which not only spontaneously knew and loved the will of God but had the power to do it."[13]

In an arresting statement, God acknowledged that, despite delivering his beloved Israel from Egypt, he eventually "showed no concern for them" since "they did not continue in my covenant" (Heb 8:9; Jer 31:32 LXX). Another way of translating the verb "showed no concern" would be "neglected."[14] Zerwick and Grosvenor suggest the translation "I lost interest

---

[12] P. Hughes, *Commentary*, 299. The difference comes down to a variant in the Greek text, *autois* ("it") versus *autous* ("them"). Most translations follow the latter, but the former has much earlier support in Greek manuscripts (Johannes L. P. Wolmarans, "The Text and Translation of Hebrews 8:8," *ZNW* 75 [1984]: 139–44).

[13] Bruce, *Hebrews*, 190.

[14] BDAG, s.v. "ἀμελέω."

in them."[15] Because Israel had been faithless to the covenant, God found himself feeling no concern and showing no attention to his people, and thus he allowed the covenant curses to consume Israel. "A fundamental flaw of the first covenant would appear to be, then, its fragility and uncertainty, on both sides. The new covenant, says the prophet, will not be 'like that one.'"[16] The promises of the new covenant are these:

1. God would write his law on the hearts of his people (v 10). The first covenant was *supposed* to be written on the hearts of God's people (Deut 30:11–14), but unlike the righteous (Pss 37:31; 40:8; 119:11; Isa 51:7), most Israelites under the old covenant did not take it to heart (Deut 5:29). Likewise, "I will be their God, and they shall be my people" is not a new development; in the Old Testament, God had made the same claim (Exod 6:7; Lev 26:12). However, what would be different under the new covenant was that a new heart would be given to the people to make this claim a reality. "Thus says the Lord GOD: … I will give you a new heart, and a new spirit I will put within you. And I will remove the heart of stone from your flesh and give you a heart of flesh. And I will put my Spirit within you, and cause you to walk in my statutes and be careful to obey my rules" (Ezekiel 36:22, 26–27).

Within this new heart of flesh—a heart indwelled by the Spirit—the law of God would be written. The ordinary Greek verb meaning "to write" (*graphō*) is used here, but with the prefix *epi*, giving it the meaning of "to write upon." Imagine the wood-burning sets of yesteryear; I'm old enough to have had one. The way those sets worked was that you drew an outline on a piece of wood and then took the hot electric pen and used it to trace over the lines, permanently burning the wood with your words or design.[17] God does not merely write his word in our hearts; he brands it there permanently. Of course, bearing God's law on our hearts under the new covenant versus living under the external legal code of stone under the old covenant means we have no excuse whatsoever for disobedience.

---

[15] Max Zerwick and Mary Grosvenor, *A Grammatical Analysis of the Greek New Testament* (Rome: Biblical Institute, 1979), 2:671.

[16] Johnson, *Hebrews*, 207. Thus God proved his unwillingness "to let human faithlessness be the final word in his relationship with his people" (Koester, *Hebrews*, 391).

[17] Another way *epigraphō* can be translated is "to enter a name into a record" (BDAG, s.v. "ἐπιγράφω"), underscoring the nuance of permanence the term carries.

2. The people would "know the Lord" (v 11). By virtue of their new hearts granted by the new covenant, God's people would come to know him implicitly versus being taught explicitly. To "know the Lord" did not refer to knowledge about him, but rather to knowing him personally or intimately. Furthermore, our author may be interpreting Jeremiah's use of "Lord" as referring to Christ (e.g., 2:3; 7:14; 13:20).[18] It is undoubtedly true that through Jesus, we come to know the Father more personally and perfectly, for the Son is the radiance and imprint of the Father (1:3). In that light, to know the Lord under the new covenant means each person in God's household would have a personal relationship with him through Christ.

3. Sins would be forgiven and forgotten (v 12). In Hebrew thought, "remembering" someone didn't mean you had previously lost knowledge or memory of them, but that you went from not interacting with them to doing something to them or on their behalf, whether good or bad. When God "remembers," it's not like our forgetting where we left our car keys and then recalling their location. When God "remembers," God acts. Though the Bible is replete with examples of people begging God to remember his mercy and covenant,[19] we do *not* want him to remember our sins. Remembering our sins means God must act against us; that he has forgotten them means "his grace has determined to forgive them—not in spite of his holiness, but in harmony with it."[20] Though God formerly "showed no concern" for his faithless covenant people, he extends mercy to us.

Our author, in verse 13, draws the logical conclusion from Jeremiah's prophecy: the "demise [of the old covenant] is a foregone conclusion."[21] The verb translated "makes ... obsolete" (*palaioō*) in its simplest form can mean "to become old."[22] Earlier in Hebrews, our author quoted Psalm 102:25–27, noting that all created things would "wear out [*palaioō*] like a garment." Thus the old, obsolete covenant is "ready to vanish away."

Scholars are divided as to whether verse 13 is proof that Hebrews was written before the Romans' destruction of Jerusalem. On the one hand, our

---

18 Lane, *Hebrews 1–8*, 210.
19 Gen 9:15; Exod 2:24; 6:5; Pss 25:6; 74:2; 89:50; 106:4; Luke 1:54, 72.
20 Bruce, *Hebrews*, 192.
21 Guthrie, "Hebrews," 972.
22 BDAG, s.v. "παλαιόω."

author focuses on the tabernacle and not the temple, which explains (as the argument goes) why he doesn't mention the temple's destruction. Plus, other ancient writers spoke of the temple in the present tense even after it was destroyed.[23] On the other hand, as Raymond Brown concedes, while verse 13 itself might not prove definitively that the temple was still standing, 10:1–2 is especially hard to explain away if the temple were already gone.[24] In my estimation, it is unconscionable, had the temple already fallen when Hebrews was written, that our author would not mention it since "it would have provided the perfect capstone to his attempt to persuade his readers not to return to Judaism."[25]

HEBREWS 9:1–10

In 2000, Electronic Arts released the video game *The Sims*. Over the last twenty years of the franchise's existence (it's now in its fourth generation), it has sold over 200 million copies. In the game, players direct an avatar through life (e.g., working, eating, sleeping, dating). I admit that I became a huge fan of the game when it first debuted, spending quite a bit of time living vicariously through my "sim." However, the game lost much of its allure when it dawned on me one day that I had come to prefer playing a simulation of life rather than living in the real world. How sad would it be for someone to miss out on real life by frolicking in a fake one?

You know what's sadder? Thinking that access to God via an intermediary ministering in an earthly sanctuary is better than direct access in the spiritual realm. But that was the temptation before the Hebrews audience, the allure of which our author sought to dispel. He now turns his attention to the Old Testament tabernacle (not the temple[26]) to demonstrate the former covenant's deficiencies. Using the tabernacle as a springboard, our

[23] *1 Clement* 41.2; Josephus, *Antiquities* 4.224–57.

[24] Raymond E. Brown, *An Introduction to the New Testament*, ABRL (New York: Doubleday, 1997), 696, n. 36.

[25] Donald A. Hagner, *The New Testament: A Historical and Theological Introduction* (Grand Rapids: Baker Academic, 2012), 652.

[26] "The reason for this is almost certainly to be traced to the prior use of Exod 25:40, instructing Moses to erect a sanctuary according to the pattern God showed to him on Mount Sinai (8:5). ... It is only natural, therefore, that the tabernacle be used rather than the temple because of the association of the desert sanctuary with the establishment of the old covenant at Sinai" (William L. Lane, *Hebrews 9–13*, WBC 47B [Dallas: Word, 1991], 218).

author will demonstrate that Christ offered a superior sacrifice because it was made (1) in a superior sanctuary (in heaven, vv 2–5), (2) with superior blood (Christ's, v 7), and (3) with superior finality (once for all versus repeatedly, vv 6–7).

First, our author refers slightingly to the tabernacle as "an earthly place of holiness" and then proceeds to give us the fifty-cent tour. He mentions the Holy Place and its contents (v 2), the curtain, or veil, separating the two areas (v 3), and the Most Holy Place and its contents (vv 3–5), including the ark of the covenant and the items in it. All of this was a way of illustrating how "even the first covenant had regulations for worship" (v 1)—that access to God was restricted and regulated. Under the old covenant, "Everyone but the high priest was barred from the [divine] presence, and even he entered in terror."[27] This truth becomes both ironic and poignant when we realize God's great desire in the Old Testament was to dwell in the midst of his people (Ezek 37:27; Zech 2:11). After the fall, and except for a few brief appearances, God never again walked the earth until he came to redeem it.[28]

Our author briefly notes three things in the Holy Place: (1) the lampstand and (2) the table on which was placed (3) the bread of the presence (v 2). The lampstand, or menorah, was on the south side of the Holy Place opposite the table (Exod 26:35). The menorah had three branches extending from both sides of the main stand, making seven lamps in all, and it was kept burning at all times (Exod 25:31–39; 27:21). On the table for the bread of the Presence, twelve loaves were placed weekly (Exod 25:23–30; 1 Chr 9:32).

Moving beyond the curtain (Exod 26:33; 40:21)—the same curtain torn in two at Christ's death—into the Most Holy Place, our author draws our attention to the altar of incense, the ark of the covenant, and the cherubim above the ark. For the Jews, the ark of the covenant (including the mercy seat and cherubim) represented the throne of Yahweh and symbolized his immense glory (Exod 25:22; Num 7:89). Hebrews contains the

---

[27] Barclay, *Hebrews*, 120. "The cultic regulations of the 'first' covenant, therefore, made sure that the nation kept its distance from God, building a hedge of punishments for encroachment and an aura of taboo around the holy of holies so as to protect the holiness of God—or, more accurately, protect the nation *from* the holiness of God" (deSilva, *Perseverance*, 299; emphasis his).

[28] Thanks to one of my editors, Melissa McFerrin, for this great observation.

only biblical text where all the contents of the ark are mentioned in one passage. Our author's comment concerning the stone tablets, manna, and Aaron's rod certainly reflects historical reality during the Exodus period, but by the time the ark was brought into the temple in Solomon's day, it contained only the stone tablets (1 Kgs 8:9).[29]

Unlike Philo and Josephus,[30] the author of Hebrews does not linger on the tabernacle elements in order to allegorize them. His statement, "Of these things we cannot now speak in detail" (v 5), indicates his disinterest "in any hidden significance of the two compartments or the sanctuary furnishings."[31] Indeed, his refresher omits several details. Our author's immediate agenda for mentioning the tabernacle is to call attention to the Holy Place versus Most Holy Place and "the impenetrable boundary separating" the two.[32]

Continuing the contrast, Hebrews notes how the priests had access to the Holy Place. He stresses that the priests performed their duties "regularly" (v 6) or "repeatedly" (csb). Note that there was no blood required for the priests to enter daily into the Holy Place. But the same was not true for the Most Holy Place. Only the high priest was permitted to enter, only on the Day of Atonement[33] (Lev 16:2, 32–34), and only armed with the blood[34] of a goat to atone for both his sins and the sins of the nation (Lev 16:3–17). The blood he brought atoned for sin and purified the tabernacle from a year's worth of defilement caused by Israel's transgressions (Lev 16:16). The high priest sprinkled this blood above the mercy seat, the top of the ark.

Our author's exact words, "unintentional sins" (v 7), prompt an important question: Did the atonement granted on Yom Kippur extend

---

[29] By the first century BC, the ark itself had disappeared, leaving behind a stone slab only three fingers high (*Yoma* 5.2). When the Roman general Pompey trespassed into the Most Holy Place in 63 BC, he found several objects, none of which was the sacred ark. Tacitus reports that it was "common knowledge that there were no representations of the gods within, but that the place [i.e., the Most Holy Place] was empty and the secret shrine contained nothing" (*Histories* 5.9; Josephus, *Wars* 5.219). One tradition maintained Jeremiah had hidden the ark in a cave before the fall of Jerusalem in 586 BC (2 Maccabees 2:4–5). That said, Hebrews shows no interest in the fate of the ark, the temple, or any Jewish speculation about their restoration.

[30] Hugh Montefiore, *A Commentary on the Epistle to the Hebrews*, BNTC (London: Black, 1964), 146.

[31] Lane, *Hebrews 9–13*, 221.

[32] Cockerill, *Hebrews*, 372.

[33] This is Hebrews' first mention of the Day of Atonement, "which becomes the dominant image for interpreting the sacrifice of Christ" (Thompson, *Hebrews*, 183).

[34] "Here for the first time the author mentions 'blood' in a cultic context. In the material that follows, he repeatedly draws attention to sacrificial blood as imperative for drawing near to God" (Guthrie, *Hebrews*, 299; see also Lane, *Hebrews 9–13*, 222–23).

to intentional sins? Various Old Testament passages would suggest not (Num 15:30; Deut 1:43; 17:12–13), though Leviticus 16:16 does read "all sins" (see also *Jubilees* 5:17–19). Koester notes that the rabbis had a saying: If one said, "'I will sin and the Day of Atonement will effect atonement,' then the Day of Atonement effects no atonement." He then concludes, "Hebrews assumes that Christ's death offers complete atonement for all sins, not just inadvertent sins, while recognizing that people can spurn the grace Christ offers (Heb 6:4–8; 10:26)."[35]

Our author makes a subtle yet significant point in his choice of "offer" (9:7). Given his familiarity with the LXX, I can't imagine this was accidental. Nowhere in the Greek Old Testament is this word used to describe what the priest did with the blood on the Day of Atonement; instead, terms such as "sprinkle" and "apply" are used. But our author uses "offer" (*prospherō*) here and in verses 14, 25, and 28 and in 10:12 to refer to Jesus' death. By using "offer" of the Old Testament high priest, our author is connecting the shadow of the Yom Kippur ritual to Jesus' sacrificial, atoning death.

By calling attention to the Most Holy Place and the Day of Atonement, our author emphasizes three facts he will develop further: (1) All Israel, including the high priest, was prohibited from entering the Most Holy Place except for one day a year. (2) On the Day of Atonement, the high priest's entry into God's presence was permitted only because he carried sacrificial blood with him. Entry without blood meant sure death, for "even he [i.e., the high priest] entered only in the power of another life."[36] (3) The blood he carried, though sacrificial and critical to entry, provided no lasting effect; "fresh blood had to be shed and a fresh entry made into the holy of holies year by year."[37] A more permanent sacrifice was necessary. This last claim was somewhat scandalous to the Jews. Leviticus explicitly says sacrifices would grant forgiveness to the people and atone for their sins (4:20, 26, 31, 35; 5:10, 13, 16, 18); never in Jewish literature is there the suggestion that these sacrifices were "fundamentally ineffective and destined to become obsolete."[38]

[35] Koester, *Hebrews*, 397.
[36] Westcott, *Hebrews*, 251.
[37] Bruce, *Hebrews*, 208.
[38] Thompson, *Hebrews*, 185.

It seems the Spirit gave our author a particular revelation (9:8) pre-viously unknown to Old Testament Israel. The Holy Place was symbol-ic—another translation would be "a parable"—for the age of the Mosaic covenant (i.e., "the present age"[39]). Just as the Holy Place was closed off from the Most Holy Place by a curtain of cloth, God's people under the law were closed off from the Most High by a curtain of conscience. All the gifts and sacrifices offered, all the blood sprinkled, all the kosher laws observed faithfully, all the ritual purifications performed—none of these could "per-fect the conscience of the worshiper" (v 9). This meant—and it's crucial you understand this—access to God was restricted for Israel because *without a clean, or perfect, conscience, entry into the divine presence is impossible.*

For "conscience" (vv 9, 14; 10:2, 22; 13:18), our author used a word (*syneidēsis*) that generally meant "awareness" in both a moral and a non-moral sense. It refers to our inner intuition that helps us discern right from wrong (you have my permission to think of Jiminy Cricket at this point). The conscience is one's awareness, or cognizance, of sin (Acts 23:1; Rom 2:15; 2 Cor 1:12; 1 Tim 3:9); deSilva describes it as "an internal knowl-edge of whether or not one has acted virtuously and honorable, and it is intimately connected with the juridical sense of 'guilt.'" He then points to Paul's use of the word in Romans 2:14–16 to denote the force within us that condemns or exonerates us.[40] In Hebrews, "conscience" refers to our memory of sin and the subsequent guilt we carry within ourselves ("I'm beating myself up").[41]

To be sure, there was forgiveness of, as well as atonement for, sins in the Old Testament. So it was not one's sin per se that stood between an Israelite and God, for that sin would have been forgiven each Yom Kip-pur. But sin was not *forgotten.* The memory of sin remained not only with

---

[39] "The 'present time' mentioned in verse 9 does not mean the time present to our author and his hearers, but rather the time concurrent with the old covenant system of worship" (Guthrie, *Hebrews*, 300). This is confirmed by the ESV marginal note, "Or which is symbolic for the age then present."

[40] DeSilva, *Perseverance*, 301; see also Gary S. Selby, "The Meaning and Function of συνείδησις in Hebrews 9 and 10," *ResQ* 28 (1985–86): 145–54; Gary T. Meadors, "Conscience," in *Baker Theological Dictionary of the Bible*, ed. Walter A. Elwell (Grand Rapids: Baker, 2000), 113–14.

[41] "Modern readers are liable to underestimate the psychological importance of what is involved here. The mental pain of a sense of guilt is too great to be dealt with internally, and needs to be objectified in practical action and to be shared with others who can help to bear the burden. Hebrews knows this well, and this is why he has repeatedly emphasized the humanity and compassion of Jesus as high priest" (Barnabas Lindars, *The Theology of the Letter to the Hebrews* [Cambridge: Cambridge Univ. Press, 1991], 85).

God but also with the individual. From our perspective, a defiled con-science brings terror and shame. From God's perspective, in addition to his heartache over our predicament (as any loving father would ache over the suffering of his children), he does not receive the highest form of worship from a defiled conscience. We cannot enter his presence to praise him. A heart burdened by sin isn't in the mood to bless the Lord. If someone en-tered the presence of God, smothered by his holiness, that person would be immediately condemned by the conscience. Peter's words would be ours: "Go away from me, Lord; I am a sinful man!" (Luke 5:8 NIV).

Without Jesus and the atonement only he can offer, entry into God's presence would trigger debilitating fear, hopelessness, and vulnerability in all of us. We feel naked and exposed before the One who sees and knows all. We know we cannot hide any longer; like our first parents, we panic (Gen 3:8–13). Without Jesus, a snowball has far greater odds of surviving hell than we do of receiving grace and mercy. We don't deserve it; our sins are too abhorrent. Though we try desperately for much of our lives to assuage our consciences in an attempt to make ourselves feel better about our sins, we know the truth all along. "Always let your conscience be your guide"? Without Jesus, the conscience guides one to unmitigated shame and fo-ments unrelenting terror.

Thus there was a need for "reformation" (v 10). The term (*diorthōsis*) could refer to the repeal or correction of a law (e.g., "the act of straighten-ing what has become disordered or correcting what is wrong"[42]) but more broadly referred to a "new order."[43] Through Jeremiah, God had made the bold promise that a new covenant would be written upon the hearts (i.e., the consciences) of his people, and he would "remember their sins no more" (31:34; Heb 8:12).

HEBREWS 9:11–14

I'm about to reveal something rather stupid about myself. For much of my time reflecting on Hebrews, I searched in vain for a way to illustrate

---

[42] Silva, "ὀρθός," *NIDNTTE* 3:540.
[43] BDAG, s.v. "διόρθωσις"; e.g., Josephus, *Against Apion* 2.183.

why it should matter to us that the new covenant is better than the old. I considered comparing it to the advantages of travel by horseback versus automobile, to the advantages of foraging for your food versus shopping at the grocery, to the advantages of wireless high-speed internet versus the dark age of dial-up via a modem. (You're thinking of that annoying modem sound, aren't you?) In the same way, the new covenant is superior to the old: a once-for-all sacrifice versus daily, repeated sacrifices. Right?

However, it occurred to me that the new covenant's better promises have nothing to do with advanced technology, personal convenience, or a simpler way of doing things. The insufficiency of perpetual sacrifices wasn't because of the frequency. The frequency was a direct symptom of our spiritual cancer: a defiled conscience. Should our consciences have remained as pure as on the day we were born, perpetual sacrifices would have been unnecessary since the foundation of the world. As it is, perpetual sacrifices were necessary because they never eradicated the real problem.

Imagine you have a horribly stained shirt. You love the shirt. You love the way you look in the shirt. You have no desire to part with the shirt; it would be the end of you. Every day, you have to wash the shirt by hand in the local river, but although the shirt has been washed, the stain does not come out. You think to yourself, "Boy, it would be nice if I could somehow make this process easier, even automated." At that point, you return home and see advertised a shiny, new thingamajig called a washing machine. You order one, have it delivered, and wash your shirt in it for the first time.

When the shirt emerges from the machine still stained, you wouldn't say, "Well, at least this process is automated! I don't have to do this myself down at the river every day anymore." This wouldn't be satisfactory. You would say, "My shirt is still dirty!" The real problem isn't the mechanism for washing. It's, and forgive me for yelling, YOU HAVE A STAINED SHIRT. Until the stain is removed, you can wash it in an automatic washer all you want, yet nothing will change.

Christ's death wasn't like installing a washing machine to relieve the hassle of repeated manual labor. That's not the significance of a once-for-all sacrifice versus daily and repeated. Instead, the death of the supreme

Son means the permanent removal of the most horrid stain that has infected every human being since our first parents—the stain of sin.

>———◇———<

The new covenant was inaugurated when "Christ appeared" (v 11). What the old covenant could never do, Jesus has done. In Christ, God corrected every inadequacy of the old covenant and brought good things (2 Cor 1:20). Upon Jesus' ascension into heaven and inauguration as our high priest, the new covenant was enacted and its better promises initiated.

Note the four claims of our author in 9:11–14 that are sharply contrasted against the Old Testament. As high priest, Christ entered:

›   into "the greater and more perfect tent" in heaven, not on earth (v 11)—*a better sanctuary*.
›   to offer atonement "once for all"; another will never be necessary (v 12)—*a better atonement*.
›   "by means of his own blood," which is far superior to that of animals (vv 12–13)—*a better blood sacrifice*.
›   to effect "an eternal redemption," a permanent purging of sin (vv 12–14)—*a better cleansing*.

A Better Sanctuary. The old covenant stipulated that the Most Holy Place was the one location on earth where God's presence resided, and Aaron and his successors could enter just once a year. But as the high priests performed their solemn ceremony annually, how many of them through the centuries wondered if the God of their fathers was really present? Imagine that dark room filled with a smoky haze from burning incense and the ripe stench of animal blood—such was as close as anyone on earth could get to the presence of God.

However, with his ascension, Jesus entered a better Most Holy Place, a heavenly one, where he meets with God. He is not limited to a dark room where he performs his duty before a being he cannot see; he is face-to-face with the Father. He does not discharge his duty in terror that one wrong move will bring instant death; he instead sits at his Father's right hand, the seat of highest honor as the supreme Son. Jesus' priesthood is performed in a better sanctuary: the throne room of heaven in the immediate presence of God.

That both the tabernacle and the temple were made by men's hands from the physical materials of the earth meant neither building would last forever. The tabernacle had long ago ceased to exist, and the Jews saw the first temple burn in 586 BC; the second would soon be destroyed also. One of Jesus' claims had been that he would tear down the temple and build another "not made with hands" (Mark 14:58), for no building made by men can contain the glory of God (Acts 7:48; 17:24). Christians, therefore, have access to a sanctuary that "is free from the ravages of time."[44]

A Better Atonement. Though the Old Testament high priest was required to enter the Most Holy Place every year to secure atonement for Israel, Jesus offered himself only once to secure atonement for the people of God. In other words, Jesus' sacrificial offering of himself was definitive; another will never be necessary. This is arguably why those who insisted on circumcision so nauseated Paul that he wished they would go all the way and emasculate themselves (Gal 5:12)—how dare anyone suggest something else is required to reconcile us to God in addition to what Jesus did at the cross! His once-for-all atonement is why circumcision is no longer necessary, why works are no longer required for salvation. Jesus' atonement paid it all.

A Better Blood Sacrifice. Jesus did not literally bring his physical blood into the heavenly places; mention of his blood is merely a reference to his passion. "Christ's entry into God's presence was through the violent and bloody death on the cross."[45] But Jesus' blood made a better sacrifice because his sacrifice was offered voluntarily and in total obedience to the Father's will whereas that of animals was given passively and involuntarily.[46]

N. T. Wright notes the absurdity—even blasphemy—Jews would have assigned that claim. Animal sacrifices were necessary for atonement,

[44] Wiersbe, *Bible Exposition*, 2:310.

[45] Johnson, *Hebrews*, 237. "The blood of Jesus" in Hebrews refers not only to his shed blood on the cross but also more broadly to the obedient death he died in keeping with the Father's will.

[46] Lane, *Hebrews 9–13*, 238.

sure. *Human* sacrifices, on the other hand, had never been orthodox. Such had been associated with idolatry throughout the Old Testament and were abhorrent to the righteous[47] (Lev 18:21; 20:2–5; Deut 18:9–12; Jer 19:5). How, then, could human sacrifice be superior in God's eyes to that of an animal?

The answer is found in Hebrews' mention of Jesus being "without blemish" (9:14; Isa 53:9; 1 Pet 1:19). Even animal sacrifices under the law were required to be without blemish, for "nothing stained or faulty is worthy to be given to God."[48] However, Jesus' perfection was fulfilled in the fact that he "owed nothing to the justice of God on his own account,"[49] not in the lack of physical defects. An unblemished animal is good and all, but an animal has no moral conscience. An animal cannot sin. On the other hand, martyrs might spill their blood voluntarily in obedience to the Father, but they are not without moral blemish. In contrast, Christ was tempted as we are, yet he emerged without sin. "The sinless high priest (4:15; 7:26) was also the spotless victim."[50] As Bruce puts it, "Our Lord's complete holiness, his 'active obedience' to God, is essential to the efficacy of his sacrifice."[51] Our author will explore this idea further in 10:5–10.

What empowered Jesus to be that unblemished sacrifice? "The eternal Spirit," our author says (v 14). There is much disagreement on what this means. Is it a reference to (1) Jesus' spiritual nature[52] ("through eternal spirit") or (2) the Holy Spirit and his anointing of Christ[53] ("through *the* eternal Spirit")? The definite article "the" isn't present in the Greek text, though that scarcely settles the issue. The second option seems more likely. For one thing, the Jews believed the Holy Spirit sanctified the high priest

---

[47] Wright, *Hebrews*, 95. He adds, "Apart from the powerful and deeply mysterious passage in Isaiah 53.10, which speaks of the sacrificial death of God's servant, the closest that Judaism comes to such an idea is the story of Abraham sacrificing Isaac at Mount Moriah (Genesis 22), a story which played a considerable role in Jewish thinking at this time, and which Hebrews will refer to in 11.17–18; but the point there, of course, was that God stopped Abraham actually killing Isaac" (*Hebrews*, 95).

[48] Maclaren, *Expositions*, 30:73.

[49] C. H. Spurgeon, "Our Lord's Entrance within the Veil," in *The Metropolitan Tabernacle Pulpit Sermons* (London: Passmore, 1889), 35:148.

[50] Lane, *Hebrews 9–13*, 240.

[51] Bruce, *Hebrews*, 218.

[52] Attridge, *Hebrews*, 250–51; P. Hughes, *Commentary*, 358–59; Johnson, *Hebrews*, 236. Contra Lindars: "Hebrews nowhere contrasts Jesus' spiritual nature with his human nature" (*Theology*, 57–58).

[53] Bruce, *Hebrews*, 217; Ellingworth, *Hebrews*, 457; Lane, *Hebrews 9–13*, 240.

so that he could enter the Most Holy Place.[54] In addition, our author may have Isaiah's Suffering Servant in mind. The Lord placed his Spirit upon his Servant (Isa 42:1), and "it was the power of the eternal Spirit which enabled Christ to be at the same time both high priest and offering."[55] Regardless of how we interpret this, the point is that "Christ's sacrifice is based on the power of God."[56] Jesus's ability to fulfill his Father's commission, live a sinless life, endure his suffering, and offer himself as an atonement to secure our redemption—this was all due to an eternal, not earthly, power.

A Better Cleansing. Our author will soon speak of what animals' blood could *not* do (10:1–4). Here, using an *a fortiori* argument, he reasons that if animal blood could purify the flesh, imagine what Christ's blood can accomplish. Our high priest offers us a better, deeper cleaning—he purifies the inside and not just the outside. The flesh no longer corrupts, yes, but the conscience no longer condemns, either (Rom 8:34; 1 John 3:19–21).

Our author's phrase "the ashes of a heifer" is an allusion to the Old Testament ritual of purifying an Israelite that had contacted a corpse (Num 19:1–10). Hebrews' interest in this passage is to demonstrate that such defilement was a barrier to worship (Num 19:13, 20) and that purification rituals affected only the flesh (the external), not the conscience (the internal).

The dead works from which our consciences have been purified are not the rituals of the law or futile works of righteousness meant to merit salvation. Instead, they are the works of the flesh at which Paul took aim in Galatians 5:19–21, works that defile the conscience. Our author does not enumerate precisely what he has in mind, but it's safe to assume (in keeping with the overall tone of his sermon) that it would include everything from wavering faith to outright apostasy.[57] His audience had once repented of these dead works in the early days of their Christian walk (6:1).

---

[54] Martin Emmrich, "'Amtscharisma': Through the Eternal Spirit (Hebrews 9:14)," *BBR* 12 (2002): 25–31. He concludes, "The Holy Spirit sustained the high priest ... in the execution of his most critical cultic appointment" ("Amtscharisma," 32).

[55] Ellingworth, *Hebrews*, 457.

[56] Cockerill, *Hebrews*, 398.

[57] Ellingworth, *Hebrews*, 458.

In the previous chapter, our author brought up the prophecy in Jeremiah 31 of a new covenant. Remember that 9:1–10:18 is an exposition of all this new covenant entails. It's written on hearts, not stone. It promises a real and total cleansing versus a symbolic and largely ineffectual one. This is not to say Old Testament saints were not forgiven or did not enjoy a spiritual connection to God. At the same time, however, how can people fully move on from their sin if there's an annual reminder of it? This would be like the credit card company's forgiving your massive debt while still sending you a statement in the mail each month, reminding you of the charges you racked up and left unpaid. They've forgiven you—but have they really?

A cleansed conscience, on the other hand, is only half of the process; it is the *purpose* for which our conscience has been cleansed that deserves greater consideration. Liberated from dead works, our cleansed conscience is then equipped to worship and serve the living God. This is not a service rendered grudgingly by a slave to his master, but willful worship lifted up by one eternally grateful for the atonement only a perfect Priest and supreme Son could offer. According to Paul, this worship—this life of service—has been our destiny from the beginning (Rom 12:1; Eph 2:10). How we glorify and serve God with a cleansed conscience under the new covenant will be explored beginning in 10:19.

HEBREWS 9:15–17

Much of the difficulty of this section of Hebrews lies in our author's abrupt change of scenery. He takes us, in an "almost kaleidoscopic fashion,"[58] from an imaginary attorney's office, with talk of wills and inheritance (vv 15–17), to the base of Sinai and the notion of a blood covenant (vv 18–22), and finally to the heavenly sanctuary, where Jesus now performs his priestly intercession before the Father on our behalf (vv 23–28).[59] As is so often the case with studying the Bible, the tougher the nut to crack, the

[58] Koester, *Hebrews*, 424.
[59] Koester, 424.

sweeter the meat inside; the more difficult a passage is to understand, the greater the truth that will be revealed. So hang with me!

In verses 15–17, our author merges the themes of atonement and covenant.[60] The "therefore" of verse 15 means that being High-Priest Jesus and Sacrificial-Lamb Jesus qualifies him to be Mediator Jesus. His death not only expunged our record of sin under the law (an atoning death) but also makes this new covenant legally valid (a ratifying death). To unravel these difficult verses, let's start in verse 17 and work our way back to verse 15.

The claim of verse 17, "a will takes effect only at death, since it is not in force as long as the one who made it is alive," seems self-evident. Upon our death, a will transfers our estate to our survivors. A last will and testament is a legally binding document, though it isn't in effect until the death of the testator.[61] On the surface, therefore, it seems our author is saying Jesus' death was necessary for his own will or testament to take effect.[62] However, there may be more to it than that.

Scholars cannot agree whether *diathēkē*—almost always translated "covenant" in Hebrews—should be rendered "will" or "covenant" in verses 16–17. I'll admit that "will" (as in a "last will and testament") appears to fit the immediate context, yet "covenant" (NASU) is more consistent with the rest of the epistle.[63] In Hebrews, *Jesus* is the heir (1:2), and we are only benefactors of his inheritance as his brothers and sisters through his death (2:10–13; Rom 8:16–17). So "will" or "testament" can't be in view because the subsequent logic—"*we* inherit these things because *Jesus* died"—doesn't make sense. Plus, the context of verses 16–17 indicates our author is focused

[60] "In order to show that what has been achieved really is permanent in its effect, Hebrews must make the point that it has an essentially permanent character. This is why he takes up the idea of the covenant, because, whereas an atonement sacrifice deals with past sins, *a covenant sacrifice inaugurates a permanent arrangement for the future.* Once a covenant has been solemnly inaugurated with the sanctions of a sacrifice it can be expected to remain in force. That is what is argued in 9.15–28" (Lindars, *Theology*, 95; emphasis mine).

[61] Be cautious about pressing the metaphor of "last will and testament" too far. First, it wasn't uncommon in ancient times (nor today) for someone to bequeath his estate *prior* to death. In addition, we die and stay dead, and our heirs will die one day and pass on to their heirs what we once passed down to them. Jesus, however, died to live forever, and our inheritance is life with him forever (R. C. H. Lenski, *The Epistle to the Hebrews and the Epistle of James* [Minneapolis: Augsburg, 1966], 306–7).

[62] N. T. Wright expresses this typical interpretation: "The word for 'covenant' is the same Greek word as 'will' in the legal sense. Before somebody dies, they make a 'will' or 'covenant', disposing of their assets as they please. This legal document is binding, but (obviously) it does not come into effect until the death of the testator has been established. With great daring, it seems, the writer now proposes that the new covenant itself only comes into force after the relevant death … which means, of course, the death of Jesus" (*Hebrews*, 99).

[63] Cockerill, *Hebrews*, 405–6; see also "A Lawyer Looks at Hebrews 9:15–17," *EvQ* 40 (1968): 151–56.

not on death as it leads to inheritance, but rather on death as it leads to Jesus' intercession.[64] Moreover, if our author is speaking of a will in verses 16–17, his comments do "not conform to any known legal practice (Hellenistic or otherwise) with respect to the validation or ratification of a will."[65]

Finally, the notion of "will" versus "covenant" might inadvertently introduce a nuance that does not belong to this concept. In a sense, inheritance is a right or entitlement, as in the term "birth*right*." What is bequeathed is earned, if only because one is the heir/child of the deceased. On the other hand, we in no way deserve what we have received from this new covenant. What Christ secured by his death is not a right but a gift.

Either way, how *diathēkē* is translated here may not matter. Our author's larger point is that an agreement (a covenant/will) that fulfills a promise or grants an inheritance is not in effect until blood has been shed via a violent death. But for my two cents, "covenant" is a better translation here. With that in mind, let's explore the "violent death" aspect of biblical covenants.

When a covenant was made in the Old Testament, the two parties swore an imprecatory oath upon themselves if they did not keep their end of the bargain. As mentioned earlier (6:13–20), God did this with Noah and Abraham. In the latter example, God reenacted the common practice of two parties slaughtering animals, meeting one another between the two pieces, and swearing an oath to keep their side of the covenant. In this custom, "the bloody dismemberment of representative animals signified the violent death of the ratifying party if he proved faithless to his oath" (e.g., Exod 24:6–8; Ps 50:5; Jer 34:17–20).[66] This practice was so inherent in the idea of a covenant that the Hebrew expression for making a covenant was "to cut a covenant," and a covenant was not considered in effect until this ceremony had taken place. Before that time, it "remained merely tentative. … A covenant is never secured until the ratifier has bound himself to his oath by means of a representative death."[67]

---

[64] "The author is primarily concerned with Christology, not with the soteriological blessings of inheritance" (John J. Hughes, "Hebrews IX 15ff. and Galatians III 15ff.: A Study in Covenant Practice and Procedure," *NovT* 21 [1979]: 39).

[65] Paul R. Williamson, *Sealed with an Oath: Covenant in God's Unfolding Purpose*, NSBT 23 (Downers Grove, IL: InterVarsity Press, 2007), 203.

[66] Lane, *Hebrews 9–13*, 242.

[67] Lane, 243.

In this light, our author is not arguing for the necessity of Jesus' death for the reasons we might think (i.e., a death is necessary to execute a will). "Some have attempted to demonstrate the logical necessity of Christ's death, but in Hebrews Jesus' death is the presupposition rather than the conclusion of the argument. Hebrews does not assume that God is bound by secular legal practice to make death the basis for inheritance. Rather, Jesus' death is a given, and the author seeks to disclose its significance in various ways, including reference to testamentary practice."[68] In other words, Jesus' death was necessary not for legal reasons (i.e., to validate a will) but to qualify him as our priestly mediator and ratify this new covenant.

The term "mediator" (*mesitēs*) (v 15; 8:6; 12:24) referred to "one who mediates between two parties to remove a disagreement or reach a common goal."[69] (I can't help picturing a version of Johnny Hart's *B.C.* comic where the caveman approaches the dictionary on a rock, seeking a definition of "mediator," and finds the entry to read "one who mediates.") The New Testament certainly believes Jesus to be the sole mediator between God and man (1 Tim 2:5). To borrow the image from Genesis 15, Jesus is the one who brings two parties (God and us) together; he has us meet "between the pieces" to ratify the new covenant envisioned by Jeremiah 31.

But let's not misunderstand Jesus' role as "mediator." Today, we tend to associate a "mediator" with an arbitrator, someone who effects a compromise between two opposing parties, such as a diplomat striking a peace accord between two Middle Eastern countries. In the only occurrence of *mesitēs* in the LXX, Job, beset by horrible circumstances allowed by God, lamented, "There is no mediator [*mesitēs* LXX] between us" (Job 9:33 CSB).

This association, however, isn't accurate when it comes to Christ. As Mohler explains, there is no common ground, no room for compromise, between God and man. "Far from suggesting a compromise between two opposing positions, Christ agrees with the Father that we deserve the infinite outpouring of his wrath. He agrees with the Father about the ugliness of our sin. He agrees with the Father about the necessity of a sacrifice.

---

[68] Koester, *Hebrews*, 425.
[69] BDAG, s.v. "μεσίτης."

As our mediator, he agrees to be that sacrifice even as the Father sends him for that task."[70]

Jesus brokers reconciliation, not compromise. With an oath (6:17), God guaranteed his promise of a new covenant (Jer 31:31–34). Christ is a mediator in the sense of being the guarantor of the new covenant (7:22), and his blood was necessary to qualify him as mediator/guarantor of this new covenant (Mark 14:24). No death? No covenant. No blood oath? No covenant. His sacrificial death made the promise of the covenant certain—remember that a death binds the ratifier to his oath. By the death of the supreme Son, the Father bound himself to his promise. Our mediator does more than have us meet with God between the pieces. He *is* the pieces: the slaughtered, sacrificial guarantee. Jesus' death is the length to which God went in order to assure us that all the promises of the new covenant will come to pass.

"Eternal" is a favorite word for our author. The new covenant inaugurated by Jesus' death is eternal (13:20); thus the salvation we have through Christ is eternal (5:9). According to Hebrews 9, the new covenant foretold by Jeremiah promises things the old could never deliver: "eternal redemption" (v 12), or "eternal inheritance," for those "who are called" (v 15; 3:1)—that is, heirs to the promises of Abraham (2:16; 6:12; 11:8). "Redemption" (*lytrōsis*) referred to the ransoming or liberation of someone,[71] such as when God redeemed Israel from Egypt (Deut 7:8; 9:26; 13:5 LXX). By the time of Christ, the Jews had come to expect their awaited messiah would redeem them in the sense of liberating them from Roman oppression (Acts 1:6). "The deliverance brought by the heavenly high priest, however, involves deliverance from sin's penalty and is eternal in nature."[72]

Hebrews has already established how "every transgression or disobedience [under the law] received a just retribution" (2:2). Jesus' death, however, has delivered us from suffering that retribution. Before the cross, there existed no final ransom, no total redemption. Paul says that, until Jesus' atonement, God had only "passed over"[73] previous sins "in his divine

---

[70] Mohler, *Exalting Jesus*, 136.

[71] BDAG, s.v. "λύτρωσις."

[72] Guthrie, *Hebrews*, 310.

[73] "No animal sacrifices ever purchased 'eternal redemption.' Their blood could only 'cover' sin until the time when Christ's blood would 'take away sin' (John 1:29)" (Wiersbe, *Bible Exposition*, 2:310).

forbearance" (Rom 3:25). Thus the effects of the death of the supreme Son are retroactive to Eden. Eternal redemption means the effects of Jesus' death reach back to the beginning and forward into eternity.

If "eternal redemption" represents the remission of our sins, our "eternal inheritance" is the reclamation of our destiny, once lost in the fall, now restored in Christ (2:10). This eternal inheritance is a place in the world to come. The old covenant was powerless to recover that forfeited destiny; Jesus' death, however, makes its recovery possible.

HEBREWS 9:18–22

The point of verses 16–17, then, is that a death was required to ratify the new covenant. And not just any death, "but a violent, sacrificial death."[74] The necessity of blood is nothing new; it was required to institute the old covenant. We are transported back to Sinai and reminded that, once the law had been mediated to Israel by Moses, it was ratified or sealed by blood.[75]

> Moses took half of the blood and put it in bowls, and the other half he splashed against the altar. Then he took the Book of the Covenant and read it to the people. They responded, "We will do everything the LORD has said; we will obey." Moses then took the blood, sprinkled it on the people and said, "This is the blood of the covenant that the LORD has made with you in accordance with all these words."
>
> EXODUS 24:6–8 NIV

Note that Hebrews mentions nothing about Moses' reading the Book of the Covenant to the people or their response. Our author seems interested only in the connection between covenant and bloodshed—"the blood bound the people, on pain of death, to obey the stipulations proclaimed and now written in the 'book.'"[76] Both the people of the covenant

---

[74] Ellingworth, *Hebrews*, 466.

[75] "The close connection between covenant and blood is confirmed by the fact that, from this point on [in Hebrews], references to a covenant are regularly linked with references to blood (10:29; 12:24; 13:20)" (Ellingworth, 470).

[76] Cockerill, *Hebrews*, 408.

and the Book of the Covenant were sprinkled by blood (Heb 9:19–20; Exod 24:8), as were the tabernacle and its furnishings (Heb 9:21; Lev 8:15, 19; 16:14–19). Note that our author uses "blood" in verse 18, not "death." Blood represented not just any death but a violent, sacrificial death.

Hence our author clarifies two points in verse 22 that will allow him to draw his conclusion in verse 23: "almost everything" under the old covenant was "purified by blood," and sins are not forgiven without bloodshed (Lev 17:11).[77] This final claim was a well-known principle among the Jews; the blood requirement for forgiveness has been true ever since the fall (Gen 3:21), and it was never more true than on the Day of Atonement. It is even true of those cultures we might consider to be far removed from the culture and worldview of Scripture. Spurgeon once argued, "Blood, and blood alone, must be applied for the remission of sin. Indeed the very heathen seem to have an inkling of this fact. Do not I see their knives gory with the blood of victims? Have I not heard horrid tales of human immolations, of holocausts, of sacrifices; and what mean these, but that there lies deep in the human breast, deep as the very existence of man, this truth,—'that without shedding of blood there is no remission.'"[78]

HEBREWS 9:23–28

With verse 23, our author draws his conclusion from the two points made in verse 22. If the earthly tabernacle (and by extension all things connected to the old covenant) had to be purified with blood, the same is true for the heavenly tabernacle—not a physical building but the immediate presence of God (v 24). On the Day of Atonement, Israel's high priest entered the Most Holy Place to stand before the mercy seat and cherubim, which *represented* the presence of God. Jesus, however, stands before God himself (i.e., his immediate presence) and sees his face. That heavenly sanctuary has been purified with "better sacrifices" (v 23): the blood of the Father's supreme Son.

---

[77] "The life being in the blood in Lev 17:11 indicates that forgiveness comes from the death of victims. It is hard to avoid the idea that the death of the animal functions as a substitute for the death of the human being. The animal suffered the fate that the human being deserved, showing the seriousness of sin and the great cost of forgiveness" (Schreiner, *Hebrews*, 279–80).

[78] C. H. Spurgeon, "The Blood-Shedding," in *The New Park Street Pulpit Sermons* (London: Passmore, 1857), 3:90.

It's natural to wonder why a spiritual/heavenly tabernacle must be cleansed. How can such be contaminated with human or earthly sin? The answer is that it wasn't defiled but *would be* once sinful human beings approach the throne of grace. Jesus' cleansing of the heavenly Most Holy Place was preventative in preparation for our arrival.

Put another way, Jesus did not cleanse a literal *place*, for God does not exist in time and space as we think of it. To say Jesus cleanses the "heavenly things" is to say Jesus cleanses *us*. The language is personal, not spatial. "If sinners are to appear before God, even by proxy, through the representation of a sinless high priest, they must be cleansed from sin, or else the very presence of God would be polluted."[79] Christians are God's house or dwelling place (3:6; Eph 1:22–23; 1 Pet 2:5), though to be that dwelling place, we must be sprinkled clean by Jesus' blood (9:14). Thus, "Jesus' cleansing of the heavenly sanctum is the ritual enactment of God's promised resolution to 'remember sins no more.'"[80]

Don't move forward until you pause and ponder the last three words of verse 24—the significance of *where* Jesus is and *what* he is doing now. On the night before his death, he spoke reassuring words to his apostles' troubled hearts. His Father's house had room for all, and he was going to prepare that place for them, at which point he would return for them (John 14:1–3). Jesus' ascension wasn't to go on vacation, nor has he passed through the heavens to conduct business of greater importance. No, Jesus is before the face of God "on our behalf." His people are the reason he ascended into heaven. "Jesus' entire existence is dedicated to his brothers and sisters."[81]

Finally, our author says Jesus' sacrifice is superior to the old not only because it was his own blood that he offered to purify a heavenly sanctuary but also because it was "once for all." He is not repeatedly dying and offering himself—such is a ludicrous idea, our author claims (vv 25–26). Unlike *Star Wars*, there will never be future episodes of *The Passion of the Christ*.[82] No, Jesus came once to deal with sin decisively. If there is a passage

---

[79] Bruce, *Hebrews*, 230; contra Lane, *Hebrews 9–13*, 247–48.

[80] DeSilva, *Perseverance*, 312–13.

[81] Johnson, *Hebrews*, 244.

[82] And trying to *repeat* the sacrifice of Jesus is as futile and ridiculous a sequel as *Rocky V*!

in the New Testament that nullifies the Catholic doctrine of the perpetual offering of Christ via Mass, it's this one.[83]

>————◇————<

Late in the third century BC, a Jewish scribe from Alexandria made the pilgrimage to Jerusalem to observe the Day of Atonement. Joshua ben Sirach watched with the crowd as the high priest at the time, Simon II the Just, officiated the rituals. Sirach later recorded the anticipation of and joy over the high priest's emergence from beyond the veil once atonement had been made for another year on behalf of Israel: "How glorious he was, surrounded by the people, as he came out of the house of the curtain" (Sirach 50:5 NRSV).

As surely as a person dies just once and then faces divine judgment (v 27)—a truth our author considered to be elementary to the gospel (6:2; 4:13)—Jesus has died once and will return a second time.[84] The certainty of death in this life is matched by the certainty of the Second Coming; one is as inevitable and inexorable as the other. As the Israelites eagerly awaited the high priest's emergence from behind the curtain, so Christians eagerly await the reappearance of our high priest from behind the heavenly veil.

And like that of Israel's high priest, Jesus' reemergence from behind the curtain separating the material from the transcendent will be the ultimate affirmation that his sacrifice has been acceptable to God. Unlike with Israel's high priest, however, "those who await Christ need have no hesitancy about the adequacy of his sacrifice."[85] With his coming, the Son will bring salvation for those "eagerly waiting for him" (v 28; 10:37). Note that our author does not say *judgment* awaits those eagerly anticipating the return of our King (1 Thess 1:10; 2 Thess 1:7; 2 Tim 4:8). Instead, for the heirs of salvation, Jesus' return "will mean full enjoyment of their inheritance."[86]

---

[83] The doctrine of the perpetual offering of Christ is in "plain contradiction to the emphatic teaching of this epistle" (Bruce, *Hebrews*, 230). Plus, "the only time anything is said in the New Testament about re-crucifying the son of God, it is mentioned as a dire warning of something nobody in their right mind would wish to do (6.6)" (Wright, *Hebrews*, 113).

[84] The word "once" (*hapax*) occurs three times in vv 26–28, connecting the certainty of our dying just once to the certainty that Jesus has dealt with sin just once.

[85] Cockerill, *Hebrews*, 427.

[86] Lane, *Hebrews 9–13*, 251.

Our author affirms here an important aspect of Christian eschatology. We long for the reappearance of our high priest for countless reasons: to escape this world and its sorrows, to destroy death fully and forever, to reunite us with loved ones who preceded us, and to usher in the advent of eternity. These are all excellent reasons to anticipate Christ's return eagerly.

However, the greatest reason we anticipate the Second Coming is that it will signal the ultimate restoration of our primeval status and achievement of our destiny. We will be children of God crowned with glory and honor. We long for our high priest's return, for it will mean we taste salvation not in part but in all its fullness. As Paul put it, "Our citizenship is in heaven, and from it we await a Savior, the Lord Jesus Christ, who will transform our lowly body to be like his glorious body, by the power that enables him even to subject all things to himself" (Phil 3:20–21).

Amen. Come, Lord Jesus.

HEBREWS 10:1-10

Our author now enters the homestretch of his discussion of Jesus as high priest and mediator of a new covenant.[87] The law, he says, was but a "shadow" (i.e., an incomplete/imperfect, versus a realistic/accurate, representation) of what was to come. Our author is thinking of the law as a mechanism to grant reconciliation and access to God. In his mind, there is a great gulf between shadow and reality when it comes to the two covenants.

When I think of the "shadow" concept in Hebrews, I imagine something being extremely out of focus—as opposed to reality, which is tack sharp and crystal clear. Consider a camera lens; it has a focus ring that can make everything in the picture sharp rather than blurry (i.e., shadowy). If what we have in Christ is a sharp image, then the law was blurry and out of focus. As Calvin put it, "under the Law was shadowed forth only in rude and imperfect lines what under the Gospel set forth in living colours and graphically distinct."[88]

---

[87] "The suggestive reference to the potency of the blood of Christ to effect a decisive purging of the conscience of the worshiper in 9:14 was not developed. It is that strand of the argument which is picked up and elaborated in 10:1–18" (Lane, 269).

[88] Calvin, *Hebrews*, 222.

Because the law was only a shadow, it had no power to "make perfect those who draw near" (v 1). By "perfect," our author means "a state of right relationship with God, in which the worshipers are once and for all cleansed from sin and delivered from a nagging sense of guilt."[89] Bruce's definition is simpler: "perfect" in verse 1 is "access to God without the constant necessity of removing the barrier of freshly accumulated sin."[90] It is the presence of sin, after all, that alienates us from God (Ps 66:18; Prov 28:9; Isa 59:1–2), and "the purity that [Israel's] multiple sacrifices effected was only skin-deep."[91] The old law could cleanse the flesh, just not the conscience. In theological terms, the law could effect justification but not purification and sanctification.

As we reflect on the entirety of Hebrews to this stage, our author's point—that the law of Moses cannot make us "perfect"—becomes increasingly pregnant with meaning. The law had no power to:

> ›   reestablish our primeval destiny (2:6–8).
> ›   bring many sons to glory (2:10).
> ›   enable us to enter God's Sabbath rest (4:9–10).
> ›   cleanse our conscience to draw us near to God (9:9; 10:22).
> ›   grant us boldness to enter God's presence (4:16).
> ›   save those eagerly waiting for the Son's return (9:28).

If the law had the power to do any of this, the Day of Atonement would not have been a regular, repeated ritual. As it was, however, the Day was an annual reminder that the law could not take away the sins of the people. "Once a year" in these passages is, in effect, "year after year." Read through verse 1 and note the train of words highlighting this idea: "never," "same," "continually," and "every year." It's as if our author is saying, "There is a futility and frustration in the law and its sacrifices, for it is like a merry-go-round that never stops."[92] The rituals never ceased because it is "impossible" (a word emphasized in the Greek text) for animal sacrifices

[89] Guthrie, *Hebrews*, 327.
[90] Bruce, *Hebrews*, 236.
[91] Attridge, *Hebrews*, 272.
[92] Schreiner, *Hebrews*, 291.

to remove sins (v 4).[93] Philip Hughes explains why: "A brute beast is by its very nature unqualified to serve as a substitute for man, the crown of God's creation. Lacking both volition and rationality, it is passive and inarticulate. … Only man, who is a rational, volitional, articulate, and responsible being, can serve as a proper equivalent and substitute for man: hence the incarnation, whereby the Son of God assumed our humanity, so that as man he might offer himself in the place of our fallen humanity."[94] Or, as someone put it to me in simpler terms, God would not elevate an animal to the level of humanity to stand in for us, for that would be unnatural. Nor would he create equal men to die for us, for that would be unjust. So he took the only course remaining: to lower deity to become the perfect sacrifice, for that is mercy incarnate.

Imagine for a moment how difficult it must have been to live under such a system as the old covenant. This difficulty might not have been palpable to the Israelites since it was all they knew. But our author means more than "recall a simple fact to our conscience" when he uses the word "reminder" (v 3). He has in mind "the Hebrew sense of a burdened, smitten heart, which became most pronounced on the Day of Atonement when it was necessary to confront the holiness of God."[95] One might say a "burdened, smitten heart" is the same as a guilty conscience. Year after year, the Day of Atonement burdened the people with guilt. Recall that when *God* "remembers," he acts; the Day of Atonement reminded the people that they could *not* act on their own to cleanse the conscience in order to enter God's holy presence and serve him.

Jewish literature repudiated this sentiment, at least in part.[96] Philo asserted that only one who was not contrite enough when offering sacrifices would fail to see his sins forgiven; the sacrifices in that case "produce no remission of sins but only a reminding of them."[97] Our author, however, can't

---

[93] "The issue is not whether the blood of bulls and goats sacrificed during the annual observances of the Day of Atonement (Lev 16:3, 6, 11, 14–16, 18–19) has any power to effect cleansing, but whether it has the potency to effect a *decisive* cleansing" (Lane, *Hebrews 9–13*, 261–62; emphasis his).

[94] P. Hughes, *Commentary*, 392.

[95] Lane, *Hebrews 9–13*, 261.

[96] The claim of v 4 that animal blood could not remit sin "is unparalleled in the OT or Jewish literature. Although writers frequently noted that sacrifices were ineffective without appropriate conduct, no one made such an absolute claim as this" (Thompson, *Hebrews*, 195).

[97] Philo, *Moses* 2.107.

help but consider repeated sacrifices to be an intrinsic reminder of sin. Inherent in a repeated action is the fact that the underlying problem persists.

For example, I suffer from mental illness, the awful side effects of which are kept at bay by taking daily medication. As long as I take the prescription as directed, I don't suffer the effects of my illness. Miss a day or two, however, and I soon regret doing so. The daily repetition of taking my medicine is a reminder that the underlying problem persists. Likewise, Israel's annual sacrifices reminded them that their sin had not been fully remitted or forgotten.

Animal sacrifices treated symptoms without coming close to procuring a cure. If anything, they *exacerbated* the symptoms; R. Kent Hughes points out that "the Day of Atonement increased the burden of those with sensitive hearts."[98] For all its good intentions, Yom Kippur's lasting effect was the aggravation of one's conscience. If pardon has to be extended again and again, it "cannot convey the same peace of conscience as a pardon bestowed once for all."[99]

What the blood of bulls and goats could not do—what fifteen centuries of annual sacrificial ritual could not do—Jesus accomplished. It's worth pointing out that our author's mention of the "reminder of sins every year" (v 3) is equivocal. "Yearly sacrifices not only reminded the people of their own sinfulness but also reminded them that *God remembers sin*."[100] Whereas Israel was reminded of her sin year after year, and God pardoned it year after year, he now remembers our "sins no more" (8:12).[101] That is why we can say "good things [have] come" (10:1; 9:11). Only in Christ are our sins forgotten forever.

All those under the law were stuck in a futile cycle, a Mosaic merry-go-round, an inadequate sacrificial system in desperate need of reformation. "Thankfully, Christ came into the world to set things right."[102] The incarnation (which includes Jesus' death) was necessary because brute beasts cannot offer to God what he desires above all: volitional obedience from

---

[98] R. Hughes, *Hebrews*, 2:22.
[99] Bruce, *Hebrews*, 237.
[100] P. Hughes, *Commentary*, 392; emphasis his.
[101] P. Hughes, 392.
[102] Guthrie, *Hebrews*, 327.

the heart. The Son came to earth to obey the Father. "His very assumption of humanity was an act of obedience that climaxed in the cross"[103] (Phil 2:6–8). To prove his point our author in 10:5 turns to Psalm 40.[104]

The genre of Psalm 40 is a hybrid of sorts. The initial ten verses form a psalm of thanksgiving. David cried to God for help, and God lifted him out of the pit and established him on solid ground (40:1–2). The shepherd king then called on everyone to put their trust in his God (v 3), affirming that those who do so will be blessed (v 4) for the Lord does wondrous things on behalf of his people (v 5).

The portion cited in Hebrews is from 40:6–8, and it is reminiscent of Saul's disobedience concerning the Amalekites. Despite divine instructions to wipe out the nation, Saul preserved its king and livestock instead to present them as a sacrifice to God. The prophet Samuel, however, rebuked Saul for his rebellion. Sacrifices to the Most High are a good thing, but not at the expense of volitional, whole-hearted, absolute obedience (1 Sam 15:22).[105]

In Psalm 40, King David declares his belief that God is not as interested in sacrifices and offerings (v 6) as he is in those who obey his law and do his will (v 8). The second line of verse 6, "you have given me an open ear," is different in the Hebrew Masoretic Text (MT) than in the LXX, which reads "a body you restored to me." That's why Psalm 40:6 and Hebrews 10:5 read slightly differently in your Bible. Barclay explains that "'You have given me an open ear' means: 'You have so touched me that everything I hear I obey.' It is the obedient ear of which the psalmist is thinking. 'A body you have prepared for me' really means: 'You created me so that in my body and with my body I should do your will.' In essence, the meaning is the same."[106] Cockerill explains further, "He [i.e., the Hebrews author] could have built his case on the more literal translation [i.e., 'ear' in Hebrew versus 'body' in the LXX] which would have been in full

---

[103] Cockerill, *Hebrews*, 434.

[104] The phrase, "'See, I have come' [v 7] furnishes the basis for attributing these verses of the psalm to Jesus at the moment when he entered the world" (Lane, *Hebrews 9–13*, 262).

[105] "God's dissatisfaction with the conventional sacrificial offerings because they failed to express a corresponding desire to obey his will is a recurring motif in the prophetic Scriptures" (Lane, 263; e.g., Isa 1:10–13; 66:2–4; Jer 7:21–24; Hos 6:6; Amos 5:21–27; Mic 6:6–8).

[106] Barclay, *Hebrews*, 135.

agreement with the obedience of the Son. However, 'body' allowed him to tie this obedience more readily to the incarnation and final offering of Christ's 'body' on the cross."[107]

More significant for the context, Hebrews deduces an essential theological point in the use of "then" in Psalm 40:7. David dismissed the old law and its sacrificial system[108] because he wanted a new covenant "within my heart" (v 8). David wished he could do God's will perfectly, rendering sin offerings unnecessary. But this was impossible; his moral failures were well documented (v 12). Jesus, on the other hand, has done what David (as well as with every other human being) could never do: render voluntary and complete obedience to the will of God. "David's desire exceeded David's ability. ... What David desired, Christ accomplished."[109] That's why our author can place the words of Psalm 40 in Jesus' mouth (Heb 10:5). Once Jesus made a perfect, obedient, bodily sacrifice, the old law became null and void,[110] the sacrificial system became unnecessary, and Psalm 40 was fulfilled.

Hence, Hebrews says, "He [God] does away with the first in order to establish the second" (v 9). By employing Psalm 40, our author claims that God's people (represented by David) have understood for a thousand years the inadequacy of animal offerings in comparison to obedience to God's voice. The divine will or desire that God's anointed (Christ) came to do, according to Hebrews, was to sanctify us "once for all" (v 10) through his body (i.e., the incarnation). This claim deserves special attention.

First, as was the case in 7:27, "once for all" (*ephapax*) translates a Greek adverb that is stronger in intensity than the "once for all" (*hapax*) used in 9:26–28. While the latter term meant "pertaining to a single occurrence and decisively unique,"[111] the adverb used in 10:10 meant "taking place once and to the exclusion of any further occurrence."[112] Not only did Jesus'

---

[107] Cockerill, *Hebrews*, 436.
[108] "The list of conventional sacrifices [in Ps 40:6] alludes to the whole cultic system" (Attridge, *Hebrews*, 274).
[109] Karen H. Jobes, "The Function of Paronomasia in Hebrews 10:5–7," *TJ* 13 (1992): 189. "In Christ, therefore, man stands before God as obedient" (Coffman, *Hebrews*, 216).
[110] The phrase "does away" (*anaireō*) in v 9 "is the strongest negative statement the author has made or will make about the OT cultus." (Ellingworth, *Hebrews*, 504).
[111] BDAG, s.v. "ἅπαξ."
[112] BDAG, s.v. "ἐφάπαξ."

offering happen only once, but also it would not—could not—happen again. Second, the word occurs at the very end of verse 10, placing it in an emphatic position. Finally, the adverb modifies "we have been sanctified." That is to say, our author "is not merely reasserting the 'once-for-all' nature of Christ's sacrifice. He is saying that its 'once-for-all' character has provided a 'once-for-all' and thus sufficient sanctification of the people of God. *The benefit derived from Christ's sacrifice is as definitive as the sacrifice itself.*"[113]

Back in verse 7, the phrase "as it is written of me in the scroll of the book" adds an important nuance to our author's point. The prophets foretold Jesus' passion; as he was arrested in Gethsemane, he said, "Let the Scriptures be fulfilled" (Mark 14:49). But Bruce notes, "It was not simply that he found his duty set down plainly in the written record and set himself to carry it out: it was at the same time the dearest desire of his heart to fulfil that special service which was his Father's will for him. While it was indeed his Father's will, it was also his own spontaneous choice. And therefore his undertaking and fulfilling it constituted a sacrifice utterly acceptable to God."[114] In other words, Jesus' obedience was perfect and acceptable not only in that it did not deviate from the plan but also in that he rendered that obedience volitionally.

Under the Old Testament, God did not find pleasure in sacrifices and offerings (which he had commanded) because they were not ultimately coupled with obedience to his will. "There was nothing appealing to him in the sight of a dying animal. God had no pleasure in the moans and death-throes of lambs or bulls."[115] Ironically, burnt offerings (acts of worship) did not please him because they had to be coupled with sin offerings (acts of repentance). In God's eyes, the ultimate act of worship isn't one coupled with an act of repentance but with complete and voluntary obedience to his will, which Jesus accomplished through the incarnation. Hence, in Christ, there is a perfect *obedience*. God's will for his Son was to sacrifice

---

[113] Cockerill, *Hebrews*, 445; emphasis mine.

[114] Bruce, *Hebrews*, 242. He later adds, "The terms of the new covenant include the provision that God's law will henceforth be engraved in his people's hearts; and it was supremely fitting that this should be preeminently true of him through whose obedience and blood the new covenant has been ratified. 'I have come to do your will' is written over the whole record of our Lord's life; this was his attitude from first to last" (*Hebrews*, 243).

[115] R. Hughes, *Hebrews*, 2:23.

his physical body to achieve what animal sin offerings never could. In turn, because he offered a perfect obedience, Christ was a perfect *sacrifice*.

HEBREWS 10:11–18

At long last, our author summarizes the primary claim of Hebrews. He observes again how the priests of the old covenant, even as our author was speaking, were standing and offering "the same sacrifices" as their predecessors had done for a millennium and a half. They could not sit (Deut 10:8; 17:12; 18:7); their job was never done because those same sacrifices could not remit the sins of God's people.

Jesus, however, did so with one offering. When his job was done, he entered into God's rest and sat down at the Father's right hand—"theirs [i.e., the priests'] is the position of a servant; his is the position of a monarch."[116] Not even angels sit in God's presence (Isa 6:2; Rev 7:11). Hebrews draws once more on the imagery of Psalm 110; the Father has invited his Son to sit at his right hand precisely because the Son's obedience is now complete. "From the shame of the cross he has been exalted to the place of highest glory. With the more confidence, therefore, may his people avail themselves of his high-priestly aid, assured that in him they have access to all the grace and power of God."[117] At God's right hand, Jesus awaits the subjugation and consummation of all things to be initiated by his return in the clouds (9:28; 1 Thess 4:16–17; Rev 19:11–16). But until then, he intercedes on our behalf as a supreme Son and perfect Priest, a merciful Mediator and gracious Guarantor.

As stressed in verse 10, our author reiterates that Jesus' definitive offering has produced a definitive perfection for "those who are being sanctified" (v 14). The tense of that last participle is present and passive. While Jesus' sacrifice (and thus our "perfection," or justification) was a past, one-time event, the process of our becoming holy (i.e., sanctified) is present and ongoing. The Spirit who sanctifies (Rom 15:16; 1 Cor 6:11; 2 Thess 2:13)

---

[116] Barclay, *Hebrews*, 140. "In the OT, to stand in God's presence was considered an honour; but the exalted Jesus sits as a sign that he shares the authority of God himself" (Ellingworth, *Hebrews*, 508).

[117] Bruce, *Hebrews*, 246.

is the same Spirit who also testifies, along with Christ, to the superiority of the new covenant and the decisiveness with which it deals with our sin. Returning to Jeremiah 31,[118] our author notes for a final time that this covenant is written not in stone but on hearts and minds, and thus it "provides a means for the process of sanctification."[119] Also, don't miss the fact that our author has slightly changed the wording of Jeremiah's prophecy from the last time he quoted it. Whereas before it was "the house of Israel" (8:10), now it is a more inclusive "them" (10:16)—by this, "the author allows for a connection between the new covenant and all for whom Christ's blood was shed."[120]

Clara Barton, the founder of the American Red Cross, was well known for never harboring a grudge against those who wronged her. When someone once tried to prompt her memory as to a past slight, she failed to recall it. Her friend asked, "Don't you remember the wrong that was done you?" Barton replied, "No, I distinctly remember forgetting that." As it was with Clara, so it is to a much greater degree with Christ.[121] Our sins are both forgiven and forgotten—what Bruce calls an "irrevocable erasing of sins from the divine record"[122]—making further offerings unnecessary. In this way (v 18), our author draws the argument at the heart of Hebrews to a close.

>———◇———<

The Gospel writers tell us that during Passover, the Romans prepared three crosses on which they planned to crucify three "robbers" (Matt 27:38). It's

---

[118] Our author quotes again from Jer 31 for both literary and theological reasons. First, repeating the prophet's words as he did in chapter 8 serves as an *inclusio*—bookends or brackets for all that lies between. (For ancient writers, an *inclusio* was the same as section or paragraph headers today.) Second, quoting Jeremiah here was our author's way of underscoring his main point since chapter 8, that sins are now completely forgiven under this new covenant by the decisive atonement of the supreme Son (Guthrie, "Hebrews," 978–79).

[119] Guthrie, *Hebrews*, 330.

[120] Koester, *Hebrews*, 435.

[121] R. Hughes, *Hebrews*, 2:26.

[122] Bruce, *Hebrews*, 248. "The removal of sins from the divine memory is the strongest possible way of affirming their total abolition" (Cockerill, *Hebrews*, 458). Undetectable in English, our author in 10:17 has changed verb tenses from 8:12 with his repetition of "I will remember their sins … no more." Whereas he used the aorist subjunctive in 8:12, he now uses future indicative, a change that adds even greater emphasis to the statement. In a general sense, aorist subjunctive prohibitions are categorical, while future indicatives are "typically solemn, universal, or timeless" (Daniel B. Wallace, *Greek Grammar Beyond the Basics* [Grand Rapids: Zondervan, 1996], 723). In effect, "God says definitively that he will no longer remember all of their former misconduct no matter how 'lawless' it may have been" (Cockerill, *Hebrews*, 458).

more likely these were three political insurrectionists or anarchists (i.e., "rebels" NIV), what we today would call "terrorists."[123] In the commotion surrounding Jesus' illegal trial, the crowd demanded that one of these terrorists (probably a Jewish Zealot) be released and the Galilean rabbi crucified in his place. Don't miss this: A terrorist deserved to die but didn't. Jesus didn't deserve to die but did. He was crucified in the place of another "according to the definite plan and foreknowledge of God," as was asserted in the first gospel sermon (Acts 2:23).

As the bleating Passover lambs had their necks slit on the steps of the temple, their blood running down a trough into the Kidron Valley, the supreme Son—the Lamb of God—willingly shed his blood for every sin that had been committed since the fall and for every sin that would be committed henceforth. In him, "the wrath of God was satisfied, for every sin on him was laid."[124] Having atoned for every sin in perfect obedience and submission to the will of the Father, having cleansed our conscience that we might serve the living God, having restored our eternal inheritance as sons crowned with glory and honor, he cried out, *Tetelestai*—

"It is finished" (John 19:30).

SUMMARY

» Jesus ministers on our behalf in a heavenly sanctuary free that is free from the world's decay.

» Jesus' sacrifice achieved for us what the old covenant could not: a clean conscience and forgotten sins.

» Jesus had to suffer a violent death to secure our eternal salvation and inheritance.

» Jesus' perfect obedience on earth means his sacrifice on our behalf was acceptable to God "once for all."

---

[123] BDAG, s.v. "λῃστής."
[124] Stuart Townend, "In Christ Alone," in *New Irish Hymns* (Kingsway Music, 2001).

TALKING POINTS

THE ATONEMENT of Christ cannot be appreciated, let alone cherished, in the least without a full sense of our sinfulness. Accepting responsibility for our transgressions means confessing that we deserve to suffer every bit of God's punitive wrath. "To be blind or oblivious to this wrath of God against sinners is incredibly dangerous, like not being able to smell the gas leak gathering around the pilot light of your water heater, ready to blow your basement to smithereens and burn your house to the ground."[125] The Lord will not grade on a curve; the moral average of our peers will not be the standard by which we are judged. Nor can we hope to "make the cut" by having more good deeds than bad. Recall my earlier point: without Jesus, the conscience guides one to unmitigated shame and foments unrelenting terror. This horrible realization is the presupposition of the gospel—we are great sinners in need of great salvation from a great Savior. To a culture that rejects moral accountability of any stripe, Christians must be faithful in pointing to the very real and devastating power sin holds over every child of Adam[126]—and then quickly pivot to the good news that Jesus, through his own violent death, has secured for us eternal salvation from God's just punishment (9:12).

><>—<

IF THE PRESENT world were to assign a content rating to this central section of Hebrews, it would be deemed "For Mature Audiences Only." Disturbing themes are implicitly and explicitly traced throughout 8:1–10:18. An explicit theme is that of blood sacrifice; it is often difficult for a modern reader to comprehend such a practice, so accustomed are we to humane treatment and the disclaimer, "No animals were injured in the production of this film." Yet, under the law, the life of an animal was sacrificed in place of the sinner. In his holiness, God mandated that the life of the guilty be

---

[125] John Piper, "Perfected for All Time by a Single Offering," *Desiring God*, 16 February 1997, http://www.desiringgod.org/messages/perfected-for-all-time-by-a-single-offering.

[126] "The consequences of sin are threefold: debt which requires forgiveness, bondage which requires redemption, alienation which requires reconciliation" (Westcott, *Hebrews*, 316).

taken to atone for their sins. In his grace, God allowed an animal to be sub-stituted for the life of the guilty party. This idea implies a theme even more disturbing to many modern readers: the notion of God's wrath. Though we aren't fond of thinking about it, "God's anger at sinners is the biggest prob-lem in everyone's life, whether we know it or not."[127] Our society's aversion to any notion of God's wrath has infiltrated Christianity, where there has been a sustained quest to shape a bloodless gospel by denying the doctrine of substitutionary atonement—the teaching that Jesus took our place and suffered the wrath of God on our behalf to pay the full penalty for our sins (2 Cor 5:21; Heb 2:9; 5:1; 7:27). This doctrine must be defended lest God's righteousness be made a mockery and his grace cheapened. God is just. We deserve his full wrath as penalty for our sins. But the Father asked the Son to take our place and bear that wrath, and the Son willingly obeyed. This is proof of the immense love the triune God has for us. This is the message of the gospel.

›——◇——‹

IT SEEMS EACH passing day brings with it another absurd example of the cancel culture in which we now live. It's not only what was recently said or done that can land one in hot water; more than a few grown adults have been called to answer for sins committed many, many years ago in their high school years, no matter how frivolous. The fact that all of us did some ill-advised things in our younger years seems very much beside the point. Caught in the crosshairs of cancel culture, the "forgiveness" of the world lasts only as long as one is willing to grovel in humiliation. Make no mistake: the witch hunt our culture has embarked upon will not end until we have thoroughly cannibalized ourselves. In a society where nothing is forgotten, it is refreshing to know that God both forgives and forgets our sins. Scripture assures us that our sins are removed from us "as far as the east is from the west" (Ps 103:12); that they are cast "into the depths of the sea" (Mic 7:19). Through Isaiah, God reminded Israel, "I am he who blots out your transgressions *for my own sake*" (43:25; emphasis mine). Our

[127] Piper, "Perfected for All Time."

Father blots out our sin that his name might be glorified to the ends of the earth. At a time when the church struggles to be culturally relevant, imagine the glory God would receive if we became bastions of mercy and fortresses of forgiveness in the wasteland of arrogance, hatred, and resentment!

>———◇———<

IF OUR SINS are truly forgotten, what is it that should take their place in our respective remembrance? It should be Jesus' blood (i.e., his death or sacrifice). On the night before his crucifixion, Jesus invited his disciples to drink from a cup, "for this is my blood of the covenant, which is poured out for many for the forgiveness of sins" (Matt 26:27–28). The blood Jesus shed for us has secured such eternal forgiveness that another sacrifice is totally unnecessary, and it is this great truth that we celebrate each Lord's Day in the observance of the Lord's Supper. An altar on which animals are slaughtered and sacrificed has no place in our houses of worship; in its stead is a table. As we commune and fellowship with Christ and with one another, we are reminded that our great sin was no match for our greater Savior. In humility, we examine ourselves; in joy, we reflect on the Father's mercy. Each Lord's Day and through the Supper, the gospel transforms our remembrance of sin and feelings of guilt into remembrance of grace and feelings of gratitude.[128] The next time you see a communion table with the words "Do this in remembrance of Me," recognize that those words were etched into the wood because of our faith in what Hebrews teaches— and then pray that God will continue to etch into your heart the promises, purposes, and power of the new covenant (8:10).

>———◇———<

INTO THE HEART of Christians inevitably creeps doubt as to whether they are really saved. Such a feeling can be triggered by the haunting memory of past sins, denied answer to prayers, or frustration that we are not yet as mature as we ought to be. But recall Cockerill's statement, that

---

[128] P. Hughes, *Commentary*, 394.

"the benefit derived from Christ's sacrifice is as definitive as the sacrifice itself."[129] Jesus has dealt decisively with sin, and we are thus encouraged to speak confidently in God's presence. Living in the bold assurance Hebrews commends to us means forgiving ourselves just as God has forgiven us, as well as praying with the confidence that we've been reconciled to God and Christ is pleading our case for us. This same confidence concerning salvation and prayer should also be applied to our expectations concerning spiritual growth. The new covenant promises include both atonement (8:12) and equipment to live the godly life that pleases the Lord (8:10).[130] "Instead of putting his laws on stone tablets, they are placed in the very center of the believer's being, so that there is an inner impulse that both delights in knowing his law and doing his will."[131] As long as we draw breath, we remain a work in progress. Yet, in another sense, our spiritual growth has already been accomplished: "we *have been* sanctified through the offering of the body of Jesus Christ once for all" (10:10; emphasis mine). In Christ, our attainment of spiritual maturity is as much a *fait accompli* as is his utter sovereignty over all things (10:13).

>———◇———<

MUCH IS MADE in Hebrews of Jesus sitting at the right hand of God. His atoning work is done; no more sacrifice remains. Our author says that Christ will remain in that position until all his enemies are subjugated (10:13). But Maclaren draws our attention to an exception to this. When Stephen had drawn to a close his speech before the Sanhedrin, and as the whole council stewed in their rage against him, the church's first martyr saw the heavens open with "the Son of Man *standing* at the right hand of God" (Acts 7:56; emphasis mine). "The seated Christ, we might say, had sprung to His feet, in answer to the dying martyr's faith and prayer, and granted him the vision, not of calm repose, but of intensest activity for his help and sustaining."[132] May it be that we, like Stephen, catch a glimpse

---

[129] Cockerill, *Hebrews*, 445.

[130] DeSilva, *Perseverance*, 326.

[131] R. Hughes, *Hebrews*, 2:24–25.

[132] Maclaren, *Expositions*, 30:80.

in our final moments on earth of the exalted Son standing eagerly as a demonstration that he is with us until, and beyond, the end. Maybe he rises from his seat at our passing to affirm that our death does not mean that it has won the victory—quite the opposite. He beckons us to fear no evil, to join him "beyond the curtain" in the immediate presence of God. In our final moments, Jesus rises as the final assurance of our faith.

Chapter 8

THEREFORE

Judah felt something stir deep inside him as Timothy transitioned from his exposition of Jeremiah's prophecy to its implications for the congregation. He was beginning to understand the greatness and glory of Jesus as a great high priest. By virtue of his confession, Judah enjoyed access to many more blessings than the cessation of annual sacrifices and atonement rituals.

Through Jesus, he had a clean conscience before God and no longer stood condemned. Through Jesus, Judah's many sins had been forgotten, not just forgiven. Through Jesus, he could draw near to God in confidence instead of hanging back in fear of the divine presence. Through Jesus, he had confidence and hope that better things had and would come. Through Jesus, he had the courage and endurance to meet the challenges ahead. Even after burying his son, Judah's future was hopeful as long as Jesus was his Master.

Through Jesus, he was part of a community of fellow believers intent on encouraging one another through the darkest of days. True, some had left the Way in recent years due to a number of pressures—many more had remained, however. As Judah looked around the assembly in Stephen's house, he realized for the first time in a long while how much he genuinely loved this spiritual family. He had lost sight of that in recent weeks, but the family he had lost in leaving Moses, Judah had regained in choosing Jesus. Truth be told, he needed them. By nearly turning back to the faith of his fathers, Judah had almost thrown away something very precious.

That's when he heard Timothy say, "Consider how to stir up one another to love and good works…"

For many reasons, Hebrews has been my most difficult writing project to date. As I mentioned in the introduction, Hebrews' content might be the most obscure and mysterious in the New Testament—more so than that of Revelation, in my opinion. The density of Hebrews 7:1–10:18 is incredibly daunting. I am fascinated by the Christology and new covenant theology in the previous chapters. As I studied them, however, I kept wrestling with the "So what?" Making this two-thousand-year-old sermon relevant to today's Christians isn't easy. Yet our author makes it eas*ier* by drawing out three primary points of application.

In hopes of encouraging you, I want to confess something mildly embarrassing. There is much of Hebrews and the nature of Christ that I did not understand until this study. I say that as one who was raised in a godly home, who planned to be a preacher since I was four, who has been in ministry for over fifteen years at the time of this writing, who has been a Christian for over twenty years, who is a seventh-generation Christian and third-generation preacher, and who has stayed at a Holiday Inn Express on numerous occasions! Despite that [mostly un]impressive résumé, it was only when I began to research, reflect, and write on Hebrews that I began to understand some of its glorious truths.

For example, I didn't understand what it meant for God to forget—not just forgive—my sin. Some Christians in my past proved capable of forgiving—but not really forgetting—my many moral failures, and I learned from their example (in how I treated both others and myself). What I've discovered in Hebrews, however, is that the only way to move past the guilt and shame Satan loves to hang over our heads is to accept by faith this claim of Hebrews: those in Christ have had their consciences purged and hearts cleansed.

I didn't understand how Christ's faithfulness to the Father in his suffering could inspire my own faithfulness in difficult times. When the storms of life battered my ship against the rocks, I was content to wring my hands and cry, "Woe is me!" instead of securing myself to the Anchor of the soul, a merciful and faithful high priest who knows exactly how I feel because he's "been there." The more we fix our eyes on Jesus and consider him, the better we are at maintaining our confidence, endurance, and hope.

Finally, I didn't understand how laying claim to the benefits of the Son's high priesthood also meant accepting my place and participating in the family of God.. Several years ago, I was required to read a very short book for graduate school, *A Little Exercise for Young Theologians.* In it, Helmut Thielicke aptly wrote that Christ "can only be regarded rightly if we are ready to meet Him on the plane where He is active, that is, within the Christian church."[1] I've never forgotten those words. If anyone ever wished Christianity could be lived out legitimately in isolation, it's me. But it can't. It just *can't.* Refusing to stir up and encourage one another (10:24)—refusing to assemble with the church (v 25)—is a repudiation of Jesus' high priestly work. Eagerly awaiting our high priest's reemergence from behind the curtain is a corporate, not just an individual, endeavor.

If at any point in your previous study of Hebrews 7:1–10:18 you felt lost and gave up, let me encourage you to return again…and again…and yet again if necessary. Patience is a necessity in Bible study. What doesn't make sense today might make a lot of sense tomorrow. As you observe our author unpacking his three "So what?" imperatives, go back to understand how they flow from the priestly and mediating ministry of the supreme Son. Recall from my comments on 6:1–3 that our author wants us to see how Christian principles find their root in Christ. In this passage, we discover the Christological "why" for much of Christian living.

HEBREWS 10:19–25

The English word "therefore" is an important signpost. It's often explained (usually in a very cheesy way) that when one sees "therefore," one should stop and ask, "What is it there for?" Groan-worthy as it is, that's a helpful way of remembering the word's significance. "Therefore" often translates the Greek *oun*, a word that notes what follows it is the result of what preceded it.[2] Our author has used *oun* several times already and will continue to do so.[3] Use of it in verse 19, however, may be his most important.

---

[1] Helmut Thielicke, *A Little Exercise for Young Theologians*, trans. Charles L. Taylor (Grand Rapids: Eerdmans, 1962), 23.

[2] BDAG, s.v. "οὖν."

[3] Heb 2:14; 4:1, 6, 11, 14, 16; 7:11; 8:4; 9:1, 23; 10:35; 12:1; 13:15.

There is an eventual movement in almost every New Testament epistle from the indicative to the imperative: "Here is what is true" to "Here is how we should live." In verses 19–25, which is one long sentence in Greek, our author transitions away from the book's main theological argument and now "earnestly appeals for the community to apply the blessings of Christ's high priestly ministry to its own daily life."[4] Specifically, what follows is predicated on two beautiful realities: (1) "We have confidence to enter the holy places by the blood of Jesus" (v 19), and (2) "We have a great priest over the house of God" (v 21).

As used previously (3:6; 4:16), "confidence" refers to the boldness with which we draw near to God. "Christians can approach God confidently, feeling completely at home in the situation created for them by Christ's saving work."[5] While Israel's access to God was restricted and characterized by fear (12:18–21), ours has been opened up by our champion-pioneer and is marked by boldness (Eph 3:12). There is now no need to approach in trepidation, anxious that one wrong move could spell our doom.

While only Israel's high priest could approach the divine presence, of which the ark was merely a symbol, our high priest allows any Christian to approach God's throne. Cockerill calls this "the most fundamental privilege that God's people now have."[6] What was once closed (9:8) is now open. The blood of Jesus has cleansed our consciences, granting us the boldness to go where his blood has prepared the way (6:19–20). It is a "new" way, for it was previously unavailable to the saints of God; it is a "living" way, for it isn't fouled by the stench of our dead works (6:1; 9:14).

As our forerunner, Christ opened up that new and living way when the temple curtain was torn in two. When our author equates the curtain with Jesus' flesh (v 20), he has in mind both the incarnation and the passion of Christ. In his life and death, he chose to identify with humanity (John 1:14); in his life and death, he also demonstrated obedience to the Father's will (Heb 5:7–9). Through the "curtain" of Jesus' life and death, therefore, we are led to glory (2:10), we enter God's rest (4:11), we

---

[4] Lane, *Hebrews 9–13*, 281.
[5] Reese, *Hebrews*, 176.
[6] Cockerill, *Hebrews*, 466.

approach the throne (4:16). And we do not stand at the throne hesitantly asking for more like Oliver Twist; we are those whom Christ has chosen to call "brothers" (2:11–13). Our confidence before God is not rooted in the incarnation alone but also in Jesus' obedience to the Father. The Father favors us because he favors his obedient Son.[7] *There thus remains no reason our confidence in our relationship with God should be any less than the supreme Son's confidence in his relationship with the Father.*

To the saving and intercessory function of Jesus' high priesthood is now added his authority and rule (v 21). As our priest-king, Jesus rules over the house of God (3:6; Eph 1:22; Col 1:18). While Christ is the head of God's house as Son in 3:6, he also serves that function as priest. He now takes responsibility for the house (i.e., the church) exclusively. His present work at the Father's right hand is not on behalf of those who have not obeyed his gospel. Our author's audience was likely preoccupied with the handful of disadvantages of being members of the church of Christ, yet he would have them see the myriad blessings. On earth, it is of great benefit to be part of a family of wealth or power, but it pales significantly compared to the privilege of being a member of the spiritual family of Christ. Entering into the holy places (i.e., drawing near to God) is a family, not an individual, affair.[8]

Since we possess this confidence and this great priest:

Let us draw near (v 22). If the supremacy and priesthood of Jesus is Hebrews' greatest truth, drawing near to God is the epistle's greatest imperative of that truth. Our author longs for his readers to draw closer to or lean harder upon God in their trials. His words here remind us of those spoken earlier: "Let us then with confidence draw near to the throne of grace" (4:16). Access to God is no longer restricted—but neither can we approach the Most High in any way we please.

We are to come *with a true, or sincere, heart* (Ps 51:6, 10; Matt 5:8; 1 Tim 1:5). Recall that the heart is the center of our being (Prov 4:23), "the

---

[7] "Because he lives, we shall live also. We shall not die in the holy place, unless he dies. God will not smite us unless he smites him" (C. H. Spurgeon, "The Rent Veil," in *The Metropolitan Tabernacle Pulpit Sermons* [London: Passmore, 1888], 34:180).

[8] All our author has to say beginning in v 19 concerns a corporate endeavor (note his use of "brothers"). "It is only as part of God's household and in union with its other members that God's people can draw near and persevere" (Cockerill, *Hebrews*, 472).

reservoir of inner resources [that] determines outward behavior."[9] Through Ezekiel, God promised to give his people a new heart to replace theirs of stone (36:25–29). Thus to have a true, sincere heart means we have opened our hearts to the transformation God longs to work in us (Eph 2:10; Phil 1:6). It means we are eager to be in his presence and do his will instead of using "drawing near" as little more than a "Get Out of Jail Free" card.

We are to come *in full assurance of faith* (6:11). Our author will have much to say about faith in the next chapter, and there he will inform his readers that the faith necessary to draw near to God must believe that God exists and God rewards (11:6). "Full assurance of faith" is a "conviction of things not seen" (11:1), which in turn equips us to endure hardship (10:36–39). Christians' faith and hope gives us the assurance we are indeed saved to the uttermost (7:25; 1 John 5:13), the confidence to approach and speak freely at the throne (4:16), and the conviction that God will keep his promises in Christ (7:21).

We must come *with sprinkled hearts and washed bodies*. Again, God promised to "sprinkle clean water" upon his people, cleansing them from their uncleanness (Ezek 36:25). Whereas under the law, material things were purified with sprinkled blood or special washing (9:18–22), Christians, via baptism, have their consciences, or hearts, sprinkled clean by Jesus' blood (1 Pet 1:2; 3:21; 1 Cor 6:11; Eph 5:26; Titus 3:5). There is no reason to be hesitant before our Father. Casting our sins into the farthest depths of the sea (Mic 7:19), he no longer has any memory of them. However, once cleansed, we must pursue righteousness in order to draw near to God.[10]

Let us hold fast (v 23). Our author repeats another key exhortation of his sermon: "hold fast" (3:6, 14; 4:14; 6:18). His concern has been that his audience had started wavering in their commitment to the Name. Since there is glory, honor, and rest to be found by those who draw near to the Father, we must hold fast, lest we drift away (2:1).

---

[9] Guthrie, *Hebrews*, 343. "We remember how the failure to respond to God through obedience by the wilderness generation was due to a wicked, hard, wandering, and faithless heart (3:8, 10, 12; 4:7), and how the word of God was described as discerning the thoughts and intentions of the heart (4:12), and how the new covenant was to be one inscribed on the hearts of humans (8:10; 10:16)" (Johnson, *Hebrews*, 257–58).

[10] "The perfect participles indicate that not only having been, but continuing to be, cleansed is prerequisite for entrance into the divine presence" (Cockerill, *Hebrews*, 475).

Our grip is on our confession of Jesus as the supreme Son and perfect Priest, the object of our hope. Hiding or giving up on our hope demonstrates we consider God to be unfaithful.[11] Calvin wrote that "as hope is born of faith, so it is fed and sustained by it to the last."[12] Thus our confession is that all our faith and hope—our trust and confidence, our belief and boldness—rests in who Christ is, what he has done for us, and that he even now reigns over all. It is the confession we made when washed and cleansed in baptism (v 22). In the face of adversity, an unwavering faith can be a nonverbal confession of our hope, but biblical confession must also make its way from the heart to the mouth (Matt 10:32–33; Rom 10:10).[13]

We are thus urged to safeguard ("hold fast … without wavering"), rather than shy away from (v 39), such a confession. This is the only occurrence of the term *aklinēs* ("without wavering") in the New Testament, but it appears twice in 4 Maccabees with the sense of inflexibility or unyieldingness (6:7; 17:3). Philo used it to refer to God's immutability.[14] Likewise, our faith and hope are to be inflexible, unyielding, and immutable, not based on our ever-changing circumstances but rather on God's faithfulness, his commitment to honor his oath (6:13–20; 7:20–21, 28), which Lane considers "the strongest incentive."[15] We can be faithful because God is (11:11).

Some of God's promises have been fulfilled (e.g., the new covenant) while others remain (entering his rest). All his promises, however, "are the basis for Christians' hope."[16] The reality of past fulfillment is our assurance that unrealized faith will become future fact. For example, as certain as Jesus died and rose again, so we can be assured that he will return (9:28;

[11] DeSilva, *Perseverance*, 341.

[12] Calvin, *Hebrews*, 238.

[13] "This hope in us … cannot remain dumb; it must speak, and give a reason both to friends and enemies of its own existence" (Franz Delitzsch, *Commentary on the Epistle to the Hebrews*, trans. Thomas L. Kingsbury, [Edinburgh: T&T Clark, 1876], 2:180).

[14] Philo, *Giants* 49; *Alleg. Interp.* 2.83.

[15] Lane, *Hebrews 9–13*, 289. That God is faithful is one of the most consistent claims of Scripture (Ps 145:13; 1 Cor 1:9; 10:13; 2 Cor 1:18; 1 Thess 5:24; 2 Thess 3:3; 1 Pet 4:19; 1 John 1:9; Rev 1:5; 3:14; 19:11). "On the other hand, this statement lays a foundation for the warning to follow in 10:26–31: those who turn aside are doing nothing less than denying the faithfulness of God. … Faithful obedience is the only appropriate response to divine faithfulness" (Cockerill, *Hebrews*, 477–78).

[16] Attridge, *Hebrews*, 289.

1 Thess 4:14). Likewise, if God's promise is so sure, "why should we not cherish it confidently and confess it boldly?"[17]

Let us consider (vv 24–25). In inviting us to "draw near," our author drew our gaze *upward*. In exhorting us to "hold fast," he directed our gaze *inward*. And in his directive to "stir up," he urges us to look *outward*.

One of my childhood homes had a large wood stove in the living room. During the winter, we used it daily to heat that part of the house. Each night, a large green log was thrown in to provide heat during the night; every morning, it was often my responsibility to take the big iron poker and stir the coals back to life. This is the image our author is using here in verse 24. To prevent the sluggishness and rebellion about which he has already warned his audience, he calls on them "to stir up one another to love and good works." The term translated "stir up" (*paroxysmos*) is used only one other time in the New Testament. In Acts 15:39, Paul and Barnabas had a "sharp disagreement" (*paroxysmos*) over what to do with John Mark. With its much more positive use here in Hebrews, our author intends his audience to seek ways to provoke ("spur" NIV) one another to further demonstrations of love and service. These good works stand opposed to the "dead works" from which our consciences have been cleansed.

>———◇———<

Throughout every one of my writing projects on a book of the Bible, I inevitably discover my views evolving on certain issues. Things I once advocated in a dogmatic fashion I end up relaxing on; some things I once believed casually become bold convictions. Infrequently, a conviction I held pretty firmly is impressed upon me to a far deeper level than before. In Hebrews' case, the conviction impressed deeper upon me is the exhortation not to forsake the assembly of the church (v 25).

Recall that Christians need daily mutual edification (3:13), or positive provocation (10:24). "A chief function of public worship, according to Paul, is the edification of all who come together (1 Cor. 14:26ff.). But how can men be edified when they absent themselves from the assembly?"[18]

---

[17] Bruce, *Hebrews*, 256.
[18] Lightfoot, *Jesus Christ Today*, 191.

It's easy to imagine the pressures likely causing some in the original audience to neglect the Christian assembly: spiritual laziness brought on by the passage of time, physical or emotional fatigue, arrogance and hubris, general busyness, or even fear.[19] The threats against them, however, were about to worsen.

Our author claims that assembling with fellow saints will become increasingly important as we "see the Day drawing near." This is a possible reference to the Second Coming;[20] it was commonly believed in the first-century church that Jesus would return in their lifetime (e.g., 1 Thess 4:13–17; 2 Thess 2:1; 1 Pet 4:7; 2 Pet 3:3–4). With the delay brought by each passing day, it perhaps was difficult for these Hebrew Christians to believe in the imminence of the Second Coming, and they became discouraged—how much more so today!

Though he has now tarried two thousand years, each day brings us closer to that glorious moment when the Lord himself will descend from heaven. Unknown to us is the time between Jesus' enthronement and return, but that period is known throughout the New Testament as the last days or end times, and we by faith believe that "the time is near" (Rev 1:3). Whether it occurs today or ten thousand years from now, Christians live convinced that the Second Coming is imminent.

To that end, our author exhorts us to be faithful to the Christian assembly, for it is only there that we receive the daily mutual encouragement to be eager, soft hearted, confident, faithful, and obedient versus sluggish, hardened, immature, unbelieving, and rebellious. Lest we still be tempted not to take our author seriously, remember the context of this imperative. It does not come in a long list of general dos and don'ts for Christians but in the wake of a grand discussion of Jesus as our perfect priest[21] and immediately following three critical imperatives. Assembling with the saints is vital for every Christian because it is there that we draw near to God;

---

[19] We know for a fact that arrogance and busyness kept some in the first and second centuries from attending (Ignatius, *Ephesians* 5.3; Hermas, *Similitude* 8.8.1; 9.20.1).

[20] Just as the Old Testament prophets spoke of the "day of the Lord" (Isa 2:12; 13:6; Joel 1:15; 2:31; Amos 5:18; Zech 14:1) as a time of judgment, the New Testament speaks of Christ's return as the "day of the Lord" (1 Cor 1:8; 5:5; 2 Cor 1:14; Phil 1:10; 2:16; 1 Thess 5:2) or simply "the day" (2 Tim 1:12, 18; 4:8) (Thompson, *Hebrews*, 207).

[21] "The neglect of worship and fellowship was symptomatic of a catastrophic failure to appreciate the significance of Christ's priestly ministry and the access to God it provided" (Lane, *Hebrews 9–13*, 290).

it is there that we confess our hope; it is there that we stir up one another. One cannot obey the three imperatives of verses 22–24 while ignoring the warning of verse 25.

>———◇———<

For all that, it cannot be gainsaid that this passage has suffered much abuse at the hands of well-meaning Christians who were a bit too prone to criticism and condemnation. A preacher I know once reamed out his congregation in a Sunday sermon because some had failed to assemble with the saints at a previous midweek Bible study—which fell on Christmas Day. He accused those not in attendance (specifically those who had not attended anywhere else on that particular Wednesday night) of violating Hebrews 10:25, as well as Matthew 6:33; 8:21–22; 10:34–39, and other passages.

More recently, the COVID-19 pandemic, with its subsequent social-distancing guidelines and mandatory shelter-in-place orders, prohibited most churches from assembling for several weeks or months. A few congregations defied these orders, contending the saints' assembly is mandatory regardless of government decrees. The Christians just mentioned looked down their noses at congregations temporarily opting for virtual, live-streamed worship services in lieu of a conventional assembly. They claimed any church faithful to Christ would adhere to Hebrews 10:25 no matter what, even in defiance of the government's public health and safety guidelines. After all, the early church continued to meet when their assemblies became unlawful. But is this really the sort of thing our author had in mind?

Two words in this text will help us answer that question. The first is "neglecting" (*enkataleipō*), a word that "connotes not simply neglect, but wrongful abandonment."[22] The second is "habit" (*ethos*), which refers to "usual behavior" or regular and consistent practices.[23] Thus our author is rebuking those who regularly and consistently abandon the Christian assembly.

So when has a Christian violated Hebrews 10:25? This might fall under "hard to define, but you know it when you see it." It should go without

---

[22] Attridge, *Hebrews*, 290; e.g., Matt 27:46; 2 Cor 4:9; 2 Tim 4:10, 16; Heb 13:5.
[23] BDAG, s.v. "ἔθος"; e.g., Luke 22:39; John 19:40; Acts 25:16.

saying that this verse has nothing to do with missing the assembly due to illness or other "providential hindrances." Nor does this verse condemn those who opt to be with family on Christmas instead of attending a mid-week Bible study, especially since this happens only when Christmas falls on a Wednesday (something that occurs only every five or six years). More-over, it hardly applies to churches that go virtual temporarily in response to a pandemic and out of love for their neighbor. If that's not "providentially hindered," I don't know what is!

No, our author is speaking to those who *frequently abandon* the assem-bly. It is their custom or practice to do so, and for any one of the myriad of reasons discussed above: spiritual lethargy, emotional or physical exhaus-tion, arrogance or hubris, or even fear. In my own life, there was a time when I knew I was among those to whom our author was speaking. I knew it because I had begun to make excuses not to attend; I even found myself preparing excuses in advance! I have felt tremendous shame for that.

What constitutes a habit of assembly abandonment must be deter-mined by individual Christians according to their consciences, including whether they are confident they can stand before the Lord with their an-swers. Make no mistake, however: When it is our consistent practice not to attend, we make excuses for not doing so, and we plan these excuses in advance—when that happens, we have placed ourselves in our author's crosshairs and should repent.

Yes, *repent*, for when we make it our habit to abandon the assembly, we are guilty of three things: (1) We have not taken seriously the imminence of the Second Coming, (2) we have failed to love and mutually encourage our Christian family,[24] and (3) we have arrogantly considered ourselves beyond the reach of the sluggishness, apathy, unbelief, and hard-hearted rebellion that have ensnared others. This last point is precisely where our author heads next.

[24] "It is interesting to note that the emphasis here is not on what a believer gets from the assembly, but rather on what he can *contribute* to the assembly (as he considers the others, in order to stimulate them to love and good works). A man who attends the public worship only for what he can get, and whose attendance becomes more and more sporadic because he thinks he is getting nothing from attending, has not yet grasped the significance of this oft-memorized passage from Hebrews! Indeed, he may need encouragement (we all do!); he also needs to be an encourager, and that encouragement is best given when the believers have all assembled" (Reese, *Hebrews*, 180; emphasis his).

HEBREWS 10:26–31

This is another of Hebrews' warning passages (Guthrie considers it "arguably the harshest in the book"[25]), and it has several ties to 6:4–8.[26] As with the whole of Hebrews, we assume a grave risk if we do not take our author at his word here; Bruce reminds us, "Our author is not given to wild exaggeration, and when he uses language like this, he chooses his words with his customary care."[27]

Why our author considers the Christian assembly to be so important should come as no surprise. As far back as 3:12–13, he linked falling away with an absence of mutual encouragement. In verse 26, he uses "for" to tie abandoning the assembly with "sinning deliberately," which is comparable to falling "away from the living God" (3:12). More broadly, these six verses are the antithesis of the previous seven. While verses 19–25 speak of a proper response to what Christ has done, verses 26–31 address the *im*proper one.[28]

First, consider *what* our author is discussing. In 9:7, he mentioned how Israel's high priest offered sacrifices to atone for the "unintentional sins of the people."[29] Does Jesus' blood likewise apply only to our inadvertent sins? What is an "unintentional" versus "intentional" sin anyway? In one sense, isn't all sin intentional in that it represents a choice we have made?

Guthrie says that the adverb translated "deliberately" (*hekousiōs*) "communicates the idea of willing participation in an action, something done with a clear mind and firm step, and is important to our interpretation of the passage."[30] As opposed to someone who trespassed out of ignorance or weakness, one who sinned intentionally against the law was said to have done so "with a high hand" (Num 15:30). Two classic examples of such sins were blasphemy (Lev 24:14–16) and idolatry (Deut 17:2–3); these sins were unforgivable because the perpetrator had rejected the sole means of forgiveness (the God of Israel) in the first place.

---

[25] Guthrie, *Hebrews*, 355.

[26] For more on the parallels between 6:4–8 and 10:26–31, see Lane, *Hebrews 9–13*, 291.

[27] Bruce, *Hebrews*, 261.

[28] Lane, *Hebrews 9–13*, 291–92.

[29] See Lev 4:2, 13, 22, 27; 5:2–4; Num 15:27–31.

[30] Guthrie, *Hebrews*, 355.

Likewise, to sin "deliberately" under the covenant of Christ is to tread intentionally the path of rebellion against the Lord. This is to be distinguished from sins of ignorance and weakness in that, instead of a solitary moment of indiscretion, one has joyfully made sin a habit,[31] and rebellion (e.g., blasphemy and idolatry) becomes the trajectory of one's whole life (Prov 2:13–15). "The ignorant cannot commit this sin. It cannot be committed inadvertently. It is a sin only 'church people' can commit. To such, 'no sacrifice for sins is left' because they have rejected the one and only valid sacrifice—Christ."[32]

Additionally, consider of *whom* our author is speaking. As they do with 6:4–6, some object that our author does not have in mind a genuine Christian. They argue that no true Christian can fall away. Yet note that our author uses the inclusive "we" (vv 26, 30). He is speaking of those who have received "the knowledge of the truth," which is a "technical expression [that] refers to the acceptance of life in response to the preaching of the gospel."[33] Moreover, our author refers to those who had once been "sanctified" (v 29) and "enlightened" (v 32). He has in mind those who once turned from sin to embrace the Son but have now forfeited their confidence and repudiated their confession.

For such a person, there "no longer remains a sacrifice for sins"[34] since he or she has rejected the only atonement provided—the once-and-for-all sacrifice of the high priest (v 18; Acts 4:12)—and has become one of God's "adversaries" (Isa 26:11). Such a one "not only shuts out himself from grace, but the door of repentance is shut behind him; and he has before him only the prospect of a damnation from which there is no escape."[35] In this case, "confidence" and "hope" (3:6) are replaced with "a fearful expectation of judgment" (10:27).

Our author returns to the *a fortiori* argument undergirding 2:2–3— that if the punishment for rebellion under Moses was certain, it is more

---

[31] The participle translated "sinning" (*hamartanontōn*) is present tense, meaning "the sin involved is not a single act, but a continuing rejection of Christ" (Attridge, *Hebrews*, 292).

[32] R. Hughes, *Hebrews*, 2:41.

[33] Lane, *Hebrews 9–13*, 292; e.g., 1 Tim 2:4; 4:3; 2 Tim 2:25; 3:7.

[34] This phrase "brings home both the promise and the peril of the priestly work of Jesus" (Johnson, *Hebrews*, 261). "The once-for-all nature of Christ's sacrifice is like a two-edged sword. On the one hand, it is so effective that it does not need to be repeated (7:27) but, on the other hand, it cannot be repeated, even if needed" (George Wesley Buchanan, *To the Hebrews*, 2nd ed., AB 36 [Garden City, NY: Doubleday, 1976], 171).

[35] Delitzsch, *Hebrews*, 2:185.

certain under the Son, for the privileges we enjoy under the Son are greater than those under Moses. To define more precisely what "punishment"[36] entails, our author gives three sharp juxtapositions in verse 29 that would have arrested the audience's attention.

Trampled underfoot the Son of God. This phrase "denotes contempt of the most flagrant kind."[37] This fact is compounded when we realize "trampled" (*katapateō*) is never used elsewhere in the LXX or the New Testament with God or Christ as the object.[38] Deliberate sin isn't just breaking a law; it's stomping on God! The use of "the Son of God" is intentional (see 6:6). The Hebrew Christians would not expect One so worthy of supreme honor to be shown such tremendous disdain.

Profaned the blood of the covenant. The word translated "profaned" (*koinos*) can mean "common" or "ordinary," though in specific contexts, it refers to "that which is ceremonially impure."[39] It is staggering to think anyone would consider Jesus' sacrificial, sanctifying blood to be defiling garbage.[40] His blood atoned for sin fully and finally (v 14) when no one else's could, yet those who reject Christ act as if his violent death was of no greater importance than the death of any other person.[41]

Outraged[42] the Spirit of grace. This is the final juxtaposition: "outrage" and "the Spirit of grace" don't belong in the same sentence! But Jesus said that to ascribe his miraculous power to the work of Satan, versus the work of the Spirit, was to commit the unforgivable sin (Mark 3:22–30). Isaiah lamented how Israel, after all the grace God had shown them, "had

---

[36] The Greek noun *timōria* referred to punishment that was vengeful rather than corrective (e.g., 2 Maccabees 6:26; 4 Maccabees 4:24; Herodotus, *Histories* 5.90; Josephus, *Wars* 2.155). "This is not to be confused with 'discipline' (*paideia*) that God brings upon his sons (Heb 12:7–11); it is, rather, the fearful judgment of the end time" (Johnson, *Hebrews*, 264).

[37] James Moffatt, *A Critical and Exegetical Commentary on the Epistle to the Hebrews*, ICC (Edinburgh: T&T Clark, 1924), 151; e.g., Ps 56:2; Isa 26:6; 63:3, 6, 18; Dan 8:10; Mic 7:10; Zech 12:3 LXX; Matt 5:13; 7:6; Homer, *Iliad* 4.157; Plato, *Laws* 4.714a.

[38] Ellingworth, *Hebrews*, 540.

[39] BDAG, s.v. "κοινός"; e.g., Mark 7:2, 5; Acts 10:14, 28; 11:8; Rom 14:14; Rev 21:27.

[40] "The author has argued throughout the letter that Jesus' blood secures 'eternal redemption' (9:12), cleanses the conscience (9:14; cf. 12:24), removes sin (9:25–26), gives access to God's presence (10:19), and sanctifies (10:29; 13:12). ... Those who reject Jesus, however, do not seek purification by blood. They reject his blood as unclean, tossing it aside as one would throw a menstrual cloth into the garbage" (Schreiner, *Hebrews*, 326).

[41] Bruce, *Hebrews*, 262.

[42] "Insulted," rather than "outraged," might be a better translation of *enybrizō*. Though both definitions are listed in BDAG, "insulted" emphasizes the arrogance of the insulter; "outraged" draws attention to the (potentially capricious) feelings of the insulted, while the Spirit is never capricious in any way.

turned on him; they grieved his Holy Spirit. So he turned on them, became their enemy and fought them" (63:10 Msg; see Eph 4:30). Specifically in Hebrews, the Spirit speaks words of warning (3:7–11), enlightenment (9:8), and hope (10:15–17). More broadly, the gift of the Spirit to the church (2:4; 6:4) is a demonstration of God's grace. "Rejection of the Spirit is so serious because it is repudiation of the presence and power of God in one's own life. Such rejection is tantamount to kicking God out."[43]

Our author does not have just any sin in mind, but that of willful or intentional apostasy, and these three juxtapositions in verse 29 make that clear. The fate that awaits us should we renounce Jesus is one almost too terrible to talk about. These adversaries (v 27), though futilely attempting to trample on the Son of God with their feet (v 29), are the same ones who will soon be placed under *Jesus'* feet as a footstool (v 13) in abject humiliation.[44]

The theme of humiliation and punishment continues with two Old Testament citations[45] (v 30) that come from the Song of Moses (Deut 32:35–36). This song was often quoted in the synagogue and early church, so Hebrews' original audience would have been familiar with it. In it, God (through Moses) lamented Israel's unfaithfulness and warned what awaited them (32:19–25) if they persisted in the rebellious ways of their fathers who lay buried in the wilderness. However, the two lines our author cites come in the context of God's swearing vengeance on Israel's *enemies* for their cruelty and presumption. "'Vengeance is mine, and recompense, for the time when their foot shall slip; for the day of their calamity is at hand, and their doom comes swiftly.' For the LORD will vindicate his people and have compassion on his servants, when he sees that their power is gone and there is none remaining, bond or free" (32:35–36). Placed together in Hebrews, our author uses Deuteronomy to warn his audience that the fate of *Israel's enemies* also awaits *Christians* who sin deliberately and renounce Jesus. Not to be missed is the particular responsibility God assumes in punishment and deliverance. This is not something he delegates; rather, as a jealous God,

---

[43] Cockerill, *Hebrews*, 490.

[44] "The ἐχθροί ['enemies'] of Ps 110:1, mentioned at 1:13 and 10:13, now become more precisely defined" (Attridge, *Hebrews*, 293, n. 23).

[45] Our author's odd introduction to these citations ("we know him who said") "undercuts any plea of ignorance, making a refusal to heed the message all the more severe" (Koester, *Hebrews*, 453).

he takes it personally when his Name is dishonored and specifically sees to judging the transgressor himself.

The final verse of this section reinforces this idea of personal vengeance. "It is a fearful thing to fall into the hands of the living God" (v 31; 4:13), a sentence that "is chilling in its simplicity."[46] To fall into someone's hands means they have overpowered you in a negative sense (Judg 15:18; Luke 10:36; Sirach 8:1). There is sometimes mercy or reassurance to be found in falling into God's hands (2 Sam 24:14) but not always (Acts 13:11)—particularly not for someone opposed to Jesus. Verse 31 has been repeated countless times through the centuries as a warning to the wicked unbeliever who refuses to obey the gospel. Keep in mind, however, that it was spoken here to Christians.[47] If a dreadful fate awaited both rebellious Israel and her enemies, exponentially greater dread awaits the apostate Christian when he or she comes face to face with a holy God without any claim to Jesus' blood.

Koester summarizes verses 26–31: "This passage is unsettling because it warns that God's people can become God's adversaries through persistent sin. Listeners do not appear to be guilty of heinous crimes, but they are susceptible to drift (2:1) and neglect (2:2; 10:25). The author's words are designed to cut through the vagueness of the listeners' situation and bring them to a zeal for God that is a fitting response to his zeal for them."[48]

HEBREWS 10:32–39

Our author now offers an encouraging word on the heels of a warning, as he did in 6:9–12.[49] In the former passage, however, he had merely expressed confidence in "better things" from his brethren and made slight mention of their good works (6:10). Now he calls on them to remember the boldness they demonstrated when they first became Christians. Their "past is to be an example to their present"[50] (1 Cor 4:17; 2 Tim 1:6).

---

[46] Johnson, *Hebrews*, 266.

[47] Bruce, *Hebrews*, 265.

[48] Koester, *Hebrews*, 456.

[49] For the parallels between 10:32–39 and 6:9–12, see Lane, *Hebrews 9–13*, 296–97, Figure 1.

[50] Ellingworth, *Hebrews*, 545. "The encouragement to continue on comes in two parts—first, to *remember* the past (vv. 32–34), and second, to *respond* in the present (vv. 35–39)" (R. Hughes, *Hebrews*, 2:51–52; emphasis his).

Following their baptism, these Christians had formerly demonstrated perseverance[51] during hardship and "sufferings" (10:32). Recently these
same struggles had prompted some to renounce their confession and to
forsake the church. For those that remained, their confidence and endurance were flagging. Our author urges them to return to their original
conduct as Christians. When he refers to their "hard struggle" (v 32), he
lays the groundwork for his race metaphor in 12:1–2; the term *athlēsis*
referred to athletes' intense competition in the arena.[52] "A criminal was
expected to bear up passively under blows inflicted for punishment, but
an athlete remained active and resistant when receiving blows in a boxing match. Accordingly, the author says that the listeners suffered, not as
mere victims, but as athletes who persevered in the hope of future glory"[53]
(1 Cor 9:24–25).

"Reproach[54] and affliction[55]" (v 33) imply that these Christians had suffered verbal and physical abuse for their faith, which would have brought
shame upon them in the eyes of their neighbors, perhaps convincing some
saints to defect and dissuading others from converting. If this abuse was
public enough, local authorities might have punished these Christians because their ill treatment at the hands of the populace presumably made the
saints appear guilty of some crime or another.[56] "Publicly exposed" (*the-
atrizō*) is another term that occurs only here in the New Testament. The
verb originally meant to "perform in the theatre,"[57] but by the first century,
it had gained the figurative meaning "to make a spectacle of someone."[58]

[51] "Endured" (*hypomenō*) in v 32 "retains the meaning of remaining on the field of battle instead of fleeing" (Ellingworth, *Hebrews*, 546); i.e., "stand one's ground" (BDAG, s.v. "ὑπομένω"; e.g., Homer, *Iliad* 15.312).

[52] Polybius, *Histories* 5.64.6; 7.10.2–4; 27.9.7–11.

[53] Koester, *Hebrews*, 464.

[54] The noun *oneidismos* and verb *oneidizō* were used throughout the LXX and New Testament to describe the verbal insult of God's people, including Old Testament saints (Pss 69:7–20; 89:50–51), Christ (Matt 27:44; Rom 15:3), and Christians (Matt 5:11; 1 Pet 4:14). "Describing the listeners' experience in this way connects them to a tradition of righteous suffering" (Koester, 459).

[55] "This probably entailed the kind of physical abuse associated with imprisonment (Matt 24:9; Acts 7:10; 20:23; Rom 8:35; Phil 1:17), beatings, and deprivation (2 Cor 6:5; 8:2; Phil 4:12–14; Col 1:24; 1 Thess 1:6; cf. 2:14–15; Rev 2:9–10). Punishments could include being whipped and beaten with rods (2 Cor 11:23–24; Acts 5:40). These were sometimes administered by officials against those who had not been convicted of a crime (Acts 16:22–23) or by a mob (Acts 18:17; cf. Heb 11:37). Affliction could also include emotional dis-tress generated by difficult social relations (2 Cor 1:4; 2:4)" (Koester, 459–60).

[56] Koester, 465.

[57] LSJ, s.v. "θεᾱτρίζω."

[58] Lane, *Hebrews 9–13*, 299; e.g., Polybius, *Histories* 3.91.10; 5.15.2; 11.8.7.

Those Christians who escaped such public humiliation chose to hold fast their confession and identify with their abused brethren.

They also had never wavered in showing "compassion" (*sympatheō*)—"not mere feeling but concrete assistance"[59] in line with how their high priest sympathized with them (4:15). Care for prisoners (v 34; 13:3) was critical in the first century. Even innocent prisoners could be beaten by officials (Acts 16:22–23) or suffer violence by the mob (Acts 18:17). These Christians, however, had insisted on showing solidarity with "the least of these" (Matt 25:36, 40) since the Son of God had shown solidarity with humanity and risked reproach and affliction by becoming incarnate (Heb 2:11–13). Indeed, "throughout the whole age of imperial persecution of the church the visiting of their friends who were in prison was a regular, though dangerous, duty of Christian charity."[60]

Yet no good deed goes unpunished. Those who weren't imprisoned suffered violent confiscation of their property, which could have resulted from judicial rulings or mob violence. The most significant loss of property, of course, would have been one's home, leading to long-term poverty and loss of dignity in the community.[61] Later, our author will invoke the patriarchs' faith in the face of homelessness (11:8–10, 13–16, 38).

All of this suffering—verbal and physical harassment, property confiscation, and imprisonment—would have triggered an overwhelming sense of shame for some of these early Christians. If we are right in assuming that they were experiencing persecution at the hands of the local Jewish community, then their confession and baptism would have precipitated disinheritance, property forfeiture, and all sorts of economic hardship.[62] Yet the loss of wealth was arguably second to the loss of honor and reputation, "and such dishonor was difficult to bear in an honor/shame culture."[63]

I know all about feeling shame from identifying with a group of people. Every year, when the calendar turns to January and the Dallas Cowboys

[59] Cockerill, *Hebrews*, 502.

[60] Bruce, *Hebrews*, 270; e.g., Phil 2:25; 4:14–18; Aristides, *Apology* 15; Tertullian, *Apology* 39.6; Eusebius, *Church History* 4.23.10.

[61] Koester, *Hebrews*, 465.

[62] P. Hughes, *Commentary*, 427; see Paul's post-conversion treatment at the hands of fellow Jews (Acts 9:23–25; 14:2, 19; 21:27–36; 22:22–23; 23:12–22; 26:21).

[63] Schreiner, *Hebrews*, 331.

once again break my heart in the NFL playoffs, I have to bear the "reproach" every other fan feels (e.g., a long offseason of tired jokes, recycled memes, and the occasional "Cowgirls" slur). Take this shame for being a fan of a sports team, multiply it until your calculator can't handle more zeros, and you get somewhat close to the scorn these early Christians must have felt for associating themselves with the religious cellar-dwellers of the first-century Greco-Roman world.

In his Sermon on the Mount, Jesus cautioned his followers about storing up treasures on earth versus in heaven (Matt 6:19–20; 19:21). When his people see their earthly possessions stripped away, they have assurance that things far greater await them;[64] that the vulnerable and temporary will one day give way to the secure and permanent. As the Son has a "better" name than the angels (1:4) and guarantees a "better" covenant (7:22) by a "better" sacrifice (9:23), so our inheritance is "better" than anything on earth (10:34). And it is not only "better" but also "abiding" (*menō*), the same term used of Jesus' priesthood (7:24). Our inheritance is as secure as Jesus' office of perfect and permanent priest.

Thus we ought to imitate the response of these Christians: joyful acceptance. Such reciprocation to shame and violence is entirely consistent with Christian teaching (Matt 5:12; Jas 1:2; 1 Pet 4:13) and practice (Acts 5:41; Rom 5:3), but it remains quite at odds with the American ethos that mocks turning the other cheek. Whenever I taught this passage in Bible class in Texas, joyful acceptance of property confiscation was always a topic of debate—it might have something to do with the "Come and Take It" flag that still waves in the state's collective zeitgeist. Nonetheless, joyful acceptance in hardship is the Christian ethos. Our author will speak soon of how Jesus despised the shame of the cross "for the joy that was set before him" (12:2). If nothing else, clinging too tightly to the material or physical exposes the fact that we have lost sight of our destiny, that we have "put too much hope in the city of man and have forgotten about the city of God."[65]

---

[64] "It should always be a mark of the spirit of the Christian that he should own nothing, outside himself, to which he cannot say goodbye with a smile" (Theodore H. Robinson, *The Epistle to the Hebrews*, MNTC [New York: Harper, 1933], 151).

[65] Schreiner, *Hebrews*, 333.

Having reminded them of their once-vibrant faith, our author prescribes the way forward (10:35–39). Recall that "confidence" carries the idea of openness or frankness throughout this epistle. Christians must maintain their boldness in associating with fellow Christians and in their proclamation of the gospel (e.g., Acts 4:13, 29, 31). Our confidence—our anchor of the soul—is predicated on Jesus' blood and his intercession at God's right hand. In the immediate context, our confidence is sustained by the invitation to draw near (10:22), by a Master who has proven trustworthy (v 23), and by the support of our spiritual family (vv 24–25).

As in the beginning of their faith (v 32), endurance was also required to claim the reward promised to God's people (6:12; Luke 8:15; Rom 2:7; Rev 3:10), particularly endurance in their obedience to God. "Christians will never advance two paces without fainting, except they are sustained by patience"[66] (Jas 1:2–4). Given the disparagement and abuse coming from all sides, it must have been challenging to continue in their worship, confession, and good works. But the Hebrews audience couldn't throw away ("abandon" NRSV) their confidence, endurance, and obedience in the face of disappointment and discouragement. To do so would be to dispose of something quite valuable. The "great reward" awaiting the people of God is nothing less than realization or fulfillment of all that "is promised" to them (v 36). So far in Hebrews, "promise" has been mentioned often (4:1; 6:12, 17; 8:6) and will be particularly highlighted in the next chapter (11:13, 17, 33, 39). Christians have a place in the long tradition of those who were promised something remarkable by the Lord and waited patiently for it. Moreover, the promises made to us are superior to any made to the Old Testament saints (8:6). Specifically, we have been promised an "eternal inheritance" (9:15) of entrance into God's rest (4:1).

Though the ideas of confidence, endurance, and obedience in verses 35–36 are distinct, they are also interrelated. When confidence is coupled with obedience to "the will of God" (v 36), endurance is produced, which in turn leads us to inherit all the promises God made to us. The type of obedience required is the same that the supreme Son offered to the Father (vv 7, 9), the obedience that sanctified us (v 10). Active exercise of our faith

---

[66] Calvin, *Hebrews*, 256.

through obedience makes possible the maintenance of our endurance, and endurance will pay off when our Lord returns. Only then will we realize our destiny, enter God's rest, and be crowned with glory and honor.

The Hebrews audience had a choice as to which direction they would take, and so do we. To choose to throw it all away will have disastrous consequences, as we've already seen (vv 26–31). To bring this home, our author invokes another passage from the Old Testament. He takes a phrase from Isaiah and tacks it onto a quote from Habakkuk 2:3–4.[67] The statement from Isaiah has the prophet calling his people to hide until God's fury against wicked Israel "has passed by"; he assures them that they need to shelter themselves only "for a little while" (26:20). By connecting this phrase with the prophecy of Habakkuk, the Hebrews author reminds his readers that Christ's return will be without "delay." In the interim, God's people are to move forward in faith versus shrink back in fear.

In Habakkuk, God made known to his prophet that he was sending the Babylonians as judgment against Judah and Jerusalem (1:5–17). In 2:2–3, Yahweh assured Habakkuk that the vision of destruction presented to him would come to pass. "In Hebrews, however, the author sees the judgment on Judah as typological of the final judgment. In other words there is an escalation between the historical judgment on Judah and the final judgment to come. What is coming in Hebrews, therefore, is not merely the realization of the vision in Hab 2:3 but Jesus himself."[68]

One will notice that the Habakkuk quote is different in verses 37–38 compared to that in the Old Testament. This is due to the fact that the Greek LXX (the Old Testament translation available to our author) varies from the Hebrew Masoretic Text. The LXX reads, "Because there is still a vision for the time, and he will appear at an end, and not in vain; if he is late, wait for him, because one coming will be present, and he will not tarry. If he draws back, my life does not find pleasure in it, but the righteous one will live by my faith." Drawing on this rendering, where Habakkuk reads *"it* will surely come" (2:3), our author clarifies with *"the coming one* will

---

[67] "The two passages probably were brought together by virtue of their common reference to 'the coming,' the author again working on the principle of verbal analogy" (Guthrie, "Hebrews," 982).

[68] Schreiner, *Hebrews*, 334.

come" (emphasis mine). Furthermore, comparing the LXX of Habakkuk to Hebrews, notice the two phrases are inverted: "my righteous one" is now first instead of "if he shrinks back."[69] Doing so makes "righteous one" the subject of the verse. If the people of God live by faith, they will be approved; if they shrink back, as did the wilderness generation, they will be rejected.[70]

Overall, these quotations from Isaiah and Habakkuk depict God as promising that he would intervene on behalf of his people in due time if they would wait patiently and live by faith. As he has consistently done, our author interprets both passages messianically just as John the Baptist did (Matt 11:3; Luke 7:19). Unlike John, however, the Hebrews author believes this "coming" to be Jesus' return, not his incarnation. The people of God are called to wait not for fulfillment of a vision (as in Habakkuk's case), but for a coming one who will deliver them. His coming is assured; what remains to be seen is whether he will find faith on the earth at his return (Luke 18:8). Such reminds us of another statement our Lord made in the Gospel of Luke: "By your endurance you will gain your lives" (21:19).

The final verse of chapter 10 is both a perfect summation of this section and a segue into the next. Our author expresses confidence in his audience that they will imitate their faithful ancestors and thus inherit the promises rather than withdraw and invite the fury of God.[71] In presenting this dichotomy, "Hebrews does not allow for a neutral space into which the listeners can retreat."[72]

>———◇———<

In the opening of chapter 6 of this book, I talked about the disappointment we all experience in life. We've discovered that our childhood disappointments concerning candy or Christmas toys pale in comparison to the

---

[69] For more on the differences between the Masoretic Text, the LXX, and Hebrews, see Ellingworth, *Hebrews*, 554–55; Guthrie, "Hebrews," 983; Koester, *Hebrews*, 462; Lane, *Hebrews 9–13*, 303–6.

[70] Bruce, *Hebrews*, 274. Just as Ps 110:4 was the key to understanding the Old Testament passages in 7:1–10:18, so Hab 2:3–4 will be the key to understanding the Old Testament passages in 11:1–12:24 (Koester, *Hebrews*, 464).

[71] The verb "destroyed" (*apōleia*) in v 39 is used frequently in the New Testament of the fate of unbelievers (Matt 7:13; Acts 8:20; Rom 9:22; Phil 1:28; 3:19; 1 Tim 6:9; 2 Pet 2:1, 3; 3:7, 16; Rev 17:8, 11).

[72] Koester, *Hebrews*, 468.

disappointments that come our way as adults. There were most certainly those in our author's audience who had experienced more disappointment as Christians than they ever thought possible. As is true of us, they were struggling with how to bridge the chasm that exists between expectation and reality. Our author would have them and us understand that the worst thing that could ever happen to us in this life is not disappointment but disbelief. When the supreme Son—the Coming One—returns, will he find faith in us?

Hebrews is an epistle about the spoken word of God. Our Father has communicated in these last days fully and finally through his beloved Son. Are we listening to that word, and are we doing so daily so as to be encouraged to endure? Faith has its reward in the life to come, yet maintaining that faith is no easy task. We learn to endure in the context of the household of God, a place where we find Jesus' solidarity with humanity lived out in the words and deeds of his people. That community, however, is not limited to those still living. Those who have gone before gave us an example of faith to follow, and they also constitute a cloud of witnesses cheering us on—exhorting us, even now, not to give up the fight or quit the race.

SUMMARY

- » Drawing near to God, holding fast our confession, and encouraging one another in the assembly are how Christians live out the implications of the new covenant.

- » It is impossible to live the Christian life apart from the local church.

- » Deliberate sin is the same as stomping on Jesus, considering his blood to be worthless, and outraging God's Spirit.

- » If we endure difficulty, we have a great reward waiting for us.

- » Faith in God is the source of our endurance.

TALKING POINTS

THE COMMAND not to abandon the assembly (10:25) is an opportunity to pause and ponder. On the one hand, there are those whose attendance to the assembly of the church is nearly perfect. They are present, as we often put it, "every time the doors are open." On the other hand, note that one can be faithful in attendance and still not be in obedience to 10:24–25. The imperative not to forsake is only one side of the coin; the other is the command to stir up or encourage others. John is a busy man; he always attends worship with his family, but he is scarcely present mentally during the worship and never engages with other church members before or after services. His mind is always elsewhere. Janet hasn't missed one worship service or period of Bible study since she had surgery thirty-nine years ago, though several church members wish she'd skip every now and again—you see, Janet is a chronic malcontent who is constantly tearing down rather than building up. Jacob was raised as a child to always be in church, but his family was never involved in the *life* of the church. As he was trained, he arrives precisely two minutes before worship begins, slips into his traditional spot on a back pew, and is out the door as soon as "Amen" is said. He neither knows nor cares to know anyone else in the congregation. While he would never put it like this, his attendance is just one of many proofs of his checklist approach to Christianity. These individuals are under the impression that they are in obedience to Hebrews 10:25, but they are not since they do not have the slightest inclination to engage in mutual encouragement with the body of Christ. The Lord wants us to be faithful in gathering with our spiritual family to worship, but that includes being faithful to encourage them as well.

>———◇———<

IT'S THE OBLIGATION of every Christian to assemble with their Christian family as often as possible. At the same time, however, it is incumbent upon that family (i.e., the congregation) to ensure that its members are being stirred up or mutually encouraged at each assembly. Any congregation relying on obligation or fear/guilt to keep people coming will soon die before it even knows it's dying. If we are not careful, our corporate worship can become as mechanical as the instruments we so rightfully eschew. God forbid we fall into such a rut. There is a time to warn and admonish, but on the whole, does the preaching encourage and inspire? Does the singing of the body foster joy in the heart of each member? Does communion draw the family together and strengthen it with grace? Do public prayers leave the audience with a profound sense that they have approached the holy? From leaders to laypersons, everyone should engage in introspection as to what they are doing personally to make each assembly an occasion for positive provocation. When my participation in corporate worship is dull or lazy, it's not just me who suffers. Guthrie reminds us, "Those of us who live in Christian community struggle, often in dark solitude, against discouragement as a result of sin, conflict with culture, physical fatigue, relational discord, and other dynamics that close in around us. When we come out of our solitude into the light of Christian fellowship, we need to experience applause and encouragement from others in the body of Christ. This gives us the courage to go back to our struggles with new energy and hope. From a human point of view such affirmation can make all the difference in holding 'firmly till the end' the confidence that began our Christian commitment."[73]

>———◇———<

THOUGH MUTUAL encouragement is critical, it is not the only reason why attending the Christian assembly is important. R. Kent Hughes notes four others: (1) Christ is present in the gathered church in a way that he is not present with the individual Christian (see Rev 1:9–20). Though Matthew 18:20 was never meant to be a quorum for worship services, it is nevertheless true that "we meet Christ in a special way in corporate worship."[74] (2) Corporate worship is a more intense experience than individual worship. If you don't believe me, consider that most people (all else being equal) would rather watch a football game in the stadium with sixty thousand of

[73] Guthrie, *Hebrews*, 147.

[74] R. Hughes, *Hebrews*, 2:34. "Those who neglect assembling together cut themselves off from the very means whereby Christ feeds, assures, and protects his people. To say, 'I can do this alone,' is to defy the very command of Christ. Some may claim that they can hear better preaching on the Internet or that they are too busy to attend church, but these excuses reveal the reality of a disobedient heart" (Mohler, *Exalting Jesus*, 158).

their closest friends than watch it alone in their living room. As Martin Luther put it, "At home in my own house there is no warmth or vigor in me, but in the church when the multitude is gathered together, a fire is kindled in my heart and it breaks its way through."[75] (3) We learn greater spiritual truths when gathered together versus in isolation. God intended his Word to be interpreted in the context of community rather than in isolation. Paul prayed that the Ephesians "may be able to comprehend with all the saints what is the length and width, height and depth of God's love" (Eph 3:18). "Great theological truths are best learned corporately—'with all the saints.'"[76] (4) The assembly is where we learn to live the Christian life; it is thus imperative to our spiritual development. Since the second greatest command is to love others, the church (rather than the world) is the best environment to practice that. "One theoretically may be able to develop *faith* and *hope* while alone (though even this is questionable), but not *love!*"[77]

>———◇———<

WHILE RESEARCHING and reflecting on Hebrews, I was startled by the number of commentators who essentially explained away Hebrews' various warning passages. Whatever our author meant by them, there's no reason (so those writers reasoned) to be unsettled by these "threats."[78] To be sure, some Christians need to hear more about the eternal security we have in Christ—and Hebrews makes much of that (e.g., 7:25). But we *all* must take seriously the potential in each of us to fall away and suffer eternal punishment. Hebrews, "like no other book of the New Testament, [is] relentless in its warnings about the dangers of carelessness in the Christian life. And the warnings are not that we might forfeit a few heavenly rewards, but that we might forfeit our souls in the fury of God's wrath."[79] The hope and promises Hebrews extends to us, rather than making us lax or sloppy in our

[75] Robert G. Rayburn, *O Come, Let Us Worship: Corporate Worship in the Evangelical Church* (Grand Rapids: Baker, 1980), 29–30.

[76] R. Hughes, *Hebrews*, 2:35.

[77] R. Hughes, 2:35; emphasis his.

[78] "We are so unused to thinking of judgment at all, or of God as in any way wanting to be angry with anyone, that we bend over backwards to downplay warnings like this one and suppose that they only apply in the most extreme cases" (Wright, *Hebrews*, 120–21).

[79] John Piper, "Woe to Those Who Trample the Son of God," *Desiring God*, 13 April 1997, http://www.desiringgod.org/messages/woe-to-those-who-trample-the-son-of-god.

Christian walk, are intended to stir within us a fervent thirst to honor and obey our great high priest. As mentioned above, deliberate sin for Christians is an intentional and rebellious rejection of God's will, but we cannot underestimate how easy it is for any one of us to commit such sin. And the context of this repeated warning is most arresting. Such rebellion does not have to take the form of grievous sin (e.g., murder, sexual assault, adultery); no, deliberate rebellion can take the innocent form of quietly abandoning the people of Jesus Christ because our affections lie elsewhere.[80]

>————◇————<

WHEN ALLEGIANCE to Jesus seems too difficult, what can be done to keep us tethered to our Anchor? (1) *Remember past performance.* Hebrews reminds its audience that they had been faithful in the past in the face of similar circumstances (10:32–34). "You *can* do this because I know you once *did* it," he says. If the story of our life has been one of faithfulness, why would we want to give up now? (2) *Tell yourself the truth until you believe it.* For her first two years of life, my middle daughter could *not* stand to be separated from her mommy. But as she got older, my daughter learned to self-soothe by repeating a phrase she'd learned from a TV show: "Grownups come back." Amid the ashes of a destroyed Jerusalem, and when all of his hope in God was gone (Lam 3:18), Jeremiah learned to self-soothe: "This I call to mind, and therefore I have hope: The steadfast love of the LORD never ceases…" (3:21–22). Holding fast our confession requires that we remind ourselves of important truths over and over again—something we do each week in the assembly. (3) *Fall deeper in love with Jesus.* The Hebrews author was right in believing that knowing more about Jesus' high priesthood could sustain the weary Christian (5:10–14). As we learn more about Jesus' person and work (past and present), our affection for him will deepen, and as our love for him increases, we soon realize no hardship can silence our confession.

---

[80] "While Jewish tradition identified the deliberate sin with blasphemy against the Torah or the deity, Hebrews identifies it with abandoning the community where God's saving gifts are received" (Thompson, *Hebrews*, 201; see also Ellingworth, *Hebrews*, 530–31).

Chapter 9

FAITH HALL OF FAME

The flickering flame of an oil lamp—and then the blazing torch on the far wall—caught Judah's eye. His mind briefly strayed to memories of his youth, around the evening fire in the courtyard, listening to his grandfather tell stories of Israel's heroes and heroines. While his Gentile playmates had looked up to Achilles and Hercules, Judah had always harbored a deep reverence for Noah, Abraham, Moses, and others. It didn't hurt that Judah's beloved *saba* had been a master storyteller, constantly changing his voice and gesturing demonstratively as he perpetuated those legends of the faithful.

Judah then thought back to being a young boy playing in the countryside around Antioch, carrying a small pouch and slingshot, pretending to be David venturing into the Elah Valley against a blaspheming giant. How great his faith had been as a child! How strong he knew he could be in the face of danger!

Where had that young boy gone? What had happened? Though he had been flirting with returning to the covenant of his fathers, Judah knew it was out of fear, not faith. He was intimidated by the ostracism he felt outside of Judaism. He feared further retribution from the Name over his forsaking Moses. Not for the first time, Judah realized that when he had buried his son in a tomb, his faith had been buried as well. *What would I do if I were to live by faith, not fear?* Judah thought to himself.

His attention returned to the homily as he heard Timothy exhort the small audience, "But we are not of those who shrink back and are destroyed, but of those who have faith and preserve their souls."

>———◇———<

In September 2017, I checked off a childhood bucket-list item: visiting the Pro Football Hall of Fame in Canton, Ohio. The displays of memorabilia, equipment, jerseys, and football cards were a delight. It was a joy to revisit the history of the game I have loved since I was seven. But the capstone on the entire experience was the Hall of Fame itself, where the bronze busts of so many gridiron greats were on display.

Of the over three hundred inductees, I had memories of less than half (the others' careers predated me). What I lacked in memories, however, I could make up for in stories I had heard from my dad and other football fans, particularly fans of the Dallas Cowboys. I made sure to locate the busts of Landry, Staubach, Lily, Dorsett, and others, as well as the heroes of my childhood: Aikman, Irvin, and Smith. As I left the hall, there was no doubt in my mind that I had just been informed of what greatness was—at least on the gridiron.

What Canton's Hall of Fame did for my football fandom, Hebrews 11 does for my faith. It increases it. No, it *compounds* it. Exponentially. Infinitely. Like Judah's, memories of my early childhood are saturated with Dad telling me bedtime stories of Israel's faithful heroes: Noah, Abraham, Moses, and David. As did Judah, I remember the faith of my childhood: robust, daring, unflinching. And just as with Judah, suffering and death and sin made me a coward, one who could feel his soul shrinking back into the shadows of fear versus walking boldly into the sunlight of faith.

This is Hebrews' most famous chapter and among the most beloved in the New Testament. For very good reason, Hebrews 11 has been called the "Hall of Faith" or the "Faith Hall of Fame." This chapter is to faith what 1 Corinthians 13 is to love—it defines and illustrates; it demands yet inspires. Remarkably, Hebrews 11 may also seem unnecessary, at least to the dispassionate analyst. Our author could have moved directly from 10:39 to 12:1, but "the faith *exhorted* in 10:19–39 is the faith *defined* in 11:1 and the faith *illustrated* in 11:3–38."[1] This master preacher knew that echoes of the examples of faith from the childhood of his audience would do what raw exegesis, exposition, and exhortation

[1] Michael R. Cosby, "The Rhetorical Composition of Hebrews 11," *JBL* 107 (1988): 260; emphasis his.

could not—rally them to stand firm and persevere versus shrink back and be destroyed.[2]

HEBREWS 11:1–7

The initial two verses of Hebrews 11 provide the framework for understanding the rest of the chapter. Our author offers what has become the classic definition of faith in verse 1 (though it is by no means comprehensive) and introduces his main point for the chapter in verse 2. Together, verses 1–7 illustrate that *biblical faith believes in the invisible.*[3]

The word *hypostasis*, translated as "assurance" (ESV) or "substance" (KJV), can also be rendered "realization" or even "title deed."[4] It refers to tangible evidence of an intangible reality, yet no single English word can capture it.[5] The term "originally referred to 'that which stands under,' the 'basis,' from which developed a range of meanings in secular Greek: 'basis, foundation, support, guarantee, possession, existence, deposit.' The last-mentioned meaning in turn led to the philosophical usages 'realization, presence, reality.'"[6]

In Hebrews, the word has been used twice previously. In 1:3, Jesus is the imprint of God's *hypostasis*, meaning he shares the same essence or reality with the Father. In 3:14, our author says we share in Christ if we hold our initial *hypostasis* (i.e., confidence, resolve) to the end. In Hebrews 11, the term carries more or less the same meaning as it does in 3:14. I like Cockerill's rendering—"Faith is living as if the things hoped for are real."[7] It's critical to note, however, that such confidence is not subjective (believing it *makes* it true) but objective (believing it *because* it's true).

Somewhat easier to translate is the second key term. The noun *elenchos* ("conviction") referred to proof or verification of something. Just as one's

[2] Some of the material in this chapter first appeared in my lecture "What Should Every College Student Know about Faith?" in the 2019 Freed-Hardeman University Lectureship book, *Out of Egypt: Liberation and Covenant in Exodus* (Henderson, TN: Freed-Hardeman Univ., 2019), 298–303.

[3] Hagner notes that "the reality of the unseen is a controlling theme in the present chapter" (*Hebrews*, 187). See Heb 11:1, 3, 6, 7, 8, 10, 13, 14, 16, 26, 27.

[4] BDAG, s.v. "ὑπόστασις."

[5] *Hypostasis* is "one of the most intractable translation problems in Hebrews" (Attridge, *Hebrews*, 308).

[6] Harm W. Hollander, "ὑπόστασις," *EDNT* 3:407.

[7] Cockerill, *Hebrews*, 521.

eyesight provides proof of present and physical reality, one's faith provides proof of future and spiritual reality.[8] In this context, Philip Hughes says conviction "is not a static emotion of complacency but something lively and active, not just a state of immovable dogmatism but a vital certainty which impels the believer to stretch out his hand, as it were, and lay hold of those realities on which his hope is fixed and which, though unseen, are already his in Christ."[9] This was the way our spiritual ancestors lived and were approved by God (v 2). Our author will go on to unpack and illustrate what this means throughout the chapter.

Verses 3–7 confront us with faith's irrationality. One of the more radical claims of Scripture, especially in our cultural climate, is that God created the world from nothing. He is "the living God" (3:12; 9:14; 10:31) whose own word is "living" (4:12), and thus he spoke all things into existence. The Greeks believed the universe had been created from preexistent matter, something Jewish tradition vigorously opposed.[10] Biblical faith believes the invisible, what can't be observed or discerned by physical senses.[11] No one was around to witness creation. Though rational arguments can be made to support the existence of a creator, we still believe by faith in God's Word that God created the world *ex nihilo*.

The mention of Abel, Enoch, and Noah—the first three "busts" in our Hall of Faith—continues the theme of faith's irrationality. By faith, Abel offered a sacrifice in obedience to a God he could not see, trusting God would commend him (Gen 4:3–4). He desired to draw near to God in worship and did so with a sacrificial offering, understanding that bloodshed was necessary to atone for his sins. "The description of Abel's sacrifice enables us to see him as one exemplifying faith's perception of a power greater than that of the world, to whom the best of what is created should be offered."[12] Jewish literature remembered Abel as the first martyr

[8] Bruce, *Hebrews*, 277. "Some realities are unseen because they belong to the spiritual realm and some because they lie in the future, when that realm will break into the earthly sphere. In either case, the person of faith lives out a bold confidence in God's greater realities" (Guthrie, *Hebrews*, 375).

[9] P. Hughes, *Commentary*, 440–41.

[10] Gen 1:3, 6, 9, 11, 14, 20, 24, 26; Ps 33:6, 9; 2 Maccabees 7:28; *Jubilees* 12.4.

[11] "This is the most fundamental of insights, the one that distinguishes believers and atheists: this sensory world is not self-contained, self-derived, or self-sufficient, but derives from a power greater than itself, which remains inaccessible to the senses, even as it brings forth everything that the senses encounter" (Johnson, *Hebrews*, 280).

[12] Johnson, 281.

(e.g., Matt 23:35). Though dead, he "still speaks" to God's people, meaning he was brought through death, and his example now encourages us to trust and obey an invisible God, even to the point of violent death, with the confidence that God sees and rewards such faithful obedience.

Enoch, too, by faith walked with a God he could not see and won God's approval. He is noteworthy in the Old Testament for being one of two people who did not see death; within the morbid refrain of "and then he died" in Genesis 5, Enoch is the sole exception. As a result, much speculation was made about him in extrabiblical Jewish literature (e.g., *1–2 Enoch*), though our author confines his remarks to the Genesis record. Enoch fulfills Habakkuk's prophecy that the righteous "live" (i.e., continue to exist in the spiritual realm) by faith, a fact our author mentions in several different ways in verse 5. Surviving death will become part of the undercurrent of this chapter. "Every person who lives by faith identifies with both Abel and Enoch. All, like Abel, will die without receiving the fullness of what God has promised. All, like Enoch, are promised triumph over death."[13]

Our author expounds on his definition of faith before moving to the next example. There's no question that biblical faith is "lively and active," as Hughes put it; it is an active trust or reliance. On the other hand, biblical faith also demands we believe in particular principles such as the existence and providence of God (v 6). Like Jesus and unlike wilderness Israel, those mentioned in this chapter lived with the conviction that God is who he claims he is and will do as he promised.

Noah, enduring derision from his neighbors, obeyed God's command to build an ark to save his family when the threat of a global flood was unimaginable, or "invisible," to him. Like Christ's (5:7), the patriarch's obedience was a product of his reverence.[14] Noah took an invisible God at his word and thus made "practical preparations against the day when that word would come true."[15] Implicit in this is the idea that trust in God's invisible world automatically puts one at odds with our material world.

---

[13] Cockerill, *Hebrews*, 526.

[14] "Noah's faith involved the whole person: his *mind* was warned of God; his *heart* was moved with fear; and his *will* acted on what God told him" (Wiersbe, *Bible Exposition*, 2:318; emphasis his).

[15] Bruce, *Hebrews*, 287.

Those who emulate Noah will themselves be heirs "of the righteousness that comes by faith" (v 7).

HEBREWS 11:8–22

Following the busts of Abel, Enoch, and Noah, our author ushers us into the Hall of Fame's grand exhibit spotlighting Abraham. For good reason, Abraham is remembered as the father of the faithful, though he also resembled the father of the *fearful* at times. So, while his appearance on this list is no surprise and definitely merited, it is not without its irony. Nonetheless, our author's theme in verses 8–22 is that *biblical faith beholds the impossible*.

Our author lauds Abraham's obedience in departing his father's house, not for definite GPS coordinates but for a land the Lord would eventually show him (Gen 12:1). "It is a no [*sic*] ordinary trial of faith," Calvin wrote, "to give up what we have in hand, in order to seek what is afar off, and unknown to us."[16] To paraphrase Luther, biblical faith means having no idea where we are going, what we are doing, or why we are suffering, but still following "the bare voice of God" and allowing it to lead and drive us.[17] The significance of "inheritance" (v 8) would not have been lost on the audience. By leaving Haran, Abraham eschewed his father's estate in favor of God's promises. "This corresponds to the situation of the listeners, who await an eternal inheritance from God (1:14; 9:15), a heavenly gift that they had tasted, but had not fully received (6:4)."[18] In surrendering his family inheritance for God's promises, the patriarch embraced the vulnerable status of an immigrant. The verb "live" (*paroikeō*) in verse 9 ("sojourned" NJB) occurs in the LXX for "inhabiting a place without possessing actual ownership or citizenship."[19] The only piece of Canaan Abraham ever called his own was his grave (Gen 23:17–18; Acts 7:5). Once he arrived, God further explained that the land would be given to his descendants instead of Abraham, and then not until four centuries had passed of their living "in

---

[16] Calvin, *Hebrews*, 279.

[17] Martin Luther, *Luther's Works*, ed. Jaroslav Pelikan (St. Louis: Concordia, 1968), 29:238.

[18] Koester, *Hebrews*, 495.

[19] Johnson, *Hebrews*, 290; e.g., Gen 12:10; 17:8; 19:9; 20:1; 21:23–34; Exod 6:4; Deut 26:5; see also Silva, "πάροικος," *NIDNTTE* 3:642–45.

a land that is not theirs" (Gen 15:13). *Biblical faith trusts that God's promises will be fulfilled, though not necessarily in our lifetime.*

Thus, our author says, Abraham's faith was not in eventually inheriting Canaan, for he never did. Instead, he continued to live in tents, as did Isaac and Jacob, for they saw beyond the physical world to the promise that they would one day inherit a place in the city of God. The verb translated "was looking forward to" in verse 10 (*ekdechomai*) means "to expect with absolute confidence" and, being in the imperfect tense, "expresses continuous expectation"[20] (e.g., Jas 5:7). It is the same verb used in 10:13 of Jesus' waiting until he can prop up his feet on his enemies. In the face of numerous setbacks, the patriarchs maintained absolute confidence that they would receive an eternal inheritance from the Lord.

Sarah,[21] too, had a faith that believed in impossible promises (v 11). At the not-exactly-fertile-Myrtle age of ninety, Abraham's wife gave birth to a promised son. The story of Sarah's derisive laughter over the thought of having a child (Gen 18:1–15) is well known. In the scene, the narrator notes the advanced ages of Abraham and Sarah and that she was past menopause, and he has her acknowledging that she and her husband had ceased being intimate (18:11–12). Despite her initial doubt, Sarah eventually believed the promise concerning Isaac because she considered the Source of the promise to be faithful (Rom 4:20). *Biblical faith believes impossible promises because of the reliability of the Promise maker, not because of the probability of the promise itself.*[22]

Thus "from one man, and him as good as dead, were born descendants" too many to count (v 12; Rom 4:19), of which our author's readers were a part (Heb 2:16). When God repeated his promise of descendants to the patriarch, Abraham complained about his lack of a child. In response, the Lord beckoned Abraham outside to gaze at the heavens. "Look at the sky and count the stars, if you are able to count them. ... Your offspring will be that numerous" (Gen 15:5 CSB). After Abraham had proven his

---

[20] Lane, *Hebrews 9–13*, 351.

[21] Following most English translations, I take Sarah to be the subject of v 11 (see Johnson, *Hebrews*, 291–92; Koester, *Hebrews*, 487–88; J. Harold Greenlee, "Hebrews 11:11: 'By Faith Sarah Received Ability,'" *AsTJ* 54 [1999]: 67–72).

[22] Philo quotes Sarah as confessing, "He who has promised is my Lord, and is older than all creation, and him I must of necessity believe" (*Names* 166).

willingness to sacrifice Isaac, God reaffirmed that promise: "By myself I have sworn, declares the LORD, ... I will surely bless you, and I will surely multiply your offspring as the stars of heaven and as the sand that is on the seashore" (22:16–17). *Biblical faith believes God will fulfill his promises far beyond our wildest imaginations.*

>———◇———<

Our author then pauses with a sigh to express his "deepest feelings on the Christian's true home"[23] (vv 13–16). In this interlude, we catch a glimpse of the conclusion, in verses 39–40, that in the days of Abraham, Isaac, and Jacob, the promise of land was just that: a promise. It remained without fulfillment in their lifetimes.[24] They lived and died in faith, though, in the sense that they considered God's promises so real that they "greeted them from afar."[25]

But the delay in fulfillment is not the point, our author essentially says, for the pleasure and safety of a home were not what our ancestors valued most. For example, Hebrews tells us, if an earthly place to call home was what the patriarchs really wanted, they would have referred to themselves differently. As it was, they identified themselves late in life as "strangers and exiles" (v 13; Gen 23:4; 47:9), and—don't miss this—*they did so while living in the land of promise!*[26] Even David considered himself "a sojourner ..., a guest [*parepidēmos* LXX], like all my fathers" (Ps 39:12) while reigning over the land of promise as king!

Wherever Abraham went, it seems he "incurred the stigma of a stranger and a foreigner."[27] In verse 9, our author referred to the patriarch as an *allotrios* ("stranger" NIV, "foreigner" CSB). In verse 13, he employs the terms *xenos* and *parepidēmos* or "strangers and exiles" (ESV, "foreigners and temporary residents" CSB). The three Greek words are effectively synonymous

---

[23] Lightfoot, *Jesus Christ Today*, 211.

[24] "The author's central concern is to show that it was in a condition of faith, not of fulfilment, that the OT characters died" (Ellingworth, *Hebrews*, 593). "There is no contradiction to Hebrews 6:15, where it reads 'he obtained the promise'—for that refers only to the birth of Isaac" (Reese, *Hebrews*, 201).

[25] Bruce, *Hebrews*, 298.

[26] "Many understood Canaan to be Abraham's inheritance (Ps 105:11), but Hebrews maintains that Abraham receives his true inheritance in God's heavenly city" (Koester, *Hebrews*, 484).

[27] Lane, *Hebrews 9–13*, 350.

in this passage and "indicate that someone is not a full participant in civic rights in this place, and suggest that they do have such rights elsewhere. It is precisely this last nuance that the author exploits. If [the patriarchs] were aliens in the land of Canaan, even though it was theirs by promise, where was their real homeland?"[28] If the patriarchs had considered their old home (Mesopotamia) to be their *real* home, they could have returned to it (v 15). If they had considered Canaan their true home or their ultimate destination, they would have put down roots, as Lot did (Gen 13:11–12), instead of "living in tents." If the pleasure and security of this life were what motivated men like Abel, Enoch, Noah, and Abraham, they could have certainly enjoyed their fair share of it.

Instead, their greatest desire in life—their objective or destination—was something different: the "city that has foundations" (v 10; 12:22; 13:14). "Although this city can be described as 'heavenly' (12:24), it does not derive its enduring nature merely from its location. It is permanent and utterly superior to the cities of this world because its 'architect and builder is God.'"[29] Note that our author says the patriarchs were seeking and desiring this better country (vv 14, 16). "This pursuit was no mere hobby or pastime. It was much more than insurance against damnation while they attended to their own affairs. It was the passion and the main business of life because its object was the only true source of blessing and 'rest.'"[30] Home is where the heart is, they say, and in this case, their heart was with God. To that end, he has prepared a "better country," a heavenly city in which the faithful will dwell forever with him (1 Cor 2:9). It is a city where Jesus has gone before us as our forerunner to prepare for our arrival (John 14:2). It is a city that we call home.

With such people, God is not ashamed to be associated (Gen 28:13; Exod 3:6; 4:5). By confessing "that they were strangers and exiles on the earth," the patriarchs confessed the Most High as their God. In turn, God was unashamed to be their God and will prove such when his Son, unashamed to call us brothers (Heb 2:11), confesses or acknowledges the

---

[28] Johnson, *Hebrews*, 292–93.
[29] Cockerill, *Hebrews*, 541.
[30] Cockerill, 553.

righteous before his throne on the final day (Matt 10:32–33). Confessing our home to be the city of God, and holding fast to that confession, means God gladly confesses that we belong to him.

In this way, our author homes in on a crucial aspect of faith most relevant for his audience: *Biblical faith looks forward, not backward.* For these Hebrew Christians, all they knew of late were dangers, toils, and snares. They were struggling to see past their present persecution to the power of the divine presence that awaited them on the other side of Jordan. They could not turn back to the place from whence they came, as the wilderness generation so often wanted to do. On the other hand, they had not yet reached their destination before them. Faith required them to acknowledge the reality of their objective as true and sure, even if they wouldn't see it in this lifetime. Faith required them to live as their ancestors had done.

Such faith will be rewarded.

>————◇————<

The ultimate test of Abraham's faith came when he was called to sacrifice Isaac (Gen 22:1–19). The patriarch had plenty of reasons to reject God's command, including the presumed integrity of God's own word when laid beside his previous promise. The Lord had vowed that, through Isaac, he would bless the world (v 18; Gen 12:3; 21:12); if Isaac died, would it not prove God either a liar or a failure?

Nevertheless, Abraham obeyed; he journeyed to the mountain and was prepared to offer his son on the altar, all the while convinced that the Lord would either preserve Isaac or raise him from the dead (v 19). The living God had given him a son when Abraham had been "as good as dead" (v 12), so, "since death was not the last word for Abraham, he could be confident that it would not be the last word for Isaac."[31]

Note Abraham's words to his servants—which "are not incidental or accidental"[32]—as he and Isaac went the final way alone: "Stay here with the donkey while I and the boy go over there. We will worship and then *we*

---

[31] Koester, *Hebrews*, 499. "As a man of faith, [Abraham] held tenaciously to the conviction that what appeared to him to be an insoluble problem was for God no problem at all" (P. Hughes, *Commentary*, 483).

[32] Schreiner, *Hebrews*, 357.

will come back to you" (Gen 22:5 NIV; emphasis mine). This was how certain the patriarch was that God's promise concerning Isaac would stand. *Biblical faith does what God says, though it may appear to contradict what God has promised.*[33]

As did his father, Isaac lived by faith, and this faith led him to bless his two sons, Jacob and Esau[34] (v 20; Gen 27:28–29, 39–40), with confidence that God would follow through on the promises made to Abraham. "Blessing is an act of faith because Isaac cannot give the recipient what is promised, but must rely on God to put the blessing into effect."[35] In a similar manner, Jacob blessed Joseph's sons (v 21; Gen 48:8–22), confident they would inherit God's promises though Jacob was about to die.

Joseph (who exhibited greater faith in his life than any of his predecessors) gave his descendants clear instructions not to bury him in Egypt but in his home in Canaan (v 22; Gen 50:24–25)—a command pregnant with conviction of God's faithfulness. While the Exodus was a future hope as Joseph lay dying, the eyes of faith made it a firm reality. Like Joseph, our author will assure his audience that their destiny lies where God has promised (12:22–24). Note especially that our author could have pointed to many things in Joseph's life as an example of faithfulness. Yet he chose literally Joseph's last act in Genesis as his single anecdote. Looking with certainty into the unknown future with eager expectation of what God will do is fundamentally what faith is all about. *Biblical faith entrusts the future to the Lord, confident that one's own death does not mean the death of God's promises.*

HEBREWS 11:23-31

In the previous two sections of Hebrews 11, our author has highlighted how faith believes the invisible and beholds the impossible. Now, in a brief

---

[33] Schreiner, 356.

[34] "It may seem strange that [our author] mentions Esau along with Jacob. ... By associating him here with the people who lived by faith, [our author] prepares for the way he will use him as a warning in 12:14–17. ... [Our author] anticipates this ominous role by the fact that Esau does not pass on the blessing to anyone" (Cockerill, *Hebrews*, 560).

[35] Koester, *Hebrews*, 500.

exposition of Moses' life, he speaks to his audience of how *biblical faith braves the unimaginable.*[36]

Moses' parents refused to obey Pharaoh's deadly holocaust edict (Exod 1:22) and instead protected their son. "That Moses was born at all was an act of faith; that he was preserved was another. He began by being the child of faith."[37] By faith, Amram and Jochebed "recognized that the future role of Moses was more real than the threats of the king."[38] Many in our author's audience would have been nervous about embracing a faith that left them at odds with legal authorities. Yet Christ gives his people boldness and confidence. *Biblical faith answers to a higher power* (Acts 5:29).

By becoming a basket case(!), Moses was adopted as a son of Pharaoh's daughter (Exod 2:5–10), and no conceivable privilege was spared him. Jewish tradition remembered Moses the Egyptian as a man of wisdom and military valor (Acts 7:22). Philo claimed that Moses, as Pharaoh's adopted grandson, was heir to the Egyptian throne.[39] If true (Scripture doesn't say), this means it was all the more remarkable that Moses opted for "the reproach of Christ" versus the riches of Egypt (Heb 11:24–26).

The "fleeting pleasures of sin" (v 25) are undoubtedly the advantages of apostasy that would accrue to any Christian who abandoned Christ and his church. Our author uses Moses' example to urge his audience to continue partnering with those suffering mistreatment.[40] "The author is sure that abuse is always associated with Christ, that to be a Christian is even to expect such abuse (13:13); and he is sure, as he looks at Moses, that it has always been that way."[41] Hebrews invites its audience to recognize that Moses' perspective was always forward looking and he saw all the way to the glory of Christ that resulted from the shame of Christ[42] (12:2; 13:13).

---

[36] "In the previous section the principal challenge to faith was that the patriarchs had to resist disappointment at not possessing an earthly inheritance. Now the challenge shifts, as Moses' generation experiences conflict with unbelievers. Recalling the various challenges faced by Israel's ancestors would have been helpful to those addressed by Hebrews, for whom both disappointment and conflict were threats" (Koester, 506).

[37] Barclay, *Hebrews*, 184.

[38] Thompson, *Hebrews*, 240.

[39] Philo, *Moses* 1.13; see also Josephus, *Antiquities* 2.232.

[40] Johnson, *Hebrews*, 300.

[41] Lightfoot, *Jesus Christ Today*, 216.

[42] "To say that Moses endured the 'abuse of Christ' may be, strictly speaking, an anachronism, but the author wants to emphasize the community of suffering that spans the centuries" (Thompson, *Hebrews*, 241).

To an audience tempted to *turn back to* Moses, there is the call instead to *look forward with* Moses. The lawgiver's example reminds us of Paul's admonition, "This light momentary affliction is preparing for us an eternal weight of glory beyond all comparison" (2 Cor 4:17). *Biblical faith knows that temporary suffering will eventually give way to eternal joy.*

A cursory reading of Exodus 2:11–12 may lead one to believe that Moses struck down the Egyptian taskmaster in a temporary fit of anger. Not so, our author argues; the incident "signaled where Moses' loyalties were."[43] After killing the taskmaster, Moses fled to Midian, and our author claims he did so without "being afraid of the anger of the king" (v 27). This seems to contradict the account in Exodus 2:14–15. Is our author fuzzy on the facts? Hardly. More likely, Hebrews means "Moses' fear was not the ultimate reality in his life. Yes, he feared dying, but at a deeper level he trusted that God would protect him and that his life would be preserved."[44]

In other words, Moses *overcame* his fear to live in faith, and that point would not have been lost on our author's audience. He persevered, claims Hebrews, "as one who sees him who is invisible" (v 27). That is, the divine presence was real to Moses, and he thus held firmly to his confession and God's purpose. "A man may be surer of God than he is of the material universe that he touches and handles and beholds. The vision that a trustful heart has of God is as real, as direct, and, I venture to say, more assured, than the knowledge which is brought to us through sense."[45]

Finally, Moses acted by faith when he instituted the Passover on Israel's final night in Egypt. He ordered the entire nation to brush lamb's blood on their doorposts so that the Angel of Death would "pass over" their homes and spare the lives of the oldest sons. "Thus when, to all appearances, the people were destined for destruction, 'the sprinkling of blood' expressed confidence in God's promises."[46] *Biblical faith obeys the voice of the Lord and leaves matters of judgment and redemption to him.*

[43] Schreiner, *Hebrews*, 362–63; see Philo, *Moses* 1.33, 40.

[44] Schreiner, *Hebrews*, 364. Some interpreters try to harmonize this perceived inconsistency by equating this flight from Egypt with the Exodus, but it's clear only Moses leaves on this occasion (see Koester, *Hebrews*, 503–4).

[45] Maclaren, *Expositions*, 30:161.

[46] Thompson, *Hebrews*, 243. Moses' faith is further demonstrated in his command to Israel to observe the Passover once they arrived in Canaan (Exod 12:25–27), so sure was he of the enterprise's success (Barclay, *Hebrews*, 187–88).

Inspired by Moses' leadership, Israel passed through the Red Sea on dry land and watched as Pharaoh and his army subsequently perished. "For our author, the faith of the Israelites has two dimensions: walking into the sea was an act of 'not knowing where they were going,' a step as dangerous and unpredictable as Abraham's leaving for a land he did not know; it was also a step that brought them to the brink of death, as did Abraham's offering of his son Isaac. But once again, God brought them to life out of a place of death."[47] *Biblical faith believes deliverance can be had by passing through suffering, not avoiding it, if God is there.*

Inspired by Joshua's encounter of and obedience to the commander of Yahweh's forces (Josh 5:14), Israel witnessed the collapse of Jericho's mighty walls. In the realm of common sense, Israel stood no chance against the mightiest fortified city in Canaan. Yet the battle belonged to the Lord, so nothing else mattered. *Biblical faith has no room for crippling fear, so confident is it that the Lord goes before us and consumes his foes on every side* (Ps 97:3; 2 Cor 10:4).

Inspired by what Israel's God had done to past enemies, Rahab showed hospitality to Israel's spies and thus did not perish with her neighbors. Her statement of faith in Joshua 2:9 is remarkable since Israel scarcely seemed (to worldly eyes) like a threat, but Rahab saw with the eyes of faith. Her occupation, which Hebrews does not attempt to downplay, is also noteworthy. That she was a prostitute[48] and a Gentile makes it all the more amazing that Rahab became an ancestor of Jesus (Matt 1:5). *Biblical faith believes "a sordid past does not preclude one from enjoying forgiveness and a future reward"*[49] (Matt 21:31).

HEBREWS 11:32–40

More than thirty verses into the Faith Hall of Fame (and presumably with a church deacon pointing at his watch!), our author knows he must soon bring this sermon to a close. The phrase "time would fail me to tell" is, in

---

[47] Johnson, *Hebrews*, 303.

[48] "It would then be disgraceful," Chrysostom exhorted his audience in relation to this verse, "if you should appear more faithless even than a harlot" (*Homilies on Hebrews* 27.3).

[49] Schreiner, *Hebrews*, 366; emphasis mine.

my estimation, the greatest single argument proving Hebrews originated as a sermon.[50] It explains why he speeds through the remaining examples so quickly. There are the heroes of the books of Judges and 1–2 Samuel: Gideon, who defeated the Midianites with a small group of three hundred; Barak, who defeated the Canaanites at Deborah's urging; Samson, whose strength was a thorn in the side of the Philistines; Jephthah, who liberated Israel from the Ammonites; David, who became Israel's greatest king; and Samuel, who led Israel back to God; as well as Israel's many righteous prophets (e.g., Elijah, Isaiah, Jeremiah, Daniel).

In verses 33–38, the exploits of these faithful men and women are enumerated in staccato fashion—what A. T. Robertson called "sledge-hammer style."[51] "With this rapidly changing imagery [our author] leaves his hearers overwhelmed and breathless before the accumulated mass of testimony presented to their senses."[52] Though Israel "conquered kingdoms" (v 33) under several military leaders, David is likely in mind here; the verb *katagōnizomai* ("conquered") doesn't occur elsewhere in the Greek Bible, yet Josephus used it to refer to David's defeating the Philistines.[53] Wise rulers in Israel like Samuel, David, and Solomon established God's justice in their realm (1 Sam 7:15–17; 2 Sam 8:15; 1 Kgs 3:6; 10:9). Some "obtained promises," including the promise of Canaan (Josh 21:43–45) and of the Davidic dynasty (2 Sam 7:13–16).

"Stopped the mouths of lions" points directly to Daniel, who was delivered because he was "found blameless" (Dan 6:22), though it could also include Samson (Judg 14:6) and David (1 Sam 17:34–35). Daniel's three friends—Hananiah, Mishael, and Azariah—"quenched the power of fire" (v 34) by their faith (Dan 3:27). Many "escaped the edge of the sword," including David (1 Sam 21:10), Elijah (1 Kgs 19:1–8), Elisha (2 Kgs 6:31–7:2), and Jeremiah (Jer 36:19, 26). Untold Old Testament saints "were

---

[50] There are several parallels to this phrase among ancient orators (e.g., Isocrates, *Oration* 1.11; 6.81; 8.56; Demosthenes, *Oration* 18.296). "It is true that the use of λέγω ['I say'] does not prove that this passage was originally spoken. ... But the use of λέγω in combination with a rhetorical question, the use for the first time of the first person singular [see 13:19], and the reference to lack of time produce a cumulatively oral effect" (Ellingworth, *Hebrews*, 623).

[51] Archibald Thomas Robertson, *Word Pictures in the New Testament* (Nashville: Broadman, 1932), 5:428.

[52] Cockerill, *Hebrews*, 587.

[53] Josephus, *Antiquities* 7.53.

made strong out of weakness, became mighty in war, [and] put foreign armies to flight," for Yahweh had promised Israel that by their faith, "Five of you shall chase a hundred, and a hundred of you shall chase ten thousand, and your enemies shall fall before you by the sword" (Lev 26:8). Such serves to illustrate that *biblical "faith is the response of all who are conscious of their own weakness and accordingly look to God for strength."*[54]

Both the widow of Zarephath and the woman of Shunem "received back their dead by resurrection" (v 35; 1 Kgs 17:17–24; 2 Kgs 4:32–37). But not all the faithful were rescued from the fangs of death, for others "were tortured, refusing to accept release, so that they might rise again to a better life." The word translated "tortured" (*tympanizō*) is specific and quite rare; it referred "to a form of torture in which a person was stretched out on a rack, and then his taut stomach was beaten as one beats a drum ... until the muscle-walls collapsed and death occurred from internal injuries."[55]

Hebrews may allude here to the martyrdom of the righteous in 2 Maccabees. Though not a part of the inspired Old Testament canon, these stories would have been well known to the original audience. One particular example often mentioned by commentators is that of a righteous, ninety-year-old scribe named Eleazar. He was punished for refusing to eat pork and rejected his friends' pleas to pretend to acquiesce to the king's edict. He was tortured and executed in the way described above. His last words were, "It is clear to the Lord in his holy knowledge that, though I might have been saved from death, I am enduring terrible sufferings in my body under this beating, but in my soul I am glad to suffer these things because I fear him" (2 Maccabees 6:30 NRSV). In 2 Maccabees 7, a mother and her seven sons refused to eat pork upon the order of the king and were tortured. Before the second son was executed, he cried out, "You dismiss us from this present life, but the King of the universe will raise us up to an everlasting renewal of life, because we have died for his laws" (7:9 NRSV).

Arguably some in the original audience had "suffered mocking and flogging, and even chains and imprisonment" (v 36; 10:32–34), as did Jesus. If our author has in mind a particular Old Testament person, it could

---

[54] P. Hughes, *Commentary*, 510; emphasis mine.
[55] Lane, *Hebrews 9–13*, 388; see LSJ, s.v. "τύμπᾰνον."

be Micaiah (1 Kgs 22:27), Hanani (2 Chr 16:10), or Jeremiah (Jer 20:2; 37:15; 38:6). Our author means to say that "this has been the experience of God's faithful witnesses in every generation—apostles, prophets, martyrs, reformers, and innumerable disciples whose names, though unknown to men, are well known to God (2 Cor. 6:9)."[56]

The priest Zechariah was among those who "were stoned" (v 37; 2 Chr 24:21), as was Jeremiah.[57] Isaiah is said to have been martyred by being "sawn in two," according to Jewish tradition.[58] And while some escaped the sword (v 34), others did not, such as the prophet Uriah (Jer 26:23) and James, the brother of John (Acts 12:2). Even the faithful who escaped the sword lived meager lives of survival at times, being poorly clothed and, like Moses and Abraham, having no permanent home on earth (vv 37–38). All these examples illustrate that "faith in God carries with it no guarantee of comfort in this world. … But it does carry with it great reward in the only world that ultimately matters."[59]

Though these remarkable men and women endured the unimaginable, and despite God's commendation (v 2), none realized their full inheritance in this life. Such will not occur without us (vv 39–40). By holding fast to our confession, we have something that not even the heroes of old possessed during their lifetimes: direct access to God. Therefore,

> may God grant that, if the saints of these latter days are to perfect the history of the Church of Christ, the end may not be less heroic than the beginning was! A true poem should gather force as it grows, and its waves of thought should roll in with greater power as it nears its climax; so should the mighty poem of faith's glorious history increase in depth and power, as it gets nearer to its grand consummation, that God may be glorified, yet more and more, through all his believing children.[60]

---

[56] P. Hughes, *Commentary*, 513.

[57] Tertullian, *Scorpiace* 8; *Lives of the Prophets* 2.1.

[58] *Ascension of Isaiah* 5:1b–14; *Sanhedrin* 103b; *Lives of the Prophets* 1.1. During the siege of Jerusalem, the Romans executed a Jewish man by tying him to a sawhorse and sawing him in two (*Genesis Rabbah* 65.22).

[59] Bruce, *Hebrews*, 329. "If the readers expect to be accepted and praised, they need to rethink matters in light of the OT. The people of God have always been a minority people, a pilgrim people, and often despised and forsaken" (Schreiner, *Hebrews*, 373).

[60] C. H. Spurgeon, "Unbelievers Upbraided," in *The Metropolitan Tabernacle Pulpit Sermons* (London: Passmore, 1904), 50:324.

One doesn't have to be a Christian for very long before the popularity of Hebrews 11 becomes apparent. It's considered to be among the most beloved and the most important chapters in Scripture. This is partly because of how it celebrates the Old Testament heroes of our Sunday school childhood. It's also because of the style of the chapter. The ending builds to a glorious crescendo; one can almost hear the preacher's voice growing stronger and deeper—"conquered kingdoms, enforced justice, obtained promises!"—it reminds me of that final fusillade of fireworks in the summer night's sky. The chapter is a literary and rhetorical masterpiece. It tugs at the heart like arguably nothing else in Hebrews. This chapter itself—not just its players—rightly belongs in the Faith Hall of Fame.

On the other hand, I have come to appreciate Hebrews 11 for another reason, one I was blind to until halfway through this project. Before you get too excited, I'll say candidly that the revelation wasn't exactly deep or profound; remember, I'm from Mississippi and was homeschooled, so manage your expectations! What I have to offer here won't blow your mind, but something doesn't have to blow your mind to change your life, as it did mine.

Halfway through my study of and reflection on Hebrews, I found myself wondering why our author had to write to a group of Christians about the deeper realities of our faith: the supremacy of the Son, the priesthood of Christ, the advantages of the new covenant that accrue to us. If these profound and blessed truths were experienced automatically, why talk about them? Why did he place so much emphasis in his homily on drawing near to God, particularly if this is something every Christian experiences via the atonement and intercession of our Lord?

That's when I realized—they don't. Not every Christian experiences that nearness, that intimacy, that wonder of being beckoned to intrude boldly into the divine presence amid many dangers, toils, and snares. What was true of the Hebrew Christians has also been true of myself and almost every other Christian. While we might have been "in Christ"—we had become "sons"—we were unaware of the glorious realities of that status. We were unaware of the access we had obtained.

I once applied for and received a credit card because of the travel points offered to whoever enrolled—the "introductory offer," as it's sometimes known. I knew the other perks offered by this card were pretty good, though I was in it for the points, so I didn't take the time to scour the brochure and memorize every single benefit the card conveyed. It was over a year later that I learned I had been paying unnecessarily for "access" or "perks" that were already mine simply by owning the credit card. For example, the card granted me access to airport lounges where I might rest a while before a flight. The card gave me rental car insurance for free so that I didn't have to use the agency's or rely on my own carrier. The card covered me with purchase protection (e.g., extended warranty) instead of having to obtain it from the store or a third party. I already had access or could lay claim to numerous benefits, but I wasn't doing so *because I was uninformed*—despite the company sending me the brochure, no less![61]

I think that was the Hebrews audience's problem; it has been my problem and likely yours also. When we emerge from baptism's waters, it's not as if an angel waves a magic wand and makes us instantly aware of all the spiritual blessings granted to us in Christ Jesus. Aside from the emotion of it all (and the emotional high from becoming a child of God is quite powerful and can last a long time), it's common not to *feel* any difference in our lives post-conversion, at least after a while. For the first few weeks, yes, everything seems different. However, when we come down from the clouds, the rhythm of day-to-day living returns to its familiar pattern. We begin to walk less by faith and more by sight. We can't help but focus on what's immediately in front of us: family matters, work responsibilities, financial struggles, health issues. Perhaps that's Satan's most common tool—not ensnaring us in some grave moral failure as much as diverting our attention and thereby blinding us to the blessings bestowed upon us by the supreme Son.

The only way to experience these blessings is by faith. It's that simple. And that hard. Remember our author's words in Hebrews 2, that we do not yet see everything under the feet of Jesus, but by faith we see the Son crowned with glory and honor (2:9), and by faith we know that he will

[61] Recall our discussion of *nōthros* (5:11; 6:12) in chapter 5 and its meaning of "slow to recognize and act on advantages."

one day soon reign over all. Likewise, we do not yet see every burden lifted from our shoulders, we do not yet see every storm dispelled to stillness, but by faith we see a faithful and merciful high priest dealing gently with us and granting us access so that our pleas and petitions and prayers might be heard at the throne. Most certainly, there are times for each of us when we do not *feel* every sin forgiven, every transgression forgotten—the prince of this world loves to broker in shame and guilt. By faith, however, we know our high priest has atoned for all our misdeeds once and for all.

The world's retort to this is to dismiss it as a mere psychological mind game, an immature "believing it makes it so" mentality that gets you nowhere. But if we believe the world was fashioned out of nothing; that a floating barge delivered eight souls from a global flood; that seas have separated, mountains have moved, and fortresses have fallen apart; that a man three days dead rose from his grave to be declared the supreme Son—then I have no issue believing in the blessings God says are mine in Christ Jesus. The problem isn't with being unrealistic; it is with being uninformed. Only in knowing about these blessings can we embrace them.[62]

Yes, all the magnificent claims of Hebrews are true. Claims of sin and salvation, fear and faith. Claims of sacrifice and suffering, perseverance and priesthood, drawing near versus shrinking back. The heroes of the Faith Hall of Fame longed to see the consummation of all these claims. We can experience them in a way they never did. We merely have to read the "brochure"—the final word God has spoken through his Son—and then live with its truths written on our hearts.

SUMMARY

» God's faithful have always lived between promise and fulfillment.

» Faith believes in the invisible—in things beyond the senses.

» Faith will witness God do impossible things.

» Faith braves unimaginable hardship for the sake of future reward.

---

[62] "As so often in the Christian life, *reminding* yourself of *truth*, not trying to conjure up feelings of this or that sort, is the way to keep going in faith and patience" (Wright, *Hebrews*, 150; emphasis his).

TALKING POINTS

THE PRIMARY objective of this famous chapter in Hebrews is to demonstrate that faith is what enables us to endure hardships. Consider for a moment the myriad challenges one may face in life. Chronic or terminal illness. Financial calamity. Broken relationships. Abuse. Temptation. Grief. In all these things, faith sustains us from beginning to end. Faith is the abiding voice within us that says with confidence, "There is another realm where it is clear, beyond any shadow of a doubt, that my God is sovereign. I cannot peer into that realm with the eyes of flesh, yet it is real nonetheless. In that realm, my big brother and perfect priest prays urgently on my behalf. My own name is kept before the Father at all times. Whatever impossible circumstances stand against me, my God is the God of the impossible. If he created the cosmos, parted waters, and destroyed fortresses with a word, he will make short work of my challenges as well. But if he should choose not to do so, I am ready to endure any hardship, trusting that he knows he will receive greater glory through my suffering than my success. Because I trust God, I trust him to do what is best for him, and that will be what's best for me. Even in my suffering, I experience a fellowship with the triune God that transcends the material world around me. Nothing can jeopardize that fellowship but by my will alone. When my life is over, may it be said that grace through faith preserved my soul to the very end."

>———◇———<

REFLECTING ON THIS passage, Schreiner notes, "One of the striking features of the list is the weakness and sins of those identified as people of faith. ... Indeed one may sin dramatically and still persevere in faith."[63] Noah was a drunk, Abraham was a liar, Jacob was a cheat, and both Moses and David were murderers. Others on the list—notably Gideon, Jephthah, and Samson—were worse. Yet each received commendation from our author because of their faith. Such reminds us that to be faithful in God's eyes is not the same as being morally perfect or flawless. "In all the saints, something

---

[63] Schreiner, *Hebrews*, 369.

reprehensible is ever to be found; yet faith, though halting and imperfect, is still approved by God. There is, therefore, no reason why the faults we labour under should break us down, or dishearten us, provided we by faith go on in the race of our calling."[64] Thanks be to God that it is faith, not moral perfection, that justifies us in his eyes, and that such faith is also the means by which we endure until we meet him face to face. Because Jesus has offered perfect atonement through his perfect obedience, it does not matter how far or how often we have fallen if we take hold of his nail-scarred hand extended to us (2:16) and allow him to set us back on our feet to finish the race before us.

>———◇———<

TO REPEAT LUTHER'S phrase, to live by faith is to be led and driven by "the bare voice of God." Believing the invisible, beholding the impossible, and braving the unimaginable are only possible if we take God at his word. That divine word beckons us forward into an unknown future fraught with danger. There will be times when seemingly all other evidence says God is wrong—will we believe? There will be times when circumstances seem to prevent God from fulfilling his promises—will we trust? There will be times when it feels our faith comes at too painful a price—will we endure? In all such moments, we must remind ourselves that, while faith is the *hypostasis* of our hope, God's word is the *hypostasis* of—"that which stands under"[65]—our faith. If we believe Christ sustains the universe by his word (1:3), we must acknowledge and allow his word to define our reality. His word (1) spoke all things into existence (11:3), (2) is the means of our salvation (2:1–4), and (3) will judge us at the last day (4:12–13; 12:25–29). Consequently, obedience to that word is paramount if we are to survive this life in any true sense. As we have seen throughout Hebrews, faith and obedience go hand in hand. What remains lacking in your faith in—and obedience to—the bare voice of God?

---

[64] Calvin, *Hebrews*, 303.
[65] Harm W. Hollander, "ὑπόστασις," *EDNT* 3:407.

Chapter 10

TALE OF TWO MOUNTAINS

A s Judah walked the short distance to his home, he thought more about Timothy's sermon. If he'd ever heard teaching that resonated in his soul this deeply, he couldn't recall it. Tears began to stream down his face, but—for the first time in four months—these were tears of joy. He saw Jesus in a new way. Israel's God had always seemed too distant to Judah. He now realized the same God was inviting Judah to live and rest in his presence through the person and work of Judah's heavenly high priest.

His heart still ached. It would for a long time—maybe forever. Yet the Name had never intended for Judah to carry his burden alone. Judah saw that now. More than that, he knew God had not been silent these last few months. Through his people in the Way, the Son had been inviting Judah to share his burden in community rather than bear it in isolation. All this time, he'd taken his Christian family for granted.

He considered for a second how close he had come to neglecting the saints' assembly that evening. Even now, he didn't know exactly why he had attended, though he was certainly glad he'd done so. He'd very nearly walked away from the saints. The consequences of abandonment that Timothy had enumerated still made Judah shudder. He'd come close to ignoring what God had been saying to him. He'd come so very close.

As Timothy brought his homily to an end, Judah found himself resolving no longer to live in fear and bitterness and regret but in faith and gratitude and hope. Less guilt; more grace. If the Most High had forgotten Judah's sins through Jesus' once-for-all atonement, Judah ought to forgive himself and forget his sins also.

As he lay down to sleep, thoughts of his son returned. *One day*, Judah thought. *One day, I will receive my dead back from resurrection.* By faith, he saw that Day in the future as if it were unfolding before him in the present. His great high priest's emergence from behind the heavenly curtain would signal the shaking of the cosmos that Haggai had predicted. Judah was confident that, when the dust settled, he would remain because his Champion remained.

Before a deep sleep overwhelmed him, Judah saw his son's face among the cloud of witnesses. A crowd of angels and people stood behind Daniel. They were cheering, calling out for Judah to endure. Judah then saw Jesus seated on his throne, shining with incomprehensible glory, a scarred hand extended downward. Judah's last conscious thought was of a line from the evening's homily: "You have come to Mount Zion and to the city of the living God…"

<hr />

A well-crafted sermon ends with both a call to action and a vision of what could be if the lesson is put into action. The author of Hebrews does both as he brings his homily to a close. In these final chapters, he urges the audience to allow Christ to perfect their faith by enduring suffering and walking in holiness. More specific instructions are given in chapter 13, but not before we are allowed a glimpse behind the curtain into the spiritual realm that Christians occupy though, for now, we see it only with the eyes of faith (12:22–24). Mohler considers those verses to be "the crescendo of the book of Hebrews,"[1] and I agree.

The many themes and characteristics of Hebrews are brought together as the author nears his close. As our champion-pioneer and forerunner, Christ is now the one who finishes, or perfects, our faith (12:2). The Old Testament, which has spoken to the community through our author multiple times, will speak again with renewed relevance (12:5–6, 26; 13:5–6). Blood and covenant are mentioned twice more (12:24; 13:20). The obedience the Son learned via suffering becomes our inspiration in our own suffering (12:5–11). Throughout the section, the Hebrew Christians are called to endure their suffering (12:1, 7) rather than lose faith, as did the

---

[1] Mohler, *Exalting Jesus*, 212.

---

wilderness generation; they are exhorted to heed the voice that sounds forth from heaven (12:25). Heed—and not take their eyes off him who speaks.

HEBREWS 12:1-3

If one is not careful, Hebrews 11 can seem to encourage us to look to the examples of the great heroes of faith to receive the inspiration and strength necessary to endure. That's when Hebrews surprises us. "Therefore, since we are surrounded by so great a cloud[2] of witnesses, … let us run with endurance the race that is set before us, looking to *Jesus*" (vv 1–2, emphasis mine). The supreme Son remains our objective and focus. In the marathon that is life, and as we turn in the "stadium" to acknowledge the cheering crowd filled with the faithful gone before us, we must fix our eyes on Jesus and keep them there.

The New Testament is replete with race metaphors for the Christian life (e.g., 1 Cor 9:24–27; Gal 2:2; Phil 2:16). To run and run well, we must rid ourselves of every weight and every sin. "Weight" (*onkos*) could refer to "mass, weight, heaviness, [or] bodily fat."[3] Ancient runners shed as much extra weight as possible before running a race, often even removing their clothes (the verb rendered "lay aside" is used in this sense in Acts 7:58). Today, each Olympiad sees greater advances in the science and aerodynamics of the suits used by swimmers and track runners, each hoping to shave a few hundredths of a second from their time with new technology. Like extra weight, "sin," though it might be attractive temporarily (11:25), is excess baggage and will hijack our endurance (Rom 13:12; Eph 4:22; Col 3:8; 1 Pet 2:1). The difference between "weight" and "sin" here is that

> there are many things which may be perfectly all right in their own way, but which hinder a competitor in the race of faith; they are "weights" which must be laid aside. It may well be that what is a hindrance to one entrant in this spiritual contest is not a hindrance to another; each must learn for himself what in his case is a weight or impediment. But there

[2] "Cloud" was an ancient way of referring to "a compact, numberless throng" (BDAG, s.v. "νέφος").
[3] Guthrie, *Hebrews*, 397.

are other things which are not perfectly all right in their own way but are essentially wrong; there is "sin which so readily ensnares us."[4]

In this marathon of life, every Christian faces the clear and present danger of being burdened or tripped up by weight and sin. Whether it's the "weight" of spiritual laziness (5:11–14) or the damnable sin of outright apostasy (6:4–8), there is a wide array of things that can keep us from the finish line. To answer these threats requires more than our best effort, for "we are beset with weaknesses. What endurance we run with is entirely of Christ. *We only endure because we belong to him.*"[5]

In our darkest hour, Jesus is our inspiring example par excellence. For the second time, he is called *archēgos*, our champion-pioneer. The supreme Son is the forerunner, or leader, of our faith in that he is the first to reach faith's end: realization of the divine promises and subsequent exaltation to God's immediate presence. Before Christ, all the other faithful "did not receive what was promised" (11:39). Christ is the first for whom faith became sight.[6] And to *archēgos*, our author now adds *teleiōtēs*, or "perfecter." To lead us to glory, the Father knew he must perfect the Son through suffering (2:10). As we mature in our faith, it is Christ who helps that faith grow until it is brought to completion. Because he can sympathize with us, Christ prays for us to come to faith (John 17:20); he prays that our faith will not fail (Luke 22:32). What was begun in us will be completed in us before Christ returns (Phil 1:6). In just a few verses, Hebrews will discuss how God matures the faith of his children through discipline (12:5–11).

As we "press on toward the goal for the prize of the upward call of God in Christ Jesus" (Phil 3:14), we focus on the Son as he focused on "the joy that was set before him" (Heb 12:2). This joy is a theme of Jesus' upper room discourse in John's Gospel (16:20–24) and culminates in this statement to the Father: "may [they] have *my* joy fulfilled in themselves" (17:13; emphasis mine). Jesus' joy for which he endured is not a possession he keeps to himself (Rev 3:21).[7] The joy that Jesus sought via

---

[4] Bruce, *Hebrews*, 335–36.

[5] Mohler, *Exalting Jesus*, 195; emphasis mine.

[6] Attridge, *Hebrews*, 356.

[7] Bruce, *Hebrews*, 339.

suffering was the joy he would experience by becoming and serving as our high priest, the joy of leading us to glory—the joy of seeing us share his reign and rule (Rev 5:9–10).

It was for this joy that Jesus did much more than endure; he despised, or disregarded, the shame of the cross. Crucifixion was so common in ancient times (people witnessed it on their daily commute; see Mark 15:29) that no one among Hebrews' original audience would have needed an explanation as to the connection between the cross and shame. Cicero found crucifixion so distasteful that he once remarked, "Let the very mention of the cross be far removed not only from a Roman citizen's body, but from his mind, his eyes, his ears."[8] Judaism considered anyone crucified to be cursed by God (Deut 21:22–23; Matt 27:43). Bruce explains further:

> To die by crucifixion was to plumb the lowest depths of disgrace; it was a punishment reserved for those who were deemed most unfit to live, a punishment for those who were subhuman. From so degrading a death Roman citizens were exempt by ancient statute; the dignity of the Roman name would be besmirched by being brought into association with anything as vile as the cross. For slaves, and criminals of low degree, it was regarded as a suitable means of execution, and a grim deterrent to others. But this disgrace Jesus disregarded, as something not worthy to be taken into account when it was a question of his obedience to the will of God.[9]

We must not ignore the fact that many in the ancient world knew the *pain* of the cross, but only the supreme Son knew its full *shame* since he bore unjustly on that cross the full measure of the sins of all humanity[10] (2 Cor 5:21). No mention is made here in Hebrews of the physical toll of crucifixion, only the psychological one. By saying that Jesus disregarded the cross' shame, Hebrews turns the entire concept of shame in suffering on its head. The shame we may feel directed at us by the world matters little compared to the esteem we receive from our Father.

8 Cicero, *Rabirius* 5.16.
9 Bruce, *Hebrews*, 338.
10 P. Hughes, *Commentary*, 525.

Having endured faithfully, Jesus was exalted to God's right hand (12:2). Such a declaration echoes our author's introduction (1:3; also 8:1; 10:12), but the image here is more expansive. In first-century stadiums, there were few seats (most spectators stood), and those seats were reserved for VIPs[11] (think of the difference between box seats and the nosebleed section). "In an ordinary stadium an honored guest would sit on a platform at the edge of the track, about midway along its course."[12] That Christ is seated is a mark of distinction, but consider also that he is the one on whom we focus or look as we run. For us, the supreme Son and perfect Priest is enthroned at the finish line, waiting to give us a crown of righteousness (2 Tim 4:8). That is why we are called to focus on Jesus (Heb 12:3) for the second time in as many verses; we are invited to compare our situation to his. The struggle as we enter the "home stretch" is daunting, but Jesus endured hostility from the world, and we also can endure. Don't "grow weary or fainthearted!" Aristotle used both these terms, *kamnō* and *eklyō*, to refer to runners' collapsing after surging victoriously past the finish line.[13] The message is, "Don't give up too soon; don't collapse until the winning post is passed."[14] One day, we will arrive in Jesus' presence "if indeed we hold our original confidence firm to the end" (3:14).

HEBREWS 12:4–17

This is one of the more overlooked and/or misunderstood sections in Hebrews. What some might mistake as a curmudgeon's timeworn moral railings are actually vibrant words of encouragement rooted in Jesus' sonship.[15] Recall the familial metaphors previously employed: Christians are "holy brothers" (3:1) who comprise "God's house" (3:6), and our older brother (2:11–13) has been made "a great priest over the house of God" (10:21). As Christ has been given an inheritance from the Father (1:2), so have we

[11] Koester, *Hebrews*, 524.
[12] Koester, *Hebrews*, 536; e.g., Virgil, *Aeneid* 5.290.
[13] Aristotle, *Rhetoric* 3.9.1409a.
[14] Barclay, *Hebrews*, 205.
[15] Johnson, *Hebrews*, 319.

(1:14; 6:12, 17; 9:15). But it was the will of God to perfect his Son through suffering, and as the "many sons" being led to glory (2:10), we must expect the same (Acts 14:22; 2 Tim 3:12). Being members of God's household has critical implications.

As he has been throughout the epistle, our author remains concerned his audience will surrender to spiritual discouragement. Jesus, he says, is the antidote for that. Christ's endurance is meant to spur us on to patient faithfulness, especially since we have not yet endured anything near what he suffered. Yes, times were tough for the Hebrews audience, but they had not yet been asked to lay down their lives for their faith.

It's important to clarify the type of suffering our author has in mind: "He is not speaking of disease or illness, domestic abuse, poverty, or subjection to an oppressive regime. He is speaking particularly of the censure, insult, abuse, and deprivations suffered by the believers as a result of their association with Jesus and the people of God. If the hardship is not encountered as a result of remaining faithful to Christ, it is not included under this heading."[16]

At this juncture, our author believes his audience would benefit from being reminded (since they seem to have forgotten) of the exhortation of Proverbs 3:11–12: "My son, do not regard lightly the discipline of the Lord, nor be weary when reproved by him. For the Lord disciplines the one he loves, and chastises every son whom he receives" (Heb 12:5–6). We might summarize these lines from Proverbs in this way: (1) Do not scorn God's discipline. (2) Do not allow God's discipline to make you spiritually weary. (3) Do not interpret God's discipline as evidence of God's animosity toward you. Rather, his discipline proves his love. Our author will go on to explain in verses 7–11 (1) the *relationship* of discipline—we are God's children (vv 7–8), (2) the *result* of discipline—holiness and life with God (vv 9–10), and (3) the *realization* of discipline—painful for a moment versus peace for a lifetime (v 11).

1. The Relationship of Discipline. When Christians endure trials, uncertainty and despair are sometimes our only companions. We interpret our poor circumstances as evidence that God is out to get us or

---

[16] DeSilva, *Perseverance*, 450.

that we have done something wrong. The negative nuance of the word "discipline" can reinforce such a notion, but Hebrews dispels that idea. To paraphrase Chrysostom, the very things that might cause us to believe we have been deserted by God should make us confident that we have not been deserted at all.[17] Paul impressed on the Thessalonians that their suffering made them worthy of God's kingdom (2 Thess 1:4–7). Suffering should trigger joy because of what it produces: "We rejoice in our sufferings, knowing that suffering produces endurance, and endurance produces character, and character produces hope" (Rom 5:3–4; see also Jas 1:2–4).

God's discipline in this life is instructive, not punitive.[18] It would be helpful to think of this sort of "discipline" as training or education. This is more consistent with the meaning of the noun *paideia*, which is used four times in this section (vv 5, 7, 8, 11) and occurs only twice elsewhere in the New Testament (Eph 6:4; 2 Tim 3:16; the verb *paideuō* is used in Heb 12:6, 7, 10). *Paideia* refers to "the act of providing guidance for responsible living" and "the state of being brought up properly."[19] God trains us because he loves us as his children.

On the other hand, if we reject God's training, then we are not acting as bona fide children. We are "illegitimate" (v 8). This is the only occurrence of *nothos* in the New Testament. Though it offends modern sensibilities, the KJV's "bastard" retains the shock and shame of such a status in ancient times. "A father would spend much care and patience on the upbringing of a trueborn son whom he hoped to make a worthy heir; and at the time such a son might have to undergo much more irksome discipline than an illegitimate child for whom no future of honor and responsibility was envisaged, and who therefore might be left more or less to please himself."[20] An absence of discipline means we are not among those sons being led to glory. Recall that even Christ, the supreme Son, though he

---

[17] Chrysostom, *Homilies on Hebrews* 29.2.

[18] In contrast, Spellman argues that the Greek *paideia* ("discipline") in this passage can be both punitive and non-punitive, and that the Hebrews author is intentionally exploiting the multifaceted sense of the term (Ched Spellman, "The Drama of Discipline: Toward an Intertextual Profile of *Paideia* in Hebrews 12," *JETS* 59 [2016]: 487–506).

[19] BDAG, s.v. "παιδεία." For more on the non-punitive sense of *paideia*, see Koester, *Hebrews*, 526–27.

[20] Bruce, *Hebrews*, 342–43.

was morally perfect, nonetheless needed to learn "obedience though what he suffered" (5:8).[21]

2. The Result of Discipline. Using another *a fortiori* argument, our author calls us to compare our earthly fathers and our heavenly One (12:9–10). My dad spanked me until my early teens, after which I was grounded a lot. As I got older, I realized these forms of discipline were meant to train me to be a better person. For that, my father was always a man I respected. And if I respected my earthly father for his discipline, shouldn't I also respect my heavenly Father? Taking the metaphor further, our earthly fathers disciplined us "as it seemed best to them" (v 10), the implication being that they disciplined us at times in the wrong way or for the wrong reason, but they did their best. Earthly parents are not perfectly just. Our spiritual Father, however, is *always* just; his discipline is always what we need and always has the intended result of making us more godly.

3. The Realization of Discipline. Yes, discipline is painful. Dad would use a large wooden paddle about two feet long and a half inch thick, one he had crafted in my grandfather's woodworking shop. That thing hurt, and it was a great day when the spankings stopped and the groundings started! But whatever good is in me today is partially due to my earthly father's discipline. Like God's, his intent was to produce in me "the peaceful fruit of righteousness" (v 11; 5:13–14; 6:7–8). Again, discipline is painful; with time and maturity, I now realize it was necessary and rejoice that I received it. A similar realization is reflected in the Psalms: "Before I was afflicted I went astray, but now I keep your word. ... It was good for me to be afflicted so that I could learn your statutes" (119:67, 71 CSB).

It is here that the ideas of discipline and suffering merge with Hebrews' theme. Since there is no way to merit our salvation, suffering is not a pathway to reconciliation with God. On the contrary, Hebrews is clear that what has restored us to God's presence is the atonement of Christ. However, while suffering (as a form of training) does not *reconcile* us to the Father, it trains us that we might *remain* there. Suffering helps to maintain our holiness that we might live (v 9). Recall our author's words in 10:14:

---

[21] "When the author declares in 12:7 that 'God is treating you as sons,' he means also that 'God is treating you as God treated his own beloved Son'" (Johnson, *Hebrews*, 321).

"For by a single offering he has perfected for all time those *who are being sanctified*" (emphasis mine). It is Jesus' once-for-all offering that justifies, or puts us right with God; it is the Father's discipline that constitutes the ongoing process of sanctification.

With all this in mind, our author called his audience to respond in three ways:

1. Stand up (vv 12–13). Instead of being ready athletes in their struggle against sin (vv 3–4), the congregation was plagued with feeble arms, weak knees, and lame feet—all traditional metaphors of exhaustion.[22] The image of these two verses is one of the boxing ring. After boxers have been pummeled in the face and absorbed multiple body blows, it's difficult to remain standing. Their hands droop and knees sag. At any moment, a wicked uppercut could knock them out. They have to dig deep and keep fighting rather than throw in the towel. (If you aren't humming *Eye of the Tiger* at this point, we can't be friends.)

Our author's words may be derived from Isaiah 35:3–4: "Strengthen the weak hands, and make firm the feeble knees. Say to those who have an anxious heart, 'Be strong; fear not! Behold, your God will come with vengeance, with the recompense of God. He will come and save you.'" In 10:37, Hebrews exhorted the audience to endure for "the coming one will come and will not delay," the same sentiment expressed in Isaiah. Christians live in perpetual hope of the return of the supreme Son, who will right every wrong; in the meantime, we receive the timely help we need by virtue of his high priestly intercession (4:16). As we noted in chapter 4, our ability to hold fast and endure faithfully depends upon the priestly work of Christ.

The words of Proverbs 4:26 LXX are also invoked here in Hebrews 12: "Make straight paths for your feet." While drooping hands and weak knees pointed to exhaustion brought on by external trials, lame feet is a metaphor for the spiritual lethargy triggered by temptation and sin (similar to "weight" and "sin" in v 1). This is a call for the audience to rededicate themselves to the pursuit of holiness. "They were to walk in a straight line, they were to live honestly and openly, without moral or

---

[22] Attridge, *Hebrews*, 365.

spiritual inconsistencies in their lives."[23] Should they continue in their sluggishness, their lame feet would become a permanent handicap (i.e., apostasy and loss of eternal salvation); should they straighten up, however, they would "be healed" (v 13). With the coming of God, "the lame will leap like a deer" (Isa 35:6 CSB).

2. Strive (v 14). We are to "strive for" (i.e., pursue, aspire to, or seek after[24]) both peace (Ps 34:14; 1 Pet 3:11) and holiness (Isa 51:1; Rom 6:22; 1 Thess 4:7). Peace seems to be an ever-elusive thing. Calvin wrote, "Men are so born that they all seem to shun peace; for all study their own interest, seek their own ways, and care not to accommodate themselves to the ways of others. Unless then we strenuously labour to follow peace, we shall never retain it; for many things will happen daily affording occasion for discords."[25] Among his beatitudes, Jesus promised, "Blessed are the peacemakers, for they shall be called *sons of God*" (Matt 5:9; emphasis mine), and Paul encouraged the church in Rome, "If possible, as far as it depends on you, live at peace with everyone" (Rom 12:18 CSB). For our author's audience, there was no escaping conflict and confrontation with neighbors and civic authorities, and it's no secret that external oppression can foster internal division. That's why he urged them to pursue peace "with everyone."

Holiness is also to be our pursuit. If holiness is an intended purpose of God's training, how sad it would be to endure suffering but not bear its fruit! I love Westcott's definition of holiness: "the preparation for the presence of God."[26] Hebrews previously implied that sharing in God's holiness equates to eternal life (12:9–10), and it now says unequivocally that without holiness, "no one will see the Lord" (v 14). Here again we are reminded of another of Christ's beatitudes: "Blessed are the pure in heart, for they shall see God" (Matt 5:8).

3. See to it (vv 15–16). Striving for peace and holiness begins with the individual, but it also must become a group endeavor. In the spirit of the

---

[23] Lightfoot, *Jesus Christ Today*, 234.
[24] BDAG, s.v. "διώκω." This verb, "which is a stronger term than the more usual ζητεῖν, 'to seek,' connotes an earnest pursuance" (Lane, *Hebrews 9–13*, 449).
[25] Calvin, *Hebrews*, 324.
[26] Westcott, *Hebrews*, 406.

daily, mutual encouragement already mentioned (3:12–13; 10:24–25), the church is to keep watch[27] that none in its midst drifts into apostasy. Discouragement, division, and disobedience each present a clear and present danger of failing to obtain, or falling short of, God's grace. It's possible that by the phrase "grace of God," our author is referring to grace in the sense of divine help granted to those in need, but it's more likely he is referring to our final salvation—"the grace that will be brought to you at the revelation of Jesus Christ" (1 Pet 1:13).

In the absence of grace, bitterness takes root.[28] "Root of bitterness" echoes Moses' warning to Israel on the doorstep of the Promised Land:

> Be sure there is no man, woman, clan, or tribe among you today whose heart turns away from the LORD our God to go and worship the gods of those nations. Be sure there is no root among you bearing poisonous and bitter fruit. When someone hears the words of this oath, he may consider himself exempt, thinking, "I will have peace even though I follow my own stubborn heart." This will lead to the destruction of the well-watered land as well as the dry land. The LORD will not be willing to forgive him. Instead, his anger and jealousy will burn against that person, and every curse written in this scroll will descend on him.
>
> DEUTERONOMY 29:18–21 CSB

In view are those who lead themselves and others astray not only by seeking after false idols but also by stubbornly refusing to obey the word of God. Such people bring on the whole land the covenant curses enumerated in Deuteronomy 28. Moreover, no forgiveness exists for them. Their sin has consequences not just for themselves but for the entire covenant community.

Roots grow slowly and spread deep and wide. Those beaten down by discouragement or infected by disobedience will cause trouble if they are not encouraged. There were likely some in our author's audience who were

---

[27] "If such holiness is to be pursued, then care must be taken to detect and nip in the bud any tendency that would be inimical to it. … If some incipient sin manifests itself in their midst, it must be eradicated at once; if it is tolerated, this is a sure way of falling short of God's grace, for many, if not the whole community, will then be contaminated" (Bruce, *Hebrews*, 349).

[28] Cockerill, *Hebrews*, 637.

about to abandon their faith in Jesus; their stubborn bitterness was "causing severe friction within the community, and relationships were breaking down."[29] If just one member of the congregation were to surrender in the struggle against sin, it would defile and devastate the entire community like cancer (1 Cor 5:6).

Genesis does not remember Esau (Heb 12:16–17) as a sexually immoral person—unless Hebrews is speaking of his marrying outside the covenant family (Gen 26:34–35; 28:6–9)[30]—meaning our author may not have in mind fornication per se. Rather, the term may be a euphemism for spiritual adultery or unfaithfulness.[31] It is the use of "unholy" (*bebēlos*) that clarifies our author's point—it referred to having a worldly mindset versus "having an interest in transcendent matters"[32] (see Col 3:2). Because Hebrews invokes Esau here, it's clear that "it is not what they [i.e., the Hebrew Christians] are drawn to *but what they might give up* that concerns our author."[33] In contrast to Moses (11:25–26) and ultimately Christ (12:2), Esau gave up something quite valuable and lasting (his birthright) for something fleeting and of significantly less value (a bowl of stew). He disregarded the wrong thing. Though he later regretted doing so, seeking "[the birthright] with tears"[34] (v 17; Gen 27:34–38), he was denied. The point by the Hebrews author is striking: "A second repentance is simply not an objective possibility."[35]

Esau's folly reinforces our author's previous exhortation, "Do not throw away your confidence, which has a great reward" (10:35), as well as his warning that continuous sin leaves only "a fearful expectation of judgment, and a fury of fire that will consume the adversaries" (10:27). In our struggle against suffering and sin, we cannot exchange our eternal inheritance for present respite. We cannot give in.

---

[29] Guthrie, *Hebrews*, 404.

[30] If our author was indeed saying Esau was guilty of actual fornication, he was relying on Jewish tradition, not Scripture, in doing so (e.g., Philo, *Virtues* 208; *Jubilees* 25.1–10; *Genesis Rabbah* 65.1).

[31] Deut 31:16; Judg 2:17; Jer 2:20; 3:6–9, 20; Hos 1:2. Fornication (i.e., sexual activity outside the marital covenant) will be condemned later in the strongest terms (13:4).

[32] BDAG, s.v. "βέβηλος"; Silva, "βέβηλος," *NIDNTTE* 1:501–3.

[33] Attridge, *Hebrews*, 369; emphasis mine.

[34] "His was not the 'godly grief' which produces 'repentance that leads to salvation,' but the 'worldly grief' which produces death (2 Cor. 7:10)" (P. Hughes, *Commentary*, 541).

[35] Attridge, *Hebrews*, 370.

HEBREWS 12:18–29

Throughout Scripture, mountains were considered sacred sites (e.g., Gen 22:1–14; Exod 3:1–5; 1 Kgs 18:20–40). In addition, our author's words, "you have ... come" (12:18, 22), are a translation of the verb *proserchomai*, a term that "is always used in Hebrews of worship or nearness to God."[36] We've encountered this term already:

> › we "draw near [*proserchomai*] to the throne of grace" (4:16);
> › we "draw near [*proserchomai*] to God through" Christ (7:25);
> › the law could not "make perfect those who draw near [*proserchomai*]" (10:1),
> › but in light of Christ's once-for-all atonement, we must "draw near [*proserchomai*] with a true heart" (10:22)
> › and must be among those who "would draw near [*proserchomai*] to God" through faith (11:6).

The Sinai scene (vv 18–21) serves as a metaphor for worship under the old covenant, and three things are stressed: God's majesty, his unapproachability, and his terror.[37] Throughout the Old Testament, Sinai (also called Horeb) is commonly known as "the mountain of God/the LORD" (Exod 3:1; Num 10:33; 1 Kgs 19:8). Sinai represents both the tangible and temporal. Ironically, though the mountain could be touched physically, it was *un*touchable by command to the Israelites—"may be touched" refers to possibility, not permission.[38] It's as if Sinai is meant to be a parable for the entire old covenant (similar to the tabernacle in 9:8–9).

The remaining descriptions of Sinai echo Moses' recounting of the scene (Exod 19:16, 19; 20:18; Deut 4:11–12; 5:22–23). The most intimidating part was hearing God's voice. After Israel spent two days consecrating themselves (including taking a bath, doing laundry, and abstaining from sex), God spoke to the people (Exod 19:9–15). Yet his voice was so terrifying, "the people were afraid and trembled, and they stood far off

---

[36] Ellingworth, *Hebrews*, 671.
[37] Barclay, *Hebrews*, 219.
[38] John F. MacArthur, Jr., *Hebrews*, MACNT (Chicago: Moody, 1983), 411.

and said to Moses, 'You speak to us, and we will listen; but do not let God speak to us, lest we die'" (20:18–19). "The cumulative effect … is an indelible impression of the majestic presence of the God who is unapproachable. … Sinai was not an occasion for revelation so much as for dread."[39] Even Moses shook in his sandals (Deut 9:19). The word translated "terrifying" in Hebrews 12:21 (*phoberos*) was also used in 10:27 and 10:31 to describe the fearsome judgment of God. Altogether, we have a scene of fear, judgment, and condemnation—and to think that Israel was there to worship God (Exod 3:12)! For good reason did Paul describe the old covenant as "the ministry of death, carved in letters on stone" (2 Cor 3:7).

How great it is, then, that the mountain of Christian worship is the heavenly Zion, not earthly Sinai. When Christians approach the throne through song, supplication, sermon, or the Supper, we encounter something completely different than Israel did. Note our author's seven-fold description of this second mountain:

Zion. The first three phrases are intended to be one unit—"city of the living God" and "heavenly Jerusalem" are our author's way of clarifying what he means by "Mount Zion." In the Old Testament, Zion was the mount on which the old city of Jerusalem was located, the Jebusite stronghold conquered by David (2 Sam 5:6–9). There the king placed the ark of the covenant in a tent. As Jerusalem expanded, "Zion" became another term for the temple mount and all of Jerusalem. Just as Jerusalem became a meeting place for all Israel (Ps 122:3–4), "so the heavenly Zion is the meeting point for the new Israel"[40] (Rev 14:1). The priest-king in Psalm 110, one like Melchizedek, was to rule from Zion (110:2). Zion is Yahweh's chosen home, his "resting place forever" (132:13–14).

In chapter 11, our author "spoke of the patriarchs as designating themselves as sojourners and aliens because they were seeking a city with foundations, and in 11:16 he asserted that God had indeed prepared a city for them."[41] The heavenly Jerusalem is that city. Though the earthly, first-century Jerusalem would soon feel Rome's wrath, the heavenly one will never be destroyed.

---

[39] Lane, *Hebrews 9–13*, 460, 462.
[40] Bruce, *Hebrews*, 356.
[41] Johnson, *Hebrews*, 331.

Angels. In the Old Testament, ten thousand angels witnessed the covenant of Sinai (Deut 33:2). "Ten thousand times ten thousand" stand before the throne (Dan 7:10; Rev 5:11). In the new covenant age, they "celebrate the fact that what the law had not been able to do has been accomplished through the son of God."[42] The noun *panēgyris*, translated "festal gathering" or "joyful assembly" (NIV), occurs only here in the New Testament. In its secular use, the word referred to "the celebratory atmosphere at the annual athletic competitions, such as the Olympics. In the LXX, it speaks of a multitudinous gathering to celebrate an occasion of joy or delight, often associated with a feast (e.g., Ezek. 46:11; Hos. 2:11; 9:5; Amos 5:21). Thus, the word communicates a sense of excitement, revelry, and well-being."[43] Recall that the "Sabbath rest" awaiting the faithful (Heb 4:9) is one of celebration. Whereas angels are "ministering spirits" appointed by God to serve the elect (1:14), they also constitute heaven's welcome party.[44] Instead of the ominous atmosphere of Sinai, Zion is filled with celebration that is as roisterous as it is eternal.

Assembly. The people of God, according to the New Testament, have their names enrolled in heaven,[45] and Paul refers to our heavenly citizenship (Phil 3:20). Thus the "assembly [*ekklēsia*] of the firstborn" is the church of Christ as it has existed in every place and every time; "the church eternal and the church universal."[46] In Christian worship, we assemble with countless angels *and* with all our brethren—those living, as well as those who have fallen asleep in Christ.

That last point quickens my pulse. To think that I have the opportunity, in the worship of the church, to take my place alongside my father and my son and echo with the innumerable multitude, "Blessing and honor and glory and power be to the one seated on the throne, and to the Lamb, forever and ever!" (Rev 5:13 CSB)—such a thought prompts me not to be like Esau, who spurned the inheritance befitting a firstborn.

---

[42] Wright, *Hebrews*, 162.

[43] Guthrie, *Hebrews*, 420.

[44] Johnson, *Hebrews*, 332.

[45] Luke 10:20; Phil 4:3; Rev 3:5; 13:8; 17:8; 20:12.

[46] Mohler, *Exalting Jesus*, 211. "All the people of Christ are the 'firstborn' children of God, through their union with him who is the Firstborn *par excellence*" (Bruce, *Hebrews*, 359; see Heb 1:6).

God. Abraham referred to the Lord as "the Judge of all the earth"[47] (Gen 18:25). Hebrews has already warned its audience about the throne of judgment (4:13; 9:27) and how dreadful it will be to fall into God's hands as those who have trampled his Son, profaned his Son's blood, and outraged his Spirit (10:29–31). Even for his faithful children, "the intimacy of their covenant-union with him is not unmixed with awe before his pure holiness."[48] Ultimately, however, and in keeping with Hebrews' message, God's people "come boldly to God's throne where he bestows grace because of Jesus (4:16), and they draw near full of assurance (10:22), knowing they will escape judgment because their bodies have been washed and cleansed."[49] Indeed, the only reason we do not stand condemned before God's throne is that Jesus' blood speaks a word of pardon on our behalf.

Spirits. This is most likely a reference to the saints of God who have already crossed Jordan,[50] the cloud of witnesses that "apart from us" have not been "made perfect" (11:40). If this is the case, "assembly of the firstborn" refers to "the whole people of God, the eschatological assembly in its ultimate and complete state, ... while ['spirits'] are the aggregate of faithful men and women who have already died and faced their judgment (9:27), having been 'perfected' on the ground of Jesus' high priestly offering (10:14)."[51] In addition, it's no coincidence that the placement of "God, the judge of all" comes between "assembly of the firstborn" and "spirits of the righteous," meaning the latter, now that those spirits have been judged by God, refers to "the final state of human beings enjoying God's intimate presence without any separating barriers."[52]

---

[47] The phrase "judge of all" (Heb 12:23) reminds our author's audience of "the surpassing importance of God's evaluation of one's life in this world. Pleasing God at all times, no matter how that is viewed by others, is all the more necessary in light of the eternal effects of God's judgment. He stands at the center of the Christian's court of reputation" (deSilva, *Perseverance*, 467).

[48] Bruce, *Hebrews*, 359. "The implication is that He is a God who is not to be regarded lightly. He is not a happy-go-lucky sort of God" (Lightfoot, *Jesus Christ Today*, 239).

[49] Schreiner, *Hebrews*, 400–01.

[50] Some argue "spirits of the righteous made perfect" is limited to those saints who died before Jesus' death and resurrection. The only other occurrences of the Greek *dikaios* ("the righteous") in Hebrews are in 10:38 and 11:4, both of which contextually refer to Old Testament saints. But Cockerill disagrees, arguing "there is only one people of God" (*Hebrews*, 657).

[51] Lane, *Hebrews 9–13*, 472.

[52] DeSilva, *Perseverance*, 467.

Jesus. Christians' access to Zion is completely due to the blood Jesus shed and the atonement he provides us as the supreme Son and our perfect Priest. Recall that we "draw near to God through him" (7:25). Were it not for the new covenant he inaugurated, mediates, and guarantees, we would have no access to God or entrance into the holy city.

Blood. Only through Jesus' sprinkled blood (9:23–24) can we confidently "enter the holy places" (10:19). Thus his blood speaks a better word than Abel's because, "while Abel's voice demands justice, the blood of Christ promotes reconciliation."[53] Subsequently, "the accusing voice of [a Christian's] past wickedness is silenced forever as the blood of the cross of Jesus speaks peace to his heart (Col. 1:20)."[54]

In the last seven verses, our author has thrown into sharp contrast two mountains. Sinai projected judgment, darkness, gloom, and exclusion, while Zion is characterized by "exultation, warmth, openness, acceptance, and relationship."[55] Christians, by virtue of the atonement offered by the supreme Son, enjoy a completely different reality than Old Testament saints. Though God remains invisible to us, he is now approachable through Christ. Instead of the "come this far and no further" tone of the old covenant, the new covenant beckons us ever closer to God's immediate presence.

Once we have recovered from the spiritual high this passage imparts, it's fair to ask: "In what sense have we already come to this new city, this new spiritual reality (v 22)?" If all we see around us is a world in decay—a world not yet in complete subjection to the Son (2:8)—how can our author speak in the present tense? After all, he will later admit that we still "seek the city that is to come" (13:14); the new Jerusalem has not yet descended in its unparalleled splendor (Rev 21:10).

The answer may lie in the "yes, but not yet" aspect of our faith. If biblical faith beholds the invisible, then it is by faith that we embrace the future as if it were the present.[56] We experience the spiritual Zion in part in the here-and-now but await its fullness in the hereafter. Though that city has not yet come down from heaven, we already have access to it in a spiritual

[53] John Byron, "Abel's Blood and the Ongoing Cry for Vengeance," *CBQ* 73 (2011): 752.
[54] P. Hughes, *Commentary*, 552.
[55] Guthrie, *Hebrews*, 420.
[56] Lane, *Hebrews 9–13*, 465.

sense because Jesus has opened up the way as our champion-pioneer and forerunner (2:10; 6:20; 10:19). We are *citizens* of heaven but not yet *residents* of it. We enjoy the full rights and benefits of citizens; still, we remain as sojourners on earth until we cross into eternity,

>————◇————<

Precisely because the privileges of Christianity are greater than those of Judaism—and with the spoken word of Jesus' blood being the greatest advantage—we simply cannot "refuse him who is speaking" (12:25).[57] Our author just used the Greek *paraiteomai* ("refuse") in verse 19 when he said the voice of God at Sinai "made the hearers beg [*paraiteomai*] that no further messages be spoken to them." In verse 25, he says we must not repeat Israel's mistake and "beg off" from hearing the divine voice.

Rejecting the word delivered at Sinai carried stiff penalties, but in that case, the divine word had been mediated to God's people from an earthly mountain through an earthly representative (i.e., he "who warned them on earth," v 25). Time and again, Israel refused to heed the voice of the Lord and thus did not escape his wrath. "How much less will we escape if we reject[58] him who warns from heaven?" our author asks rhetorically. One last time, he employs an *a fortiori* argument to press home his point.[59] As beneficiaries of a better covenant and heirs of a better inheritance, we have a greater responsibility to heed God's voice. In these last days, he has spoken a final word through his Son, and to reject that word has unimaginable, inescapable consequences.

So terrifying was God's presence at Sinai that the mountain trembled (Exod 19:18); such an event was memorialized by David (Ps 68:7–8), and it was popularly thought in Jewish tradition that God shook the entire world on this occasion (e.g., 2 Esdras 3:18). The Old Testament prophets

---

[57] Debate as to who is speaking here, God or Christ, essentially doesn't matter. "It is through this Christ (cf. 8:1–2)—eternal, incarnate, obedient, exalted—that God now speaks 'from heaven,' offering salvation to his people in the present" (Cockerill, *Hebrews*, 663).

[58] Though our author uses *paraiteomai* twice in the first part of v 25 for "refuse," he uses a stronger term, *apostrephō* ("reject"), "to denote the rejection of the covenant relationship." The term "is descriptive of a catastrophic turning away from God and a rejection of his salvation" (Lane, *Hebrews 9–13*, 478).

[59] Cockerill (*Hebrews*, 661–64) provides an excellent analysis of 12:25 (our author's last use of the *a fortiori* argument) and 2:2–3 (his first).

(as well as Jewish apocalyptic literature) associated the earth shaking with "the Day of the LORD," the time when God would act in judgment either on behalf of, or against, his people.[60]

This is why our author quotes from the prophet Haggai, who spoke to the exiles who had returned from Babylon. Almost twenty years after returning, the Jews had still not rebuilt the temple, and Haggai voiced the Lord's displeasure (1:4). After the temple rebuilding project commenced, some were discouraged that the second temple didn't hold a candle to the glory of Solomon's (2:3), but God assured them he would be with them (v 4) and that his Spirit remained in their midst (v 5). He then promised, "Yet once more, in a little while, I will shake the heavens and the earth and the sea and the dry land. And I will shake all nations, so that the treasures of all nations shall come in, and I will fill this house with glory, says the LORD of hosts" (vv 6–7). Later, the Lord swore again, "I am about to shake the heavens and the earth, and to overthrow the throne of kingdoms. I am about to destroy the strength of the kingdoms of the nations, and over-throw the chariots and their riders. And the horses and their riders shall go down, every one by the sword of his brother" (vv 21–22).

Our author seizes upon the phrase "Yet once more" in Haggai 2:6. Its use in Hebrews means (1) there remains only one more "shaking," and (2) that shaking has yet to occur. In other words, Haggai's prophecy had not yet seen historical-political fulfillment. "Since God will shake the earth and heaven 'once for all,' and not merely 'again,' the author reads this as a promise of the decisive shaking and removal of the visible creation, both the earth and the visible heavens."[61]

There is coming a day when God has promised that he will do to the entire cosmos[62] (2 Pet 3:10) what he once did to Sinai. The promise of "yet once more" is that "these last days" are not infinite. Indeed, "the Day"—the return of our Priest and King—approaches at a pace known only to the Father (Matt 24:36). This is the day of "the coming one [who] will come and will not delay" (Heb 10:37). We believe by faith that "the universe was

---

[60] Günther Bornkamm, "σείω," *TDNT* 7:198.

[61] DeSilva, *Perseverance*, 471.

[62] Our author uses "heavens" as he does in 1:10; 4:14; 7:26; 11:12—it "refers to the higher part of the created universe" rather than the place where God dwells, as it does in 9:24; 12:23, 25 (Ellingworth, *Hebrews*, 687).

created by the word of God" (11:3) and that God, through the Son, "up-holds the universe by the word of his power" (1:3). So we also believe by faith that the material realm—"things that have been made" (12:27)—will be gone in an instant[63] by his same word.

Jesus predicted that prior to his coming, "the powers of the heavens will be shaken" (Matt 24:29). In John's Apocalypse, the apostle witnessed "a great earthquake, and the sun became black as sackcloth, the full moon became like blood, and the stars of the sky fell to the earth. ... The sky vanished like a scroll that is being rolled up, and every mountain and island was removed from its place" (Rev 6:12–14). On that day, there will be a "removal" (*metathesis*), the same word our author used for the abrogation of the old covenant (7:12) and the rapture of Enoch from the earth (11:5). All three uses suggest a significant—even cataclysmic—removal of something. When God shakes heaven and earth, the veil separating the two will be re-moved and Christians will be raptured to their homeland—"the presence of God in the unshakable heaven."[64]

When the cosmos is violently overthrown at the return of the Son (Rev 20:11), the church of Christ will "remain" (*menō*), for it belongs to God. We can trace this concept throughout Hebrews:

› The church, God's house over which is our high priest (3:6; 10:21), is destined to endure forever; it "cannot be shaken" (12:28).

› Our better possession or inheritance is "an abiding [*menō*] one" (10:34); "here we have no lasting [*menō*] city, but we seek the city that is to come" (13:14).

› The stability of this kingdom is due solely and entirely to the fact that our perfect priest "holds his priesthood permanently, because he continues [*menō*] forever" (7:24).

On that day and as was promised long ago, "the saints of the Most High shall receive the kingdom and possess the kingdom forever, forever and ever" (Dan 7:18; see also Luke 12:32). As long as the church has a

---

[63] "This expectation undergirds the author's consistent devaluing of worldly possessions, worldly citizen-ship, worldly status" (deSilva, *Perseverance*, 472).

[64] DeSilva, 472.

Christ, it has a future. He is indeed the one who anchors all things sure and steadfast for his people.

In light of that glorious truth, Hebrews calls for gratitude for our kingdom citizenship. Remember that this is a passage about God's judgment against those of us who "reject him who warns from heaven" (12:25). At the heart of apostasy lies the bitter root of ingratitude (Rom 1:21), so gratitude must be "the pulsating heartbeat of every positive response to the gospel."[65]

We're also called to offer "acceptable worship," which is made possible only now that Christ has cleansed the Christian's conscience. We cannot approach God in whatever way we wish, as our author reminded us in 9:1–7. Because of God's greatness and goodness to us, he deserves to be worshiped in the way he has prescribed. Much could be said on this topic, but our author seems to have in mind particularly "reverence and awe" (as well as gratitude) for the nature or character of our worship. "Reverence" translates *eulabeia*, also used of Jesus' disposition toward the Father during his earthly suffering (5:7). There is scarcely a distinction to be made between "reverence" and "awe" (*deos*)—the latter term was likely employed to intensify the former (e.g., "reverent fear").[66]

Gratitude and reverential worship are necessary, "for our God is a consuming fire" (12:29; Deut 4:24). As at Sinai, so now: God's presence is marked by fire, and "consuming fire" has to do with judgment and punishment (Matt 25:41; 2 Thess 1:8; Heb 6:8; 10:27; 2 Pet 3:7). "God must not be trifled with. Those who heed the heavenly warning will enjoy the kingdom forever, but those who forsake him will face the fire of his anger."[67] Indeed, the difference between an eternity in fire and an eternity in the kingdom is Jesus' blood that has, on our behalf, satisfied God's wrath. Christ gives us confidence in the terrifying presence of God. "There is no dread, though there is reverence, and no fear, though there is awe, in the approach of those who come through Jesus Christ, and live beneath the smile of their reconciled God and Father."[68]

---

[65] P. Hughes, *Commentary*, 559.
[66] Ellingworth, *Hebrews*, 691; Attridge, *Hebrews*, 383.
[67] Schreiner, *Hebrews*, 407.
[68] Maclaren, *Expositions*, 30:241.

HEBREWS 13:1-19

Hebrews' final chapter is a collection of instructions regarding Christian ethics. This passage reminds us of those places in Paul's letters where he gives moral exhortations following his teachings (e.g., Rom 12–14; Gal 5–6; Eph 4–6). There are twenty imperatives in this chapter, covering fifteen topics;[69] all of them in one way or another reflect our author's teachings elsewhere in the epistle. They are his way of illustrating how we render acceptable worship to God in the new covenant age.[70]

Our author begins by explaining that God's people serve God by serving one another (vv 1–7). "Brotherly love" (*philadelphia*) is a hallmark of Christians' relationship with one another[71] (Rom 12:10; 1 Thess 4:9; 1 Pet 1:22; 2 Pet 1:7). "Such brotherly love is no mere sentiment; it can be a very costly thing," as reflected in 1 John 3:16.[72] The next several verses discuss how such love should be demonstrated. For a community dealing with antagonism from without and discouragement from within, expressions of brotherly love are essential because they fortify the hearts of all Christians.[73] When our author calls for this love to "continue," he uses the verb *menō*, the same term used in 12:27. Through our enduring love for one another, God ensures his people endure also.

Like brotherly love, hospitality[74] (v 2) was another important expression of Christianity (Matt 25:35–46; Rom 12:13; 1 Pet 4:9), but it was not limited to Christians. "Among Jews and Gentiles alike hospitality to

---

[69] Floyd V. Filson, *"Yesterday": A Study of Hebrews in the Light of Chapter 13*, SBT 2:4 (Naperville, IL: Allenson, 1967), 14. Later, Filson warns, "It is neither necessary nor right to find reflected in each exhortation a serious failure in the life of the recipients. ... But each point is one which the author thinks the recipients need to take seriously if they are to live loyally and faithfully" (*Yesterday*, 77).

[70] "Worship itself has not become obsolete since it is commanded in Heb 12:28, but what form should such 'acceptable worship' take? Structurally, Heb 12:28–29 links the practical admonitions of chapter 13 to the rest of the book" (Joshua Caleb Hutchens, "Christian Worship in Hebrews 12:28 as Ethical and Exclusive," *JETS* 59 [2016]: 507).

[71] The Greek *philadelphia* "is a relatively rare term outside of Christian literature, referring primarily to the affection of natural siblings" (Attridge, *Hebrews*, 385). "The relationship between siblings was the closest, strongest, and most intimate of relationships in the ancient world" (deSilva, *Perseverance*, 486).

[72] Bruce, *Hebrews*, 370.

[73] "There is a tendency in times of persecution to allow one's brotherly love to cool, to show indifference to those being persecuted, and thus escape any suffering ourselves" (Reese, *Hebrews*, 234).

[74] The Greek words for "brotherly love" and "hospitality" are linked linguistically. "To the first hearers these two exhortations would have sounded something like, 'Love of brother let it continue; love of stranger ... do not forget.' They are not just to remember 'hospitality' but the 'love of hospitality'" (Cockerill, *Hebrews*, 680).

strangers ranked high as a virtue; it was, indeed, a religious obligation."[75] Early Christians could not afford to be less hospitable than their unbelieving neighbors. Hospitality was important in antiquity because inns were expensive and often plagued by thieves and prostitutes. Sadly, our modern age has seen hospitality fall by the wayside; perhaps the most relevant words for us in verse 2 are "do not neglect." Showing hospitality must be an intentional act; it will not happen automatically.

For Jews, the greatest example in this area was Abraham (Gen 18:1–8), who demonstrated remarkable hospitality in three ways: (1) he had a meal prepared in the middle of the day when everyone would normally be napping; (2) the meal included a tender calf (a delicacy fit for a prince in that day), curds, milk, and bread; (3) he did all of these things "quickly." Unbeknownst to Abraham, he was showing hospitality to angels (Gen 18:22; 19:1), and Hebrews uses that fact to encourage its readers.[76]

Circumstances place some in particular need of hospitality. Prisons (v 3) in ancient times were not used for long-term punishment but as short-term holding places for those awaiting trial or execution.[77] "Prisoners were not well treated, and they depended—often even for necessities like food—on sympathizers. Sometimes people withheld help for fear of identifying themselves with the prisoners and suffering similar punishment."[78] It was incumbent on the church, then, to care for their incarcerated brethren as if the free Christians were incarcerated themselves! This care, however, was not to be limited to prisoners but to include all "those who are mistreated." Our author's words, "Remember ... as if you yourselves were suffering" (v 3 NIV), reflect Paul's: "If one member suffers, all the members suffer with it" (1 Cor 12:26 CSB). Expressing solidarity with those of Jesus' body who are oppressed remains an obligation since Jesus expressed solidarity with us.

Marriage (v 4) is to be held in the highest esteem. While it was not uncommon in antiquity for males to practice promiscuity, homosexuality, and

---

[75] Bruce, *Hebrews*, 370; see also Koester, *Hebrews*, 558.

[76] "The reference to angels does not mean that Christians should practice hospitality with the express hope of entertaining angels. It is instead another way of saying that those who show hospitality to all often gain unexpected benefits from their guests. 'You never know,' the author says, 'what hospitality might bring'" (Lightfoot, *Jesus Christ Today*, 247).

[77] Gary L. Knapp, "Prison," *ISBE* 3:975. On first-century prison conditions, see Koester, *Hebrews*, 564–65.

[78] Leon Morris, "Hebrews," in *The Expositor's Bible Commentary* (Grand Rapids: Zondervan, 1981), 12:146.

even pedophilia, no sexual immorality is to be named among Christians.[79] Those who defile the marriage bed *before* marriage are guilty of fornication (general sexual immorality); those who do so *while* married are guilty of adultery (unfaithfulness to one's spouse). Violators should know that, according to our author, "God will judge"—which "rules out the notion that sexual infidelity is acceptable if it is not discovered."[80] "It is a fearful thing to fall into the hands of the living God"[81] (10:31).

Greed (vv 5–6), like fornication and adultery, has no place in the Christian's life.[82] Greed destroys community cohesion. It stands opposed to brotherly love and hospitality and is the opposite of contentment. Hebrews intimates that greed is rooted in a lack of faith and trust that God is present with us ("I will never leave you…," v 5; see Deut 31:6, 8; Josh 1:5) and that he will provide for our needs ("The Lord is my helper…," v 6; see 4:16; Ps 118:6; 1 Tim 6:17). Detachment from worldly possessions (which are a part of "things that have been made," 12:27) makes their loss more bearable (10:34).[83] Greed comes from anxiety or fear (Matt 6:24–34); contentment springs from a heart of faith.

>———◇———<

Three times in this final chapter (vv 7, 17, 24), leaders of this unknown congregation are mentioned. In verse 7, our author asks that they be remembered, considered, and imitated. Though the references in verses 17 and 24 are to leaders still alive, the command to "remember," etc., in verse 7 has to do with the leaders who first taught the audience the gospel (2:3) but had

[79] "Anyone who has witnessed the damage that adultery (particularly when committed by people in the same church) can do to the Christian walk of the individuals involved and to the vision and mission of the whole church will understand at once the author's concern here" (deSilva, *Perseverance*, 490–91).

[80] Koester, *Hebrews*, 566.

[81] "Thus the same threat issued against those who defile what is most holy, the 'blood of the covenant' (10:29–31), also applies to those who do not pursue the life of sanctification that that covenant demands" (Attridge, *Hebrews*, 388).

[82] "Ancient moralists, indeed, grasped the moral connection between sexual incontinence and greed. Both pointed to disordered or excessive desires. Both led to reckless behavior destructive of proper human relationships. We are not surprised, therefore, to see statements on sexual and economic behavior standing side by side as they do in Heb 13:4–5" (Johnson, *Hebrews*, 341; see Attridge, *Hebrews*, 387, nn. 45–47).

[83] Attridge, *Hebrews*, 388. "The frightening prospect of renewed suffering … may have encouraged the members of the house church to seek to secure their future through the accumulation of material resources. It is at least probable that some Christians wished to amass wealth in order to protect themselves from persecution through money" (Lane, *Hebrews 9–13*, 518).

now passed away. "The whole course of their lives, from start to finish, now lies before their disciples and followers for review and imitation."[84] The Hebrew Christians had not only the Old Testament saints cheering them on from the cloud of witnesses but also their former leaders.[85]

Though some of their leaders were no more, Jesus Christ is constant (v 8). In chapter 1, our author quoted Psalm 102, "You are the same, and your years will have no end" (1:12), and elsewhere he reiterated the Son's indestructibility (7:16, 24–25). The timelessness of our Lord is something to which Jesus himself attested while on earth: "Before Abraham was, I am" (John 8:58). "Hebrews knows of no time when the Son did not exist or will not exist."[86] Because Christ is constant, he is most qualified to be our anchor of the soul. He was with our fathers, he is with us, and he will be with our children until he comes again.

> In the current context of Hebrews 13, the author has a specific reason for interjecting this confession concerning the Son's immutablity [sic]. The key lies in the phrase "who spoke the word of God to you" from verse 7. The proclamation of the gospel had played a significant role in the founding of this church. That event, now in the distant past, perhaps has faded in the minds of those who are struggling with the faith. With this Christological statement the author reminds his audience that the same Christ who was so real to their community in the beginning, as they were ministered to by their former leaders, presently sits in his exalted state and will rule perpetually. Although their circumstances and perspectives change, Jesus Christ and his gospel do not.[87]

In stark contrast to Christ's constancy lies the prospect of being "led away by diverse and strange teachings" (v 9). Our hearts, our author says, are "to be strengthened by grace, not by foods" (see 4:16; 9:9–10). Though some see in this a reference to issues in Paul's epistles related to what foods could be eaten (see Rom 14:17; 1 Cor 8:8; Col 2:16, 21–23), I see

---

[84] Bruce, *Hebrews*, 374.

[85] "In ch. 11 the faith of men and women of earlier generations is presented for emulation, but there is something in the vivid recollection of a life that we have seen which cannot be conveyed by a record that has come to us only by reading or hearing" (Bruce, 374–75).

[86] Filson, *Yesterday*, 39.

[87] Guthrie, *Hebrews*, 439.

"foods" as a metaphor for something else (as is Esau's meal in 12:16–17). The use of "diverse" inclines me to think our author is intentionally non-specific.[88] My best guess is that this passage calls on its audience to sever all religious ties to the Jewish community.[89] After all, Christians have an "altar" (i.e., access to God through Jesus' sacrificial death) that the rest of humanity does not (v 10; 8:1).[90] Why would the Hebrew Christians sit on the fence any longer?

Sharing in that "altar" entails three things: (1) identifying with Jesus' suffering (vv 11–14), (2) confession and worship (v 15), and (3) serving the people around us (v 16).[91] That the carcasses of animal sacrifices were burned outside the camp on the Day of Atonement (Lev 16:27; see also Exod 29:14; Lev 9:11) is an Old Testament shadow our author cannot pass up. Jesus, too, was sacrificed "outside the camp" or "gate" (John 19:20) to cleanse our conscience for worship (Heb 9:14) and to sanctify us by his blood (13:12; 10:14).[92] In so doing, Jesus identified with us, unashamed to call us brothers (2:12). If Jesus, then, suffered "outside the camp," we ought to leave the world behind and unashamedly "share in the abuse of Jesus" (13:13 Msg; see also 11:26). That is the "equivalent of the call to take up the cross [Mark 8:34]."[93]

The recipients of this epistle were becoming the rejects of their neighborhoods. When Hebrews was authored, Judaism still held the status of *religio licita* ("approved religion") under Roman law; Christianity did not. By reminding them of how Jesus endured the same rejection to a far greater degree, our author essentially says, "This is what you signed up for when you became a Christian" (see 1 Pet 2:21). Since heaven and earth will soon

---

[88] "The combination of specific detail (at the level of imagery) and vague reference (at the level of history) makes this section maddening to those who want to pin down the precise situation to which this discourse was addressed" (Johnson, *Hebrews*, 346).

[89] Norman H. Young, "'Bearing His Reproach' (Heb 13.9–14)," *NTS* 48 (2002): 243–61.

[90] Like most Protestant interpreters, I do not consider 13:10 to be a reference to the Lord's Supper. See Marie E. Isaacs, "Hebrews 13:9–16 Revisited," *NTS* 43 (1997): 268–84.

[91] Attridge, *Hebrews*, 391.

[92] "The crucifixion is thus once more grounded in the purpose of God for the preparation of the 'many sons and daughters' to enter God's presence" (deSilva, *Perseverance*, 501).

[93] Attridge, *Hebrews*, 399. "As his suffering was the means of his exaltation, so identifying with him in his suffering is the means by which his people enter God's presence through him. Drawing near to God through the exalted Christ and identifying with the reproach of the suffering Christ are inseparably bound together" (Cockerill, *Hebrews*, 701–2).

be shaken as promised,[94] the people of God "have no lasting city" (Heb 13:14) in this world, for "our citizenship is in heaven" (Phil 3:20).

Simply the fact that Jesus has offered a once-for-all sacrifice, however, does not mean the Christian has no more sacrifice to offer. Since we have gone outside the gate to identify with Christ and have inherited an unshakable kingdom, we are to offer to God "acceptable worship," which our author now says is a continual "sacrifice of praise to God, that is, the fruit of lips that acknowledge his name" (v 15). Confession of faith in the supreme Son in the face of a hostile world is a most acceptable sacrifice. "Throughout this sermon he has been urging his hearers to persevere by maintaining their 'confession' of Christ before an unbelieving world (3:1; 4:14; 10:23; cf. 11:13). Now he affirms that the 'fruit of lips confessing his name' is also the 'sacrifice of praise' pleasing to God, and thus the ultimate act of worship."[95]

In addition to the fruit of our lips, doing good and sharing our blessings (both inside and outside the community of faith) constitute "sacrifices [that] are pleasing to God" (v 16; 6:10; 10:24, 34). When the Philippians sent a monetary gift to help with Paul's needs, the apostle called it "a fragrant offering, a sacrifice acceptable and pleasing to God" (Phil 4:18). James made a similar statement: "Religion that God accepts as pure and without fault is this: caring for orphans or widows who need help, and keeping yourself free from the world's evil influence" (1:27 NCV; see also Rom 12:1; Gal 6:10; 1 Pet 2:5). In this way, "The response of praise and the works of love are the only appropriate sacrifices remaining to the redeemed community."[96]

>———◇———<

In his prior reference to the congregation's leaders (v 7), it was former, deceased leaders that our author had in mind. Here in verse 17, however, it's the current ones who are in view. He has as much confidence in them as

[94] "Judaism, a religion wed to the old covenant, is depicted as an aspect of the present world that will be shaken to pieces at Christ's return" (Guthrie, *Hebrews*, 441). It's possible that in our author's words in 13:9–14 lies a prediction of Jerusalem's destruction in 70 by the Romans (Peter Walker, "Jerusalem in Hebrews 13:9–14 and the Dating of the Epistle," *TynBul* 45 [1994]: 38–71).

[95] Cockerill, *Hebrews*, 706.

[96] Lane, *Hebrews 9–13*, 553.

he did the first ones;[97] thus he urges obedience[98] and submission to them. Bruce notes that the verb translated "keeping watch" (*agrypneō*) can be rendered "lose sleep"[99] (e.g., Mark 13:33; Luke 21:36), and this stresses the incredible responsibility that leaders (i.e., elders/shepherds) have in their charge to oversee the flock. Lane notes that the verb is always used in the New Testament with an eschatological nuance (Mark 13:33; Luke 21:36; Eph 6:18).[100] Leaders keep watch over our souls in light of the Son's imminent return, knowing that nothing less than eternal life or death is at stake.

Indeed, our author saw the clouds of persecution growing darker on the horizon, and he knew that strong, effective leadership would be essential to the survival of the congregation for what lay ahead. In addition, if some of the congregation were drifting away and neglecting the assembly, the leaders needed to exercise loving discipline so that those at fault might not miss out on "such a great salvation" (2:3). Christians may not always agree with their leaders, but obedience and submission are nonetheless mandated since the Holy Spirit appointed the overseers of the flock (Acts 20:28). To reject their leadership is to reject the authority of the Spirit of God.

If standing before the throne and giving an account for our own selves is terrifying (4:13), how much more so standing before "the great shepherd of the sheep" (13:20) and giving an account for one's leadership of Christ's people![101] No wonder, then, are we called to make sure the experience of leadership is pleasant, not dispiriting. If churches abuse their leaders long enough, they shouldn't be surprised when the day comes that no one is willing to serve in this capacity. On the other hand, "The onerous work of leadership is made joyful when carried out in an atmosphere of trust and cooperation."[102]

[97] Bruce, *Hebrews*, 385.
[98] The word translated "obey" (*peithō*) has the nuance of obedience because of persuasion versus automatic obedience to established authority structures (Cockerill, *Hebrews*, 708; BDAG, s.v. "πείθω"). This suggests that such obedience is meritorious—leaders deserve respect because of their conduct and integrity (see Timothy M. Willis, "'Obey Your Leaders': Hebrews 13 and Leadership in the Church," *ResQ* 36 [1994]: 316–26).
[99] Bruce, *Hebrews*, 385, n. 101; see also Silva, "ἀγρυπνέω," *NIDNTTE* 1:141–2.
[100] Lane, *Hebrews 9–13*, 555.
[101] "They should be trusted and their authority should be respected because they recognize their place within a structure of accountability to God" (Lane, 556).
[102] Johnson, *Hebrews*, 351.

Our author also asks for his readers' prayers. It may be that he once (or currently) held a position of leadership in this same congregation.[103] His appeal to a clear conscience[104]—the very conscience cleansed by Christ's atoning work (9:14)—and honorable conduct, as well as the desire to be restored to them, may indicate that he was presently in prison (see 13:23). This defense could have been a reminder that he was suffering unjustly as a follower of Jesus. Whatever it was that prevented him from being reunited with his audience, he urged them to pray most fervently that such an obstacle be removed. It's implied that they had already been praying; our author now urges them to keep it up and with more intensity[105] (the phrase "the more earnestly" is emphasized in the Greek).

HEBREWS 13:20–25

In my estimation, there are two back-to-back endings to Hebrews. The first (vv 20–21) is a closing benediction, one that seems appropriate for the close of a sermon. It is "a prayer containing the essential elements of" the epistle.[106] For a congregation facing persecution from without and weakness from within, they were most in need of the peace only God can provide (Phil 4:7), a peace he offers through the gospel of Jesus (Eph 6:15).

Here also is the sole mention of the resurrection in the entirety of Hebrews. The supreme Son was raised on the third day "by the blood of the eternal covenant," meaning "his resurrection is the demonstration that his sacrifice of himself has been accepted by God and the new covenant established on the basis of that sacrifice."[107] It should be noted that neither of the conventional verbs for the resurrection (*anistēmi* and *egeirō*) are employed here. The one that is used reminds us of one of Hebrews' greatest claims:

[103] "The juxtaposition of references to the leaders (v. 17) and to the writer himself (v. 18) strengthens the view that the writer considered himself a leader of the community to which he writes; there is no indication that he claimed a more general, for example, apostolic, authority" (Ellingworth, *Hebrews*, 722).

[104] The appeal to a clean conscience is perhaps a hint that the author was a close associate of Paul (see Acts 23:1; 1 Tim 1:5, 19; 3:9; 2 Tim 1:3).

[105] Ellingworth, *Hebrews*, 725.

[106] Guthrie, *Hebrews*, 443.

[107] Bruce, *Hebrews*, 388.

the God who brought (*anagō*) Jesus from the dead is the same God who, through Jesus, brings (*agō*) his children to glory (2:10). Reference to Jesus as "the great shepherd of the sheep" is consistent with how our Lord was sometimes depicted in the Gospels (e.g., Matt 18:12–14; John 10:11, 14), but our author is likely thinking of Isaiah 63:11 LXX where Moses is referred to as the shepherd of God's flock.[108] One final time, Hebrews exalts Jesus above Israel's lawgiver without denigrating him. "Great shepherd" is particularly reflective of Jesus' high priestly ministry depicted in 4:14–16.

The benediction concludes with the author's wish that God would equip his people to do his will. In light of what Jesus has accomplished for us, we ought to strive to do the will of the Father, allowing him to work "in us that which is pleasing in his sight" (v 21). Hebrews has emphasized Christ's obedience to the Father's will and has called upon its readers to obey God's will; now, at the end, we learn that "people carry out God's will only as God works within and among them (13:21b), yet rather than making human work unnecessary, God's action makes right human action possible" (see Eph 2:8–10; Phil 2:12–13).[109]

Unlike other New Testament benedictions, which normally ascribe glory to God (Rom 11:34–36; Gal 1:4–5; Phil 4:20) or God through Christ (Rom 16:27; Eph 3:20–21; 1 Pet 4:11), our author ascribes glory to Jesus Christ. From beginning (1:2–3) to end, Hebrews has equated Jesus with God.

In the epistle's second ending (vv 22–25), a final greeting is extended. Remarkably, these verses are the first time our author has used language plainly indicative of an epistle and not a sermon. Oddly, however, here he first refers to his message as a "word of exhortation," a phrase that also appears in Acts 13:15 in reference to a sermon.[110] Indeed, much of Hebrews reads like a sermon (e.g., "we have much to say," 5:11; "we cannot now speak in detail," 9:5; "time would fail me to tell," 11:32). Yet, as soon as he refers to this work as a sermon, he says, "I have *written* to you briefly"

---

[108] Cockerill, *Hebrews*, 715–16.

[109] Koester, *Hebrews*, 579.

[110] "The expression appears to have been an idiomatic designation for the homily or edifying discourse that followed the public reading from the designated portions of Scripture in the hellenistic synagogues" (Lane, *Hebrews 9–13*, 568).

(v 22; emphasis mine). The verb *epistellō* means to "inform/instruct by letter."[111] How do we explain our author's speaking of his work first as a "word of exhortation," or sermon, but second as an epistle?

As mentioned in our opening Q&A for this book, I contend Hebrews was first a sermon that was preached by one person, and another copied it down and disseminated it as an epistle. This second person was probably known to the recipients, but because Hebrews was technically not his material, his identity was quickly forgotten, explaining why the authorship of Hebrews was unknown so early in church history. That the original speaker (the true author) and original writer were two different individuals may have caused the subsequent confusion.

The preacher of this sermon, I contend, was Timothy.[112] I willingly concede that my theory of Timothy's authorship of Hebrews is unprovable; as previously mentioned, knowing for sure who spoke or wrote Hebrews is neither possible nor necessary. In this second ending, however, our author mentions that Timothy has of late been released (from prison?),[113] and should he visit the recipients soon, the writer plans to join him (v 23). Some consider this mention of Timothy to exclude him from authorship, but I believe it supports it. Think of these final four verses as a postscript[114] of sorts from the "copyist." Timothy's sermon ends in verse 21; the remaining verses are our copyist's way of updating them as to Timothy's status—he was certainly known to them already ("our brother").[115] Moreover, while other New Testament epistles often conclude with a greeting from both the author and several of his associates,[116] Hebrews mentions only Timothy by name. Why? Again, I contend it was because he was somehow mutually understood to have been the preacher of this sermon.

---

[111] BDAG, s.v. "ἐπιστέλλω."

[112] Though I came to this conclusion on my own many years ago, late in this project I discovered an article by John D. Legg ("Our Brother Timothy: A Suggested Solution to the Problem of the Authorship of the Epistle to the Hebrews," *EvQ* 40 [1968]: 220–23) that also argues for Timothy's authorship.

[113] The first verse of Philemon suggests Timothy shared in at least one of Paul's imprisonments. If Timothy was arrested under Nero's rule and subsequently released upon Nero's death (June 9, 68), this would pinpoint the date of Hebrews' authorship (Craig S. Keener, *The IVP Bible Background Commentary: New Testament* [Downers Grove, IL: InterVarsity Press, 1993], 684–85).

[114] Gert J. Steyn, "The Ending of Hebrews Reconsidered," *ZNW* 103 (2012): 235–53.

[115] Calvin (*Hebrews*, 358) takes "our brother" as suggestive that Paul did not write this epistle, given that the apostle most often referred to Timothy as a son (Phil 2:22; see also 1 Tim 1:2, 18; 2 Tim 1:2; 2:1).

[116] Rom 16:21–23; 1 Cor 16:19–20; Col 4:10–14; 1 Pet 5:12–13.

Our author then concludes with the customary greeting so familiar to New Testament readers, with "those who come from Italy" specifically mentioned. Some interpret this as an indication that Hebrews originated in Italy, yet the phrase could be nothing more than a reference to those who were from Italy but not currently living there (Acts 18:2)—"those formerly of Italy." In the final analysis, the reference is decidedly ambiguous.

Hebrews' final words, "Grace be with all of you," are more than a conventional farewell. They constitute "an appropriate conclusion for a work that has promised the availability of grace from the heavenly High Priest (4:16)."[117]

One June, I took a road trip to the Dakotas, and high on my bucket list was visiting Mount Rushmore. The evening before my visit, a front moved in, carrying with it rain and fog. Conditions were rather dreary, and as I drove up to the National Memorial, it became clear that the low-lying fog would make seeing the faces quite difficult. As it turned out, it was impossible. I drove almost every road in the area, but I never saw the faces on the mountain. I knew they were there—they had to be—but I just couldn't see them.

Charles Spurgeon spoke once of visiting a friend in Newcastle. His friend told him the view was clear enough from an upstairs window to see Durham Cathedral, but only "on a Sunday." When Spurgeon asked why that was the only day of the week one could see the cathedral, his friend replied, "Well, you see all that smoke down there, all those furnaces, and so on; they are all stopped on a Sunday, and then, when the air is clear, we can see Durham Cathedral."[118]

As with Rushmore and Durham's cathedral, sometimes the fog and smoke of life can obscure our view. *Jesus is King; Jesus is enthroned; Jesus is crowned with glory and honor; Jesus has had all things placed under his feet in utter subjection.* We, however, can't always see that. Sometimes the smoke and fog obstructing our view is of our own making, whether it be sin or our

[117] Attridge, *Hebrews*, 410.
[118] C. H. Spurgeon, "Seeing Jesus," in *The Metropolitan Tabernacle Pulpit Sermons* (London: Passmore, 1867), 13:525.

preoccupation with trivial things. Sometimes the smoke and fog is Satan's work, whether it be temptation or turmoil. It's in those moments—indeed, *especially* in those moments—we must realize that just because we can't see a thing doesn't make it any less real or true. We must look with the eyes of faith (2 Cor 5:7) if we want to see Jesus.

Now that we have come to the close of Hebrews, my hope is that in this study you've seen Jesus unlike ever before, or that at least you have seen him afresh for the first time in a long while. I hope you've been inspired to walk boldly into the Father's presence to embrace the favor he now showers upon you through the Son. I hope your faith has grown stronger and your conviction has run deeper. Most of all, I hope Hebrews has brought you to your knees in worship of your Priest and King. That's what writing this book has done for me. I started this project because I needed to fall back in love with Jesus. I received far more than I ever could have expected.

Three days after my initial visit, I returned to Mount Rushmore. That day was warm and sunny; the view was as clear as spotless glass. Obviously I had no problem seeing the faces of Washington, Jefferson, Roosevelt, and Lincoln. The experience reminded me of the apostles who, on a particular day, saw their Lord crucified like a common criminal and buried—only to discover him raised, exalted, and glorified as the supreme Son of God three days later.

Three days, it seems, can change your entire perspective.

SUMMARY

» Jesus is our ultimate inspiration and example for Christian living.

» God uses suffering to train his beloved children in the ways of holiness.

» Christian worship is a preview of what we'll experience fully in heaven.

» In lieu of a sacrificial system, new covenant worship includes confession, good deeds, and ethical living.

» Timothy wrote Hebrews.

TALKING POINTS

AS EVERY GOOD Eagle Scout should, I remember the Boy Scout motto of my youth: "Be prepared." In my tenderfoot days, I thought that meant one should go out into the wilderness carrying everything except the kitchen sink. But the immense burden of my backpack—with all that unnecessary weight—taught me an important lesson: if it doesn't help you get to where you're going, get rid of it. After every backpacking trip into the wilderness, I inventory the gear I took and ask whether it's necessary for my next adventure. If it didn't help me arrive at my destination, I toss it. Like back-packers, Christians must rid themselves of all excess mass on their journey (12:1). As we discussed in the chapter, "weight" refers to those things that are not intrinsically wrong—but they are an unnecessary burden. "When we ask about a certain habit or condition, 'What's wrong with that?' the answer often is, 'Nothing in itself.' The problem is not in what the weight is but in what it does."[119] Christians know that sin has no place in our backpacks, but this "weight" is far more subtle. What one Christian finds helpful (even necessary), another may discover is a hindrance. As we grow in our faith and discernment, we begin to intuit what those weights are and why we must rid ourselves of them. We come to realize that we've held on to certain things because of our affection for them, though they serve no useful purpose. What "weights" exist in your life? How committed are you to shedding anything that doesn't help you get to where you're going?

>———◇———<

DESPITE WHAT James says, no one enjoys suffering "of various kinds" (1:2). But our author has been diligent in correcting his audience's per-spective of the role suffering plays in the Christian life (12:5–11). "Rather than viewing these challenges as occasions for them to test God, he implies that such situations might be ways in which God tests them."[120] Barclay notes five primary ways people respond to suffering: (1) *Resignation:* This is a defeated acceptance, one that views God as a tyrant versus a Father.

[119] MacArthur, *Hebrews*, 376.
[120] Koester, *Hebrews*, 342.

(2) *Defiance:* This is a rebellious acceptance, a grin-and-bear-it approach that is determined not to learn any lessons from the experience. (3) *Self-pity:* This is a selfish approach, one that will undoubtedly lead to defeat. (4) *Punishment:* This is an angry approach, one that asks "What did I do to deserve this?" because it believes suffering is always God's punishment for sin. (5) *Love:* This is the joyful approach—not because one enjoys the pain, but because the Christian recognizes suffering is proof of God's love and approval.[121] If in our suffering, we fix our eyes on the exalted, enthroned Son, we will discover (1) that God is perfecting us as he perfected his beloved Son, (2) that there is no greater way to identify and fellowship with Jesus than the avenue of suffering, and (3) that Christ not only shares in our suffering but is also actively interceding on our behalf concerning it. As I said in the introduction, no matter what you're going through, enduring it with Jesus makes it infinitely better, for *he* is infinitely better.

>———◇———<

FROM THE START, Hebrews has sought to draw its audience's affection away from material things. This world will one day wear out (1:12). Thus the reproach of Christ is of far greater value than terrestrial treasures (11:26). In Hebrews 12, this theme develops into a contrast of two mountains: Sinai can be experienced with the five senses but is limited to the physical realm; Zion is experienced in this world only by faith yet belongs to the realm that will remain when everything else is shaken. In Hebrews 13, the same theme undergirds the exhortations concerning hospitality and greed. The latter is a manifest failure to trust in God; the former acknowledges the solidarity of God's people and seeks to share the riches found in God's Son. Just as greed is more subtle than the rampant accumulation of wealth, hospitality is more than entertaining guests in the home. It is learning to "turn aside" and notice strangers, "the least of these"—those whom others never see. It's being sensitive to others' needs, embracing them fully as siblings in Jesus, and working for their welfare. Greed says that God's word concerning the fate of the cosmos cannot be trusted. Hospitality is one

[121] Barclay, *Hebrews*, 210.

of many ways we express gratitude to God for receiving a kingdom that cannot be shaken.

>———◇———<

IN CONTEMPLATING the two mountains of this chapter, R. Kent Hughes insightfully observes that few contemporary Christians "are in danger of turning back to Sinai per se and embracing the Levitical corpus of the Old Testament. ... Instead, we fabricate our own mini-Sinais with a series of mini-laws which reflect nothing of the fiery presence and which are, we think, well within the reach of our unaided powers." These mini-laws, Hughes goes on to explain, are both reductionist and judgmental— mini-laws shrink spirituality down to what can be done by our own power while, at the same time, elevating us by putting other people down.[122] Zion, however, offers us something greater and higher than our mini-Sinais. By embracing Zion, we are relieved to discover that personal holiness is not dependent on our willpower but on God's power that equips us to do his will. By embracing Zion, we don't look down on those whom we (think) are inferior; we look up to God in "reverence and awe" (12:28). Instead of obsessing over not doing the "don'ts," we focus on doing whatever glorifies Christ and serves his people. Instead of the increasing alienation caused by a judgmental spirit, we find connection within and mutual encouragement from the spiritual family (i.e., the church) God has created for us.

>———◇———<

THE 1992 SUMMER Olympics in Barcelona were the setting for one of the most inspirational moments in the wide world of sports. British track star Derek Redmond was running the 400 meters when, 150 meters in, he tore his hamstring. In agony, Derek refused help and struggled to his feet to limp his way to the finish line. His father, Jim, ran out of the stands, past security, and helped his son reach the finish line. The crowd erupted in a standing ovation, and I imagine few remember who won that race. A runner refusing to quit despite the agony; a father refusing to let his child

[122] R. Hughes, *Hebrews*, 2:190.

struggle alone—sound familiar? Throughout Hebrews, it's been made clear that we will reach our goal only with our Father's aid. The Father leads many sons to glory (2:10); the Father governs our spiritual growth (6:3); the Father trains his children in holiness (12:5–11); the Father equips us to do his will (13:21). If you have been trying to live the Christian life by your willpower alone, then you know it's a miserable way to live. Yes, Hebrews exhorts us to struggle, to endure, to hope, to trust, to hold fast—no matter the cost. But never in his wildest dreams did our author expect us to do all this alone.[123] In the race of life, as we lift our eyes to focus on God, we discover that he isn't simply waiting for us at the finish line—he's been shouldering us all along.

---

[123] "No believer runs with endurance by his own strength. We are beset with weaknesses. What endurance we run with is entirely of Christ. We only endure because we belong to him. As 1 Peter 1:5 teaches, we are being guarded by God's power" (Mohler, *Exalting Jesus*, 195).

ABBREVIATIONS

AB	Anchor Bible
ABD	Freeman, David Noel, ed. *Anchor Bible Dictionary*. 6 vols. New York: Doubleday, 1992.
ABRL	Anchor Bible Reference Library
ALGHJ	Arbeiten zur Literatur und Geschichte des hellenistischen Judentums
AsTJ	*Asbury Theological Journal*
AUSS	*Andrews University Seminary Studies*
BA	*Biblical Archaeologist*
BDAG	Danker, Frederick William, ed. *A Greek-English Lexicon of the New Testament and Other Early Christian Literature*. 3rd ed. Chicago: Univ. of Chicago Press, 2000.
Bib	*Biblica*
BJRL	*Bulletin of the John Rylands University Library*
BNTC	Black's New Testament Commentaries
BSac	*Bibliotheca Sacra*
BT	*The Bible Translator*
BTCP	Biblical Theology for Christian Proclamation
CBQ	*Catholic Biblical Quarterly*
CCE	Christ-Centered Exposition
CSB	Christian Standard Bible
DLNT	Martin, Ralph P., and Peter H. Davids, eds. *Dictionary of the Later New Testament and Its Developments*. Downers Grove, IL: InterVarsity Press, 1997.
EDNT	Balz, Horst Balz, and Gerhard Schneider, eds. *Exegetical Dictionary of the New Testament*. 3 vols. Grand Rapids: Eerdmans, 1990.

ESV	English Standard Version
EvQ	*Evangelical Quarterly*
ExpTim	*Expository Times*
FM	*Faith and Mission*
GNTE	Guides to New Testament Exegesis
HCSB	Holman Christian Standard Bible
HNT	Handbooks on the New Testament
ICC	International Critical Commentary
ISBE	Bromiley, Geoffrey W., ed. *International Standard Bible Encyclopedia*. 4 vols. Grand Rapids: Eerdmans, 1982.
JETS	*Journal of the Evangelical Theological Society*
JSJ	*Journal for the Study of Judaism*
JSNT	*Journal for the Study of the New Testament*
KJV	King James Version
L&N	Louw, Johannes P., and Eugene Albert Nida, eds. *Greek-English Lexicon of the New Testament: Based on Semantic Domains*. New York: United Bible Societies, 1996.
LSJ	Liddell, Henry George, Robert Scott, and Henry Stuart Jones. *A Greek-English Lexicon*. 9th ed. with revised supplement. Oxford: Clarendon, 1996.
LXX	Septuagint, the Greek translation of the Old Testament
MACNT	MacArthur New Testament Commentary
MNTC	Moffatt New Testament Commentary
Msg	The Message
NAC	New American Commentary
NASU	New American Standard Bible — Updated Edition (1995)
NCV	New Century Version
NDSB	New Daily Study Bible
NEB	New English Bible
NICNT	New International Commentary on the New Testament
NIDNTTE	Silva, Moisés, ed. *New International Dictionary of New Testament Theology and Exegesis*. 2nd ed. 5 vols. Grand Rapids: Zondervan, 2014.

NIGTC	New International Greek Testament Commentary
NIV	New International Version
NIVAC	NIV Application Commentary
NJB	New Jerusalem Bible
NKJV	New King James Version
NLT	New Living Translation
NovT	*Novum Testamentum*
NRSV	New Revised Standard Version
NSBT	New Studies in Biblical Theology
NTE	New Testament for Everyone
NTL	New Testament Library
NTS	*New Testament Studies*
PCNT	Paideia Commentaries on the New Testament
Presb	*Presbyterion*
PTW	Preaching the Word
ResQ	*Restoration Quarterly*
SBT	Studies in Biblical Theology
SDSSRL	Studies in the Dead Sea Scrolls and Related Literature
TDNT	Kittel, Gerhard, and Gerhard Friedrich, eds. *Theological Dictionary of the New Testament.* Translated by Geoffrey W. Bromiley. 10 vols. Grand Rapids: Eerdmans, 1964–1976.
TJ	*Trinity Journal*
TNTC	Tyndale New Testament Commentaries
TynBul	*Tyndale Bulletin*
UBCS	Understanding the Bible Commentary Series
WBC	Word Biblical Commentary
WTJ	*Westminster Theological Journal*
ZNW	*Zeitschrift für die neutestamentliche Wissenschaft und die Kunde der älteren Kirche*

ACKNOWLEDGMENTS

To Katie Gilchrist and Melissa McFerrin for making this book readable. Any remaining errors are mine alone.

To Drew Dabbs, Zack Martin, and Jack Wilkie for forbearing my endless questions about Hebrews for the last three years.

To Joey Sparks for his invaluable counsel on so many things.

To Katy Ashley Orr for providing her professional expertise during (what was for me) an awkward phone conversation.

To Shirley Eaton for providing the usual stellar research assistance. My alma mater owes an outstanding debt to thee, and so do I.

To Dan Winkler, who did not know of this book's dedication before he wrote the foreword. Thank you for your love for my family.

To Rebecca Thompson, who wouldn't allow me *not* to finish this book.

To Tim and Pam Ashley for entertaining angels unawares.

To Jeff Jenkins for insisting I "pay much closer attention" to the things I have heard.

To the Burlington-Santa Fe Church of Christ for their encouragement as they endured four months of my preaching through this magnificent New Testament epistle.

To Audrey, Mikaela, and Autumn. Daddies are for a moment, but the Son continues forever.

To my wife. When I read the words, "Women received their dead, raised to life again" (Heb 11:35 csb), I think of you. You are in my Faith Hall of Fame.

To the supreme Son and perfect Priest, who is faithful when we are faithless. Hasten that Day when heaven and earth are shaken and you save forever those eagerly waiting for you.

BIBLIOGRAPHY

Allen, David L. "The Authorship of Hebrews: The Lukan Proposal." *FM* 18, no. 2 (2001): 27–40.

—. *Hebrews*. NAC 35. Nashville: B&H, 2010.

Attridge, Harold W. *The Epistle to the Hebrews*. Hermeneia. Philadelphia: Fortress, 1989.

Bakker, Adolphine. "Christ an Angel? A Study of Early Christian Docetism." *ZNW* 32 (1933): 255–65.

Barclay, William. *The Letter to the Hebrews*. 3rd ed. NDSB. Louisville: Westminster John Knox, 2002.

Barth, Markus. "The Old Testament in Hebrews: An Essay in Biblical Hermeneutics." Pages 53–78 in *Current Issues in New Testament Interpretation: Essays in Honor of Otto A. Piper*. Edited by William Klassen and Graydon F. Snyder. New York: Harper, 1962.

Bateman, Herbert W., IV. "Two First-Century Messianic Uses of the OT: Heb 1:5–13 and 4QFlor 1.1–19." *JETS* 38 (1995): 11–27.

Bauckham, Richard "The Divinity of Jesus Christ in the Epistle to the Hebrews." Pages 15–36 in *The Epistle to the Hebrews and Christian Theology*. Edited by Richard Bauckham et. al. Grand Rapids: Eerdmans, 2009.

Beale, G. K., and Benjamin L. Gladd. *The Story Retold: A Biblical-Theological Introduction to the New Testament*. Downers Grove, IL: IVP Academic, 2020.

Bercot, David W., ed. *A Dictionary of Early Christian Beliefs: A Reference Guide to More than 700 Topics Discussed by the Early Church Fathers*. Peabody, MA: Hendrickson Publishers, 1998.

Black, David Alan. "Who Wrote Hebrews? The Internal and External Evidence Reexamined." *FM* 18, no. 2 (2001): 3–26.

Brown, Raymond E. *An Introduction to the New Testament*. ABRL. New York: Doubleday, 1997.

Bruce, F. F. *The Epistle to the Hebrews*. Rev. ed. NICNT. Grand Rapids: Eerdmans, 1990.

Buchanan, George Wesley. *To the Hebrews*. 2nd ed. AB 36. Garden City, NY: Doubleday, 1976.

Byron, John. "Abel's Blood and the Ongoing Cry for Vengeance." *CBQ* 73 (2011): 743–56.

Calvin, John. *Commentaries on the Epistle to the Hebrews*. Translated by John Owen. Grand Rapids: Eerdmans, 1949.

Carson, D. A., and Douglas J. Moo. *An Introduction to the New Testament*. 2nd ed. Grand Rapids: Zondervan, 2005.

Cockerill, Gareth Lee. *The Epistle to the Hebrews*. NICNT. Grand Rapids: Eerdmans, 2012.

Coffman, James Burton. *Commentary on Hebrews*. Austin: Firm Foundation, 1971.

Cosby, Michael R. "The Rhetorical Composition of Hebrews 11." *JBL* 107 (1988): 257–73.

Delcor, M. "Melchizedek from Genesis to the Qumran Texts and the Epistle to the Hebrews." *JSJ* 2 (1971): 115–35.

Delitzsch, Franz. *Commentary on the Epistle to the Hebrews*. Translated by Thomas L. Kingsbury. Vol. 2. Edinburgh: T&T Clark, 1876.

Denney, James. "Priest in NT". Pages 97–100 in *A Dictionary of the Bible*. Edited by James Hastings. Vol. 4. New York: Scribner's, 1911–12.

DeSilva, David A. *An Introduction to the New Testament: Contexts, Methods and Ministry Formation*. Downers Grove, IL: InterVarsity Press, 2004.

———. *Perseverance in Gratitude*. Grand Rapids: Eerdmans, 2000.

DeYoung, Kevin. "Divine Impassibility and the Passion of Christ in the Book of Hebrews." *WTJ* 68 (2006): 41–50.

Ellingworth, Paul. *The Epistle to the Hebrews*. NIGTC. Grand Rapids: Eerdmans, 1993.

———. "The Unshakable Priesthood: Hebrews 7.24." *JSNT* 23 (1985): 125–26.

Elliott, J. Keith. "Is Post-Baptismal Sin Forgivable?" *BT* 28 (1977): 330–32.

Emmrich, Martin. "'Amtscharisma': Through the Eternal Spirit (Hebrews 9:14)." *BBR* 12 (2002): 17–32.

Filson, Floyd V. *"Yesterday": A Study of Hebrews in the Light of Chapter 13*. SBT 2:4. Naperville, IL: Allenson, 1967.

Fitzmyer, Joseph A. *The Dead Sea Scrolls and Christian Origins*. SDSSRL. Grand Rapids: Eerdmans, 2000.

Gleason, Randall C. "The Old Testament Background of Rest in Hebrews 3:7–4:11." *BSac* 157 (2000): 281–303.

Greenlee, J. Harold. "Hebrews 11:11: 'By Faith Sarah Received Ability.'" *AsTJ* 54 (1999): 67–72.

Grudem, Wayne. "Perseverance of the Saints: A Case Study from the Warning Passages in Hebrews." Pages 133–82 in *Still Sovereign: Contemporary Perspectives on Election, Foreknowledge, and Grace*. Edited by Thomas R. Schreiner and Bruce A. Ware. Grand Rapids: Baker, 2000.

Guthrie, Donald. *New Testament Introduction*. 4th ed. Downers Grove, IL: InterVarsity Press, 1990.

Guthrie, George H. "The Case for Apollos as the Author of Hebrews." *FM* 18, no. 2 (2001): 41–56.

—. *Hebrews*. NIVAC. Grand Rapids: Zondervan, 1998.

—. "Hebrews." Pages 919–95 in *Commentary on the New Testament Use of the Old Testament*. Edited by G. K. Beale and D. A. Carson. Grand Rapids: Baker Academic, 2007.

—. "Hebrews." Pages 2–85 in *Zondervan Illustrated Bible Backgrounds Commentary: Hebrews to Revelation*. Edited by Clinton E. Arnold. Vol. 4. Grand Rapids: Zondervan, 2002.

Guy, Cynthia Dianne. *Journey to a Better Place: A Women's Guided Study of Hebrews*. Nashville: Gospel Advocate, 2017.

Guzmán, Ron, and Michael W. Martin. "Is Hebrews 5:11–6:20 Really a Digression?" *NovT* 57 (2015): 295–310.

Hagner, Donald A. *Hebrews*. UBCS. Grand Rapids: Baker, 2011.

—. *The New Testament: A Historical and Theological Introduction*. Grand Rapids: Baker Academic, 2012.

Harris, Murray J. "The Translation and Significance of ὁ θεός in Hebrews 1:8–9." *TynBul* 36 (1985): 129–62.

Hughes, John J. "Hebrews IX 15ff. and Galatians III 15ff.: A Study in Covenant Practice and Procedure." *NovT* 21 (1979): 27–96.

Hughes, Philip Edgcumbe. *A Commentary on the Epistle to the Hebrews*. NICNT. Grand Rapids: Eerdmans, 1977.

Hughes, R. Kent. *Hebrews*. 2 vols. PTW. Wheaton, IL: Crossway, 1993.

Hutchens, Joshua Caleb. "Christian Worship in Hebrews 12:28 as Ethical and Exclusive." *JETS* 59 (2016): 507–22.

Isaacs, Marie E. "Hebrews 13.9–16 Revisited." *NTS* 43 (1997): 268–84.

Jipp, Joshua W. "The Son's Entrance into the Heavenly World: The Soteriological Necessity of the Scriptural Catena in Hebrews 1.5–14." *NTS* 56 (2010): 557–75.

Jobes, Karen H. "The Function of Paronomasia in Hebrews 10:5–7." *TJ* 13 (1992): 181–91.

Johnson, Luke Timothy. *Hebrews*. NTL. Louisville: Westminster John Knox, 2006.

Johnsson, William G. "The Cultus of Hebrews in Twentieth-Century Scholarship." *ExpTim* 89 (1978): 104–8.

Jones, W. "Hebrews." in *The Pulpit Commentary*. Edited by H. D. M. Spence and Joseph S. Exell. Vol. 21. Grand Rapids: Eerdmans, 1950.

Keener, Craig S. *The IVP Bible Background Commentary: New Testament*. Downers Grove, IL: InterVarsity Press, 1993.

Kennedy, Charles A. "Early Christians and the Anchor." *BA* 38 (1975): 115–24.

Kistemaker, Simon J. "The Authorship of Hebrews." *FM* 18, no. 2 (2001): 57–69.

Koester, Craig R. *Hebrews*. AB 36. New York: Doubleday, 2001.

Köstenberger, Andreas J. *Handbook on Hebrews through Revelation*. HNT. Grand Rapids: Baker Academic, 2020.

Köstenberger, Andreas J., L. Scott Kellum, and Charles L. Quarles. *The Cradle, the Cross, and the Crown: An Introduction to the New Testament*. 2nd ed. Nashville: B&H Academic, 2016.

Laansma, Jon C. "Hebrews." Pages 186–99 in *Theological Interpretation of the New Testament: A Book-by-Book Survey*. Edited by Kevin J. Vanhoozer. Grand Rapids: Baker Academic, 2008.

Lane, William L. *Hebrews*. Vancouver: Regent College, 2004.

—. *Hebrews 1–8*. WBC 47A. Dallas: Word, 1991.

—. *Hebrews 9–13*. WBC 47B. Dallas: Word, 1991.

"A Lawyer Looks at Hebrews 9:15–17." *EvQ* 40 (1968): 151–56.

Legg, John D. "Our Brother Timothy: A Suggested Solution to the Problem of the Authorship of the Epistle to the Hebrews." *EvQ* 40 (1968): 220–23.

Lenski, R. C. H. *The Epistle to the Hebrews and the Epistle of James.* Minneapolis: Augsburg, 1966.

Lewis, C. S. *Mere Christianity.* New York: HarperCollins, 2001.

Lightfoot, Neil R. *Jesus Christ Today.* Abilene, TX: Bible Guides, 1976.

—. "The Saving of the Savior: Hebrews 5:7ff." *ResQ* 16 (1973): 166–73.

Lindars, Barnabas. *The Theology of the Letter to the Hebrews.* Cambridge: Cambridge Univ. Press, 1991.

Llewelyn, S. R. *New Documents Illustrating Early Christianity.* Vol. 6. New South Wales: Ancient History Documentary Research Centre, Macquarie Univ., 1992.

Luther, Martin. *Luther's Works.* Edited by Jaroslav Pelikan. Vol. 29. St. Louis: Concordia, 1968.

MacArthur, John F., Jr. *Hebrews.* MACNT. Chicago: Moody, 1983.

Maclaren, Alexander. *Expositions of Holy Scripture.* Vols. 29–30. Grand Rapids: Baker, 1984.

MacLeod, David J. "Christ, the Believer's High Priest: An Exposition of Hebrews 7:26–28." *BSac* 162 (2005): 331–43.

Malone, Andrew S. *God's Mediators: A Biblical Theology of Priesthood.* NSBT 43. Downers Grove, IL: InterVarsity Press, 2017.

Manson, T. W. Manson. "The Problem of the Epistle to the Hebrews." *BJRL* 32 (1949–50): 1–17.

McCheyne, Robert Murray, and Andrew A. Bonar. *Memoir and Remains of the Rev. Robert Murray McCheyne.* Edinburgh: Oliphant, 1894.

Meadors, Gary T. "Conscience." Pages 113–14 in *Baker Theological Dictionary of the Bible.* Edited by Walter A. Elwell. Grand Rapids: Baker, 2000,

Metzger, Bruce M. *A Textual Commentary on the Greek New Testament.* 2nd ed. Stuttgart: German Bible Society, 1994.

Milligan, Robert. *The Epistle to the Hebrews.* Nashville: Gospel Advocate, 1981.

Moffatt, James. *A Critical and Exegetical Commentary on the Epistle to the Hebrews.* ICC. Edinburgh: T&T Clark, 1924.

Mohler, R. Albert, Jr. *Exalting Jesus in Hebrews.* CCE. Nashville: Holman Reference, 2017.

Montefiore, Hugh. *A Commentary on the Epistle to the Hebrews.* BNTC. London: Black, 1964.

Moore, Nicholas J. "Jesus as 'The One who Entered his Rest': The Christological Reading of Hebrews 4.10." *JSNT* 36 (2014): 383–400.

Moorehead, William G. "Priesthood." Pages 2444–45 in *International Standard Bible Encyclopaedia*. Edited by James Orr. Vol. 4. Grand Rapids: Eerdmans, 1939.

Morris, Leon. "Hebrews." Pages 1–158 in *The Expositor's Bible Commentary*. Vol. 12. Grand Rapids: Zondervan, 1981.

Nardoni, Enrique. "Partakers in Christ (Hebrews 3.14)." *NTS* 37 (1991): 456–72.

Neyrey, Jerome H. "'Without Beginning of Days or End of Life' (Hebrews 7:3): Topos for a True Deity." *CBQ* 53 (1991): 439–55.

Owen, John. *An Exposition of the Epistle to the Hebrews*. Edited by W. H. Goold. 7 vols. Grand Rapids: Baker, 1980.

Paul, M. J. "The Order of Melchizedek (Ps 110:4 and Heb 7:3)." *WTJ* 49 (1987): 195–211.

Perry, Peter S. "Making Fear Personal: Hebrews 5.11–6.12 and the Argument from Shame." *JSNT* 32 (2009): 99–125.

Peterson, David G. *Hebrews*. TNTC 15. Downers Grove, IL: IVP Academic, 2020.

Peterson, Robert A. "Apostasy in the Hebrews Warning Passages." *Presb* 34 (2008): 27–44.

Powell, Mark Allan *Introducing the New Testament: A Historical, Literary, and Theological Survey*. 2nd ed. Grand Rapids: Baker Academic, 2018.

Raabe, Paul R. *Obadiah*. AB 24D. New York: Doubleday, 1996.

Rayburn, Robert G. *O Come, Let Us Worship: Corporate Worship in the Evangelical Church*. Grand Rapids: Baker, 1980.

Redmond, Calvin D. "Jesus: God's Agent of Creation." *AUSS* 42 (2004): 287–303.

Reese, Gareth L. *Hebrews*. Moberly, MO: Scripture Exposition Books, 2008.

Robertson, Archibald Thomas. *Word Pictures in the New Testament*. Vol. 5. Nashville: Broadman, 1932.

Robinson, Theodore H. *The Epistle to the Hebrews*. MNTC. New York: Harper, 1933.

Ryken, Leland, James C. Wilhoit, and Tremper Longman III, eds. *Dictionary of Biblical Imagery*. Downers Grove, IL: InterVarsity Press, 2000.

Schenck, Kenneth. "Keeping His Appointment: Creation and Enthronement in Hebrews." *JSNT* 66 (1997): 91–117.

Schreiner, Thomas R. *Commentary on Hebrews*. BTCP. Nashville: Holman Reference, 2015.

Scott, Brett R. "Jesus' Superiority over Moses in Hebrews 3:1–6." *BSac* 155 (1998): 201–10.

Selby, Gary S. "The Meaning and Function of συνείδησις in Hebrews 9 and 10." *ResQ* 28 (1985–86): 145–54.

Silva, Moisés. "Perfection and Eschatology in Hebrews." *WTJ* 39 (1976): 60–71.

Simpson, E. K. "The Vocabulary of the Epistle to the Hebrews." *EvQ* 18 (1946): 35–38, 187–90.

Spellman, Ched. "The Drama of Discipline: Toward an Intertextual Profile of *Paideia* in Hebrews 12." *JETS* 59 (2016): 487–506.

Spurgeon, C. H. "All of One." Pages 289–300 in *The Metropolitan Tabernacle Pulpit Sermons*. Vol. 41. London: Passmore, 1895.

—. "The Blood-Shedding." Pages 89–104 in *The New Park Street Pulpit Sermons*. Vol. 3. London: Passmore, 1857.

—. "The Deceitfulness of Sin." Pages 97–108 in *The Metropolitan Tabernacle Pulpit Sermons*. Vol. 36. London: Passmore, 1890.

—. "Depths and Heights." Pages 385–96 in *The Metropolitan Tabernacle Pulpit Sermons*. Vol. 45. London: Passmore, 1899.

—. "An Earnest Warning against Unbelief." Pages 469–80 in *The Metropolitan Tabernacle Pulpit Sermons*. Vol. 56. London: Passmore, 1910.

—. "Final Perseverance." Pages 169–76 in *The New Park Street Pulpit Sermons*. Vol. 2. London: Passmore, 1856.

—. "Our Lord's Entrance within the Veil." Pages 145–56 in *The Metropolitan Tabernacle Pulpit Sermons*. Vol. 35. London: Passmore, 1889.

—. "The Rent Veil." Pages 169–80 in *The Metropolitan Tabernacle Pulpit Sermons*. Vol. 34. London: Passmore, 1888.

—. "Seeing Jesus." Pages 517–28 in *The Metropolitan Tabernacle Pulpit Sermons*. Vol. 13. London: Passmore, 1867.

—. "Unbelievers Upbraided." Pages 313–24 in *The Metropolitan Tabernacle Pulpit Sermons*. Vol. 50. London: Passmore, 1904.

—. "The Word a Sword." Pages 109–20 in *The Metropolitan Tabernacle Pulpit Sermons*. Vol. 34. London: Passmore, 1888.

Stewart, R. A. "The Sinless High-Priest." *NTS* 14 (1967): 126–35.

Steyn, Gert J. "The Ending of Hebrews Reconsidered," *ZNW* 103 (2012): 235–53.

Swetnam, James. "ὁ ἀπόστολος in Hebrews 3,1." *Bib* 89 (2008): 252–62.

Tate, Marvin E. *Psalms 51–100*. WBC 20. Dallas: Word, 1990.

Thielicke, Helmut. *A Little Exercise for Young Theologians*. Translated by Charles L. Taylor. Grand Rapids: Eerdmans, 1962.

Thompson, James W. "The Conceptual Background and Purpose of the Midrash in Hebrews VII." *NovT* 19 (1977): 209–23.

—. *Hebrews*. PCNT. Grand Rapids: Baker Academic, 2008.

—. "The Hermeneutics of the Epistle to the Hebrews." *ResQ* 38 (1996): 229–37.

Trotter, Andrew H., Jr., *Interpreting the Epistle to the Hebrews*. GNTE 6. Grand Rapids: Baker, 1997.

van Unnik, W. C. "The Christian's Freedom of Speech in the New Testament." *BJRL* 44 (1961–62): 466–88.

Walker, Peter. "Jerusalem in Hebrews 13:9–14 and the Dating of the Epistle." *TynBul* 45 (1994): 38–71.

Wallace, Daniel B. *Greek Grammar Beyond the Basics*. Grand Rapids: Zondervan, 1996.

Westcott, Brooke Foss. *The Epistle to the Hebrews*. Grand Rapids: Eerdmans, 1967.

Whitworth, Michael. *The Epic of God: A Guide to Genesis*. Rev. ed. Bowie, TX: Start2Finish, 2014.

—. "What Should Every College Student Know about Faith?" Pages 298–303 in *Out of Egypt: Liberation and Covenant in Exodus*. Henderson, TN: Freed-Hardeman Univ., 2019.

Wiersbe, Warren W. *The Bible Exposition Commentary*. Vol. 2. Wheaton, IL: Victor, 1989.

Williamson, Paul R. *Sealed with an Oath: Covenant in God's Unfolding Purpose*. NSBT 23. Downers Grove, IL: InterVarsity Press, 2007.

Williamson, Ronald. *Philo and the Epistle to the Hebrews*. ALGH 4. Leiden: Brill, 1970.

Willis, Timothy M. "'Obey Your Leaders': Hebrews 13 and Leadership in the Church." *ResQ* 36 (1994): 316–26.

Witherington, Ben, III. *Invitation to the New Testament: First Things*. Oxford: Oxford Univ. Press, 2013.

Wolmarans, Johannes L. P. "The Text and Translation of Hebrews 8:8." *ZNW* 75 (1984): 139–44.

Wright, N. T. *Hebrews for Everyone*. NTE. Louisville: Westminster John Knox, 2004.

Wuest, Kenneth S. "Hebrews Six in the Greek New Testament." *BSac* 119 (1962): 45–53.

Young, Norman H. "'Bearing His Reproach' (Heb 13.9–14)." *NTS* 48 (2002): 243–61.

Zerwick, Max, and Mary Grosvenor. *A Grammatical Analysis of the Greek New Testament*. Vol. 2. Rome: Biblical Institute, 1979.

ὥσπερ ξένοι χαίρουσι πατρίδα βλέπειν
οὕτως καὶ τοῖς κάμνουσι βιβλίου τέλος